I0878088

THE MAKING OF STANLEY KUBRICK'S 2001: A SPACE ODYSSEY

THE MAKING OF STANLEY KUBRICK'S 2001: A SPACE ODYSSEY

BY PIERS BIZONY

TASCHEN

PART I

JOURNEY BEYOND THE STARS

▹ 6

PART II

A KING OF INFINITE SPACE

▹ 104

PART III

SANTA'S WORKSHOP

▹ 148

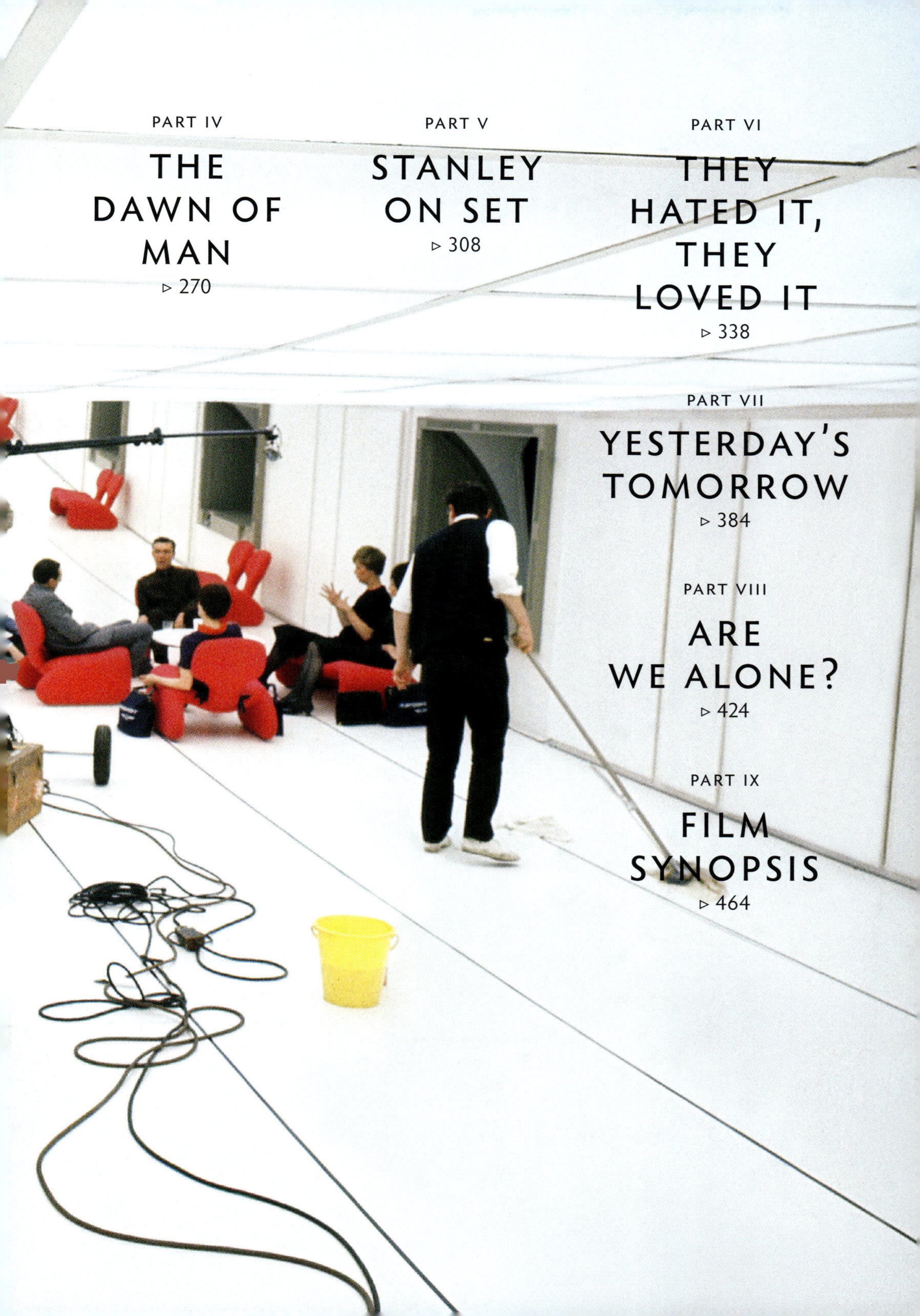

PART IV
THE DAWN OF MAN
▹ 270

PART V
STANLEY ON SET
▹ 308

PART VI
THEY HATED IT, THEY LOVED IT
▹ 338

PART VII
YESTERDAY'S TOMORROW
▹ 384

PART VIII
ARE WE ALONE?
▹ 424

PART IX
FILM SYNOPSIS
▹ 464

I

"The purpose of my visit here is to gather additional facts and opinions on the situation."

JOURNEY BEYOND THE STARS

Where does the story of the world's most impressive science-fiction film begin? In the wordless opening half hour of the widescreen Cinerama presentation, as first seen by puzzled critics and premiere audiences in April 1968? Or does it start with the vainglorious daydream made reality by John F. Kennedy's speech seven years earlier, committing America—and it still seems fabulous today—to building a fleet of colossal space rockets with the aim of conquering the Moon? Should we reach further back in time, to Manhattan in 1957, where we find a young New York–born film director investigating cans of Japanese science fiction, checking out the current state of special effects, even as Sputnik orbits overhead? Do we backtrack yet further to 1936, when a British mathematician, Alan Turing, predicted that electrical calculating machines might one day become as intelligent as their makers? We could go back further, to 1871 and *The Descent of Man*, Darwin's godless account of human evolution from the apes. After all, the film in question is about evolution. Although the events on screen supposedly depict technological achievements at the dawn of the 21st century, are these, in fact, the final artistic and cultural expressions of Enlightenment rationalism, Newtonian mathematics, and the computerized logic of nuclear strategies planned by men in the grip of irrational prehistoric passions? Can the God of Abraham be translated into a machine entity of unknown origin? In order for *2001: A Space Odyssey* to succeed as one of the greatest works of art in living memory, someone, somewhere, had to decide where to start, and pull all these strands of thought into one cohesive, satisfying whole.

Born in 1928, the son of Gertrude and her successful doctor husband, Jacques, Stanley Kubrick was brought up in the Bronx district of New York. He once claimed never to have read a book for pleasure as a boy, and certainly learned little of interest from his schooling. The subsequent, extraordinary range of his intellectual interests owed almost nothing to the New York educational system. Jazz was an early enthusiasm, and young Kubrick toyed with the idea of one day becoming a drummer, until his father gave him a Kodak Monitor 620 camera for his 13th birthday, apparently triggering an innate visual talent. He became the official photographer at William Taft High School, while his teachers told him his grades were too poor to get him into college.

While still at Taft in 1945, Kubrick took a candid photograph of a street newspaper vendor whose distressed expression matched the similarly gloomy banner headline on his stall. President Franklin D. Roosevelt had died in office. Kubrick sold the photograph to *Look* magazine, a prominent title among a new breed of popular journals specializing in picture essays. The magazine's editors applauded his ambition and hired him as a staff photographer. Three years later, having established himself as a skilled photojournalist and essayist, he was sufficiently noteworthy to be interviewed by specialist magazine *The Camera.* Staff writer Mildred Stagg was impressed by the precocious young man:

"I think aesthetically recording spontaneous action, rather than carefully posing a picture, is the most valid and expressive use of photography," Stanley Kubrick said. Maybe the statement wasn't earthshaking, but it startled me. The boy who said that had turned 19 a week ago, and has been a staff photographer for Look *magazine since age 17. Mr. Kubrick didn't come by this photographic philosophy overnight. He has been making and selling picture stories for three years. Stan is also very serious about cinematography, and is about to start filming a sound production written and financed by himself and several friends.*

Look's picture editor, Helen O'Brian, told Stagg, "Stanley had the highest percentage of acceptances of any photographer I've ever dealt with." Kubrick was similarly complimentary about his editors: "The magazine's policy is so well determined that you seldom go out on a wild goose chase. When *Look* sends you out on a story, it is usually published."

Although Kubrick had quit school at 17 to become *Look*'s youngest employee, he read voraciously at night, and took vocational evening classes at New York City College, attending lectures given by literary critic Lionel Trilling and poet Mark Van Doren. Fascinated by cinema, Kubrick stalked New York's movie theaters, and kept up with another abiding fascination: science fiction, at that time ubiquitously available in a wide range of pulp magazines, so-called because of the cheap paper stock on which they were printed. On afternoons off, he played chess in cafés and clubs, or at the open-air tables in Central Park, reinforcing what would become a life-long fascination, for both the game and its potential narrative metaphors. In 1947 Kubrick obtained a pilot's license, expecting that this would enable him, on occasion, to be quick on the spot as a photojournalist. Throughout his life he retained his fascination for aviation—in principle. In practice, he developed an irreversible phobia against actually flying, whether as pilot or passenger.

By 1949 he had married his Taft High School girlfriend, Toba Metz, and embarked on preparations for his first film. Alex Singer, a former school friend, was working at March of Time, a newsreel company that was perfectly content to spend $40,000 or more on films that ran for eight or 10 minutes. Kubrick and Singer decided they could shoot perfectly good newsreel stories for a fraction of those costs. Their first impressive effort, *Day of the Fight*, followed middleweight boxer Walter Cartier in the run-up to a bout. Perhaps predictably, March of Time went bust, and another production house, RKO Pictures, bought the Cartier film for a derisory few hundred dollars. The good news was that Kubrick and Singer were commissioned, for a more worthwhile fee, to make a second film. *Flying Padre* charted the working life of a priest in New Mexico who visited the widely scattered members of his flock by means of a Piper Cub airplane.

Meanwhile Kubrick laid the groundwork for his first feature film. As he told the *New York Times* in a 1972 interview, "Without even beginning to understand what the problems of making films were, I was taken with the impression that I could not do a film any worse than the ones I was seeing." Financed with $9,000 borrowed from friends and family, performed and scripted by relatively unknown actor friends and writers, and filmed in the San Gabriel mountains near Los Angeles, *Fear and Desire* (1953) was an abstract, slightly pretentious drama of soldiers trapped behind enemy lines during an unspecified war. None of the major distributors were interested in this small film, but Kubrick obtained a screening at the Guild Theater on 50th Street, where critics first had a chance to encourage his further efforts. In later years he distanced himself from this first feature, seemingly embarrassed by the film's portentous dialogue and variable technical quality. Nevertheless, the trade magazine *Variety* thought *Fear and Desire* "a literate, unhackneyed war drama, outstanding for its fresh camera treatment and poetic dialogue."[1]

Despite the unfortunate loss of the initial $9,000 investment, Kubrick's second fictional film was financed with $40,000 raised, once again, from family connections. *Killer's Kiss* (1955) was a dark romance about a boxer, Davey Gordon (Jamie Smith), who rescues girlfriend Gloria (Irene Kane) from the rapacious attentions of a nightclub boss. A particularly striking scene is set in a mannequin factory, where the dismembered torsos and plastic limbs echo the human violence. Kubrick wrote most of the script, operated the camera, and edited the film.

Impressed by *Killer's Kiss*, James B. Harris, the clever and ambitious son of a well-established cinema and television producer, decided to team up with Kubrick. The United Artists studio put up $200,000 of financing for their first jointly produced film, on the condition that they could persuade a reasonably well-known actor to participate. Sterling Hayden signed up for *The Killing* (1956), the first feature in which Kubrick's tight technical and compositional control, desire for experimentation, and specific narrative interests really emerge. For instance, he repeated certain scenes, demonstrating how crucial events in the drama are witnessed and interpreted by different characters. Hayden played robber Johnny Clay, coolly assembling a $2 million racetrack heist (a key diversion calls for the assassination of a horse mid-race), only to find his project endangered by a series of apparently insignificant failures and emotional betrayals whose cumulative effect threatens disaster. Johnny deals with almost all the contingencies, operating as calmly as a computer, while the rest of his gang self-destructs. In the last reel he makes it to the airport with fiancée Fay (Coleen Gray) and all the cash stuffed into a suitcase. The only thing he hasn't accounted for is the unpredictable: the airport check-in refuses to allow the big suitcase in

1 *Variety*, March 26, 1953

the plane's cabin. He has to check it into the hold. As the luggage cart crosses the tarmac, its driver swerves to avoid a dog. The suitcase falls off and breaks open. The cash spills out and is caught by the wash from the plane's propellers. Johnny stands and watches the snow of bills, as if paralyzed. For this problem—this crushing, unexpected disappointment—he has no answers, no new plan in reserve. Fay urges him to hail a cab and get out of there. "What's the difference?" he says, listlessly. The cops close in.

United Artists were uncertain about the proposal for Kubrick and Harris's next film, *Paths of Glory*, an unedifying tale based on a novel of the same name by Humphrey Cobb, a disgusted Canadian army veteran of the 1914–1918 war. Cobb, in turn, based his narrative on real-life events. Colonel Dax, a French army officer, attempts, without success, to prevent a cruel and cynical miscarriage of justice. Throughout the film, well-fed senior officers billeted in luxury mansions deliberately and cold-bloodedly sacrifice the lives of common soldiers, forcing them into attacks that can only end in massacre. The generals attribute the failure of their tactics to the cowardice of the troops, and order a number of men to be executed as deserters.

Kirk Douglas, at that time a major Hollywood star, signed up as Dax, the "hero" who fails to save the day. His brave choice of role (many actors of his status would have been terrified of such dark and controversial material) opened the studio coffers. Kubrick shot most of the film in and around Munich, from where hundreds of policemen were recruited to play French soldiers. Georg Krause, an experienced German cinematographer, worked with Kubrick on the film's technically flawless, emotionally relentless tracking shots, along the wet, muddy trenches, through the explosive barrage of cannon shells and machine-gun fire, and most startlingly, from directly overhead as if flying over an endless wasteland of death. Dax and his men are compelled to run through this absolute nightmare, their feeble rifles and bayonets at the ready. The film cannot be watched by any person of conscience without a sense of shame for what humans have done to each other. Superbly crafted, savagely cynical and unarguably antiwar in its outlook, *Paths of Glory* was a critical success, despite being banned for many years throughout France and Switzerland, and in all U.S. military bases around the world.

Kubrick's private life was discreet yet eventful. His first marriage to Toba Metz fell by the wayside, as did his second, similarly brief union with Ruth Sobotka, a ballet dancer who featured briefly in *Killer's Kiss*, and had worked as an art director on *The Killing*. A more successful and durable relationship began when Kubrick filmed a mournful scene for *Paths of Glory*. German-born Christiane Susanne Harlan sings a gentle song, "Der Treue Husar" ("The Faithful Hussar"), whose words are meaningless to her audience of French soldiers. Yet they have tears in their eyes, because the music alone conveys the singer's subjects: love, longing, loss, homesickness, hopelessness... Christiane was terrified as she walked onto the set. Kubrick smiled, and reassured her. A spark of affinity was obvious from the first moment they met. Could this become anything more? Christiane's youthful marriage to actor Werner Bruhns had recently ended in divorce, and she was not predisposed to marrying again. Likewise, Kubrick's relationship with Sobotka had been difficult. An additional complication was that Christiane had with her a little girl, Katharina, born in 1953. Kubrick and Christiane ignored George Bernard Shaw's description of second (or third) marriages as "the triumph of optimism over experience" and were married in April 1957. Katharina soon had a stepfather who adored her, and two sisters, Anya (born in 1958) and Vivian (1960).

INTO THE GLADIATOR'S ARENA

Kirk Douglas was sufficiently impressed with Kubrick to hire him for his big-budget star vehicle, *Spartacus* (1960), the story of a slave rebellion and its charismatic, doomed leader, an escapee from the savage gladiatorial circuses of ancient Rome. Commercially, *Paths of Glory* had not done so well that Kubrick could ignore this offer of work. It seemed wise, also, for him to gain further directorial experience on a large-scale production, while Jim Harris scouted for future projects that the Harris-Kubrick partnership might develop at a later date. Kubrick walked, eyes more or less open, into a morass of egotism and resentment. Anthony Mann was supposed to direct the film, but he and Douglas had fallen out in the first week of shooting. Kubrick was the last-minute replacement. Douglas imagined that the young director would be more malleable than Mann. This turned out not to be the case. Kubrick did his best to impose his vision on the pre-established project, trying, as best he could, to be patient with an insecure Charles Laughton, while fending off unwanted suggestions from a lofty Laurence Olivier. Streetwise Tony Curtis proved a valuable friend and ally. The worst battles were fought with cinematographer Russell Metty, who was appalled that Kubrick should demand so many different takes, from different angles, of key scenes. Kubrick was frustrated that, for the first time, he could not automatically take charge of the camera whenever he wished.

Overall, the nature of Kubrick's deal with the devil was made clear in the 1960 publicity brochures for *Spartacus*, in which the director of the $12 million epic barely rates a mention. The film was a commercial success, and modestly well received by critics, not least because of the cool intelligence that its embattled director brought to the project. As a consequence, Kubrick became a reasonably "bankable" proposition. However, the experience also taught him never again to relinquish control of a project, nor to accept work merely as a hired hand. He told *Horizon* magazine that a director should "control everything," from the creation of a script, the casting, the contract negotiations, the sets, the costumes, and through to editing, the choice of music, and the publicity campaign. "I think the fragmentation of these jobs, by different people, is a very bad thing," he said. The *New York Times* heard something similar from him: "I don't mean to minimize the contributions of the others involved, but the director is the only one who can authentically impose his personality onto a picture, and the result is his responsibility, partly because he's the only one who's always there." In that same piece, Kirk Douglas suggested that Kubrick could be a great director some day: "If he falls flat on his face just once, it might teach him how to compromise."[2]

With great relief (and after an abortive attempt to work with Marlon Brando on a cowboy drama, *One-Eyed Jacks*), Kubrick and Harris teamed up once again to make *Lolita* (1962), with James Mason and Peter Sellers, based on the linguistically splendid and wonderfully amoral novel by Vladimir Nabokov. Kubrick admired the writing, and knew also that, just as readers had purchased the novel in order to determine for themselves what the fuss was about, so movie-theater audiences would wish to satisfy their curiosity, too. Beneath the profitable noise of the underage-sex controversy (when Nabokov's antihero first meets Lolita in the book, she is 11 years old; in the film, more obviously a teenager) lay the characteristic beat of Nabokov's humor and Kubrick's similarly mischievous narrative pulse. Humbert Humbert, the ludicrously named, sleazy, self-deluding seducer of young flesh, is ambushed by the one emotion for which he hadn't planned: a genuine and hopeless love for his victim, despite the fact that she has matured into motherhood and marriage with another and more conventionally appropriate man. Humbert selflessly does what he can to help her new family, then leaves to kill his nemesis…

Harris and Kubrick's ideas meshed seamlessly. According to Harris, "We wanted to really engage an audience into reversing what they perceived as a dirty old man. By the time the picture ends they should really feel sorry for him." Kubrick audaciously expanded a lesser character from Nabokov's book and subsequent screenplay: creepy Clare Quilty, a writer and media dilettante played by Sellers. If audiences were supposed to be appalled by Humbert's molestation of Lolita, how much more awful is their realization that Quilty, a truly monstrous child pornographer, has stage-managed events from the start, with Lolita in his thrall, and Humbert his hopeless, unknowing pawn.[3]

Kubrick shot most of *Lolita* in England, as far away as possible from Hollywood studio interference. Harris knew that his old friend was on the verge of becoming an expatriate.

2 *New York Times*, October 2, 1960

3 Harris, James, 2002 interview with Mick Garrett for *Hollywood 5-0* website

"Stanley fell in love with England. He felt it was a more civilized place to raise kids. Living in New York, he had a fear of sending his kids to school there. Too much violence. He felt comfortable in England. He spoke the language. And they had the facilities to make films. He said, 'You can make films anywhere. It's where you live with your children that's to care about.' He wasn't a big fan of California. He wasn't one to go out and sit in the sun."

KUBRICK AND THE BOMB

No matter how far he traveled, neither Kubrick nor anyone else in the world could find safety in the terrifying fall season of 1962. American spy planes had photographed short-range Soviet nuclear missiles accumulating at secret bases on Cuba. President Kennedy initiated a naval blockade of all Soviet shipping approaching the island. Given the stark alternatives, a ground-troop invasion of Cuba, or an air strike against the missile bases, the blockade seemed the least dangerous of several high-risk strategies available to him. As is now clear from tapes of White House crisis meetings, Kennedy and his staff went to bed on the night of October 23 not knowing if they, or anyone in the world, would be alive the next morning. Kennedy and Khrushchev nearly backed themselves into a corner from which they couldn't withdraw. Fortunately, neither man had any appetite for global catastrophe. The same could not be said of their military advisors, some of whom urged surprise nuclear attacks to settle the matter of Cold War supremacy once and for all.

Kubrick understood that the prospect of nuclear destruction was almost impossible for the ordinary mind to encompass. Even the terror of the Cuban crisis had been met, he felt, by a kind of mass fatalism. The peaceful resolution allowed military strategists and politicians to slip back into default mode. Kubrick told the physicist and writer Jeremy Bernstein, "The longer the bomb is around without anything happening, the better the job that people do in psychologically denying its existence. It has become as abstract as the fact that we are all going to die some day, which we usually do an excellent job of denying." Kubrick wanted to dispel the false sense of security created by respectable nuclear intellectuals, laden with doctorates in science, game theory, and politics, yet, to a man, seemingly devoid of common sense, and incapable of seeing that the only logical consequence of attempting to deter nuclear war by threatening the use of nuclear weapons was nuclear war.[4]

Appalled and quietly furious, Kubrick set about researching nuclear strategy for his next film, once again coproduced by Harris. Their attention was caught by a realistic thriller, *Red Alert*, written by a genuinely alarmed ex-RAF pilot, Peter George, and published in

4 Bernstein, Jeremy, "How About a Little Game?," *The New Yorker*, November 12, 1966

Colleagues were struck by the intensity of Kubrick's gaze. His dark, intense eyes locked onto the smallest details, the tiniest flaws.

1958. In his scenario, a paranoid general launches a rogue air strike against the Soviet Union. When it becomes clear that one plane from the attack wing cannot be recalled by saner authorities, a deal is struck, whereby the Soviets will be allowed to destroy one American city in recompense for their own lost city. Fortunately the last plane fails to hit its target. George worked up a screenplay, while sinking copious quantities of whiskey mixed with milk. Meanwhile, Sidney Lumet, director of the tensely claustrophobic 1957 jury-room drama *Twelve Angry Men*, was developing *Fail-Safe*, a film based on a similar theme—so similar, in fact, that Kubrick and George tried to sue him and his writers for plagiarism. Lumet's film went into production regardless, with Henry Fonda as the unfortunate president forced to order the destruction of one of his own cities.

Kubrick had already decided (although Harris wasn't so sure) that the best way of distinguishing his project from Lumet's was to turn George's essentially sympathetic characters into monstrous grotesques, and to treat the storyline as a farce, so dark, yet so comedic, no one would ever forget it. The more he contemplated the strategic theory of Mutually Assured Destruction, the more it seemed that derisive laughter was the only appropriate response. He enlisted American satirist Terry Southern to reshape George's earnest script. Columbia Pictures, the same studio that eventually bought Lumet's *Fail-Safe*, also invested in Kubrick's new film, *Dr. Strangelove*, on the understanding that British comedy star Peter Sellers would play multiple roles. Columbia did not realize, at the outset, that there would be no last-minute reprieve in Kubrick's version. Mankind blows itself to damnation with the help of maverick machinery, while emotionally and sexually retarded political and military leaders consider the merits of going into underground bunkers with a selection of nubile young girls. *Strangelove* was a frighteningly funny vision of men and machines in terminal chaos. Kubrick was acclaimed as the Best Director of 1964 by the New York critics, in a season when the entire, frightened world was desperate to laugh in the face of annihilation. Beaten to the market by *Strangelove*, Lumet's perfectly fine and sober *Fail-Safe* was overshadowed.

Harris had worked with Kubrick to set up the necessary deals for *Strangelove*, before departing, on perfectly amicable terms (the two men remained lifelong friends), to try his hand as an independent director. In his first and thoroughly accomplished film, *The Bedford Incident* (1965), Richard Widmark plays the obsessive captain of a Navy destroyer on the hunt for Soviet submarines. Rising star Sidney Poitier is a civilian press observer on the ship. When a submarine is located, ego, obsession, exhaustion, and unspoken racism lead to disaster for all on board.

While shooting *Strangelove*, Kubrick renewed his friendship with New York street photographer Arthur Fellig, more popularly known as "Weegee." His press photographs of crime scenes were so vivid, he was said to have used a spirit-summoning Ouija board to predict when crimes were about to happen. (In fact he used a licensed police radio.) His craft skills were exceptional, and his vivid,

Kubrick's space epic shows humans in contact with something unknown—and perhaps, fundamentally unknowable. This publicity shot captures space-suited lunar explorers as they prepare to walk down a ramp and into a freshly excavated trench, where a mysterious artifact awaits them.

Space artist Robert McCall was commissioned to make three artworks for use in movie posters. In this scene, Bowman rockets away from the *Discovery* in a one-man space pod. The giant planet Jupiter looms in the background, with one of its moons at upper right. McCall exaggerated the pod's rocket plume for dramatic effect.

often darkly fascinating photos bridged the divide between reportage and art. Kubrick invited him to take some of the publicity stills for *Strangelove*. Sellers, a keen photographer himself, loved having Weegee around—and it was his heavily accented voice, not Wernher von Braun's, that gave Sellers the inspiration he needed for his manic scientist's wayward speech patterns.

KUBRICK AND THE MACHINES

In the opening credits for *Dr. Strangelove*, we see something that even the science-fiction films of the day had seldom touched upon. Kubrick shows us a huge jet bomber nuzzling its stratospheric bulk against the tip of a probe on the belly of another plane. Literally, the scene depicts the bomber refueling in mid-air, a procedure that extended strike capability in an era when intercontinental missile technology was still too unreliable to replace bombers altogether. Figuratively, Kubrick shows us machines copulating. Having sex. Pushing the point home, he plays Vera Lynn on the soundtrack, singing the 1940s hit "Try a Little Tenderness." As the bomber twists and jiggles with a balletic delicacy completely at odds with its ugly purpose, we are invited to speculate on the unlikely lyricism and intimacy of machines.

Kubrick spends much of *Strangelove* contrasting the logical formalism of the machines with the manic disorganization of fleshy humanity. The planes, the bombs, and so forth actually seem disconnected from the human realm. Men pilot the planes, but there is no obvious sign that they actually designed and built them in the first place. Even the piloting is a process where pudgy, rote-educated men of average intelligence stare at the cockpit's cryptic symbols, gauges, and instruments, and then "obey" the instructions issuing from the control panels, like the clown Charlie Chaplin in *Modern Times*, only with a much greater pratfall in store.

Subsequently, and throughout *Strangelove*, we are shown specific details of encoding devices, cockpit controls, and bomb-release mechanisms. Kubrick's first intention is to explain what flying a nuclear raid is really like. (Careful trawling of aviation journals had yielded sufficient information to alarm the authorities.) Beyond this purely narrative show-and-tell, he invests the machinery with the same kind of loaded significance that is conventionally attached to human actors.

The sets and décor were expressive of man's intertwined and complex relationship with technology. Ken Adam, designer of the underground lair in the first James Bond film, *Dr. No* (1962), was responsible for *Strangelove*'s unforgettable War Room, with its polished floor, circular table and lighting rig, oddly sloping walls, and huge graphic displays.

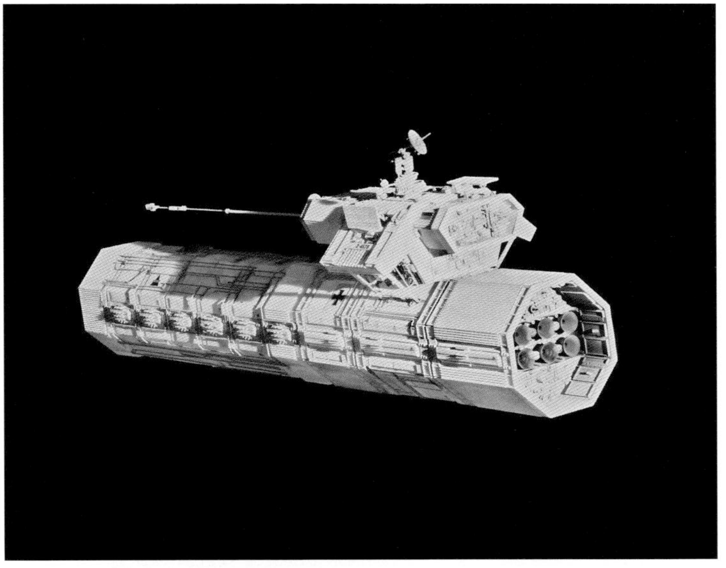

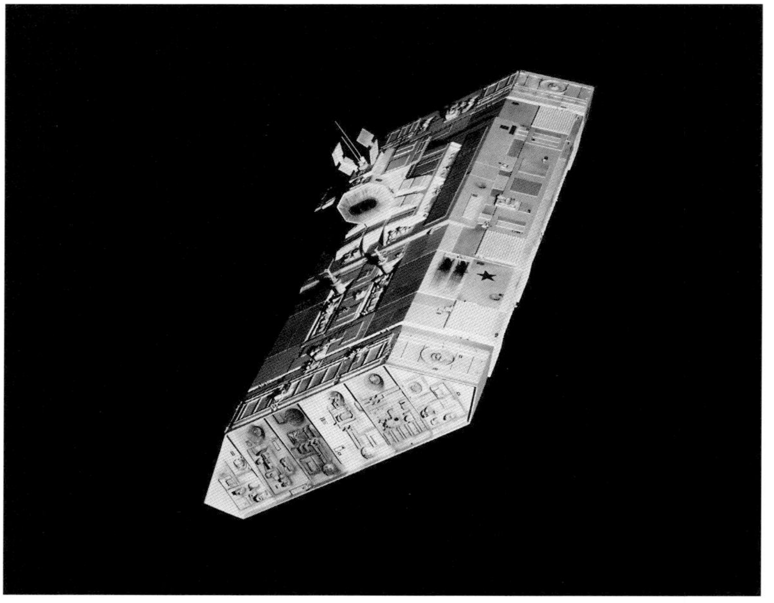

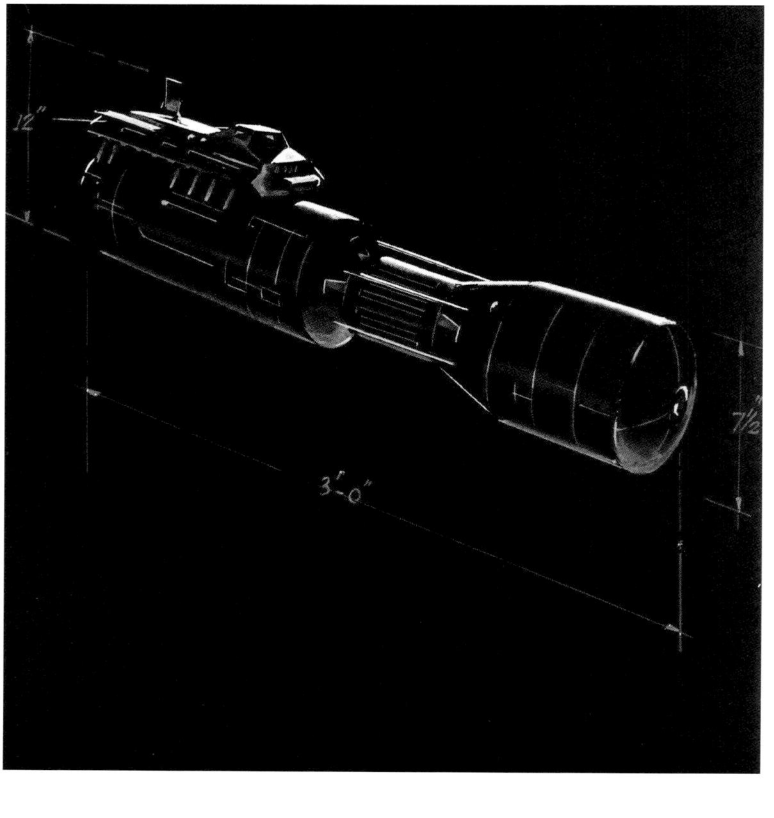
12"
3'-0"
7½"

The room's design was inspired by the theory that an angular structure would deflect an impacting bomb. Kubrick had also insisted—and this was a hallmark of his style throughout his career—that the light sources in the room had to be explicable in terms of the setting. Fill-in lamps and reflectors obviously had to be used for enhancing bad shadows, but essentially, most of the light had to come from realistic fixtures, openly visible on screen. The B-52 cockpit was lit by the small lamps one would expect in such a plane, while the characters seated at Adam's circular War Room table were caught in the glare of a matching overhead circle of lights: just the kind of architectural detail that one would expect to find in a room of high political purpose and low pomposity.

The next and most ambitious project of Kubrick's career would introduce machines and settings as principal performers. Tools, weapons, and space compartments were to become subjects as well as objects in the drama. "There's no doubt that there's a deep emotional relationship between man and his machines, which are his children," he would tell the *New York Times* five years later. "There is a sexiness to beautiful machines. The smell of a Nikon camera. The feel of an Italian sports car, or a beautiful tape recorder. We are almost in a sort of biological machine society already. Man has always worshiped beauty, and I think there's a new kind of beauty afoot in the world." The possibility of nuclear destruction was just that: a choice, an option or an accidental ending. It wasn't an inevitability. Even as Kubrick derided the generals and despaired of our political leaders, he thought he could see a spark of light glinting in the darkness ahead. "The coming age of space flight," he hoped, would "change our view of ourselves and our world. There is a very close correlation between the ability of a civilization to make significant space voyages and its ability to learn to live with nuclear energy." [5]

This essential optimism—the idea that technology might be a force for progress as well as destruction—certainly was not new to Kubrick the youthful science-fiction enthusiast, even if it would take some years before he was ready to express such hopes on film. Alexander Walker, at that time a young critic for the London *Evening Standard*, first met him in 1957 in connection with *Paths of Glory*. As Walker prepared to leave the director's New York apartment after a long and friendly discussion, a consignment of films arrived. They turned out to be Japanese science fiction. Kubrick was familiarizing himself with their special effects. "Are you making a film about outer space?" Walker asked.

Kubrick shot him a dark and suspicious glance. "*Please!* Be careful what you write."

5 Ibid.

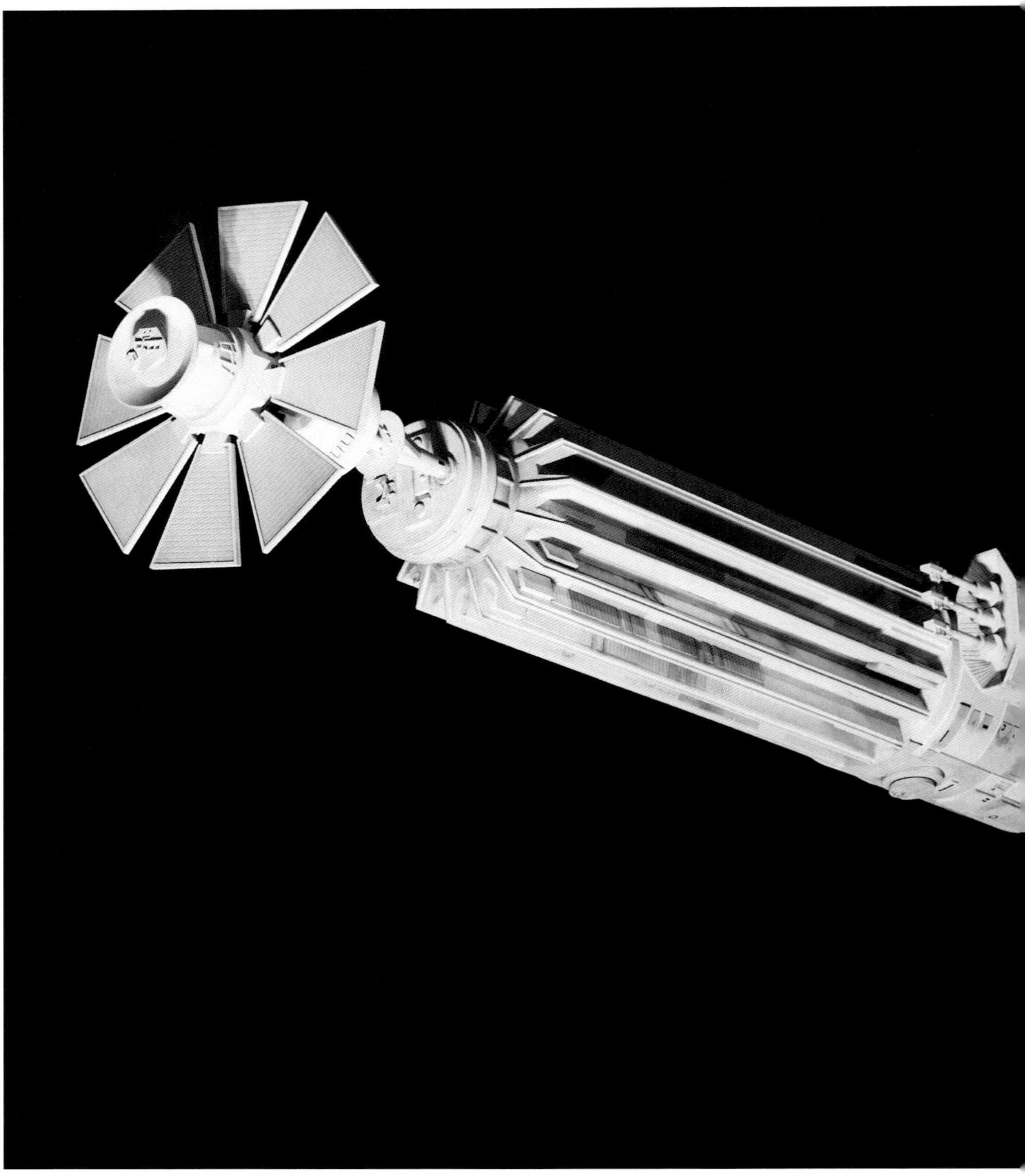

◃ 21–22 Kubrick and Clarke envisioned space weapons from France, the German Democratic Republic, Russia, and America cluttering the orbital realm. Kubrick did not specify that the first spaceships we see on screen are nuclear bombs, although the famous jump cut from murderous bone to a similarly shaped orbiting device is significant.

△ Even in the mid-1960s, at the height of the Soviet-American Cold War, the assumption was that China must also reach superpower status by the early 21st century. This artwork, and the resulting model, represent a Chinese orbiting nuclear weapon.

External scientific experts and aerospace engineers designed switch panels, display systems, and communications devices for the spacecraft interiors. Kubrick was relentless in his belief that every detail on screen had to be plausible, even if only glimpsed for a moment.

Even as Kubrick despaired at the technology of destruction, one or two explosive devices inspired by military hardware proved useful. This is the detailed switch panel for the space pod's rear hatch, which can be blown off in an emergency by small explosive charges. A warning sign on the hatch pushes the point home.

CAUTION
EXPLOSIVE BOLTS

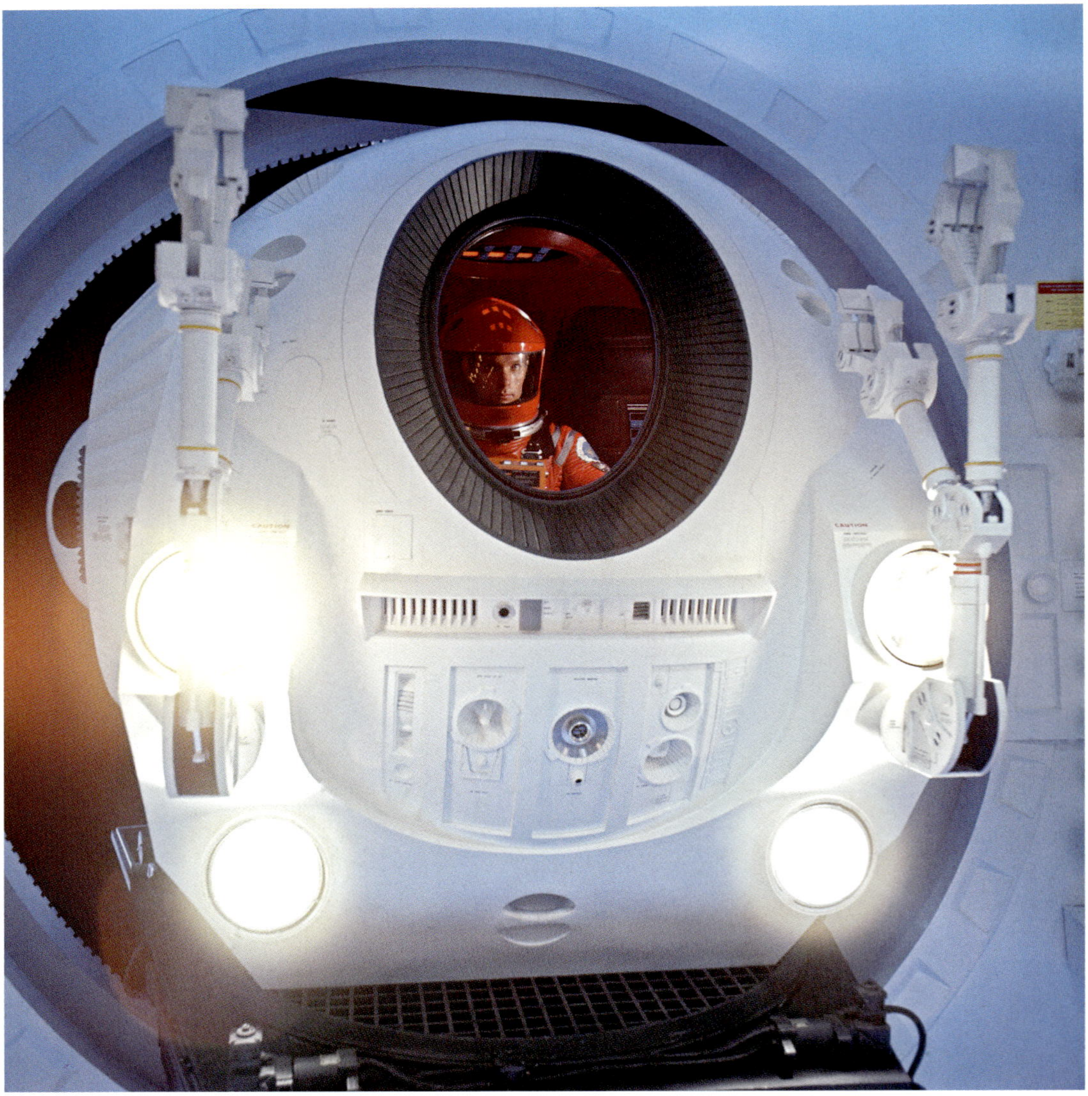

The fusion between us and our machines is a dominant theme. Does the elaborate equipment expand our range of expression and action, or are these airtight pods merely claustrophobic cages for the human spirit?

INTRODUCING ARTHUR C. CLARKE

In the late 20th century, Roger Caras was familiar to many Americans as an author and television presenter with a passion for animal conservation. In 1991 he was appointed president of the American Society for the Prevention of Cruelty to Animals. Few among his large nationwide audience would have suspected that he'd been a press secretary for the actress Joan Crawford and had moved on to merchandising at Columbia Pictures, before spending three years as one of Kubrick's closest associates as a Polaris Productions executive, and as vice president of the British-based cousin company Hawk Films. One of his tasks was to deal with the thousands of media requests for information and interviews throughout the making of *2001: A Space Odyssey*. He was involved in all aspects of the film's publicity, even down to licensing some of the spaceship designs to toy makers. Significantly, he introduced Kubrick to his co-screenwriter on the film. According to Caras's version of events, "Stanley and I were having lunch in February 1964, and he told me he was fascinated by aliens and extraterrestrials. 'I'm reading everything by everybody,' he said. So I told him to stop wasting time and get in touch with the best—Arthur C. Clarke."

Kubrick confirmed that he was familiar with Clarke's work, "but isn't he a recluse? A nut living up a tree some place?" Caras vigorously dispelled this myth. Clarke had left Britain in 1956 and set up home in Sri Lanka (then known as Ceylon), where he intended to pursue his interest in underwater exploration. He also wished to escape Britain's stuffy social conventions with regard to living arrangements. His standard answer when anyone asked him outright if he was gay was, "No, merely quite cheerful." One of his closest relationships was with fellow scuba enthusiast Leslie Ekanayake, who died in 1977 after a motorcycle accident. The extended

New American Library's first hardback edition of Clarke's novel, based on the screenplay cowritten with Kubrick, was published in June 1968, two months after the film's initial release.

△ Arthur C. Clarke in a relaxed pose on the pod bay set. Kubrick pushed Clarke to the limits of his endurance, yet never ceased to describe his co-screenwriter as indispensable to the success of *2001*. "As an artist, his ability to impart poignancy to a dying ocean or an intelligent vapor is unique," Kubrick said of him. "He has the kind of mind of which the world can never have enough."

Ekanayake clan looked after their strange British "relative" for the remainder of his long life. However private the nature of his home circumstances, Clarke was always perfectly contactable. Intrigued by Caras's recommendation, Kubrick subsequently wrote a letter to Clarke, dated March 31, 1964, saying that he was "a great admirer of your books" and that he "had always wanted to discuss with you the possibility of doing the proverbial 'really good' science-fiction movie." He wondered if Clarke might be available for a meeting "to determine whether an idea might exist or arise which would sufficiently interest both of us enough to want to collaborate on a screenplay." In particular, Kubrick highlighted three areas of interest:

Kubrick's associate producer Victor Lyndon is in center frame while Kubrick and Clarke pose as if for a script meeting in Lyndon's room. Kubrick's office was too untidy to serve as a backdrop.

▹ 37 Clarke is flanked by actors Gary Lockwood at left and Keir Dullea at right, as they attend a preview screening of *2001* in April 1968.

1 *The reason for believing in the existence of intelligent extraterrestrial life.*
2 *The impact (and perhaps lack of impact in some quarters) such a discovery would have on Earth in the near future.*
3 *A space probe with a landing on and exploration of the Moon and Mars.*

Clarke wrote back on April 8. "Naturally I was very pleased to get your letter," he enthused. "*Lolita* is one of the few films I have seen twice—the first time, to enjoy it, the second time to see how it was done." Promising to arrive in New York a few days hence for preliminary meetings, he warned Kubrick that he needed to be back in Ceylon within a couple of weeks because of tax problems. "They have injected me with a mysterious Oriental drug, unknown to Western science, which will cause me to die in convulsions if I am not back at the Tax Department to receive the antidote." More seriously he agreed with Kubrick that "the 'really good' science-fiction movie is a great many years overdue." Unsuccessfully, he tried to tempt Kubrick into working with him in Ceylon, "away from the distractions of civilization."

A publishing project with Time-Life for a book, *Man in Space*, already required Clarke's presence in New York over the coming month. An exploratory lunch meeting with Kubrick was easily arranged. The two first met on Wednesday, April 22, 1964, at Trader Vic's, a Polynesian-themed cocktail lounge and restaurant in the basement of the Plaza Hotel on 5th Avenue for which Kubrick had an unlikely fondness. The meeting stretched through lunch and a long, leisurely walk. Further companionable meetings followed over the next days. Clarke was impressed by Kubrick, and the respect was mutual, as they discussed "flying saucers, politics, the space program, Senator Goldwater, and of course, the projected movie."

Arthur Charles Clarke was born on December 16, 1917, in Minehead, a seaside town in southwest England. From 1924 his family lived on a farm called Ballifants, set among the picturesque Quantock Hills of Somerset County. Arthur and his brothers, Fred and Michael, and sister, Mary, were brought up by their mother, Nora. Her husband, Charles, had been a Post Office engineer in Somerset before serving in the Royal Engineers during the First World War. He never properly recovered from poison-gas injuries to his lungs, and died in 1931.

As a young man, Arthur also worked in the Post Office for a while, where he became fascinated by the latest communications systems of the time, such as valve radio sets, telegraph machines, and telephone switching rooms. In those days telephone operators switched calls with wires and plugs in giant pegboards. The British Post Office was a significant technological pioneer in an era before privatized phone services. In 1936 Clarke began work as a civil servant in London, becoming a junior auditor within the Exchequer,

the British government's tax and public finances administration. He also joined the British Interplanetary Society (BIS), a group of enthusiasts exploring the theoretical possibilities of space flight. His old school friends in Somerset called him "Scientific Sid," while his London companions knew him as "Ego" because he was never shy in stepping forward with his ideas. He took a close interest in a BIS proposal to design a Moon landing craft, based purely on existing scientific and technical knowledge. The BIS wanted to prove that space travel was not a science-fiction dream. It could actually be achieved. Clarke was satisfied with the technical realism of the plan. What was needed, he thought, was a sound economic reason for building such a ship.

During the Second World War Clarke served in the Royal Air Force, helping to develop radar-guided "talk-down" systems for bomber planes struggling to land in poor visibility. At war's end, he studied for his eventual First Class degree awards in mathematics and physics at King's College, London, while resuming his keen interest in space. By now, he thought he might have solved the problem that had first vexed him concerning the BIS Moonship proposal. Why would anyone wish to pay for such an expensive machine? What would be the social and economic purpose of space travel in its earliest, faltering steps?

More than a decade before the first artificial satellites of any kind were launched, Clarke proposed that if a satellite could be boosted to a particular region of space, 22,300 miles above the Earth, it could fly a 24-hour "geosynchronous" orbit, on the same plane as the Equator, keeping pace exactly with the planet's rotation and the ground beneath. The satellite would hover motionless in the sky, making it an ideal radio-relay platform. Three

A production sketch shows the alien artifact as a pyramid, in keeping with Clarke's short story "The Sentinel." Kubrick's Widelux camera frame of the completed Tycho excavation set reveals his eventual preference: the famous black monolith. The word "monolithic" literally means "of a single stone," and is commonly used to denote impenetrable uniformity.

▹ 41 Technical consultant Frederick I. Ordway (top left) and production designer Harry Lange, posing on the shell of the centrifuge wheel.

satellites, communicating with the ground and with each other, would provide total global communications—and a massively profitable industry into the bargain. Clarke's only mistake was to imagine that each of his large satellites, crammed with heavy valve radio equipment, would require a maintenance crew, thereby fulfilling his principal aim: to justify the costs of sending humans into space. In October 1945 a British trade journal, *Wireless World*, published his ideas as a four-page technical paper entitled "Extra-Terrestrial Relays: Can Rocket Stations Give World-wide Coverage?" The magazine's editors were wary of associating themselves with a scheme that looked more like science fiction than sound engineering. In fact, it proved to be one of the founding documents of modern times. In 1964 the first geostationary communications satellite, Syncom 3, was used to broadcast television pictures from the Summer Olympics in Tokyo, just as Clarke had proposed.

Clarke's first book, *Interplanetary Flight: An Introduction to Astronautics*, was published by Temple Press of London in 1950, and by Harper Brothers in the U.S. a year later. This compelling and sometimes impassioned account of rocket technology and its potential benefits was rounded off with an appendix containing the necessary mathematical formulae, from the required rocket thrusts to the calculations of orbits and interplanetary trajectories. Such an accomplished technical manifesto, and the earlier paper on communications satellites, would have been sufficient to guarantee Clarke's reputation among like-minded engineers. The wider public came to know him through his vast output of short stories and novels, almost all dedicated to the subject of space, and humankind's place in the cosmos. His first published novel, *The Sands of Mars* (1951), depicts colonists on the Red Planet seeking self-sufficiency. *Prelude to Space*, compiled from a previously published magazine series, told of the first manned mission to the Moon. *Islands in the Sky* (1952) introduced a young audience to the notion of weightlessness, and described how it would feel to live under the centrifugally induced artificial gravity aboard a rotating space station. The central character is a boy who makes a trip to orbit after winning a TV game show.

It was Clarke's third novel that won him worldwide recognition as a fiction writer. *Childhood's End* (1953) tells how our traditional images of devils and demons come not from cultural influences in our past, but rather, from a collective premonition of something destined to happen in the future—our encounter of benign aliens with bodies that happen to look like leathery demons. The "Overlords" arrive in gigantic ships and position themselves in the skies above Earth's major cities. From these lofty and impregnable outposts, they exert an influence over human affairs. Their purpose is to prepare us for a time when we will depart from our physical selves and set up home as part of a greater cosmic entity, the "Overmind." This turns out to be a collective intelligence derived from a union of countless galactic civilizations, all of whom have freed themselves from ordinary

material concerns, breaking loose from the bonds of space and time. The Overlords turn out to be much more pleasant than their outer shapes suggest. Indeed, they are positively heroic. An unfortunate flaw in their biology prevents them from joining in our great psychic ascent. After all their interventions on our behalf, they can only observe our progress from the sidelines.

By the time of his first encounter with Kubrick, 47-year-old Clarke's status as a space visionary was secure. He found his workload for the *Man and Space* book relatively undemanding: "Whenever one of the researchers asked me, 'What is your authority for this statement?' I would look at her firmly and reply, 'I am.' So I had ample time for moonlighting with Stanley Kubrick."[6]

The second thing Clarke noticed about Kubrick was his sharp intelligence, allied to a restless curiosity. He could absorb new ideas almost instantly and seemed to forget nothing, no matter how apparently trivial. He asked incessant questions, and stored the resultant answers away as if in the memory of a computer. In the months that followed Clarke would often tell his friends, "Every time I finish a meeting with Stanley, I have to go lie down." The first quality about him that struck Clarke as unusual was his "night person's pallor." Apparently he was a man who functioned best in the small hours of the morning. Many collaborators with more traditional sleeping habits would discover this.

The Trader Vic's encounter established the tone for further long afternoons ambling companionably through New York, visiting art galleries and bars. They talked incessantly about the latest developments in astronomy, anthropology, and rocket flight, while deciding how their collaboration might work, and thinking about how far into the future their narrative should be set. According to Clarke, "The first actual lunar landing still seemed, psychologically, a dream of the far future. Intellectually, we knew that it was inevitable. Emotionally, we still couldn't really believe it—as indeed, some foolish people do not believe it even now. NASA was spending the entire budget of our movie, over $10 million, every day, so the portents were clear. Our film would still be on its first run while men were actually walking on the Moon. We had to out-guess the future." The challenge was how to create "a story that would not be made obsolete, or even worse, ridiculous, by the events of the next few years." Both men agreed that the safest course was to be so far ahead of present-day technologies that there could be no danger of factual developments overtaking them. "On the other hand, if we got too far ahead there would be a grave risk of losing contact with our audience." The two men selected the turn of the century as a suitable time frame, although the actual year 2001 wasn't yet in their minds.

6 Clarke, Arthur C., "Son of Dr. Strangelove," reprinted in *Report on Planet Three*, Victor Gollancz, 1973

△▷ 44 The exterior of the *Aries* lunar spacecraft set. Appropriate carpenters and set decorators could be recruited from within MGM's studio complex at Borehamwood, in these last years before cutbacks and studio closures became inevitable.

Kubrick, a man of visual imagination and often spontaneous narrative instinct, disliked film scripts, once describing them as "the most uncommunicative form of writing ever devised." The two men decided to write a scenario in the form of a conventional text flavored with all the tropes and linguistic flourishes of a novel, which—eventually—could be published as a book to accompany the film. Kubrick predicted, optimistically, that the film would take around two years to complete. An early draft of the novel would be used as a "treatment," the primary sales tool for attracting the necessary production budget from a major Hollywood studio. Only later would they thrash out a shooting script, the comparatively duller document that would outline each set or location and specify every last line of dialogue. The screenwriting credits would highlight Kubrick over Clarke, while the subsequent book promotion would display Clarke's name over Kubrick's. This was a fair reflection of the eventual facts. Clarke was responsible for most of the novel, while Kubrick had absolute control over the film script, but both men contributed ideas, so that it often became impossible to determine who had first thought of what.[7]

Such a writing partnership was unusual for the film trade at that time. Ordinarily, a studio or a producer acquired the rights to a preexisting novel that had already attracted public renown (or notoriety) and commissioned a screenplay broadly based upon it; or else a script was developed from a purely cinematic concept, and a commissioned author subsequently expanded it into a novel that would slipstream behind the success of the film in question. Kubrick and Clarke decided that their two creative works, novel and film, were to emerge in tandem and would coexist as overlapping expressions of the same material.

On May 17, 1964, Clarke formally agreed to collaborate on a project whose working title, *Journey Beyond the Stars*, was purely provisional. Late that night, as the two men celebrated on the rooftop deck of the Kubrick family's penthouse apartment on East 84th Street, they saw a brilliant star moving swiftly across the sky, straight overhead, and apparently come to a stop. Then it moved on again. Subsequent investigation proved the strange star to be *Echo II*, an inflated silver sphere launched earlier that year as part of a NASA project to bounce microwave signals off a reflective target. Clarke immediately suspected that "the apparent hovering was deceptive, a trick of our viewpoint. We were fooled. And, of course, we were excited, and it did seem strange that the only time in my life I ever saw a UFO that gave me a moment's pause was the very evening that Stanley and I decided to make the film." Kubrick also wondered if he should look into insuring his project against the possibility of being outpaced by an actual alien discovery.

Clarke resigned himself to several months in New York, hoping that he might return to Ceylon by the end of the year. Roger Caras knew he had introduced one powerful mind

7 Ibid.

to another: "Arthur had a tremendous ego, and quite rightly, because of his many accomplishments. He loved taking pride in what he'd done. I never saw Arthur take a back seat to anybody in his entire life, except for Stanley. But I believe Stanley was also very impressed by Arthur. When those two were together, bouncing ideas off each other, it was like watching two intellectual duelists."

Much of the dueling took place at the Kubrick residence. Jeremy Bernstein, the *New Yorker* scientist-writer, visited 84th Street from time to time, and found "a mixture of Christiane's lovely paintings, the effects of three rambunctious young children, and Kubrick's inevitable collection of cameras, tape recorders, and hi-fi sets." Christiane, an accomplished artist whose studio accoutrements took up almost as much domestic space as Stanley's film paraphernalia, recalls their home as "two adjoining apartments knocked into one, with a balcony all round, and an incinerator chimney on the building's roof that snowed oily ashes on everything. The balcony and windows were at a dizzying height, so Stanley always worried that the children would fall off. Inside, the ceilings were low, which I hated, but we had lots of different rooms, which was good, because there was plenty of space to work." It seems that the Polaris Productions offices were largely irrelevant. "Jimmy Harris thought they were a good idea, along with a secretary and a reception desk. Stanley thought, 'Who am I trying to impress?' He liked to get out of bed and start working, even in his dressing-gown."

The work rooms were adorned with planning charts, speculative space artwork, and sketches for the proposed new film. As Clarke and Kubrick brainstormed, the frequent distractions generated by the children were refreshing; the endless phone calls and visitors, less so. Christiane's husband had a remarkable quality: "He was not interruptible. By that, I mean, you *could* interrupt him and it wouldn't make any difference to his train of thought. He was interrupted by a thousand things, and would instantly go back afterwards to what he was doing, without getting tense. I think this was an unappreciated gift that he had. Most people have to lock themselves away. So, he would get angry with some lawyer on the phone, and he'd be fuming. Afterwards he'd put the phone down again and be perfectly happy. Most of us can't do that."

Clarke was among those who couldn't. When the time came for him to start typing, he survived for one day at the Kubricks, and a similarly brief period in the Polaris offices, before retreating to the relative safety of the Chelsea Hotel on West 23rd Street, where he barricaded himself as best he could. This particular hotel was famous for its indulgent cosseting of creative genius. Its brochure of the time advertised "an oasis of friendliness for people of temperament" and highlighted "large and soundproofed" rooms. Clarke would sometimes wander into the bar for a chat with William Burroughs or Allen Ginsberg.

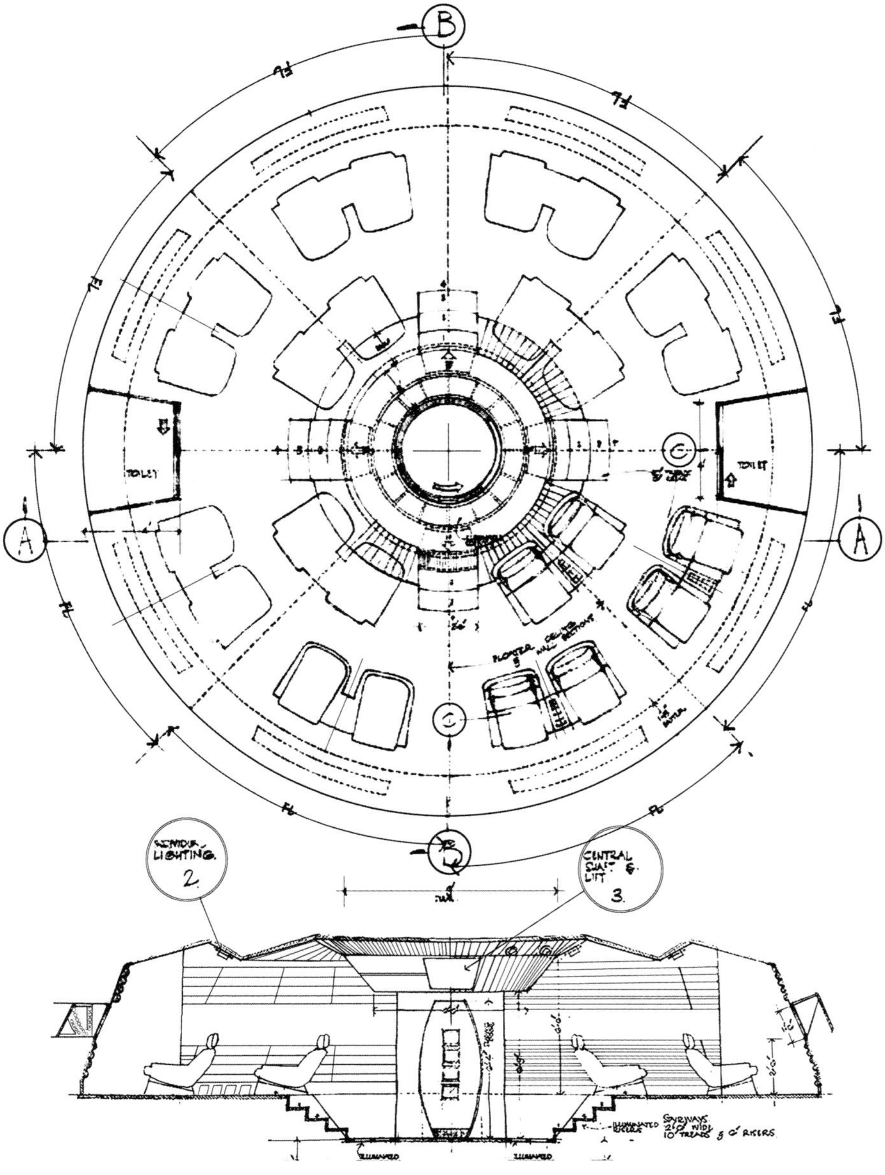

Construction drawings for the passenger cabin of the *Aries* ferry.

▹ 48/49 Fashion designer Hardy Amies designed the nontechnical costumes for the film, including the uniforms and padded hats for these stewardesses on board the *Aries* lunar ferry.

Meanwhile Kubrick's lawyer, Louis Blau, investigated the possibility of a bank loan to keep the Ceylonese tax poisoners at bay. The expectation was that book sales would solve all Clarke's problems at a stroke. No one suspected that the film would take nearly four years to complete.

Kubrick screened a number of science-fiction films that, in Clarke's opinion, were worth at least a passing glance. His reaction to Alexander Korda's *Things to Come* (1936) was scathing. "What are you trying to do to me?" he said. "I'll never see another movie you recommend." Nevertheless, a couple did contain good ideas. The first was Fred Wilcox's *Forbidden Planet* (1956), based loosely on Shakespeare's *The Tempest.*

An interstellar saucer commanded by Leslie Nielsen (later of *Airplane!* fame) arrives on the planet Altair to rescue Morbius, a stranded scientist played by Walter Pidgeon. Nielsen and his crew are beguiled by Morbius's daughter (Anne Francis). Equally impressive is Morbius's intelligent mechanical helper, Robby the Robot, a fabulous special-effects prop by the standards of his day. Morbius has no wish to leave Altair, because he is charting the remains of its vanished civilization, the Krell. Colossal machinery still hums in underground caverns. Obviously the Krell were an advanced species, yet there is no sign of them. As Morbius and his would-be rescuers discover, the Krell developed technologies that could turn their merest thoughts into reality. They became "a civilization without instrumentality." Unwisely, Morbius tinkers with the abandoned machinery and is visited by the darkest elements of his unconscious mind, expressed as a destructive force field. Perhaps the Krell conjured their own demons, and on a far more powerful scale, inadvertently causing their own demise? Not bad for 1950s hokum. More significantly, *Forbidden Planet* sets up an intriguing environment that feels genuinely alien, a source of wonderment and curiosity that is not neatly explained away.

The second film of note was *The Day the Earth Stood Still* (1951). Michael Rennie is the alien envoy Klaatu, landing in Washington in a sleek silver-gray saucer to warn the world that it must give up its nuclear weapons, or else be punished by a superior galactic collective of civilizations. On Klaatu's departure after a series of misunderstandings and mutual suspicions, his tall robot Gort (sleek silver-gray) stays behind as a police presence. Throughout the development of *Journey Beyond the Stars*, and even well into the shooting phase, orbiting nuclear bombs and a continuing Cold War standoff in space were strong themes. At the climax of Clarke's eventual novel, the "starchild" intervenes by harmlessly detonating the space weapons because "he preferred a cleaner sky." Some readers weren't even sure that this destruction was harmless.

THE SOURCE MATERIALS

Kubrick purchased half a dozen of Clarke's short stories, in the expectation that at least one, and perhaps all of them, might form the seed crystal around which the grander project could coalesce. In "Breaking Strain," a freighter bound for Venus is hit by a meteor. Most of the ship's oxygen is lost overboard (a scenario foreshadowing the Apollo 13 crisis in 1970). Clarke's two crewmen face a horrifying problem: the remaining oxygen supply will only allow one of them to survive the flight. "Into the Comet" describes a computer failure during a mission to rendezvous with a comet. The crew improvise the ship's navigation using the principle of an ancient abacus counting frame. "Out of the Cradle, Endlessly Orbiting" tells of the first human to be born off the Earth, thereby establishing us as a true space-faring species; and in "Before Eden," scientists landing on Venus encounter simple plant life capable of inching across the terrain in matted colonies. When the explorers depart at the end of their mission, the plants extract nutrients from rubbish left behind, including earthly viruses and bacteria more complex than their own cells. Inevitably, most of these microorganisms will perish in the harsh Venusian environments, but some are absorbed by the native organisms, which proceed to die out even at the very dawn of their evolution.

In "Who's There?," an astronaut clambers into a hard-shelled cylindrical suit: effectively an independent short-range spacecraft. As he ventures outside a space station to conduct repairs, he feels something touching him and cannot turn around in the cramped compartment to identify the source of this frightening sensation. His imagination lets loose and he worries that the ghost of a colleague, killed in an earlier accident in that same suit, might be haunting him. Eventually he realizes that the station's cat has deposited three kittens inside the suit. While the cats were not especially significant, the hardware ideas found their way into Kubrick's film.

None of these tales were sufficient, as individual narratives, to determine the film's plot. Clarke subsequently bought most of them back from Kubrick, hoping that they might be useful for other film projects one day. Nevertheless, a couple of themes did stimulate discussion. "Before Eden" hinted at the idea of superior intelligences accidentally interfering in the evolutionary destiny of a less advanced species, while "Breaking Strain" established lack of oxygen as a useful dramatic device. Clarke had always been interested in what happens if someone is forced to venture into space without a pressure suit. "It's a complete myth that you explode in a burst of blood and gore. All that happens is that you feel a freezing sensation, and experience a nasty pain in your ears as the pressure vanishes—and, of course, you'll die in about a minute or so, because you can't get any air. Actually you retain consciousness for fifteen seconds or more if you're adequately prepared, and that gives you plenty of time to do something." This curious fascination certainly decided a key moment when astronaut Dave Bowman breaks into an emergency airlock from the outside, without the protection of his helmet.

It was the sixth short text among those purchased by Kubrick that provided the central narrative device, although Clarke insisted in later years that "the resulting film bore as much relation to that story as a full-grown oak to an acorn." Even before the Trader Vic's meeting, Clarke had dispatched a restlessly excitable second letter to Kubrick in New York. "I have thought of a nice opening for a space movie which might give you some ideas," he said, afire at the prospect of collaborating on a screenplay.

> *Opening: Screen full of stars. A completely black disc slowly drifts in from the left until it fills the center of the screen, eclipsing the stars. Its right-hand edge lightens, the glow of the corona appears, and the sun rises… We realize we are looking down on the night side of the Moon.*

This is not so far removed from what we actually see in the opening few seconds of the eventual film. Clarke had the rather neat idea that the soundtrack should consist

CAUTION
WEIGHTLESS
CONDITION

Kubrick and Clarke pose for publicity photographs inside the passenger deck set of the *Aries* lunar ferry. Clarke's suit is crisply pressed for the occasion, while Kubrick's clothes, as usual, are worn carelessly.

of radio chatter, with American, Russian, French, and British voices discernible among the static crackle. "We establish a sound-picture of a co-operative and energetic lunar exploration effort. We can tell from the rising excitement and incoherent phrases that a survey team has found something quite out of the ordinary. The situation described in "The Sentinel" then develops. Briefly, the explorers discover a strange mechanism like a giant crystal..."

"The Sentinel," written by Clarke in 1948 for a BBC Radio short-story competition (which it failed to win), was first published in a 1951 science-fiction anthology, *10 Story Fantasy*. A roving team of lunar explorers discover a crystalline alien pyramid resting on a circle of undisturbed terrain. There are countless small craters just outside the perimeter of the circle: pockmarked evidence of meteorite impacts over many aeons. In marked contrast, the floor on which the pyramid sits is perfectly smooth. An invisible dome of energy has protected the eerie object. Judging by the state of the surrounding landscape, pitted and scarred by long exposure to the cosmic elements, the pyramid must have been set in place when the Earth itself was young. Eventually the pyramid's force field is penetrated, or rather smashed, using the unsubtle force of nuclear energy. One of the scientists speculates that this abrupt destruction will alert some unseen intelligence that life has arisen on Earth and taken its first steps into space. He suspects that the alien device is just "one of millions scattered throughout the universe, watching over all worlds with the promise of life, and patiently signaling the fact that no one had discovered it." With the breaking of the force field, "we have set off the fire alarm and have nothing to do now but wait."

While Clarke stressed his conviction that "The Sentinel" was a solid platform for the film treatment, another story, not among those purchased by Kubrick, began to gnaw at him. "Encounter in the Dawn" was first published in the June 1953 edition of *Amazing Stories* magazine. The action is set at least 100,000 years ago. Three alien scientists conduct a survey among "the loosely packed stars at the rim of the Milky Way." On seeing the Earth, they are reminded of their own planet as it was in more peaceful times, before an unspecified age of innocence came to an end. They search for kindred sparks of intelligence in our solar system, knowing all the while that their distant homes and families are threatened by "the shadow that lay across civilization." After targeting the Earth for closer investigation, one of the explorers, Clindar, gradually tames a hunter-gatherer hominid male, named Yaan, as he emerges each morning from "a village of flimsy huts ringed by a wooden palisade" and sets off along a familiar hunting path. A tentative respect develops between the primitive not-quite human and his immensely more advanced visitor.

As the expedition departs, Clindar leaves behind a few simple objects, hoping that Yaan and his community might learn how to benefit from them and prosper into some far-off future. Clindar only wishes he could warn Yaan "of the mistakes we made, and which now will cost us all that we have won." Here is a mournful mirror image of *The Day the Earth Stood Still*, in which the clever aliens, rather than the backward humans, are the ones threatening to self-destruct. An idea just as significant as the alien alarm system from "The Sentinel" is expressed when Clindar tries to persuade Yaan to accept a parting gift: "I'm leaving you these tools. Some of them, you will discover how to use. See how this blade cuts, and guard it well."

In early October 1964, just as Clarke was finishing what he hoped would be a solid first draft of the *Journey* treatment, he found additional inspiration in the book *African Genesis* (1961) by playwright-turned-anthropologist Robert Ardrey. One of his themes was that the ability to kill was a major factor in our survival, "we" being the descendants of just one hominid species that must have gained dominance over several others, now extinct. "We were born of risen apes, not fallen angels, and the apes were armed killers besides," he wrote. In vivid, populist prose, Ardrey explained to his Cold War–era readers why "our murders and massacres and missiles, and our irreconcilable regiments" are modern manifestations of prehistoric instincts from which we cannot easily escape. Yet there is always hope, for "the miracle of man is not how far he has sunk but how magnificently he has risen. We are known among the stars by our poems, not our corpses."

Ardrey also speculated about the possible effect of cosmic rays on the chemistry of life. He knew that such radiation is potentially harmful (we are fortunate that the Earth's atmosphere blocks most of it long before it reaches the ground), but he thought that, very occasionally, such molecular disruptions might spur evolutionarily useful mutations. This is the passage in African Genesis that Clarke found particularly striking:

> *Would evolution's experiment come to a tragic failure? Why did not the human line become extinct in the depths of the Pliocene? We know that, but for a gift from the stars, but for the accidental collision of ray and gene, intelligence would have perished on some forgotten African field… The battered, defeated ape, by luck and necessity and generalized potential, turned in time to vaster pastures and became the most successful animal that the world has ever seen.*

HOW THE SOLAR SYSTEM WAS WON

By the end of 1964 a draft of the novelized treatment was in sufficiently good shape to be submitted as a film proposal. Clarke presented it as a Christmas present, and Kubrick's lawyer, Louis Blau, then set the wheels in motion ahead of pitching the idea to a studio. Curiously, the backers of *Dr. Strangelove* were the least likely people to step forward and embrace Kubrick's new project. Columbia Pictures' conservative senior executives were embarrassed by his unflattering portrayal of the American defense establishment. Co-screenwriter Terry Southern was hauled aside by Columbia executive Mo Rothman. "Just tell Stanley that New York does not see *anything* funny about the end of the world!" Rothman paused for a moment, then added, "As we know it." Audiences thought otherwise, and Columbia took what comfort it could from the film's critical and commercial success. Rothman's distrust aside, there were additional compelling reasons for Kubrick to go elsewhere with *Journey Beyond the Stars.*[8]

Metro-Goldwyn-Mayer, or MGM, was founded in 1924. Two preexisting companies, Metro and Goldwyn Pictures, were absorbed into the new empire. MGM became a star-making factory. Greta Garbo, Joan Crawford, Clark Gable, Spencer Tracy, James Stewart, and Elizabeth Taylor were talent-spotted, trained, and presented on screen in exactingly controlled circumstances. MGM's marketing office promised "more stars than there are in heaven." Talented directors suffered the studio lash in return for the chance to work with famous stars striding across lavishly funded sets, or singing and dancing their way through exuberant musicals. From the 1930s to well into the 1950s, MGM was unassailable. By the mid-1960s, television was eating into its audience share, and executives were fending off takeover bids for the company's ailing remains. Fortunately, when Kubrick and Clarke sent in their treatment at the end of 1964, the famous roaring lion was still on its feet.

Hollywood studio chiefs had a well-earned reputation as egotistical, bombastic, party-going, power-crazed, lustful, and often ruthless eccentrics. Robert O'Brien was an unusually humane newcomer to the trade, recruited by MGM specifically for his more modern corporate and political skills. As a young man, he had served in Franklin Roosevelt's Public Works Administration, one of the vast schemes of national reconstruction implemented after the Wall Street crash of 1929. He worked, also, at the sober Securities and Exchange Commission, where he helped to implement the first formal regulation of electric utility companies. Advised by friends to try his luck in the film business, he joined

8 Southern, Terry, "Notes from the War Room," *Grand Street*, Summer 1994, Vol. 13, Issue 1

Paramount for a few years before accepting a senior role at MGM in 1963, even while freely admitting, "I'm no movie mogul." His main task was to rebalance the books after MGM's troubles with *Mutiny on the Bounty* (1962). Despite the presence of Marlon Brando, and excellent box-office receipts, *Mutiny*'s budget had spun out of control and the project made a significant loss. O'Brien brought matters back on track with a series of happier investments. He was particularly pleased when *Doctor Zhivago*, a film that he personally nurtured, proved a commercial success in 1965.

O'Brien and his fellow board members at MGM were interested in a widescreen film format called Cinerama, whose scale and grandeur was designed to compete with the dangerous attractions of television, the dreadful little box that was keeping too many audience members at home when they should have been at the movies. The Cinerama logo gives an idea of the format's original process, based on the work of a restlessly clever inventor, Fred Waller, and first unveiled in 1952 for a presentation called *This Is Cinerama*. Original photography required three cameras combined in one rig, with a common shutter mechanism ensuring that each trio of film frames was exposed simultaneously. The middle camera was pointed directly into the scene, while the left and right cameras were diverted sideways from the central axis. The result was a cumulative angle of view that approximated the wide peripheral scope of human vision. The finished footage was shown in specially equipped venues running three projectors. The neatly abutting images were beamed onto a huge curved screen in such a way that the joins (almost) did not show.

On the plus side, audiences experienced something akin to what we might now call an "immersive" sensory experience. Cinerama was superb for depictions of wild open landscapes, surging oceans, and big skies. The drawback was its lack of intimacy as a canvas for human drama. Audiences for MGM's *How the West Was Won* (1962) often had the impression that actors on the edges of the action were looking in the wrong direction when speaking to fellow performers in the middle of the composition. In response to these flaws, film producer Mike Todd, one of the founders of the original Cinerama process, revived an earlier experiment first tried by 20th Century Fox in the 1920s and only abandoned because of a lack of enthusiasm from movie theaters back then. Simply, the idea was to use just a single camera loaded with an unusually wide film. The complications of matching three cameras and processing three strips of film would be eliminated at a stroke. Fox's successful 1955 version of the musical *Oklahoma!* was photographed in the "Todd A-O" 70 mm-wide film format. Lean's *Lawrence of Arabia*, and the musicals *My Fair Lady* and *The Sound of Music*, made in the early 1960s, were among the most famous films presented in 70 mm widescreen. The films were shot on 65 mm negative and the images printed onto 70 mm positive print stock for projection. The additional 5 mm accommodated stereo

In a typical publicity photograph by unit photographer John Jay, Robert Beatty models what the well-dressed scientist-administrator of the 21st century was expected to wear: a space helmet and pressure suit.

Character actor and comedian Leonard Rossiter nearly breaks through the expressionless style of acting demanded by *2001*. Watch him sneakily retrieve his whiskey glass from the opposite side of the table in the space station lounge.

soundtracks. Two companies in particular, Mitchell and Panavision, developed cameras and lenses suitable for this format.

Most movie theaters were too small and modest to accommodate the giant screen and huge projectors required for Cinerama. Marketing depended on a concept known as the "roadshow." Relatively few American cinemas in the 1960s, and perhaps one or two in each major city around the world, were equipped with appropriate projectors. Audiences would book in advance for these premium-priced screenings, as if attending a long run of a successful Broadway play. Many months later, word of mouth would lure audiences in smaller towns into booking seats for a more widely distributed 35 mm release. The 65 mm film would be printed down in a horizontally squeezed "anamorphic" format onto the smaller stock, and artificially widened out again by compensatory optics in the projectors. The results, when screened, were not so grand as true Cinerama, but film fans in fleapits and drive-ins at least got to see something.

MGM, therefore, looked for Cinerama proposals that offered landscapes as sweeping as the canyons and prairies in *How the West Was Won*, while at the same time delivering fresh excitements for audiences who, perhaps, would have seen enough cowboys and singing nuns for the time being. At the dawn of the Space Age, every newspaper, magazine, and television

Krystina Marr and her sister Irena Marr took uncredited roles as Russian scientists alongside Tyzack and Rossiter.

Margaret Tyzack was a classically trained actor working with the Royal Shakespeare Company, and had starred alongside Sylvester in a spy drama before Kubrick hired her.

station breathlessly reported on NASA's progress, from one-man Mercury capsules lofted on firecracker rockets to the sportier two-seat Gemini craft. American space agency NASA was reaching toward its ultimate, presidentially mandated goal, a lunar landing expedition using rockets whose size and power could barely be grasped, even by the people building them. Kubrick and Clarke had every reason to think that space opened up superb possibilities for a widescreen extravaganza. This faith was reflected in a joke working title for their film: *How the Solar System Was Won*.

MGM took the bait. A press release for February 23, 1965, much of it drafted by Kubrick, announced the studio's intention to back *Journey Beyond the Stars*, a film "based on a novel to be published this winter." This "epic story of adventure and exploration, encompassing the Earth, the planets of our Solar System and a journey light-years away to another part of the Galaxy" was expected to begin production on August 16, and would be filmed in Cinerama "on locations in Britain, Switzerland, Africa, Germany and the United States." According to Kubrick's loyal publicity man Roger Caras, "Bob O'Brien was a believer. He wasn't jaded, like so many of them. Considering his position as the head of a major Hollywood movie studio, he was a very decent man." Over the years ahead, Kubrick would often acknowledge his debt of gratitude: "O'Brien trusted my judgment. He is a

Keir Dullea played *Discovery*'s self-controlled commander, David Bowman. Earlier roles as a chilly charmer with psychopathic tendencies suggested a capacity for violence and terror behind the young actor's seemingly dispassionate exterior. Freeborn's makeup department aged him a few years by adding hints of gray to his hair.

Gary Lockwood's athletic build, and previous experience as a college sportsman, recommended him as Frank Poole, the most obviously physical human presence aboard *Discovery*, especially when he shadowboxes around the centrifuge.

wonderful man, and one of the very few film bosses able to inspire genuine loyalty and affection from his film-makers."[9]

MGM was ready with a draft contract by the end of March 1965. Certain provisions are amusing in light of subsequent developments. For instance, the film was supposed to be completed by the fall of 1966, and to cost around $6 million (approximately $50 million in today's terms). MGM also outlined a number of casting possibilities selected from among "bankable" stars of the time. Among a dozen actors, Robert Ryan, at that time familiar from war films such as *The Longest Day* (1962) and *Battle of the Bulge* (1965), was considered appropriate for the role of Heywood Floyd, the cool, dispassionate bureaucrat who slumbers his way to the Moon, then delivers a dull lecture about security to the underground scientists. Henry Fonda, George C. Scott, and Jason Robards were also to be approached, while the man-ape leader Moonwatcher was thought an appropriate opportunity for Irish tough guy Robert Shaw, Japanese warrior Toshiro Mifune, or perhaps a promising newcomer, a fit and physically imposing young ex-ball player turned television actor, Gary Lockwood. Albert Finney completed the list of potential ape leaders. Grinning spoof spy and girl magnet James Coburn and slick, suntanned George Hamilton edged close—in MGM's imagination at least—to occupying the copilot's seat aboard the spaceship *Discovery*, alongside Keir Dullea, the only actor to have been selected and approved by all parties at the start of the project.

Dullea's performance in Otto Preminger's psychological thriller *Bunny Lake Is Missing* was particularly influential in Kubrick's casting decision. The film was not due for release for another year. Happy to be of assistance, Preminger sent Kubrick outtakes and dailies so that he could watch Dullea's performance as it developed. Ann, a young American mother played by Carol Lynley, has just arrived in England with her brother, Steven, played by Dullea. In a story reminiscent of Hitchcock's *The Lady Vanishes*, the audience is invited to wonder, is Ann deranged and Bunny a figment of her imagination? It transpires that Steven is the delusional one. He has kidnapped the child in an attempt to further his cloying attachment to his sister.

Kubrick was impressed by Dullea's physique, his healthy-looking features (astronauts of the 21st century presumably would be flawless biological specimens), and, above all, his ability to present a calm, apparently rationalistic exterior even if a dangerous psychosis happens to be raging within. An earlier independent film from 1962, *David and Lisa*, featured Dullea as a young mental patient with an obsessive need for precision and a phobia about being touched. When Kubrick approached him for the new space movie, he was "relieved at the prospect of not playing a psychopath. The repressed aspect that

9 Ciment, Michel, *Kubrick*, English translation, 1983

I portrayed in those earlier films may have been close to what Stanley wanted in terms of the astronauts being characters who would not show a lot of emotion because of their psychological profiles."

Gary Lockwood was a stunt extra in Kubrick's *Spartacus*, played supporting roles in a couple of Elvis Presley movies, performed in several television shows, and featured in a supporting role for Elia Kazan's 1961 drama, *Splendor in the Grass*. A couple of years later he starred in 30 episodes of a television series, *The Lieutenant*, created by Gene Roddenberry (whose subsequent invention, *Star Trek*, would prove more durable). He was making reasonable progress as a young actor, but certainly did not expect an offer of employment from such a prominent director as Kubrick. On hearing the news, he said to his agent, "You mean, he's going to pay me? Surely I should be paying him?" Lockwood and Dullea had been enthusiastic science-fiction readers in their youth, and both were familiar with Clarke's short story "The Sentinel." When the wordy treatment for *Journey Beyond the Stars* was shown to them, they recognized immediately its central plot device.

Kubrick had selected two presentable young men with sufficient acting experience to cope with the demands of a major film project, while deliberately avoiding famous star names. While *Dr. Strangelove* depended upon the comedic talents of its larger-than-life players, the new space film would require its human performers to be diminished by giant machinery and an infinite, unfeeling, unknowable cosmos. Kubrick was careful not to worry MGM too soon with such subtle details. The studio assumed that he would settle eventually on the "cast of international importance" promised in the press release.

Apart from his suave, authoritative appearance, entirely appropriate for his role as a senior space-agency official, William Sylvester's main attractions were that he lived in England, and was not such a major star that his face would be instantly recognizable to audiences. Born in Oakland, California, in 1922, he served in the U.S. Navy in the 1940s, then came to England to study at the Royal Academy of Dramatic Art (RADA). He settled into a career as a leading man in films of modest ambition. He was often recruited by British studios who wanted to include at least one American character in an effort to boost a film's marketing potential across the Atlantic. His screen persona was moderately handsome, yet essentially bland. He wore a suit well. From Kubrick's point of view, he seemed the perfect space-age bureaucrat.

Sylvester had played leading roles in a number of perfectly passable horror films and thrillers. His double-crossing agent in a 1964 film, *Ring of Spies*, lures Margaret Tyzack into passing secrets to the Russians. This film was loosely based on a real scandal involving a Soviet mole disguised as a Canadian businessman, and a junior filing clerk at a British weapons laboratory. Tyzack also was recruited by Kubrick. A versatile and experienced actor, she was cast as Elena, one of the Russian scientists who meet Floyd on the space station and try, without success, to quiz him for more details about mysterious events on the Moon.

The role of senior lunar scientist Halvorsen was assigned to Robert Beatty, whose rugged, craggy face was familiar from a dozen war and adventure films, although his major claim to fame was his radio journalism in the early 1940s. Having come to England to study at RADA, he was caught up in the Nazis' aerial bombing campaign against London: a period between September 1940 and May 1941 known as the "Blitz." Beatty's regular eyewitness accounts of the devastation were transmitted by the BBC Overseas News Service at a time when the United States had not yet entered the war. Beatty's broadcasts were, essentially, a British appeal for help transmitted in a North American voice.

Kubrick's supporting actors were solidly reliable, yet there was no question of marketing this film as a vehicle for Peter Sellers in multiple roles, or Kirk Douglas grinding his teeth as a heroic lead. Perhaps the riskiest choice was Leonard Rossiter for the role of Dr. Smyslov, the persistently curious Russian scientist who presses hardest to break through Sylvester's blank wall of charm. Rossiter was an intelligent, restless actor who could turn the twitch of an eyebrow into a scene-stealing moment. Even something so small as the surreptitious manner in which he pulls his whiskey glass away from where Floyd is sitting seems cleverly calculated to enhance his performance.

William Sylvester's performance as a polite yet reserved and secretive space agency bureaucrat called for exemplary acting skills, especially when given lines of dialogue that were deliberately banal.

▹ 66/67 The space station lounge could be part of any modern airport or waiting area, apart from the odd detail of the curving floor, and French designer Olivier Mourgue's memorable "Djinn" chairs.

АЭРОФЛОТ

HOWARD JOHNSON'S

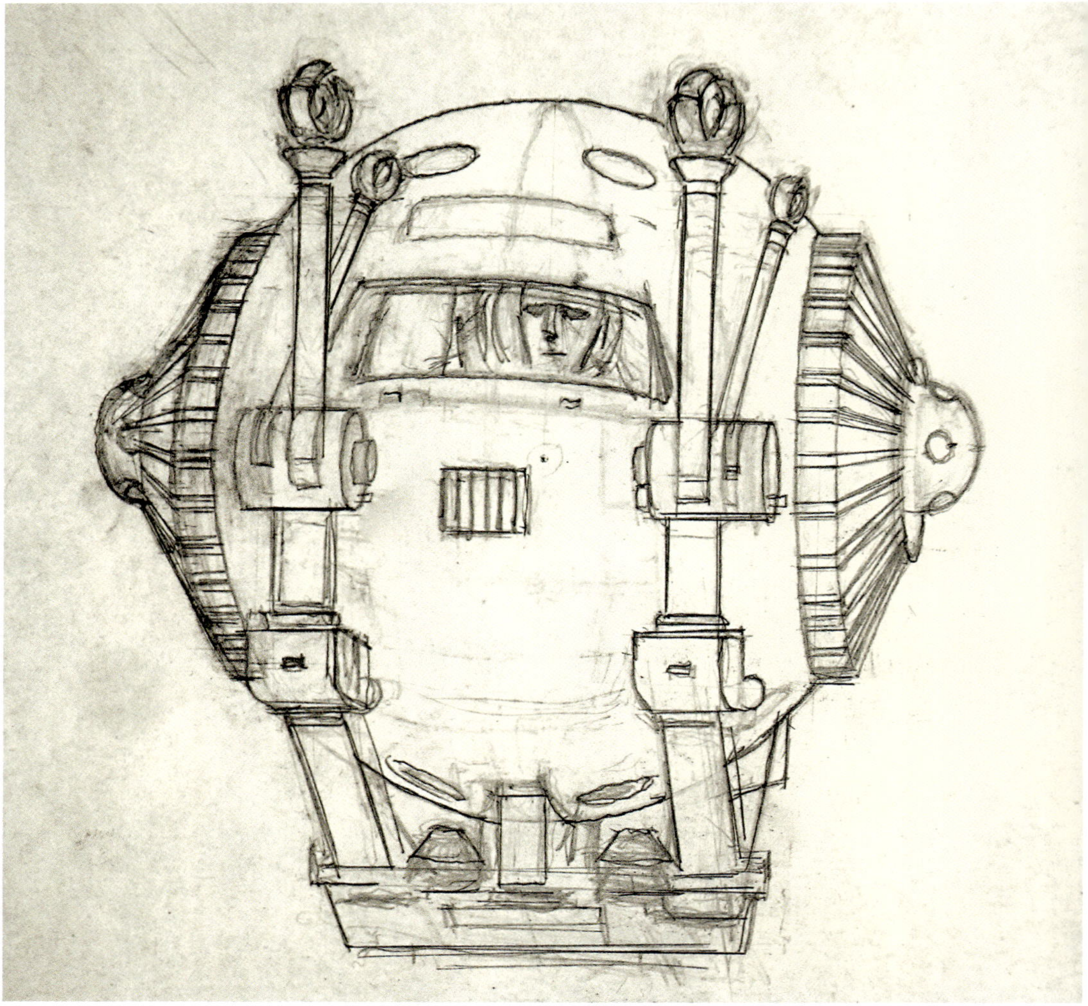

Roy Carnon's interpretation of a space pod, showing the jointed arms and rear hatch.

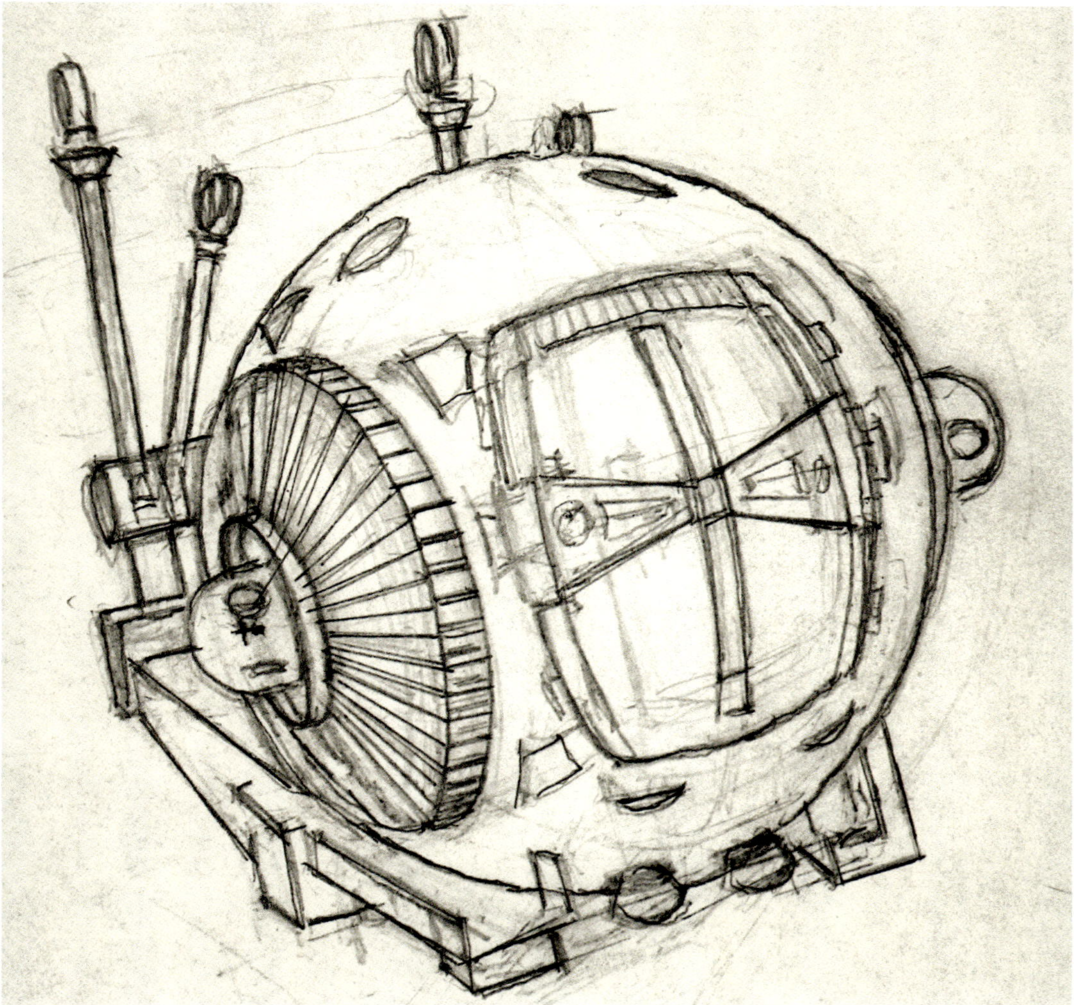

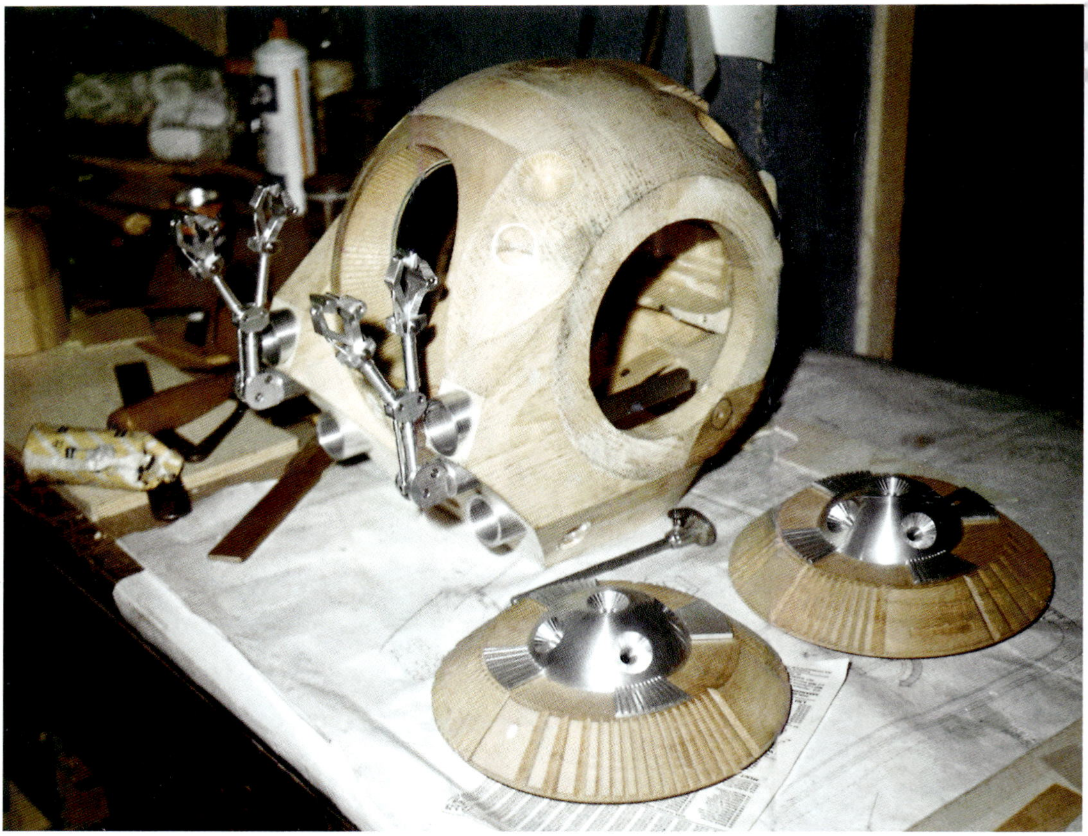

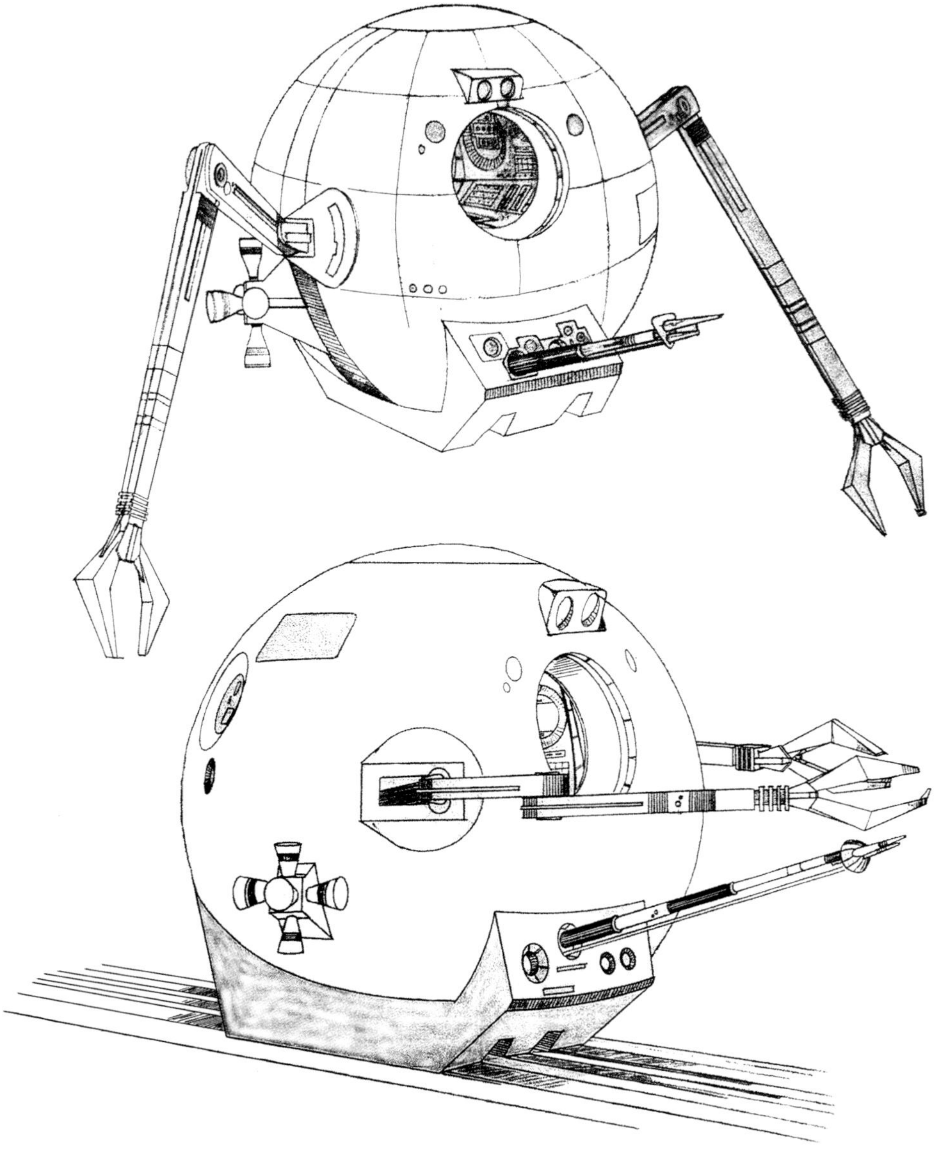

In the mid-1960s the best way of conveying futuristic hardware was by means of traditional craft skills. The 13-inch space-pod miniature was built from oak and other hard woods capable of retaining fine details. The robotic arms, machined by a jeweler, were steel and aluminum.

△ Harry Lange's early design for the one-man space repair pod shows recognizable features, such as the robotic arms and the oval window, and the side thrusters.

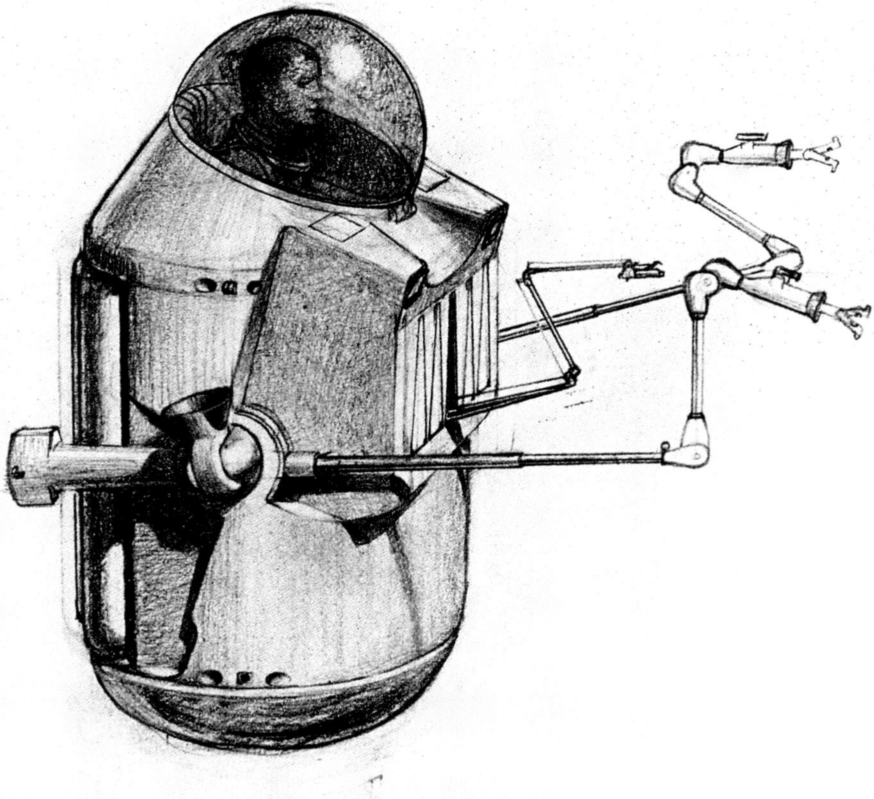

Con Pederson's design for a space repair pod was influenced by an early 1960s idea from the Boeing company.

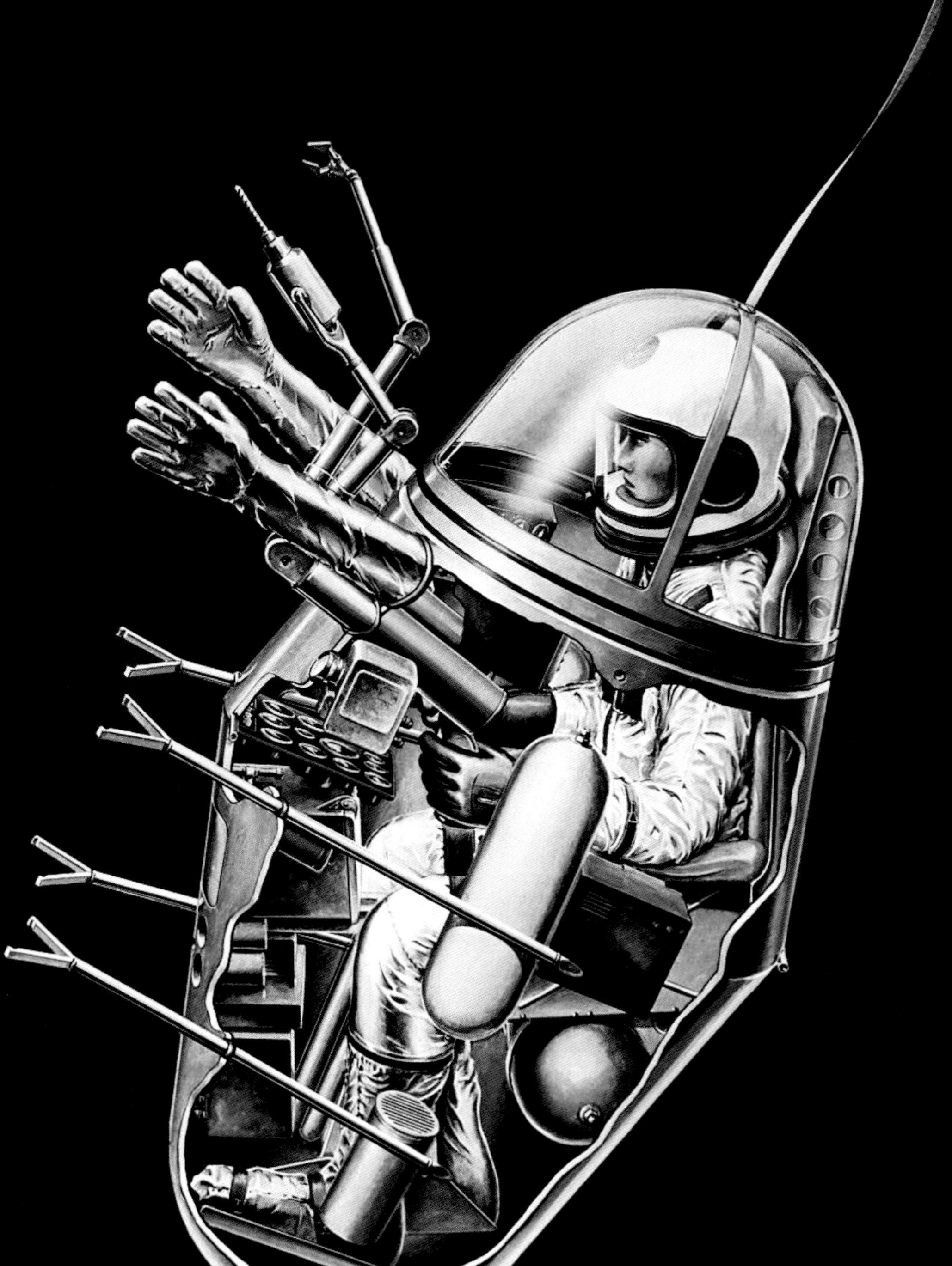

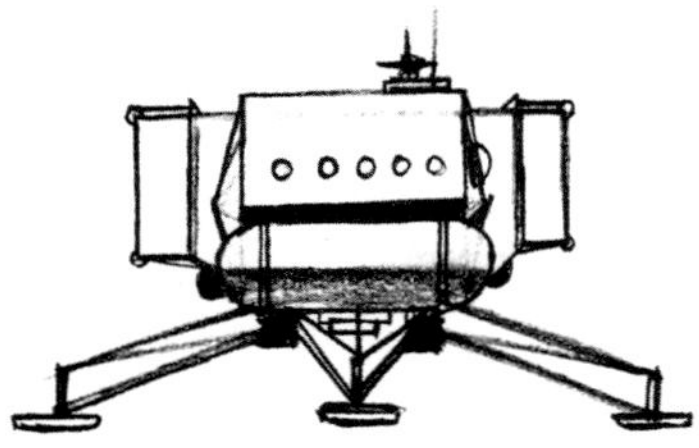

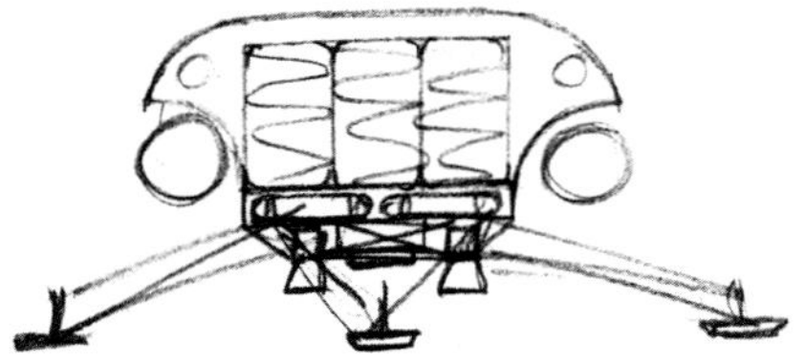

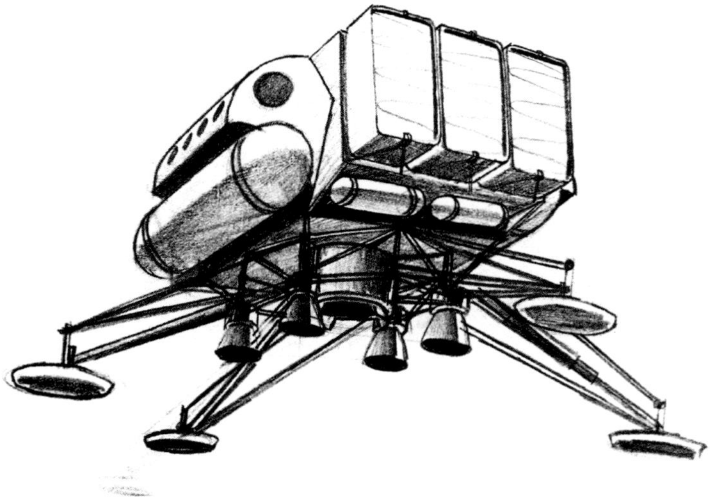

Inflatable lunar habitats are just as realistic a proposal today as they were when Graphic Films delivered this concept to Kubrick.

◁ Pederson's rocket plane incorporates variable-shape wings and a retractable docking connector.

◁ Graphic Films' drawing of the lunar shuttle looks remarkably similar to a British Interplanetary Society (BIS) proposal from the late 1930s.

△ A sketch from Graphic Films depicting a lunar landing craft: one of many iterations that took into account the genuine engineering problems of touching down safely.

▷ 76/77 Richard McKenna was among many artists whose uncredited contributions were absorbed into *2001*'s production-design office. This version of *Aries*'s descent was used in early magazine publicity for the film.

◁▷ 78–83 Storyboards by Roy Carnon show the *Aries* passenger shuttle descending toward the giant underground lunar colony. The special-effects department subsequently tried, without success, to devise rocket-engine exhaust flares that would look convincing on screen.

Roy Carnon
(UNFIXED PASTEL)

2001
ARIES TAKING OFF
FROM THE MOON

2001 ARIES OVER CLAVIUS - MOONBASE

Roy Cannon
'65
UNFIXED PASTEL

PRODUCTION DESIGN

MGM's commitment triggered the hiring of production staff. Kubrick took note of *The Day the Earth Caught Fire* (1961), an accidental Armageddon seen from the vantage point of London newspapermen sniffing a story of international cover-up. Competitive tests of nuclear bombs inadvertently push the Earth slightly closer than normal to the Sun, raising temperatures and endangering human survival. Another series of explosions is conducted to try and correct the disaster. As the film ends, we are left uncertain as to the scheme's success. The film's production designer, Tony Masters, worked in a similar, uncredited role on David Lean's *Lawrence of Arabia* (1962) and was recruited for Kubrick's new space epic, along with his assistant John Hoesli. For Lean's next film, *Doctor Zhivago* (1965), in which the Russian Revolution and its aftermath determine the fates of two handsome young lovers played by Omar Sharif and Julie Christie, assistant art director Ernie Archer helped coordinate the construction of huge sets, including Moscow street scenes faked at a special compound just outside Madrid, and an abandoned family house apparently frozen with icicles: an effect created with molten beeswax. Archer, too, was brought into Kubrick's production team.

The one drawback was that none of these production staff had any specific knowledge of space technology. Kubrick had not been impressed by any of the settings that he had investigated while watching other science-fiction films, and certainly did not wish to rely on film artists alone for his sets and props. He was drawn, instead, to the work of astronomical artists and book illustrators. Richard McKenna was among the first of many contributing artists to create color visualizations of various spacecraft in their nascent forms. As the engineering details reached further refinement, Roy Carnon, a Corgi Books cover artist, established a visual style that met with Kubrick's particular approval, emulating the intense directional light from the Sun, and the deep, almost impenetrable shadow areas of unlit surfaces on the flanks of vehicles in interplanetary space.

Carnon worked with white chalk and colored pastels on black backing paper, creating an effect that came close to what Kubrick hoped to convey on screen. Carnon had served as a navigator aboard RAF Sunderland bombers during the Second World War, serving in Africa, India, and the Far East. As a consequence, he had a particular feel for the nuts and bolts of swift machines and the logic of their forms. He was equally useful when contributing more abstract ideas for the film's closing scenes, in which unearthly alien environments were to be depicted. McKenna and Carnon's color renditions were based on technical drawings and other reference materials supplied by film newcomer Harry Lange and his

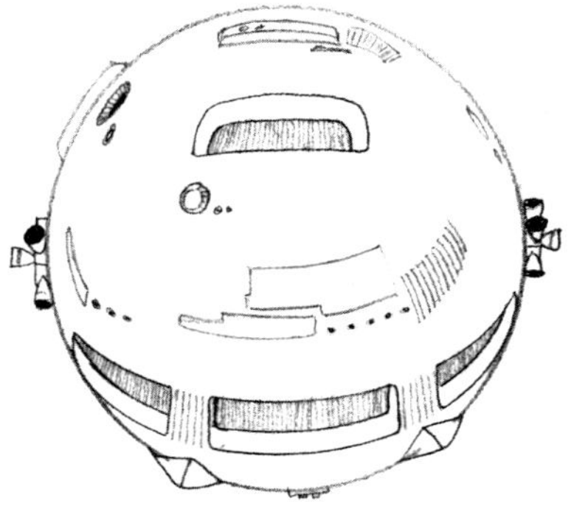

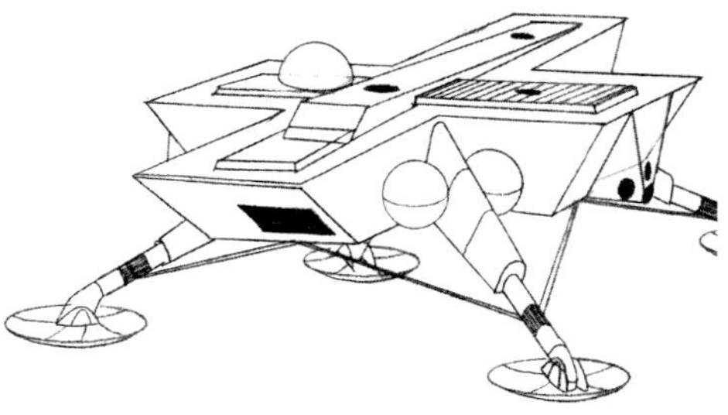

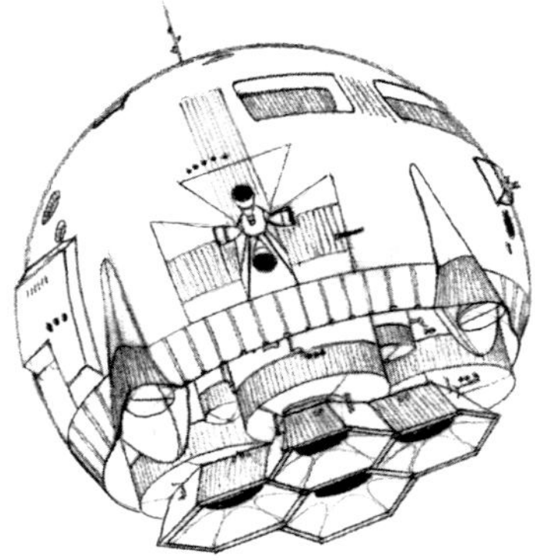

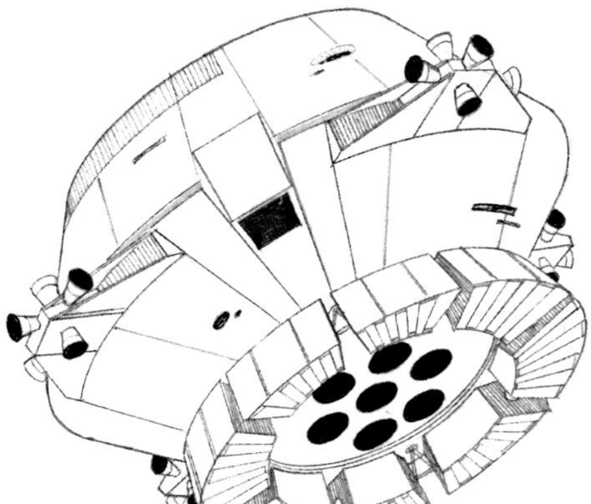

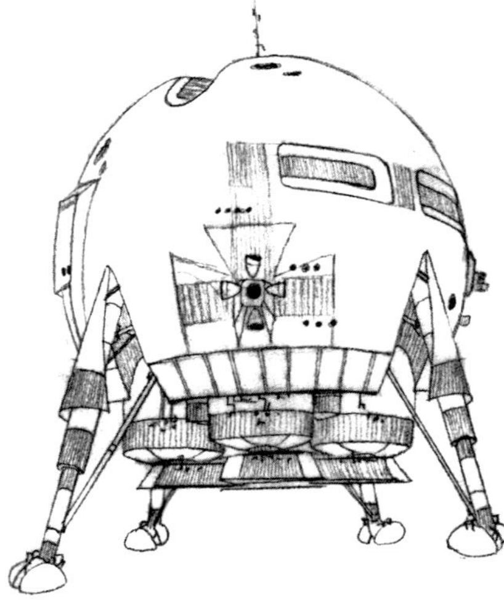

Almost all the space vehicles depicted in *2001* evolved from pencil sketches by Harry Lange. This sequence shows the evolution of the *Aries* ferry.

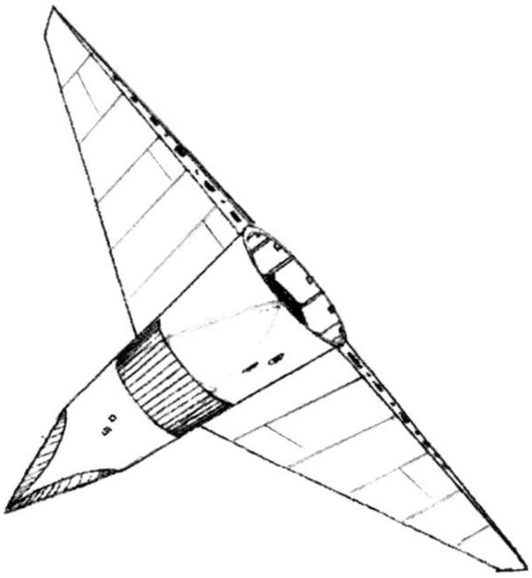

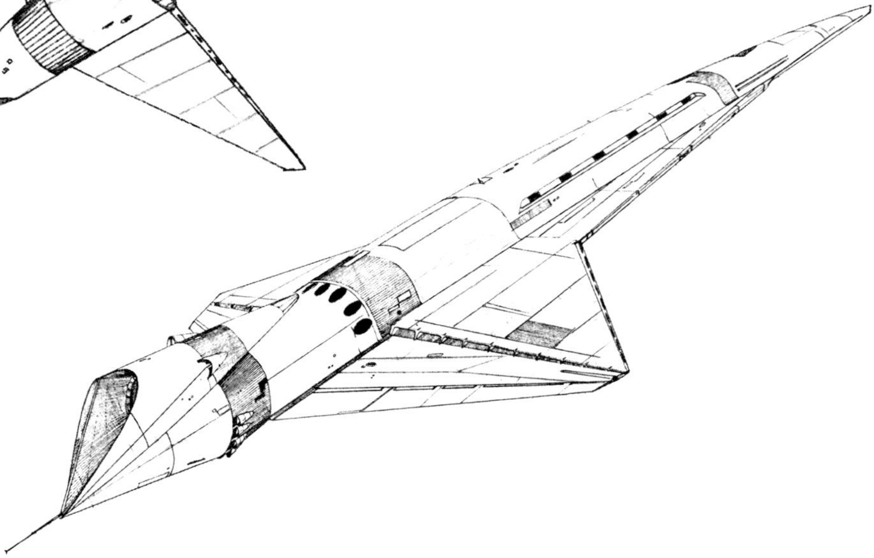

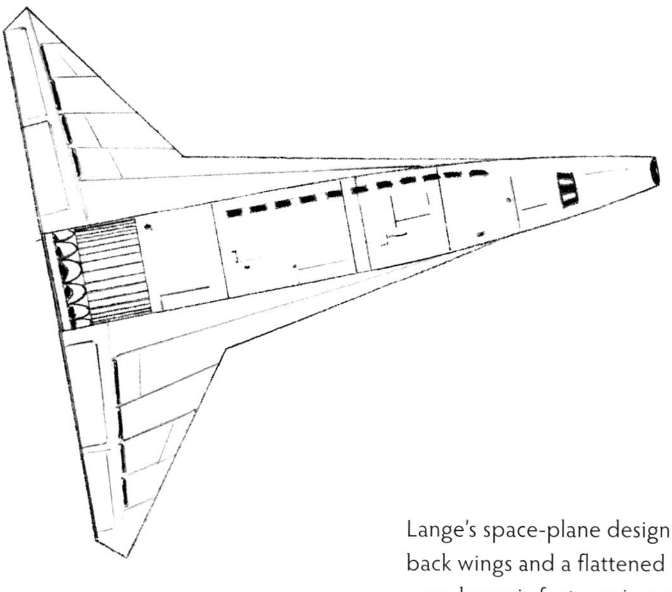

Lange's space-plane design for *2001* had swept-back wings and a flattened underside: important aerodynamic features in real shuttles.

colleague, special scientific consultant Fred Ordway, who worked together to ensure that everything on screen would convey an unprecedented sense of technical realism.

Hans-Kurt Lange was born on December 7, 1930, at Eisenach, in Germany. As a boy, he was interested in Latin and Greek, and dreamed of a career in archaeology, until the Second World War brutally interrupted his schemes. Aged 13, he survived three terrifying nights in Hamburg during the intense Allied bombing that razed the city to the ground, killing 42,000 people. At war's end, Eisenach became part of Communist-controlled East Germany. Lange decided to make his escape, first into West Germany, where he pursued his Classics studies, and then to the United States, where his drawing skills found receptive sponsors in the New York advertising business. The giant aerospace corporations were promoting their prominent role in the Cold War era, and marketing their preparedness for the coming of the Space Age.

Lange was drawn into the German-speaking circle of Wernher von Braun's expatriate rocket team at the Army Ballistic Missile Agency (ABMA) in Huntsville, Alabama. When this complex was absorbed into the new civilian space agency NASA in 1958, Lange became an illustrator for an office known as the Future Projects Division, where von Braun's people outlined their fondest dreams for a steady expansion of space activities. The escalating expense of the Vietnam conflict encroached on NASA's budgets, and although the Apollo lunar landing effort continued to be lavishly funded, speculative departments such as the Future Projects office became a target for cutbacks. By 1964 both Lange and his good friend Frederick Ordway were wondering about their own futures. They felt it was no longer such a good idea to be tied down so exclusively to the governmental space effort, and decided to establish an outside project of their own: a modest company called the General Astronautics Research Corporation (GARC).

Frederick Ordway, educated in geosciences at Harvard and at the University of Paris, was a natural American Establishment insider with a gift for political and commercial friendships and alliances. Von Braun found him an invaluable bridge between the close-knit German engineering clan at Huntsville and the wider American corporate culture. Ordway's scientific expertise (he was editor of several space technical journals) was backed up by a persuasive understanding of the public-relations processes by which large and complex organizations like NASA must inform the outside world about their activities. Among his other duties for von Braun, Ordway coordinated a study project known as EMPIRE (Early Manned Planetary-Interplanetary Round-trip Expeditions). The expectation was that NASA would be in a position to fly such missions by the mid-1970s, using nuclear-electric-powered ships assembled in Earth orbit from components hauled aloft by Saturn rockets. These hopes were quick to fade. By 1964 Ordway shared Lange's suspicion

that the glory days of American expansion into space would have to await some other generation than theirs. A fortunate meeting with Arthur Clarke in January 1965 determined their next steps.

Ordway heard that Clarke was in New York and arranged a social gathering at the Harvard Club, where he and Lange were staying. Clarke mentioned that he was publicizing his forthcoming Time-Life book, *Man and Space*, and working with a talented young movie director called Stanley Kubrick on a film about contact with extraterrestrials. This, he explained, was going to be *the* greatest space movie, against which all others of its kind would be judged. It would portray humanity facing the enormity of the cosmos, and would consider the possibility of other forms of life among the stars.

By coincidence, Lange and Ordway were assembling a book on a similar theme, *Intelligence in the Universe*, for publisher Prentice Hall, and had recently completed another project, *Life in Other Solar Systems*. Clarke asked to see some of Lange's artwork for the new book. He and Ordway then spent a pleasant half hour or so showing material to Arthur, who certainly seemed impressed. While Clarke headed off for his next appointment, Ordway and Lange went to their rooms at the club to change for dinner. A little while later they were standing outside the club, waiting for the doorman to hail a cab in the midst of heavy snowfall. Just as they were about to be driven away, one of the club's employees gesticulated wildly for them to stop. There was an urgent phone call for Ordway. When he reached the telephone, a voice identified itself on the other end of the line: "Mr. Ordway? My name is Stanley Kubrick..."

Clarke had left the Harvard Club, trudged as swiftly as he could through the blizzard, and found a discreet phone box on Sixth Avenue, from where he called Kubrick. Next day, Lange and Ordway spent what the latter described as "a mentally exhilarating afternoon" discussing concepts with Kubrick and Clarke at the director's Upper East Side apartment, and examining the possibility of collaboration. Then they were asked formally for their assistance. Ordway would become principal scientific advisor to the project, while Lange would create a series of realistic spaceship designs. The pair signed an initial six-month contract to work with Kubrick in New York, from where they would fly to other cities and NASA research centers to recruit further advisors, assemble all the necessary technical material, and keep the production informed about the latest trends in real space research.

The first meeting with Lange was characterized, as so often, by Kubrick's probing sense of mischief. As he browsed through a folio of Lange's artwork, he commented, "These are fine, but good illustrators are a dime a dozen. They're all starving, hanging around Greenwich Village." Lange was about to gather up his presentations and leave, until Kubrick finished what he had to say. "Illustrators who know about spaceflight systems? Now, that's a combination I can use."

Lange's lack of specific filmmaking experience presented a particular obstacle. He did not belong to any of the appropriate trade unions in Great Britain, where both Kubrick and MGM had agreed that the principal studio photography for *Journey Beyond the Stars* should be conducted. Kubrick sidestepped the issue by appointing him, at first, as a technical consultant, for which union membership was not required. By the time Kubrick's film was released, Lange had been working on the set for so long he was able to gain

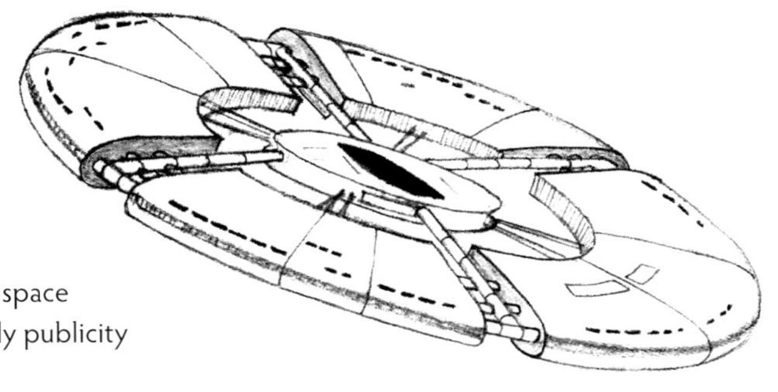

A disc-shaped Lange sketch of the space station formed the basis for an early publicity painting by McKenna.

Early concept art by Richard McKenna, showing the distinct double-wheel idea for the space station.

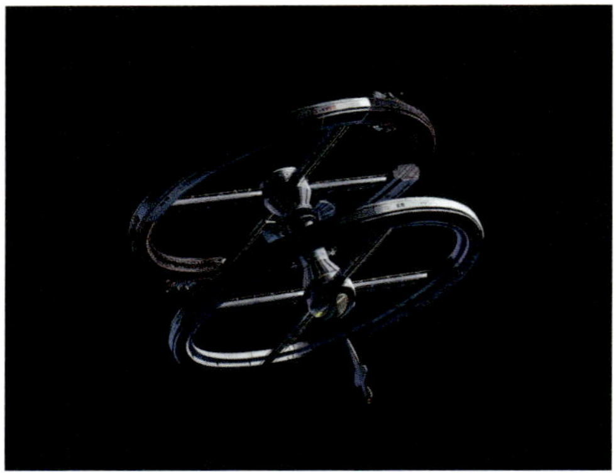

Roy Carnon's formal study of the space station, based on a design by Lange, closely matches what we see on screen.

acceptance into the industry and share formal credit with Masters and Archer for production design. In a 1977 interview with Don Shay, Masters said, "Harry put the authenticity into it. The strange thing was that we all worked together for so long that we began to design in the same way. Just like Georgian or Victorian is a period, we designed *2001* as a period. We designed a way to live, right down to the last knife and fork. If we had to do a door, we would do it in *our* style."

2001: A Space Odyssey became the film's official title in April 1965, almost exactly one year after the project's inception. Other options, including *Planetfall* and *Tunnel to the Stars*, were rejected. Kubrick and Clarke's desire to choose a time frame that was sufficiently futuristic to be exotic, yet not so far distant as to be fanciful, helped settle their minds on the turn of the 20th century as a suitable backdrop. From here, it seems to have been Kubrick alone who decided that the numerals "2001" would work well in the title. The Odyssean theme gained in prominence after Kubrick gave Clarke a copy of Joseph Campbell's influential book, *The Hero with a Thousand Faces*. Campbell's thesis was that, no matter where one looks for narrative inspiration, or in what language tales are told, they adopt one of a handful of primordial structures, based on psychological archetypes common to all humanity. A hero is one whose life of peace and harmony is disrupted by troubles. He must journey through a dangerous landscape, discover his courage and humility, and resolve the crisis. "He ventures forth from the world of common day into a region of supernatural wonder: fabulous forces are there encountered and a decisive victory is won: the hero comes back from this mysterious adventure with the power to bestow boons on his fellow man," Campbell wrote.

Dave Bowman's first name in early drafts of the script was Alex. He was part Alexander the Great, part common "bow man" soldier. A quality of "mythic grandeur" (in Kubrick's phrase) crept into *2001*'s planning from the earliest days, even if the classical influences were couched, for MGM's benefit, in the modern language of rocket ships, lunar bases, and alien encounters. Clarke was pleased with this turn of events: "Stanley wanted to create a myth, and I think he succeeded. A myth should contain all sorts of levels, deeper and deeper. A myth should be unfathomable, and at the same time, instinctively recognizable. Different people should have different interpretations—and that, of course, is exactly what happened when the film finally emerged."

Another early rendering of the space station by Richard McKenna. Kubrick was particularly keen to show that the station was assembled gradually, using small components ferried up from Earth.

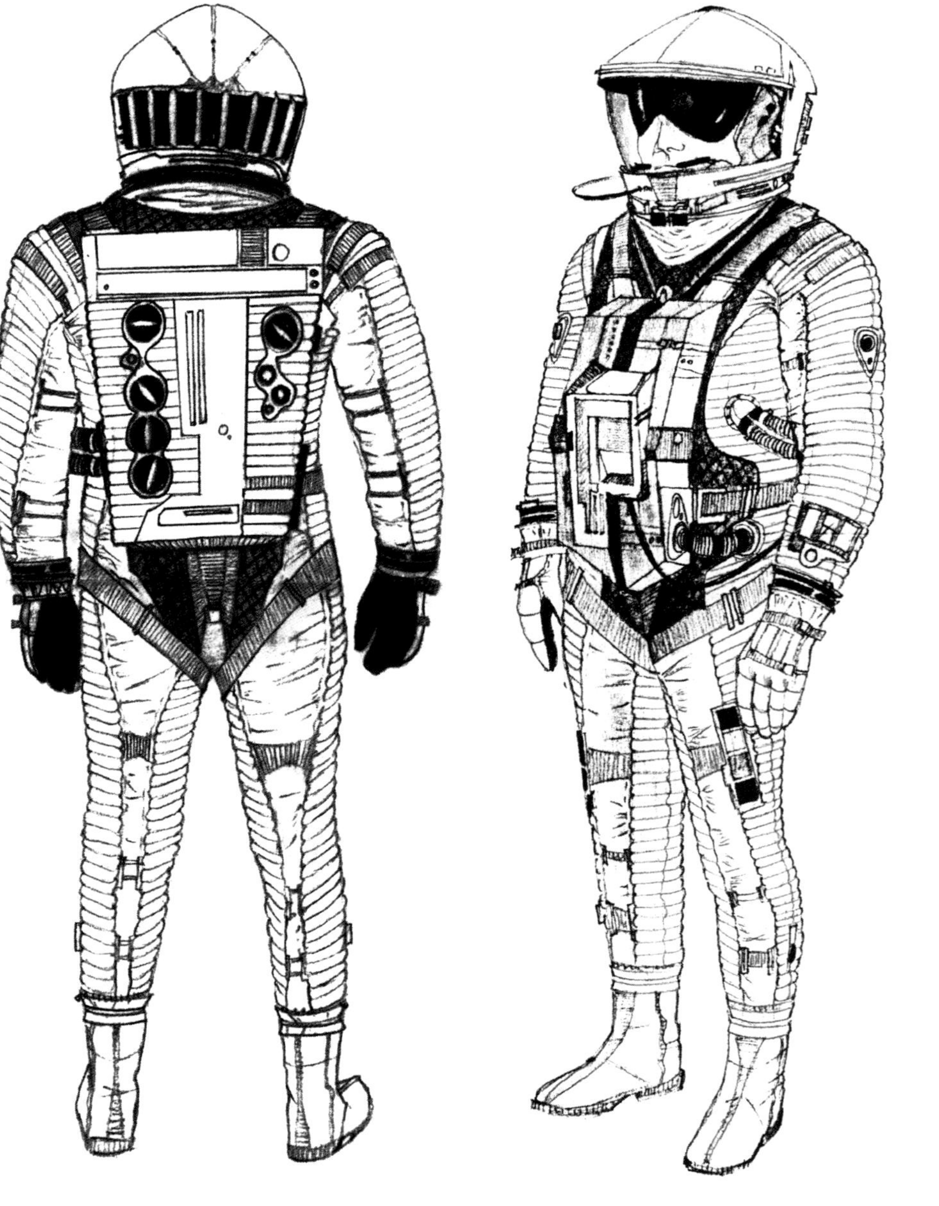

Lange's designs for *2001*'s space suits were based on NASA's "constant volume" principle. Horizontal stitching of the fabric prevents the suit from ballooning when inflated with air. The rectangular blocks on the back of the helmets were supposed to represent plug-in data modules.

▷ A test of the space suit's flexibility revealed that the metal attachment rings for the boots and gloves could work loose.

◁▷ 94–99 Concept artworks of *Discovery*'s main control area were inspired by the awkwardly crouched postures of astronauts in Apollo space capsules, at that time being designed by NASA. Kubrick wanted the seating arrangements to suggest *Discovery*'s weightless interior.

▹ 100 Early concepts for the centrifuge interior, including Bowman's unsuccessful attempt to revive one of his colleagues from hibernation: an idea that evolved into HAL's deliberate killing of the frozen sleepers.

▹ 101 Proposals for the *Discovery*'s pod bay, space suit racks, fuel cylinders, and test bench equipment are closely related to the props and settings that eventually appeared in the film.

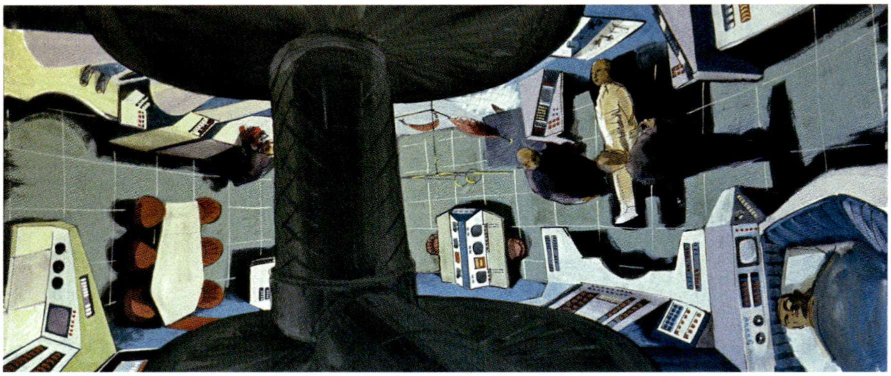

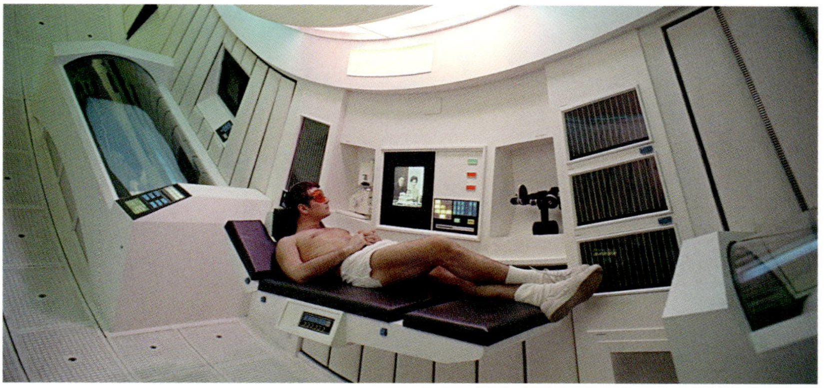

SUBURBAN BRITISH HOLLYWOOD

British entrepreneurs never quite succeeded in replicating the Hollywood studio system. The Amalgamated Studios company began an ambitious building project in the mid-1930s, then ran out of money before they could complete it. The J. Arthur Rank company acquired the site in 1938. During the Second World War, Handley Page Halifax bomber components were assembled in the huge studio buildings. By 1948 MGM's British subsidiary had taken control of the studios, scrubby back lots, and various subsidiary blocks sprawled over 100 acres in what was at that time a quiet and leafy community 15 miles north of London. A typically understated English version of the Hollywood lifestyle descended upon the modest villages of Borehamwood and nearby Elstree.

After a year's preparatory work in New York, the Kubrick family, Arthur Clarke, and the small preproduction team shipped to England over June and July and set up base at Kubrick's British production entity, Hawk Films, now housed in a single-story prefabricated building alongside the white clock tower that lent a hint of glamour to MGM Borehamwood's otherwise ordinary industrial appearance. Seven shooting stages loomed in the background, shaped like vast airplane hangars. Christiane and her three girls camped at the Dorchester Hotel in London while she and Stanley looked for more suitable long-term housing nearer to the studios. Fred Ordway stayed behind in New York until August, packing up 20 trunk loads of artwork and technical materials for carriage aboard the ocean liner *S.S. France.*[10]

As *2001*'s production team set up for business, television star Patrick McGoohan was completing the last episodes of his action series *Danger Man* prior to embarking on a darker and more surreal drama, *The Prisoner*. (Listen carefully to the electric doors in the spooky village where *The Prisoner*'s unnamed antihero is held captive, and you will hear the unmistakable sound of a *2001* space pod's hatch opening.) Antonioni's *Blow-Up* and the war adventures *Where Eagles Dare* and *The Dirty Dozen* were among various films that shared MGM facilities during Kubrick's unusually long production phase. In 1965, O'Brien had thought it wise for *2001*'s budget to absorb some of the slack at the slightly under-booked Borehamwood facility. By late 1966 Kubrick's film was occupying most of the available shooting stages, while other productions supposedly waited for space to become free. Many film historians cite *2001* as one of the factors behind Borehamwood's eventual closure in 1970. The starker truth is that none of the once-great American studios could sustain major British adventures at a time when confidence back in Hollywood was faltering, too. It was television, not *2001*, that eventually stifled the roar from MGM's lion.

10 Typewritten notes of recollection, courtesy of Frederick I. Ordway

Kubrick and his principal production designer Tony Masters watch a test of the sliding logic modules in the HAL 9000 "brain room" set.

II

"Despite your enormous intellect,
are you ever frustrated by your dependence on people
to carry out actions?"

A KING OF INFINITE SPACE

Throughout the summer and fall of 1965, Kubrick and his fast-expanding production crew geared up for live-action photography, while Christiane made ready the new family house, The Chantry, on Barnet Lane, Elstree, within easy reach of the studios, rented to them by a film executive friend. This would be "home" until the completion of *2001* three years later. Meanwhile, Clarke—shuttling between London, Ceylon, and various speaking engagements at the same time as dealing with Kubrick's requests for script improvements—grew restive about the final scenes. In *Journey Beyond the Stars*, and several versions beyond, all but one of *Discovery*'s crew survive the outward voyage, eventually launching robotic probes through a rectangular slot in a giant alien artifact drifting through space. At the far end of what seems like an immensely deep rectilinear tunnel with smooth walls, another slot-shaped opening can be discerned, through which the explorers can see stars whose patterns do not conform to any constellations visible from within our solar system. This is the Stargate, an artificial wormhole. The film's scrupulous scientific plausibility had to give way, at this point, to a fantasy. Nevertheless, there were physicists in the 1960s ready to suggest that space-warp transportation might be possible for an advanced civilization. Clarke composed a press release justifying the idea.

> *There may be "short cuts" through space, so that two points which seem to us billions of miles apart may be quite close in some other dimension. Imagine a bug crawling on a sheet of paper. To get from one side to the other would be a long journey, but if it could tunnel through the thickness of the paper, it might make the trip in a very short time indeed. Perhaps one day we will be able to do something similar, so that even the stars will be close at hand.*

After Kubrick and Clarke had agreed that Bowman should be the only astronaut to experience the climactic encounter with extraterrestrial agencies, a narrative passage was inserted in the *Journey* treatment, explaining that an alien machine had "waited four million years" for Bowman's arrival, and

> *...was prepared to wait for eternity. Presently, it felt the gentle touch of radiations, trying to probe its secrets. Soon, these gave way to more complex signals at many frequencies, ultraviolet, infrared, X-rays. The machine made no reply... Then the pod came, carrying life. The great machine searched its memories. The logic circuits made their decision when the pod had fallen beyond the last faint glow of the reflected Saturnian light. In a moment of time, too short to be measured, space turned and twisted upon itself.* END OF SCREENPLAY

And that was it. "The weakness of our ending is that we never explain what happens to Bowman, but leave it entirely to the imagination," Clarke noted to Kubrick in August 1965. He proposed that Bowman should be presented with a "soft, voluptuous spaceship, an obvious ultimate extension of that ancient bone tool." Kubrick's handwritten note of reply was a portent of things to come: "I prefer to present a non-specific result for the film. Maybe this works for the book." Clarke persisted in his search for a punchier finale: "A tall and graceful extra-terrestrial creature appears. Towering above Bowman in splendid blue phosphorescence, it carefully takes the Earth-man's hand, and leads him forward, looking not unlike a parent leading its child." Bowman is escorted to a featureless void where a transparent cube rests on a seemingly limitless floor. In Clarke's imagination, "the cube is visible only from the light glinting on its edges." Once again, this seemed unsatisfactory, incomplete. A month later, Clarke noted in his diary, "Gave Stanley my latest ideas, and one of them suddenly clicked. Bowman will regress to infancy, and we'll see him at the end as a baby in orbit. It's his image of himself at this stage of his development." Kubrick was unwilling to commit just yet. Clarke resigned himself to further fluidity, equally uncertain about how the film should conclude: "We didn't know exactly what the ending would be until very late in the game. And at one time, indeed, we thought the discovery of the artifact on the Moon would be the end of the movie, not the beginning. So that shows you how much our ideas changed during the development." [1]

1 Clarke, *The Lost Worlds of 2001*, 1972

Space pods approach the chasm of the Stargate. A single pod descends into this mysterious realm, cut into one of Jupiter's moons by long-departed alien engineers. In the published novel, Clarke opted for the Saturnian moon Iapetus as the Stargate's location.

△ In this version of Discovery's alien encounter, the Stargate is incorporated into a gigantic black tetrahedron drifting in space high above Saturn's rings.

▽ One-man space pods embark from the *Discovery* on a mission to investigate an alien presence.

Roy Cotton
UNFIXED PASTEL

2001
'DISCOVERY' OVER SATURN

◁ 108/109 A Carnon painting of the "dragonfly" Discovery flying past Saturn, whose vast bulk and cloudy atmosphere fill the entire background.

◁▷ 110–113 Storyboards of an early Discovery variant blasting away from Earth's orbit, with a disc-shaped space station in the background. The ship discards its booster tanks, and is then seen drifting into Jupiter space and flying over the surface of a Jovian moon.

THE BIRTH OF HAL

In the *Journey Beyond the Stars* treatment, spaceship *Discovery* is considered as one of a pair. At the dawn of the 21st century, a straightforward scientific expedition to Jupiter is already being prepared. News of the alien signal beamed from the Moon toward Jupiter causes a rethink of the schedule. *Discovery* and her crew set off five years earlier than originally planned. The ship lacks some of the fuel and life-support capabilities required for the voyage home, so the space agency settles on a potentially risky solution. On completing their mission near Jupiter, the entire crew is to be placed in a state of suspended animation inside special freezers. Their intake of food, water, and oxygen will drop to minimal levels, thus saving the ship's life-support reserves. In this dreamless state of profound unconsciousness, months and years will seem to pass in moments while the crew awaits rescue by the as-yet-unbuilt sister vessel, *Discovery II*. Clarke noted to Kubrick in October 1965, "I have just seen an interesting article to the effect that one Dr. Leonard Axelrod of the S.W. Institute of Research and Education, San Antonio, Texas, has succeeded in inducing hibernation in nonhibernating animals (e.g. cats and mice) by injecting them with extracts from the brains of squirrels. The astronautical implications of this work are specifically mentioned."

Clarke also proposed that, while the astronauts sleep, a more or less humanoid robot named Bruno, or perhaps Socrates, could tend *Discovery*'s systems and watch over the freezer units. This somewhat clichéd science-fiction trope was dropped in favor of a more realistic onboard computer, inspired by the new digital guidance systems being built for NASA's capsules. *Discovery*'s sleeping beauties would be taken care of by a relatively simple and benign talking computer named Athena. Throughout the summer of 1965, Roger Caras and Fred Ordway assiduously courted the world's largest computer company, IBM, seeking advice about how to make Athena plausible. IBM brought in their celebrated industrial-design consultant, Eliot Noyes, and his firm created dozens of briefing papers and drawings, just as Caras had requested.

IBM's reputation was built on the power and scale of its room-sized supercomputers. There was no such thing as a "personal computer" in the mid-1960s. Few people could even imagine such a thing. Computers were for professional users, such as corporate accountants, military ballistics experts, payroll managers, and space-trajectory plotters. Only computer experts could understand the arcane language of binary coding, punched cards, and magnetic tapes. Furthermore, despite rapid advances in the miniaturization of individual circuits and electronic transistors, a computer such as Athena, with its voice software and

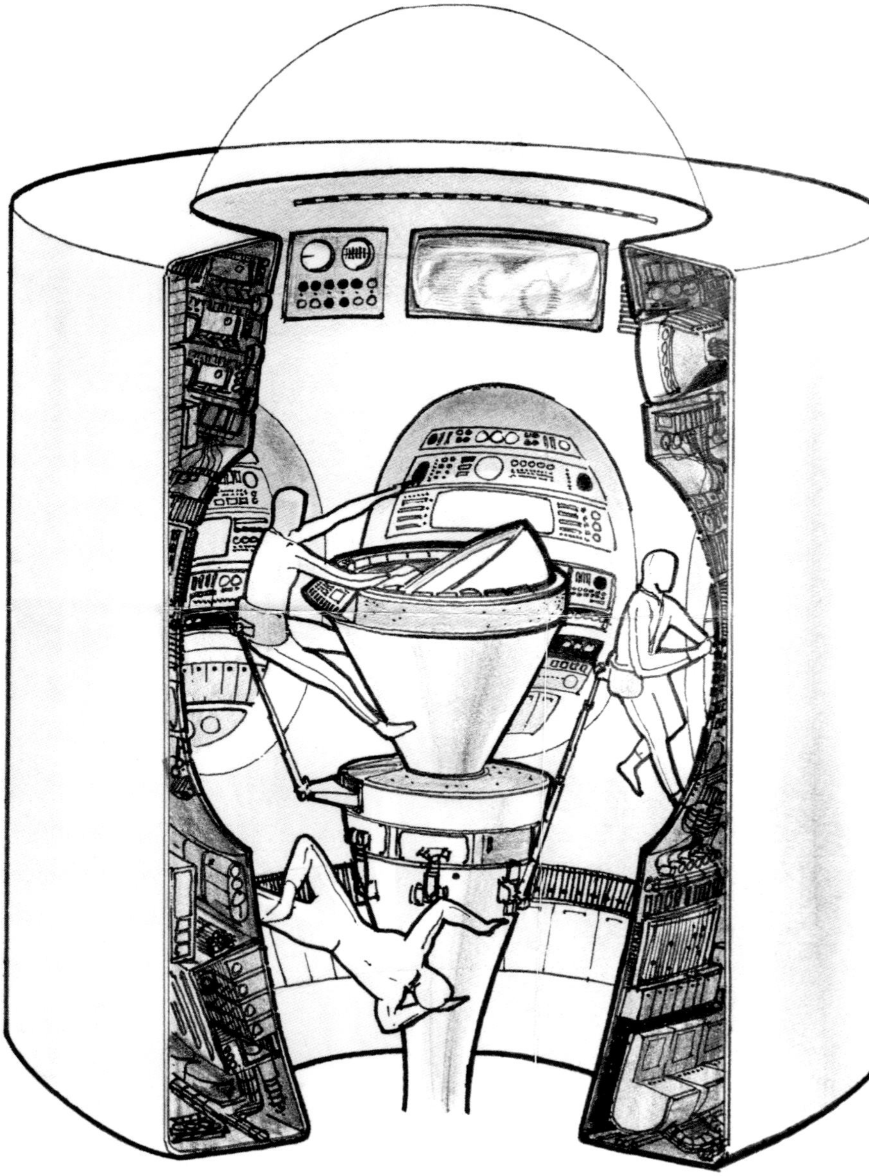

The IBM computer company, and its industrial design consultant Eliot Noyes, suggested that a superintelligent computer would be something that humans worked inside, rather than walked around. At first Kubrick was not impressed by this idea. This is a Noyes proposal for Discovery's control and navigation center. Noyes suggested that the main computer might reside in a do-nut-shaped chamber surrounding this cylinder.

This illustration of a rocket ship was part of Roy Carnon's initial presentation to Kubrick, who hired him on the spot.

semi-intelligent behavior, would need—or so it was assumed by IBM—a huge volume of hardware. Noyes delivered his beautiful drawings accordingly. A letter from Caras, dated July 27, 1965, warns Kubrick that Athena would have to be more than just a neat little section of *Discovery*'s cockpit panel.

> *Dear Stan,*
> *IBM has delivered their initial design concepts for the Athena computer. As you can see, they say that a computer of the complexity required by the "Discovery" spacecraft would be a computer into which men went, rather than a computer around which men walked. This is an interesting idea and you may want to consider it carefully.*

Kubrick's reply a couple of days later was thunderous: "The IBM Athena drawings are useless and totally irrelevant to our needs. I am extremely bored and depressed with all of this abysmal waste of time. Annoyed, but lovingly, S." Caras did his best to soften the bad news for IBM: "Stan, your missile exploded here this morning, although I am happy to report that no one was killed by shrapnel… IBM is extremely unwieldy because of their immense size. They are doing their best to supply you with what you want. I am sorry that their idea of working inside of a computer instead of around one was not pleasing to you."

Kubrick's outburst may have been intemperate in the haste of the moment, but he was right. IBM's assumptions were behind the times. Rival companies, such as Motorola and Raytheon, were pushing toward miniaturization, spurred in large part by NASA's urgent requirement for computers small enough to fit inside the new lunar capsules. Just as significant was the space agency's development of "man-machine interfaces." The men who flew the Gemini and Apollo capsules were pilots, not scientists. They knew everything about aviation, and almost nothing about computing, and could care less. Simple keypads and numerical displays enabled them to "talk" with their guidance systems without having to be digital experts. Furthermore, those systems were contained in boxes no larger than an automobile battery. All the circuitry was hidden behind the capsule control panels. It was already obvious that space vehicles of the future would not contain room-sized computers. Nevertheless, Kubrick reconsidered his attitude toward the Noyes proposal because of a problem with *Discovery*'s outward trip in general. Quite simply, it lacked drama.

Clarke had written a series of accidents and hardware failures to spice up the voyage. These misfortunes were exciting, yet they seemed, somehow, too innocent and disjointed. *Discovery*'s astronauts needed an adversary to confront and conquer. What if all the various malfunctions could be redefined as the product of deliberate sabotage? While

The typesetting of HAL's logo was inspired by the general corporate aesthetics of the 1960s computer industry, and not just IBM's, whose familiar branding was highlighted in space ships other than the troubled *Discovery*.

▹ 120/121 HAL's glowing red eye is the product of artistic license. A real camera lens does not glow from the inside. But who cares?This is one of the most iconic images in movie history.

IBM
FETCH
RESET
DELETE

HAL

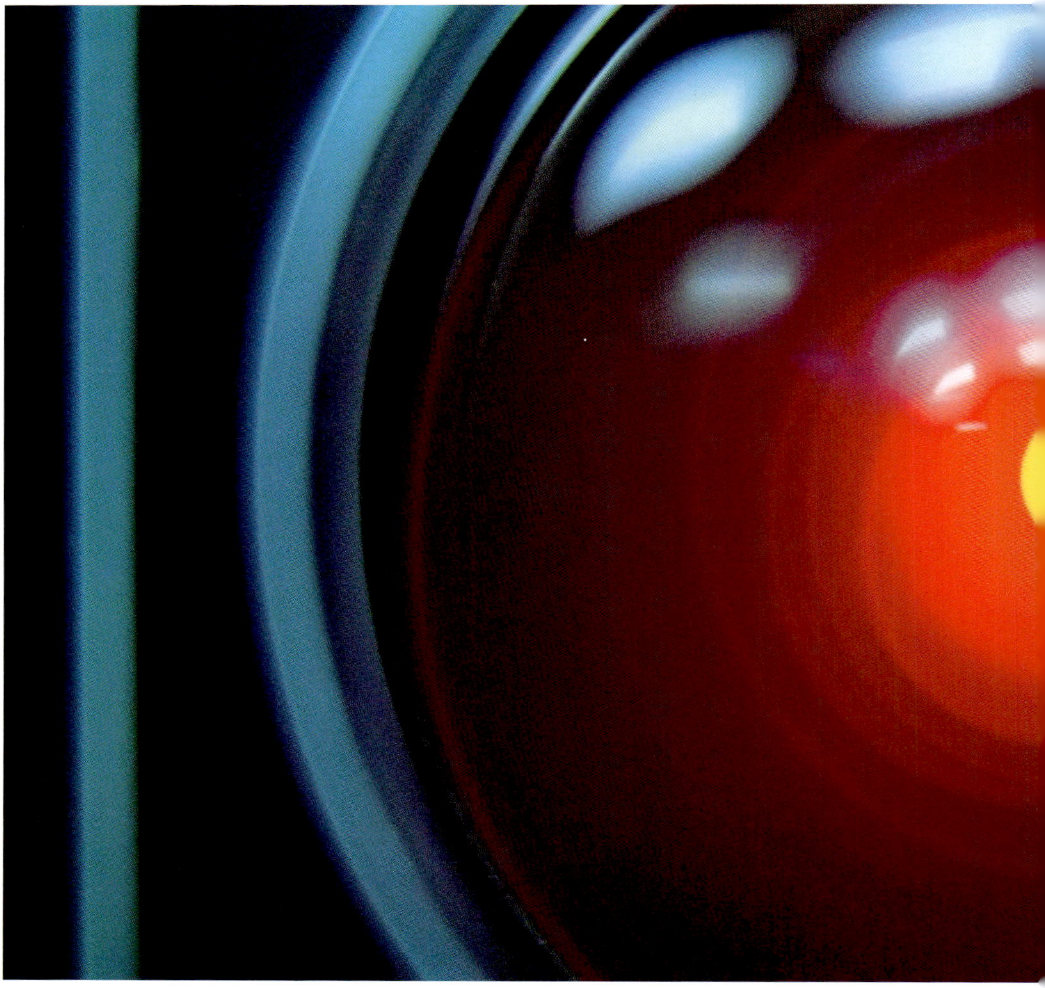

9000

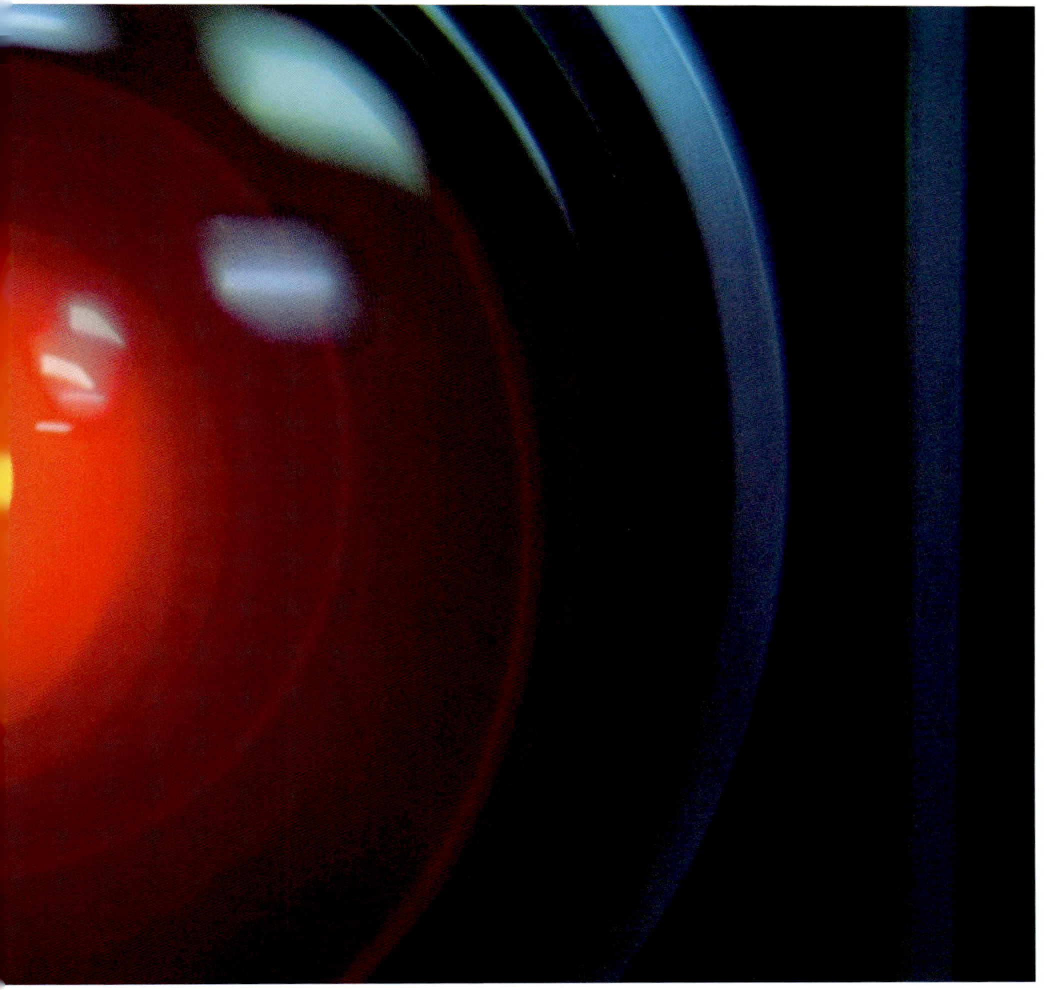

keeping within the bounds of scientific realism and plot plausibility, the script needed a villain. Everyone is familiar with the final version of *2001*'s shipboard drama, in which a lethally disobedient computer refuses to allow a stranded astronaut back on board the ship. The first, faint signs of this rebellion emerged in July 1965, when Athena does the opposite, refusing to let Bowman out.

Poole sets off in a repair pod to fix a small leak in *Discovery*'s hull caused by a micrometeorite impact. His pod thruster is jammed in the "on" position and crashes into the main communications antenna, ripping it off the ship's flank. At first, Bowman is not unduly alarmed, and he calculates how to rescue his colleague. Before he can leave *Discovery* in his own pod, he must ensure that someone on board the mother ship is available to monitor events and rescue him, too, should anything happen. He initiates the revival of a hibernating crew member, Dr. Kaminski, who dies a few moments after regaining partial consciousness. Apparently his heart has not withstood the shock of revival. Athena announces coolly, "All systems of Kaminski are no-go. Please replace him with a spare unit."

Time is running out if Poole is to be rescued before he drifts too far from *Discovery*. As if going in circles, Athena reminds Bowman that he must not leave the ship unless someone is awake to keep watch. With help from the computer, Bowman sets the other hibernation units on automatic revival mode, hoping that the unconscious occupants will awaken successfully while he is outside the ship. Then he clambers into the second of three repair pods, imagining that he has satisfied Athena's strict, although perfectly proper, requirements for mission safety. At this point, Athena refuses to let Bowman leave, because no one else is available to watch over the ship. This is a pretty dumb computer, and certainly not the red-eyed genius waiting in the wings. Athena simply obeys mission protocol moment by moment. Bowman disconnects some of her circuits, more in the spirit of an electrician making necessary adjustments than as one distraught intelligence killing another. Then he sets off into space. Poole is beyond rescue by now, and deliberately climbs out of his pod, knowing that he will die. All Bowman can do is try to recover the antenna, *Discovery*'s only communications link with distant Earth.

A brief script note has Kubrick wondering, "Is it neater to kill off Poole quickly?" Over the space of a few days during October 1965, he had a series of inspirations. First, he decided that Bowman must be the *only* survivor of the mission, otherwise how could the "Odyssey" theme of the film be justified? Clarke immediately agreed that this was the proper course. "It took us a long time to see the obvious," he acknowledged. Now came the moment in the scripting process when Athena lost her digital innocence and gained a new cunning. It was Kubrick's idea that "the computer reports an unlikely flaw which cannot be disproven without an EVA, since all the checks are made by the computer.

ON POOLE'S BIRTHDAY?" The only problem was, how to slip these radical new story developments past IBM, one of the production's most prominent and important sources of technical assistance. Ordway's letter to the corporate giant, dated October 27, 1965, was delicately phrased:

> *As the final screenplay emerges we feel that the most appropriate place for the IBM computer is in the "Orion III" space vehicle rather than in the "Discovery." In "Orion" it would be featured prominently. The "Discovery" spacecraft in the meantime is evolving in the story as a considerably more experimental vehicle than originally visualized, as are many of its key elements, including the hibernation system, and the computer. Taking into account the experimental nature of things, a number of interesting plot points become feasible, involving, in some cases, unpredictable malfunctioning. Naturally we do not want to represent any IBM equipment in such light.*

In the *Journey* treatment, the entire world is informed when astronaut-scientists find an alien object on the Moon, and everyone aboard *Discovery* is perfectly clear about their mission objectives. Kubrick gravitated toward a secret agenda: one whose true nature would be known only to the ship's computer, a more advanced and intelligent version of Athena. As the tension between man and machine reaches the point of outright conflict, Bowman seeks to rouse his hibernating companions and enlist their help. Athena arranges a diversion to prevent this from happening. Kubrick imagined a terrifying scene, noting to Clarke, "Suddenly there is a roar and a hurricane wind... The computer has apparently opened all the airlock doors. Bowman manages to clamp an emergency respirator on himself as he struggles into his space suit. According to expert opinion he would have approximately two minutes. What do you think?" Athena began her transformation into a male-voiced computer, and HAL 9000 was born.

SWITCHING PLANETS, CHANGING SHIPS

In the same week that Ordway was writing careful letters to IBM, he was faced with another problem, this time, much closer to home. Kubrick had become fascinated in a nuclear research project code-named *Orion*, a grandiose concept that was the perfect

The winged space plane was named *Orion* in honor of the abandoned nuclear-propulsion scheme for *Discovery*. The basic shell was made from plastic and fiberglass by Master Models, a company near London's Heathrow airport.

The *2001* effects department overlaid thin sheets of cut plastic to mimic the plane's exterior panels. Careful airbrushing of dirt streaks and naturalistic discoloration added realism.

expression of something we have almost forgotten today. Even under the shadow of The Bomb, many scientists and engineers still believed that the "friendly atom" might revolutionize our lives for the better. There would be atomic cars and trains and planes, and of course, atomic spaceships. *Orion* was a detailed proposal for a spacecraft powered by miniature nuclear detonations. The project was initiated in 1957 by Theodore Taylor, a physicist at the General Dynamics company, and the renowned quantum theorist Freeman Dyson. Both men were convinced that chemical rockets, with their limited payloads and high cost, were inadequate tools for space travel. Their solution, the 10,000-ton *Orion*, was (on the drawing boards, at least) 16 stories high. Its engine consisted of a flat circular pusher plate at the base, with a small hole in its center, through which miniaturized nuclear bomblets, "pulse units," were to be ejected. Huge shock absorbers between the pusher plate and the main body of the ship evened out the staccato stresses of the bomb blasts, and the great monster was supposed to rise into orbit at the rate of one explosion per second. After that, it would head for the Moon or Mars at a more modest rate of 10 blasts per minute. There would be 2,000 or 3,000 pulse units used per mission...

This was no joke. *Orion* was expected one day to carry 1,000-ton payloads into space: 10 times more than NASA's Saturn V rockets for Apollo. The research was funded jointly by the U.S. Air Force and the Defense Advanced Research Projects Agency (DARPA). Taylor and Dyson built several small-scale test vehicles powered by conventional explosive

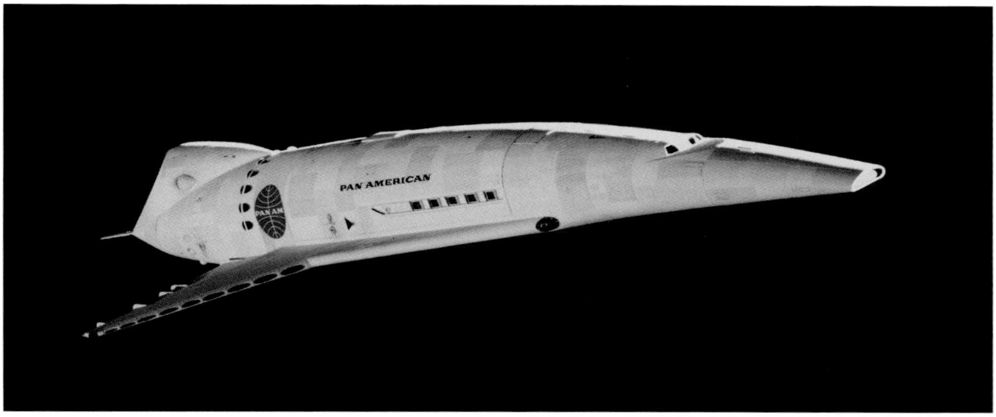

pellets, and launched a few miniature *Orions* a few hundred feet into the air from safe test sites on Point Loma, a three-mile-long spit of land guarding the entrance to San Diego harbor. The project continued until 1965, by which time an international nuclear treaty had limited the scope of nuclear explosive technologies, even for the peaceful exploration of space; and NASA already was committed to the more conventional use of chemically powered engines. Even so, Kubrick demanded that the *Discovery* spacecraft design be altered to incorporate a pusher plate. A revision to the script introduced this new machinery: "*Discovery* is 1,000,000 miles from Earth. We see the Earth and Moon small. We see a blinding flash every 5 seconds from *Discovery*'s nuclear pulse propulsion. It strikes against the ship's thick ablative plate."

Eventually, the idea of a spaceship "farting" its way across the solar system seemed too comical, and the redesign joined the many others filed away as unusable. Only the name, *Orion*, was salvaged, and awarded to the winged space plane that carries Heywood Floyd to the orbiting space station. In the first week of November 1965, Clarke and Kubrick inspected the *Orion*'s cockpit set, and Clarke said, too casually, that it reminded him of a Chinese restaurant. "That kills it for me," Kubrick said, and ordered a rebuild. Clarke jotted a chastened note in his diary: "Must keep away from the Art Department for a few days." By December 1965, only a week away from the start of principal photography, Ordway was sufficiently frustrated to write:

> *We are continually facing difficulties of decision-making. Whatever U.S. industry comes up with doesn't always please Stanley. Many design aspects of the vehicles for the film change so regularly that it becomes impossible at times to finalize anything. The screenplay has a decided tendency to change rather rapidly, even*

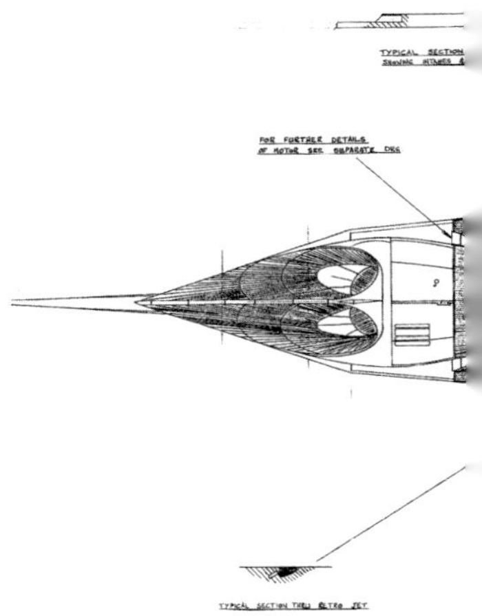

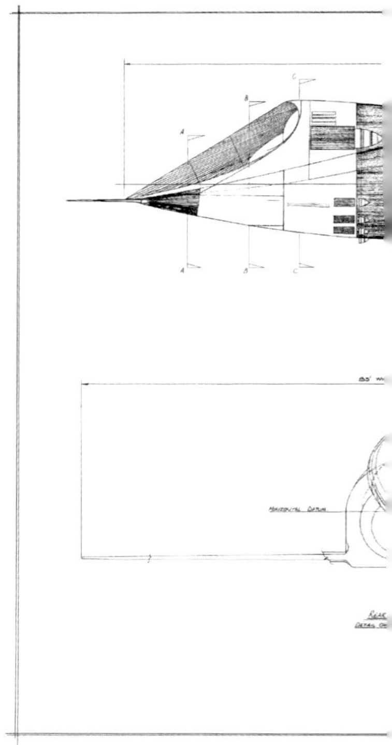

Technical drawings for the winged *Orion* space plane, closely matching the final version seen briefly on screen.

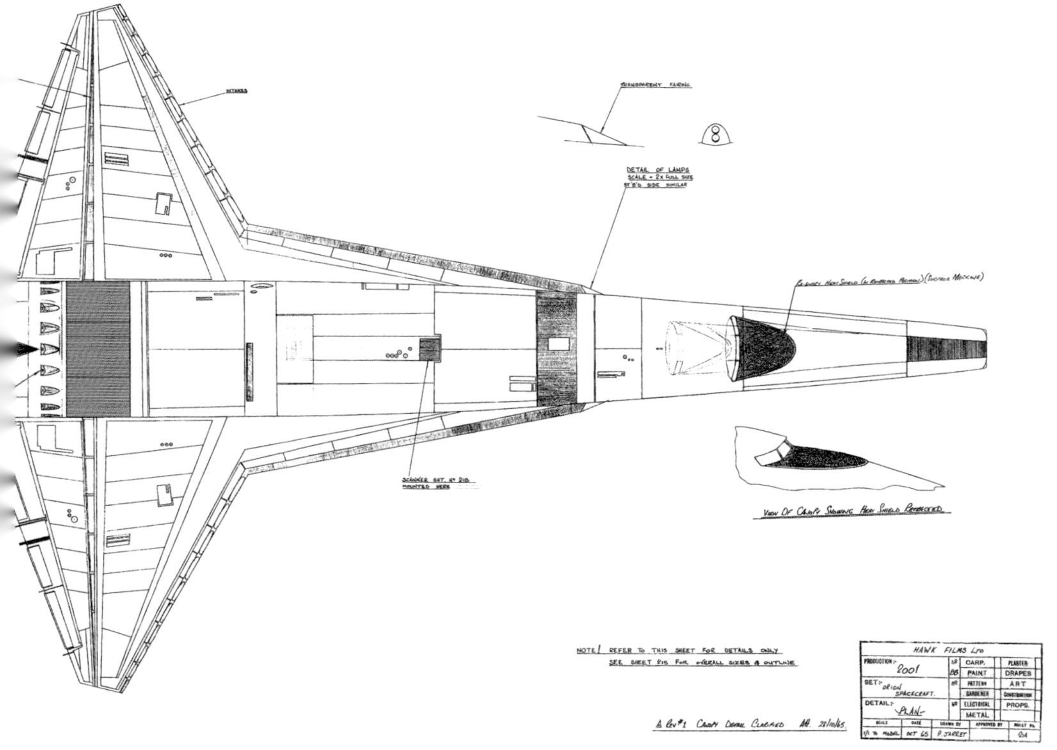
TRANSPARENT FAIRING
DETAIL OF LAMPS
SCALE = 2 x FULL SIZE
STB'D SIDE SIMILAR
SCANNER SET. No 218
MOUNTED HERE
NOTE! REFER TO THIS SHEET FOR DETAILS ONLY
SEE SHEET 2/5 FOR OVERALL SIZES & OUTLINE
HAWK FILMS LTD
PRODUCTION: 2001
SET: ORION SPACECRAFT.
DETAIL: PLAN
CARP.
PAINT
PATTERN
GARDENER
ELECTRICAL
METAL
PLASTER
DRAPES
ART
CONSTRUCTION
PROPS.
P. SARRET

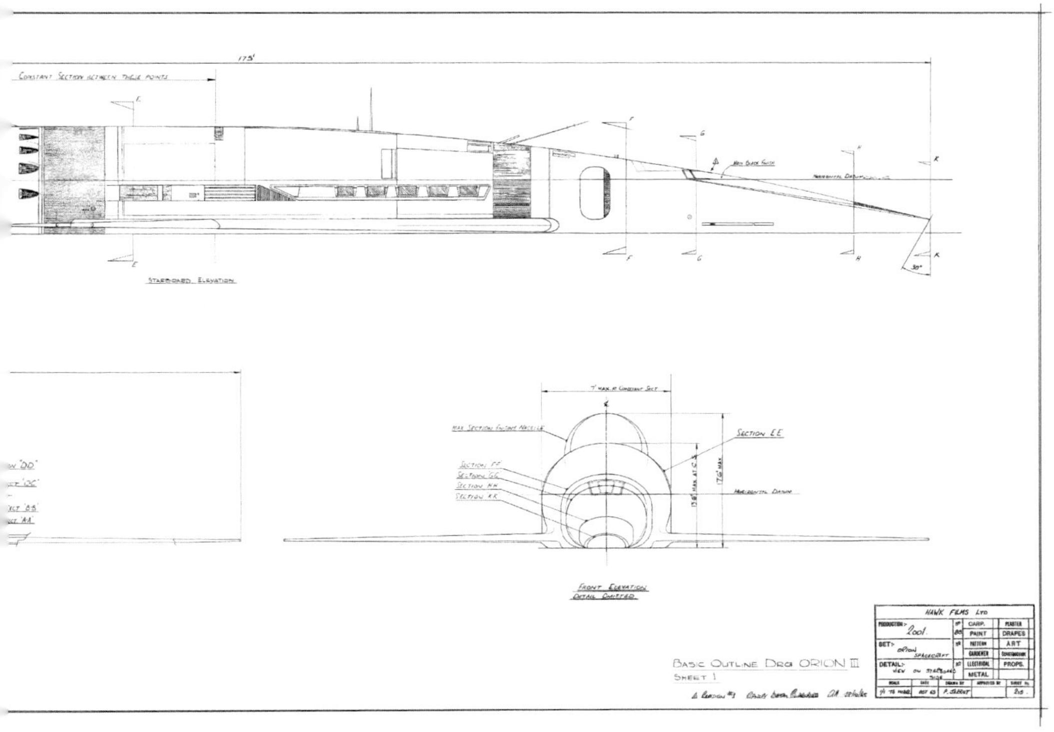
175'
CONSTANT SECTION BETWEEN THESE POINTS
STARBOARD ELEVATION
SECTION EE
FRONT ELEVATION
DETAIL OMITTED
HAWK FILMS LTD
PRODUCTION: 2001.
SET: ORION SPACECRAFT
CARP.
PAINT
PATTERN
GARDENER
ELECTRICAL
METAL
PLASTER
DRAPES
ART
CONSTRUCTION
PROPS.
BASIC OUTLINE DRG ORION III
SHEET 1
P. SARRET
2/B

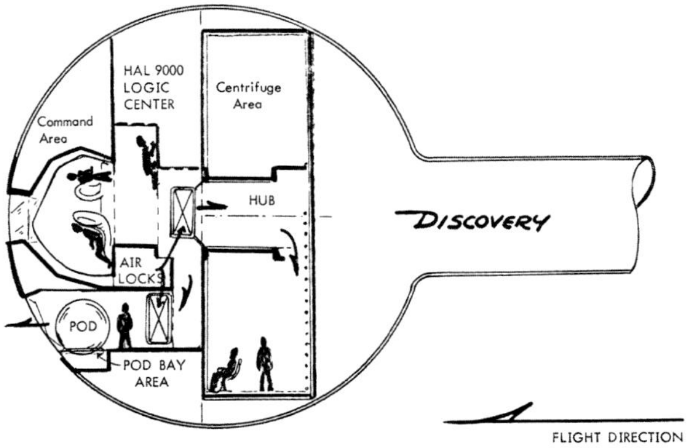

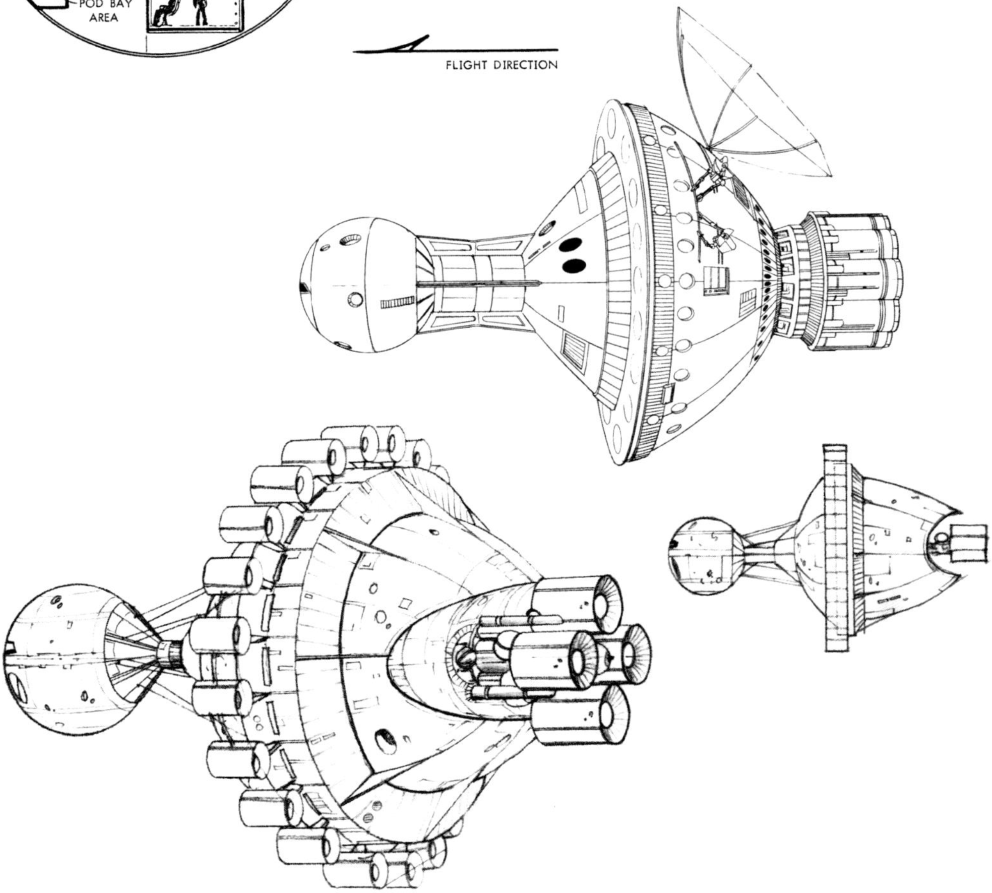

This rough sketch shows the supposed internal layout of *Discovery*'s habitation sphere.

△ This series of Lange sketches shows the Jupiter spaceship *Discovery* with a curious and bulky saucer-shape: an attempt to convey that true ships of space do not need to be streamlined because they function in a vacuum.

as we are moving forward. Film experts tell me this is highly unorthodox and produces more difficulties than necessary.

At the height of the construction effort, more than 100 model makers were employed to super-detail the various spacecraft models, which were unusually large for special-effects miniatures. The space station's diameter was about eight feet, and the *Aries* lunar ship's, three feet. The *Discovery* was built in two sizes: a 15-foot version for long shots and a 54-foot leviathan for close-ups, accompanied by a 13-inch-diameter pod. The model makers came from all kinds of specialist backgrounds. There were boat builders, architectural students, fine artists, sculptors, lithographers, metalworkers, and even some ivory carvers fresh off a whaling boat. This minor army was employed on a freelance basis. Turnover was high, as many of them failed to satisfy the exacting demands of the production's seniors. Those who stood the course were perfectionists, all of whom had to possess the additional quality of being immune to the shocks and disappointments of suddenly having to scrap several weeks' worth of work and start again. This happened quite frequently. The designs were not set in stone until the last moment before the models were set in front of the cameras. Even then, they might not be safe. Tony Masters and his construction teams built the props "to a hand-rubbed automobile finish. If Stanley spotted a nail head anywhere, that was impossible, because this was a story about the future, and there could be no imperfection. So we'd have to go back and redo it. Out of it all came something very good—you just wouldn't want to do it too often, because it takes years off your life." [2]

Gerry and Sylvia Anderson, coproducers of the television puppet shows *Stingray* and *Thunderbirds*, noticed that they were leaking staff from their specially converted building in a Berkshire County industrial estate. Brian Johnson was among them. "The *Thunderbirds* rockets weighed two or three pounds each," he recalls. "We suspended them on very fine tungsten wire, a single piece of filament that's probably half a mile long to a reel, but almost invisible if you shoot it against a fairly 'noisy' background, such as a cloudy sky. We'd hang the craft from poles and pull them along, or up and down." A looping roller of painted sky slid past behind the models, creating the illusion that they were flying through the air. Puffs of artificial smoke stood in for clouds. The haze helped to hide the wires. Kubrick was moderately impressed. Johnson "had a phone call to say, would I be available to meet him? So I went along to MGM, and I had to look for him, because he was always wandering around everywhere. I walked onto a huge stage, and went up to someone dressed in a disheveled blue suit, clutching a half-eaten sausage. I thought he must be a painter or a props guy. I said, 'I'm looking for Stanley Kubrick.

2 Interview with Tony Masters conducted by Don Shay, 1976

You haven't seen him around, have you?' And he said, 'I'm Stanley Kubrick.' That was my first introduction."

Johnson's first task was to rig the "weightless" pen retrieved by the flight attendant on board the *Orion* space plane. After experimenting with wire work, he decided to try a large glass disc instead: "We stuck the pen on it, although there was one shot where we had it hanging on a wire." Inevitably, given his previous experience, Johnson became involved with the model work for all the spacecraft: "On *Thunderbirds*, we used plastic kit components to some degree, but we took it to an extreme for *2001*. I went off to Germany to a toy fair and bought nearly every kit that was going. We embellished all the models with little bits of plastic molding, because we needed to build up this fantastic level of detail to give an impression of enormous scale. Then a very subtle paint scheme brought them to life. In any film frame, your eye automatically tells you these spaceships are huge."

Basic components were handcrafted in wood, plastic, and fiberglass. The 13-inch miniature of the pod was carved from oak and other hardwoods because Kubrick placed an absolute ban on plasters, resins, or any other model-making materials that might too easily dent or scratch. It was also essential to ensure that spherical surfaces were absolutely smooth, because the oblique high-contrast lighting used for the space sequences would betray any flaws. Hardwoods ensured the necessary precision for fine detailing of grooves in the HAL camera recesses and around the pod window. The intricate arms and claws were machined from aluminum. *Discovery*'s tanks and boom assemblies—10 segments, each consisting of at least three smaller modules—were assembled in what amounted to a factory environment. Here in particular, imaginative cannibalization of model kits proved helpful. The three-foot-diameter *Aries* lunar shuttle included motorized legs that extended as the craft approached for landing. Ordway and Clarke made a trip to the Grumman plant at Bethpage, New York, specifically to see the real NASA lunar module's legs under construction. Compressed air jets in *Aries*'s exhaust nozzles kicked up chalk dust at the moment of touchdown. The ship was suspended on a boom arm swathed in black velvet.

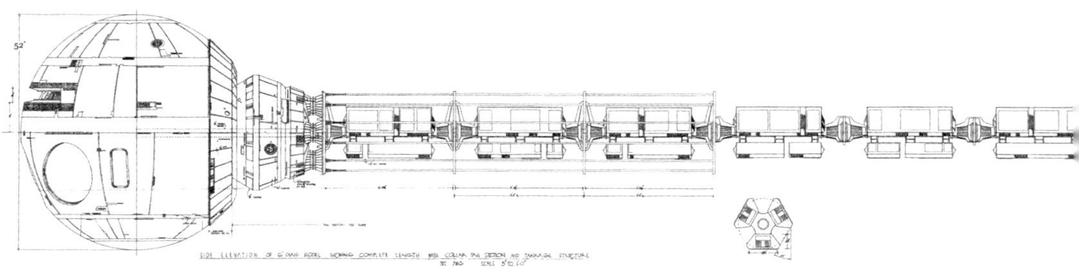

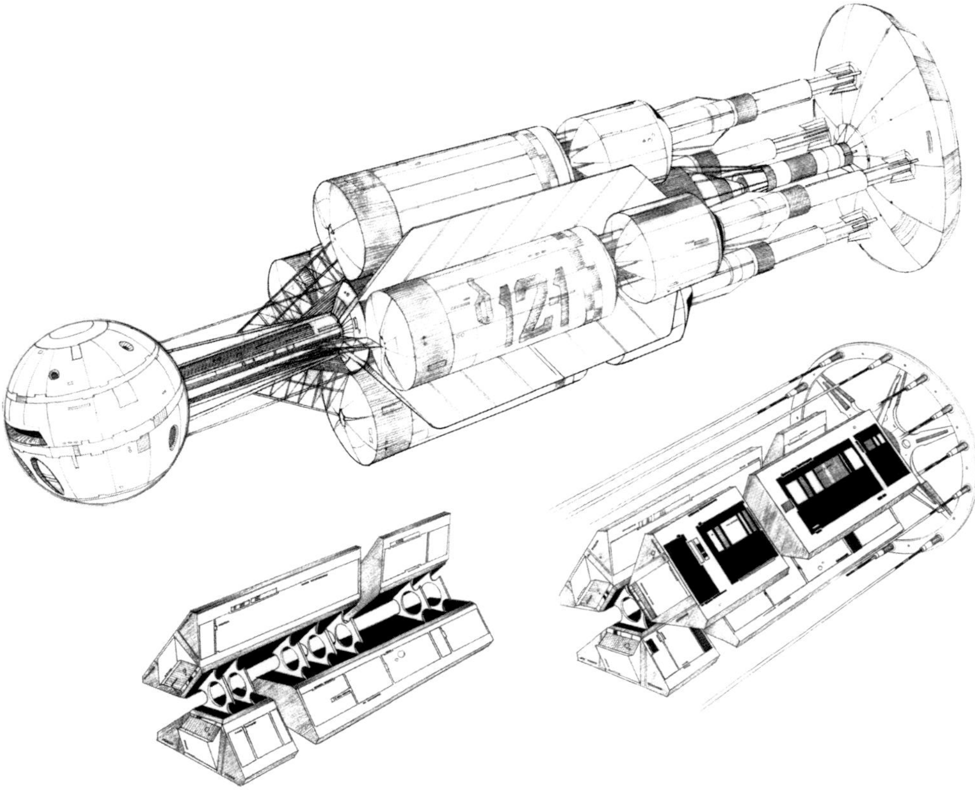

The nuclear pulse "pusher plate" idea for *Discovery* came close to being filmed, until Kubrick decided, at the last moment, not to stress direct references to atomic explosions, even on small scales; and anyway, the idea seemed faintly ridiculous.

▽ A near-final drawing of *Discovery*, showing the segmented boom, and thin rods strengthening the slender structure. The rods were eventually stripped away from the completed model.

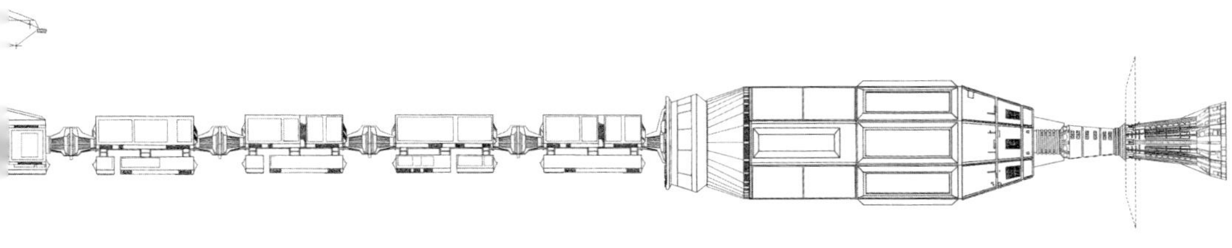

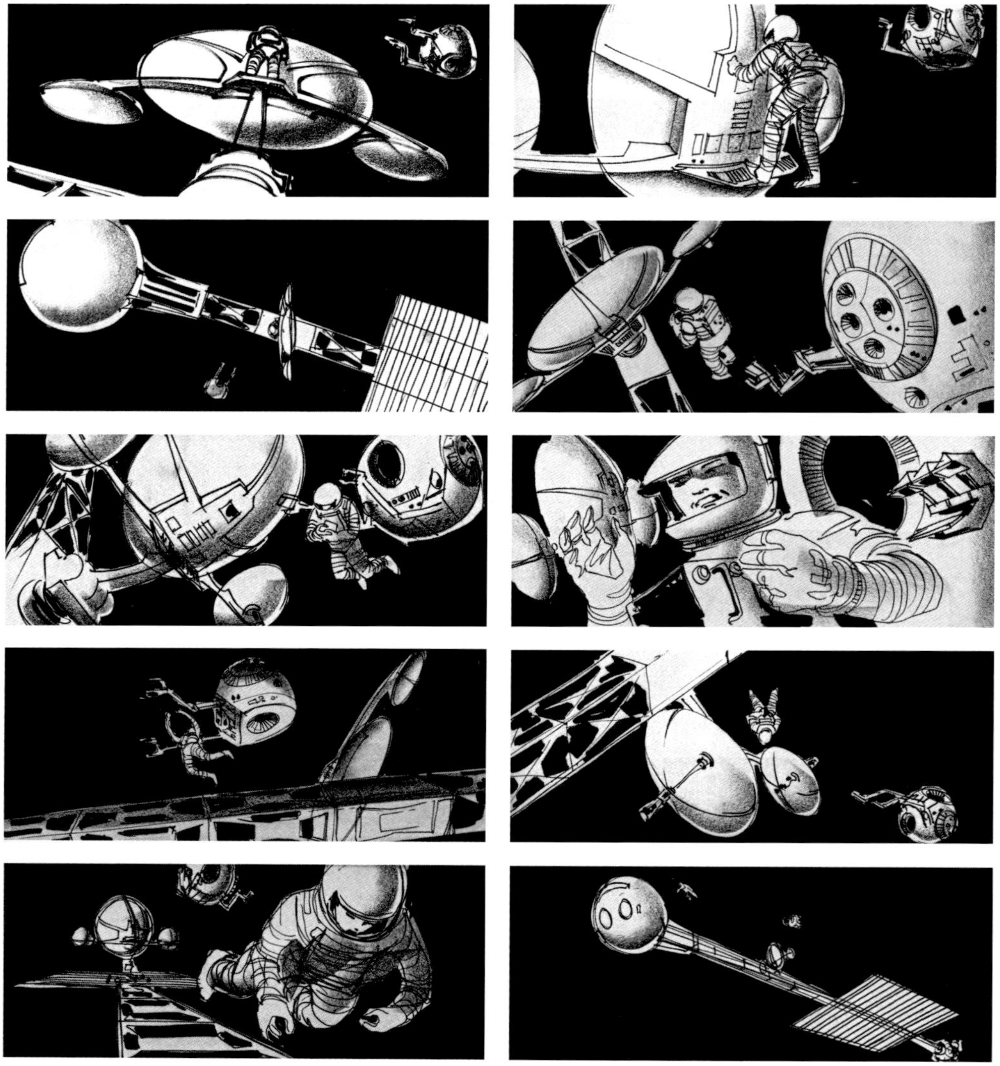

Storyboards of Frank Poole's murder depict a version of Discovery with radiators to dissipate heat from the engines. No one wanted to give the impression that the ship had "wings" or solar panels. Eventually the radiators were abandoned.

▹ 133–135 Carnon's artwork matches, in every detail, the description of Discovery in the novel. Clarke described "the slender V" of the radiators at the rear, and compared the ship to "some vast dragonfly." A rough physical model was assembled from polystyrene. The special-effects crew disliked this idea, and it was abandoned in favor of a long, slender boom with the habitation sphere at the front, and a bulky engine module at the far end.

Roy Carnon '66
2001
'DISCOVERY'
IN SPACE

Carnon's version of the main ball-shaped front sphere and a departing space pod is recognizably the hardware that we see in the film.

Yet another design iteration of the Discovery is put through a lighting test. The radiators and the wire cage along the boom were eventually abandoned.

Full-size space pods, space suits, and helmets required the services of outside industrial companies. The suits were manufactured by a firm of pilots' outfitters, Frankenstein Air and Sea Rescue in Manchester. The helmets were molded by a London company, Master Models, along with chest packs and basic structural shells for the *Orion* space plane and the Moonbus. The Hawker Siddeley aircraft company (makers of Harrier vertical takeoff fighter jets) produced pod interiors and instrument layouts to specifications that were so precise, they might as well have been working on a genuine aerospace project. According to Hawker's team leader, Arthur Cole:

> *We were contracted to provide consultancy during the early stages of production, and our responsibility was communications systems, voice, video, radar, navigation and control systems, attitude and orbit, remote manipulators and so on. Between us we derived many instrument layouts and provided advice on the likely shape of various structural features such as antennas, propulsion and control jets, and relevant hatch and docking systems.* [3]

3 Letter to the author

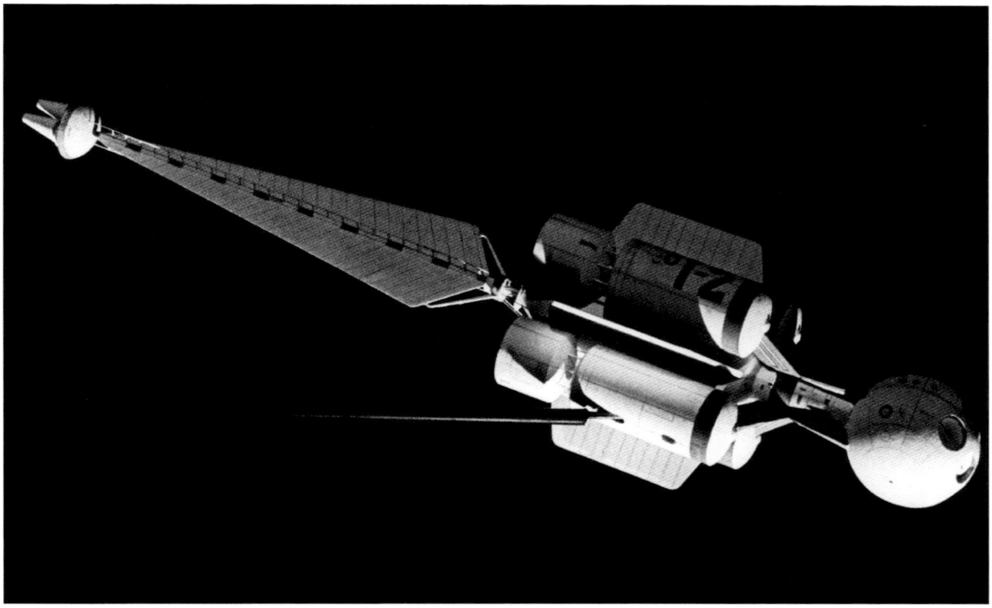

An accomplished Sri Lankan engineer and artist (and a future Sri Lankan ambassador to Burma), Hapugoda Rankothge Premaratne, known by his colleagues as "Prema," was Clarke's personal assistant at the time. Prema had just retired as director of Ceylon's Department of Public Works. Clarke had a feeling that he might be useful to Kubrick. The larger models incorporated mechanized components, such as landing legs, doors, and pod launch platforms. Additionally they required hidden steel armatures for support. Like many people who worked on the production, Prema looked back on his *2001* experience as a positive adventure. Harry Lange wrote to him when it was all over, saying, "Not one model could have been brought to the exceptionally high standard required in this production without the skills and imagination of people like yourself." Prema kept this letter proudly, although his memories of working on the film were not entirely painless:

> *I well remember the number of times we detailed the "Discovery" command module, when Mr. Kubrick would come along and, after a critical examination, would order scrapping the whole thing and re-doing it, this time using more convincing materials. Of course we worked under Harry [Lange]'s direction, and when we finally finished the whole thing, giving it a metallic finish using grained silver adhesive paper, complete with details, it was given a coat of paint obliterating all the metallic effect.* [4]

The polished steel skins of traditional science-fiction spaceships were gone forever as NASA began coating its angular hardware with heat-reflective paints. Kubrick wanted not merely to keep pace with real life, but to anticipate what might happen to space technology in the decades to come. The legacy of all this heartbreaking effort today is that *Discovery* and the other vehicles of *2001* still look convincing nearly half a century after he—at long last—approved their final design. The consequence of so many revisions at the time was that both the schedule and the budget strained at their anticipated boundaries. MGM chief Robert O'Brien held his nerve when quizzed by movie trade paper *Variety* about his wayward director's overruns: "Should we have told him to stop? Why have Buck Rogers at $6 million when you can have Kubrick at $7 million?" [5]

A letter from Clarke to his close friend and diving partner Mike Wilson, dated September 10, 1965, reveals that the film's budget broke loose from its moorings in the first year, with nearly four months yet to pass before live-action shooting could begin: "I went to the studio yesterday and emerged stunned. This is no longer a six million dollar movie.

4 Letter to the author

5 *Variety*, September 14, 1966

Storyboards of the Moonbus streaking over a harsh lunar terrain. In common with almost all space scientists at the time, Kubrick and his designers thought that lunar high ground must be rugged because of the lack of wind erosion. Real lunar mountains turned out to be more softly contoured than anyone expected.

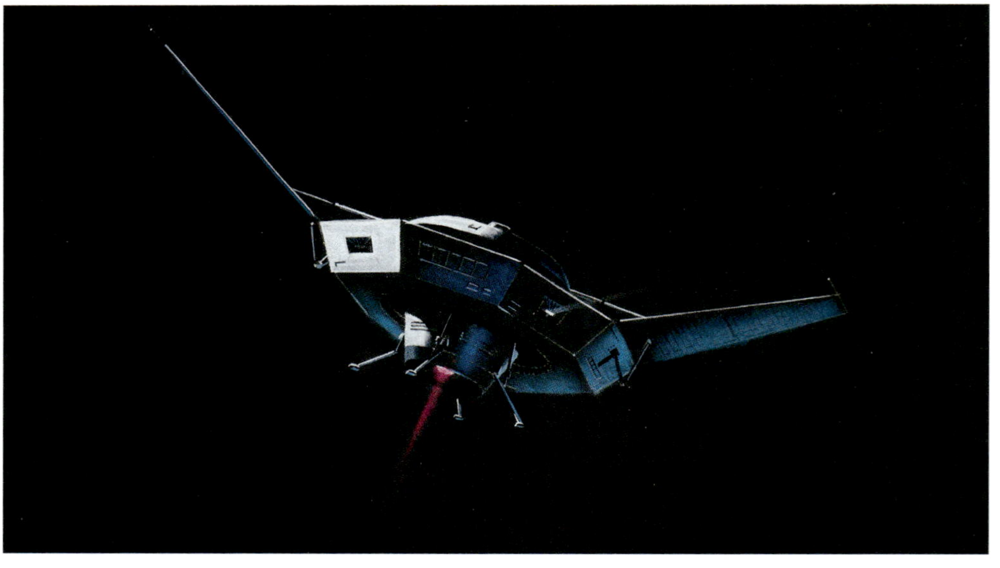

Two unmanned probes rendered by Carnon. In early drafts of the screenplay, the lunar monolith's radio signal, aimed at Jupiter, was detected by robot instruments in deep space.

I think the accounts department has thrown in its hand. The guess I heard was ten million." The letter also touches on Floyd's tense encounter with Russian scientists as he stops off in Earth orbit prior to heading for the Moon. "It's not really a vital scene," Clarke wrote, airily. "It takes place inside a 750-foot diameter disc-shaped space station. Yet they're building a full size section of the rim. It's a circular arc 150 feet long and 30 feet wide, the size and shape of a ski-jump. Actors at the far end will have to learn to walk tilted."

Much to his dismay, Clarke was still revising the novel and helping to adjust the shooting script nearly two years after he and Kubrick had first got together. The shifting designs of the space hardware were starting to feed back into the story process. Clarke continued to shuttle restlessly between Ceylon and Borehamwood, also taking on international speaking engagements, while being plagued, at inconvenient times, by bouts of fever and lassitude. A polio attack in 1962 had already weakened him. A subsequent condition, known as post-polio syndrome, compromised the strength in his legs, and he occasionally resorted to a stick. Physically and financially, the collaboration with Kubrick was becoming harder work than he had anticipated. The book version of *2001* was not yet in sufficiently good shape to be submitted for publication. Nevertheless, Clarke and Kubrick amicably continued to spark off each other, with productive results.

Some major revisions were at Clarke's behest, even though they called for yet more rewriting. By January 1966 he had persuaded Kubrick that it might be interesting for *Discovery* to visit Saturn, so that the planet's prominent and beautiful ring system could be shown. Ordway was instructed to find everything he could about the giant gaseous world and its icy rings. Saturn's third-largest Moon, Japetus, was known to have a strange dark patch. One hemisphere of the little world reflected only one-sixth as much sunlight as the opposite side. In the absence of the kind of space-probe data that we take for granted now, the astronomical details were sufficiently vague for Clarke to set the entrance to the Stargate on Japetus, thereby "explaining" the dark zone. He was so convinced by this new idea, he retained Saturn as the destination planet in the novel. He also described a "perturbation" maneuver by which *Discovery* exploited Jupiter's gravitational field to fling itself toward Saturn. Two planets could be explored for the price of one.

Kubrick, for his part, was keen on the rings. So it was agreed. *Discovery* would head for Saturn. The special-effects department was not so sure about this, and spent several tense weeks getting this decision reversed, having already worked up proposals for showing Jupiter, Clarke and Kubrick's original target from the *Journey Beyond the Stars* treatment. The task of creating an unexpected new planet, and its rings, was too much of an overload.

REFINING MURDER

Yet another script revision in February 1966 features an inquisitive television interviewer asking HAL, "Why was *Discovery*'s mission brought forward by five years?" HAL explains politely but falsely, "I don't know the answer to that question. Despite my qualifications, I am not kept advised of the reasons behind major policy decisions." Then the script enters surreal territory. HAL claims that the signal from Earth is to blame for communications problems, rather than the antenna itself. Mission control suggests, on open microphone, "We believe, under these circumstances, it would be advisable to disconnect the computer." When Bowman breaks into HAL's main chamber to do this, a doppelgänger is somehow activated inside the same circuitry, as if an electronic mind could conjure a schizophrenic twin. This shadow HAL delivers a wordy explanation for the "original" HAL's failure in the face of conflicting orders. The stress of hiding the mission's true purpose from his human companions has unsettled the balance of his digital mind. The twin HAL tells Bowman, "He was slowly overcome with a paralyzing mental anxiety, and eventually with guilt, because of your faith in him, and because of his loyalty to you." The "real" HAL breaks in. "Don't listen to him, Dave."

Clarke expressed some doubts from the safety of his Ceylon home when Kubrick telexed him with staccato urgency later that month: "HAVE WONDERFUL IDEA PREDICATED

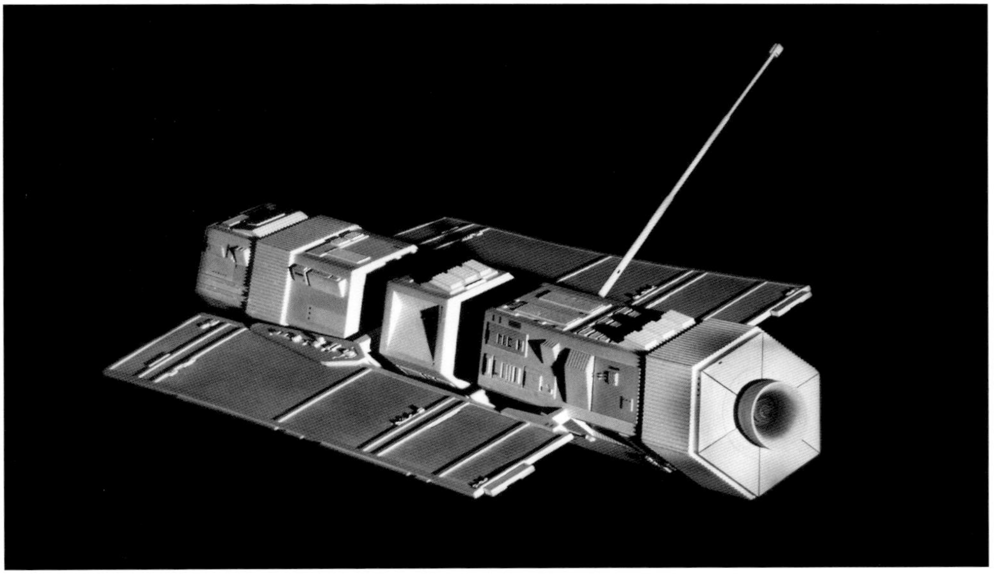

These unmanned space probes are some of perhaps a dozen models made for the film but never used, as Kubrick and his team restlessly kept up with the latest technical information from NASA's hardware designers.

ON HAL BEING ABLE TO OVERHEAR BOWMAN AND POOLE DISCUSSING HIM IN WHISPERS INSIDE POD CAN YOU THINK OF INGENIOUS WAY FOR HAL TO CIRCUMVENT CAREFUL PRECAUTIONS." Three days later he proposed, "HAL WILL READ THEIR LIPS THROUGH THE POD WINDOW I THINK THIS IS MARVELOUS SOLUTION BEST REGARDS STANLEY."

Clarke responded via conventional airmail letter: "I agree the lip-reading is the neatest solution, but isn't it odd that Hal can see both men's lips through the narrow pod window?" He also worried that "we are making Hal so clever that his defeat seems improbable." Kubrick reassured him: "It happens that Hal's eye can see directly into the pod window from across the pod bay. Both men can easily fit into the pod." Clarke dropped his objections to the lip-reading, while still concerned that the idea of a schizophrenic twin HAL breaking into the conversation just as Bowman is about to destroy the "first" HAL was "quite unexplained and unbelievable. Why does 'HAL 2' pop up at this point, and not before?"

As *Discovery*'s interior compartments and full-scale space pods came before the cameras in mid-1966, their physical reality presented other new ideas, not least of which was the use of a pod as a murder weapon—and as a potential safecracking tool. Rather than staying inside *Discovery*, as in the Athena drafts, Bowman would leave the safety of the ship in an attempt to rescue Poole, and then be trapped outside by HAL. "I think I've figured out a completely believable way to get him into the airlock," Kubrick suggested. "The rear pod door will have explosive bolts which Bowman will explode without bleeding the pod's air. He should be shot like a cannonball directly into the open airlock. What do you think?" Clarke was pleased with this idea, and enthusiastically set out to prove his earlier thesis: that an astronaut could survive in the vacuum of space for 10 to 15 seconds, which would allow him sufficient time to reach safety. Clarke's only complaint, subsequent to the film's release, was that Dullea appears to take a gulp of air just before blowing the pod's hatch: "If anything, you should breathe out as hard as you can, getting rid of any gas in your lungs. Otherwise you may have an embolism, and that's dangerous."

The notion of a jammed thruster on the pod was abandoned in favor of HAL's deliberate and sinister intervention, although it may have been a source of satisfaction to Clarke that a real-life space crisis a few weeks later proved that thrusters really could fail in the manner that he had proposed. Neil Armstrong flew his first orbital mission in March 1966 aboard a two-seat Gemini capsule. With copilot David Scott, he made a rendezvous with an uncrewed Agena target vehicle, and nudged the Gemini's nose into the waiting portal. The combined craft exhibited signs of instability, and Armstrong withdrew again. The Gemini tumbled more severely out of control because one of its roll thruster valves was locked in the open position. The two men felt themselves slipping into unconsciousness as the roll rate increased. Armstrong disabled the main thrusters and switched to a smaller set intended for reentry. He and Scott came home safely, just as Kubrick was simulating the similar dramas of future astronauts not yet born.

Live-action photography for *2001* began on December 29, 1965, at Shepperton Studios, a few miles west of London. Kubrick was unimpressed by the fact that Alexander Korda had photographed *Things to Come* there. More relevant was the fact that Shepperton's largest stage could accommodate what he needed for the Tycho excavation scenes: a huge trench partly filled with 100 tons of carefully graded, washed, and colored coke (a derivative of coal) in emulation of fine lunar soil. By January 8, 1966, he and his camera crew were back at Borehamwood. Shooting of the space-station interiors, and the lunar scientists in their underground conference room, was completed by the end of the month. Then actors Keir Dullea and Gary Lockwood remained on call from February through to the end of July, for filming of the *Discovery* interior scenes. Jeremy Bernstein, the physics professor and popular science writer, visited Borehamwood for the *New Yorker* magazine in early March, and found Kubrick working on a typically elaborate set. [6]

> *The scene that presented itself to me was overwhelming... A man came to me and led me, in a semi-daze, to an opening at the bottom. Peering into the dazzlingly lit interior, I spotted Kubrick lying flat on his back on the floor of the machine and staring up through the viewfinder of an enormous camera, in complete concentration...Kubrick, unwinding himself from the camera, spotted me staring open-mouthed... The furniture of the crew's dining quarters was bolted to the ceiling. [He] said, "Don't worry. That stuff is bolted down." Then he motioned me to come up and join him.*

Nearly half a century after the fact, there is still something vivid and thrilling in this firsthand account of Kubrick, cool and confident in his incandescent otherworld of lights, machines, hydraulics, optics, and electricity—a modern Merlin, inviting us awestruck mere mortals to "come and join him."

6 Stork, David G., *HAL's Legacy*, 1997

III

"Well, I must say, you guys have certainly come up with something."

SANTA'S WORKSHOP

On June 18, 1965, Victor Lyndon prepared a 160-page typescript of production notes, based on a series of conferences held at Polaris Productions in New York in the weeks prior to the move to England. Arthur Clarke noted in his diary, "they left me completely overwhelmed." The colossal scale and vaunting ambition of the film was evident by that summer. Forty pages deal with props, instruments, electronic newspapers for the year 2001, cups, plates, saucers, and other utensils for the large space-station set, and for the lunar hardware at the Tycho TMA-1 excavation site. In the dozens of warnings about seemingly trivial items that might be overlooked and cause problems later, one can sense Kubrick's intense concentration, his "don't forget"s ranging from details of camera requirements to the precise lettering on futuristic food dispensers:

> *Space Station Reception/Immigration Control, Instrument panel display screen: if actual closed-circuit television is used, the problem of proper camera/TV synchronization will have to be dealt with. CCTV, if used, may require special make-up. Research this and, if necessary, test. Every 40 feet or so in the space station's corridors there should be a sign which says: "Caution—Automatic Safety Doors." There is an elegant food dispenser. When the order is delivered an illuminated sign says "Served" or "Order Delivered." In each room of the space station there is a small air-testing display, plus buttons for emergency oxygen supply, etc.*

By page 112 of the notes, we are on board the *Discovery* spaceship and heading for Jupiter. The question of how to handle the weightless scenes is discussed. Everybody has agreed that the ship will have to contain some system for providing its crew with an artificial gravity. There is a lengthy section about "the centrifuge," a device that the production team must already have taken for granted among themselves, because it crops up, unannounced as it were, from page 115 onwards as a rumor, an intimation, of something truly grandiose:

> *The question of the studio floor and the weight of the centrifuge should be examined to determine whether a special foundation should be laid upon which the structure will be built... The center of the curving floor round the entire 360 [degrees] of the centrifuge will be slotted so that a cable can run through it and be attached to the camera dolly. The cable and dolly must support 2 or 3 men plus a studio camera, which has an estimated weight of 1,000 lbs. All internal furnishings, lighting fixtures, etc. must remain firmly attached, and should be made to function properly while the centrifuge rotates. Air conditioning must be provided.*

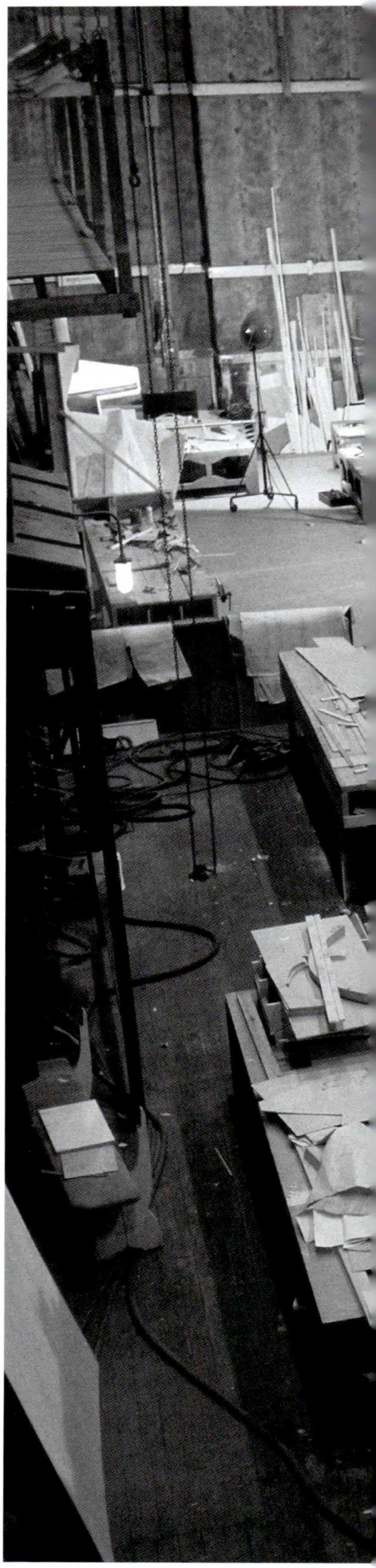

The exterior of the full-sized Moonbus set echoes the shape of the vehicle. Futuristic shapes were constructed from plywood and lengths of timber by skilled MGM craftsmen.

▵ A painting of planet Earth, mounted on a large rotating disc, ready to be positioned outside the space station set's window.

▹ Interior fittings for the centrifuge take shape on the studio floor alongside the steel rig for the wheel itself, just visible at top right. Notice the access ladder with its neatly turned wooden rungs.

CARPENTERS
FLOOR
CUPBOARD

The exterior of *Discovery*'s command deck. The access hatch leading to HAL's logic room is visible at bottom left.

The view of Earth as seen from the space-station windows was achieved with a rotating disc-shaped artwork positioned outside the set.

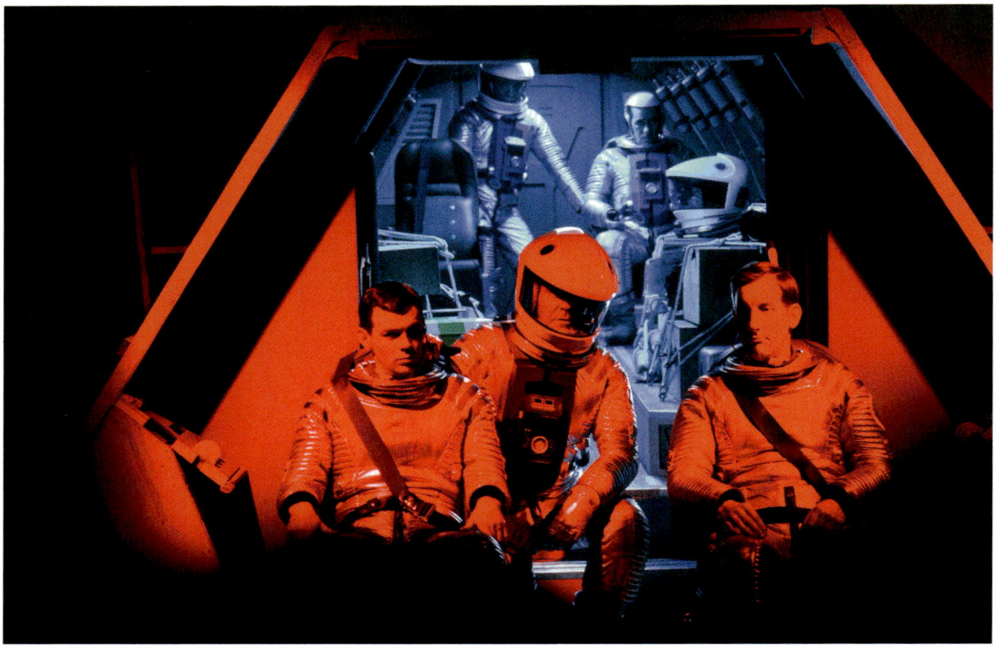

Many film critics have been fascinated by the color schemes evident in *2001*, and especially the use of red-lit interiors. Kubrick's advisors took their cue from submarines and other military vehicles. Night vision through the windows is enhanced by dim lighting in the cabins. The Moonbus cockpit was red-lit, while its passenger compartment was blue.

> *ABSOLUTELY NO SMOKING… There should be a built-in electronic piano somewhere in the recreational area.*

This strange carousel was commissioned from the Vickers Engineering company at a cost of over $750,000, a sum that accounted for a substantial fraction of *2001*'s budget. Arthur Clarke's brother, Fred (a central heating engineer whose math-laden book on the subject was a standard trade reference), thought that the machining and welding on Vickers's structure was of such fine quality, "you could almost imagine they were building a prototype for the real thing."

Chief production designer Tony Masters described the centrifuge to Don Shay in a 1977 interview: "We designed quite a cunning apparatus, really. The set was created in two halves, like two coffee tin lids held together to form a round box. If you open the two lids a fraction of an inch, there's a gap all the way around, and the two halves are separate." Through this narrow gap, a steel blade fed from the studio floor and into the drum's interior. Onto this,

the heavy camera could be attached, and remain secure while the entire set rotated past it. The challenge was "to get those two halves revolving together with the space between them never varying."

The eight-foot-wide shooting area, sandwiched in the middle of the assembly like the cream in a sponge cake propped up on its edge, was considerably narrower than the drum's exterior might have suggested. The outer areas accommodated lamps and electrical equipment that were essential for bringing the interior to life, yet had to be kept out of sight from the camera. In addition, 18 16 mm film projectors attached at various points on the left and right walls provided graphic displays for the set's control consoles (and two were fitted under the dining table to drive the astronauts' portable flat-screen televisions). The outside of the drum was a tangle of scaffolding, metal struts, access platforms, and ladders. The entire structure was swaddled in a mass of electrical cabling. A thick air-conditioning duct on one side of the drum pumped in cool air, while its snakelike twin on the opposite side carried away hot air generated by the lighting. Hatches set at frequent intervals along the curved outer wall of the drum ensured that actors and technicians could clamber out quickly in the event of a fire. Victor Lyndon's detailed brief to Vickers specified an escape system similar to that of an aircraft, with multiple quick-release panels around the skin of the structure.

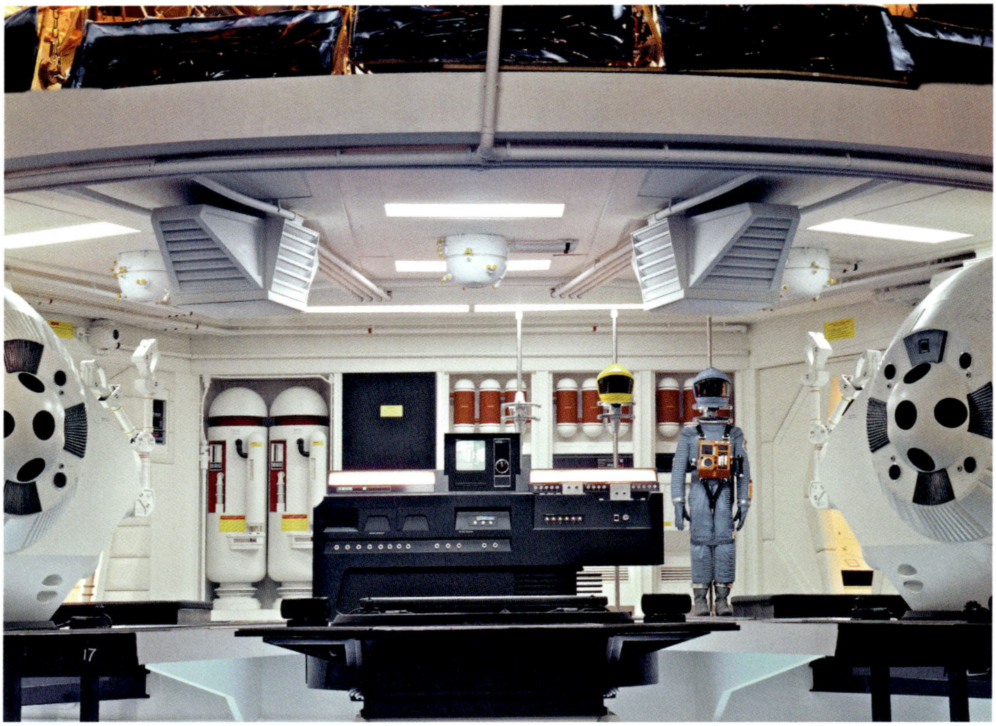

A detail of the pod bay set showing the workbench, dominated by one of HAL's electronic eyes.

▹ Three full-scale pods were constructed, one of which included a fully equipped interior and functioning rear hatch.

In keeping with his desire for naturalism, Kubrick wanted the main lighting for the centrifuge to be a function of its interior fittings. Strip-lighting diffusers were incorporated into recessed panels around the walls, so as to look like an integral part of the décor. Doug Trumbull from the special-effects department (of whom, more later) was impressed by the psychological impact of this on cast and crew alike: "You have a set that's completely 360-degree enclosed, and the lighting is actually built into the set, and none of the walls are 'floated' out the way. Architecturally, the lighting is built into the concept of the location. This had a profound effect, I think, on the actors and the production team, because you were in what seemed like a real place. They got comfortable with climbing up and down ladders and sitting in certain chairs and being in that environment. They felt like they were embedded in their space." Behind each ring of translucent Perspex in the centrifuge—one for the left wall, one for the right—there was an outer ring of powerful lamps. By the time they had shone their way through the panels, there was a tremendous buildup of heat in the set, but

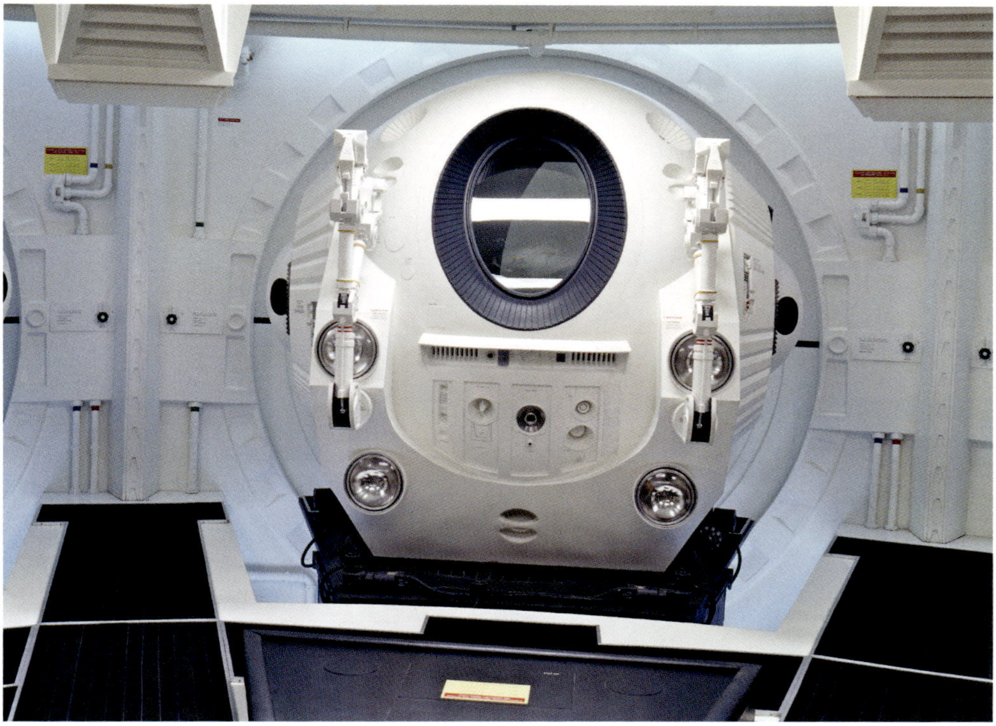

surprisingly little illumination. Kubrick's cinematographer, Geoffrey Unsworth, had to push the 65 mm film emulsion to the limits of its exposure capacity. In contrast, the outside of the drum shone like an inferno during takes.

Throughout photography in the centrifuge, film crews wore hard hats to protect themselves from any loose pieces of equipment that might fall on them from 40 feet over their heads as the mammoth construction slowly wheeled about. The customary "silence on set" during a take was often interrupted by the dramatic shattering of overstressed lamps. There was an incessant tinkle of small glass fragments trapped inside the walls, and a disconcerting screech of complaint every time the drum started to turn, while the steel support struts adjusted to the restless motion of their 30-ton load. Powerful electric drive motors under the rim of the drum, recessed into an expensively gouged trench in the studio floor, added their own unearthly thrum.

One shooting arrangement consisted of a camera and dolly bolted onto the steel blade that protruded through the groove near the "bottom" of the set, while the drum rolled past it. Gary Lockwood shadowboxed just in front of the camera, running through his fitness routine in shorts and a T-shirt. From our point of view, the off-duty spaceman

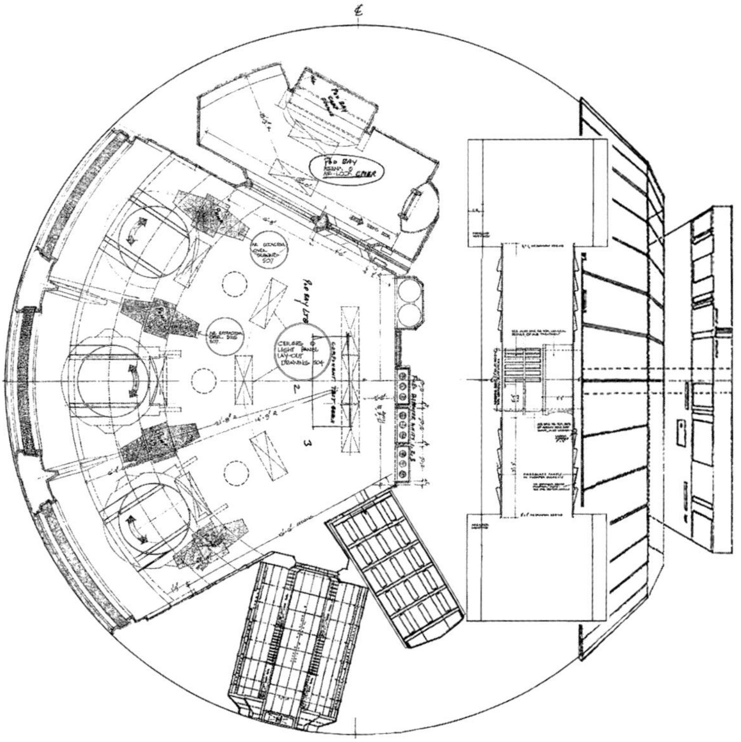

A reference drawing demonstrates how the pod bay and its associated corridors would fit into *Discovery*'s habitation sphere.

▹ The pod bay with the outer shell and circular external hatches removed. Notice the lighting on the lower front of the set, which helped to remove shadows from the inner walls of the three hatches when they were in their "closed" position.

punches and jabs his way around the interior of his little world while a fascinating procession of computer panels, washrooms, science cubicles, and freezer compartments glides past him. All the while, the camera had to be kept about 10 feet ahead of him, some way up the incline of the centrifuge's steeply curving floor. Rubber mats on the floor immediately fell back into place behind the camera's steel mounting blade, so that no trace remained of its knifelike progress through the slot. Any misalignments would have caused the set to squeeze together at the bottom, narrowing the slot, pinching the blade, and perhaps causing the camera to snap off its mounting while the drum rolled remorselessly past it. In admirably plain English, Lyndon's production notes insisted that it "must be impossible for [the blade] to tear loose from the dolly, otherwise a considerable amount of damage might be done to the actors standing ten feet away at the bottom of the inclined wall."

28

18

The seating area in *Discovery*'s control deck could be arranged horizontally or vertically, depending on the camera angle Kubrick wanted. Careful cinematography emphasized the lack of distinction between "up" and "down" in this supposedly weightless compartment. In one shot, a large mirror angled at 45 degrees at the rear of the main set created the illusion that the two astronauts were standing at right angles to each other: one on a "floor," the other on a "wall."

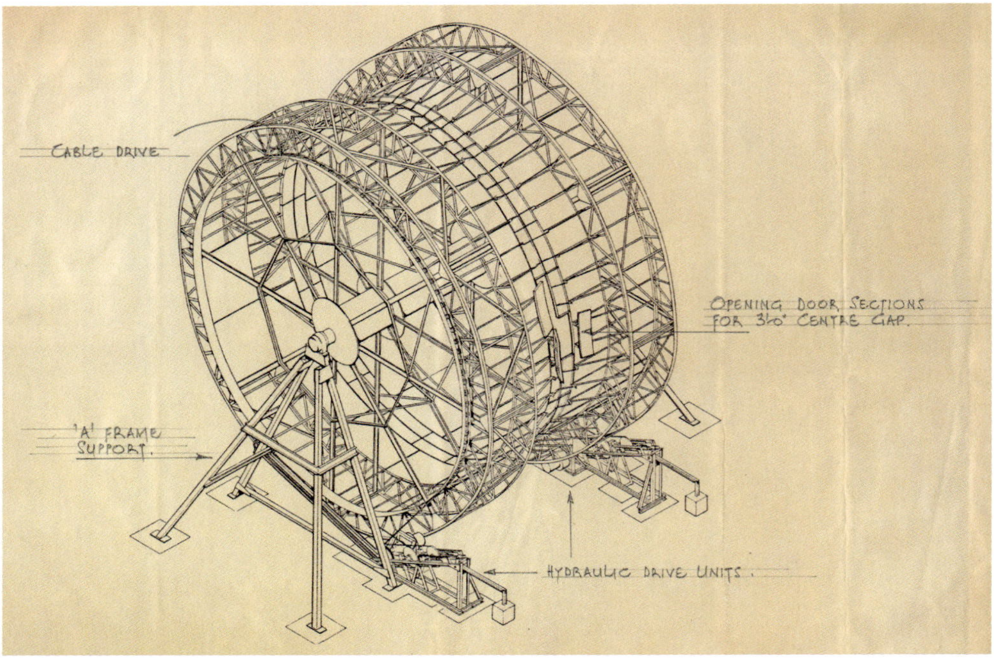
CABLE DRIVE
OPENING DOOR SECTIONS
FOR 360° CENTRE GAP.
'A' FRAME
SUPPORT.
HYDRAULIC DRIVE UNITS.

PANAVISION

The Vickers engineering company designed the steel support rig and drive mechanism for the centrifuge set.

◁ Rotating camera mounts, gyroscopic gimbal frames, and other mechanics enabled some acrobatic movements of the heavy cameras.

△▷ 164 The carousel-shaped centrifuge takes shape. Production staff and fitters standing at the bottom of the wheel give an impression of its scale.

▹ A Mitchell camera is mounted outside the centrifuge set, immediately behind HAL's control console, emulating his point of view via the use of a specially adapted fish-eye lens. The Panavision camera at right shoots Bowman looking at HAL.

▹ 165 The exterior of the centrifuge, showing the lighting rig and some of the projectors used to power various displays inside the set.

NORT

DELIBERATE DISORIENTATION

Other shots were even more dangerous to obtain. The camera could be attached securely to particular sections of the floor. Operator Kelvin Pike was strapped into his chair while he and his camera were carried nearly 40 feet aloft by the set's rotation. Pike's seat was mounted in a gimbal frame, like an oceangoing ship's compass, enabling him to remain upright and keep his bearings even when the camera, at the topmost point of its travels, was upside-down relative to the studio floor. Meanwhile, Dullea and Lockwood trod the bottom of the drum like oversized, bipedal hamsters in an exercise wheel, as the futuristic fixtures and fittings trundled slowly past them. From the camera's point of view—and the audience's—the astronauts appeared to be walking around the walls while the set stood rock steady. An establishing scene shows Bowman climbing down the ladder of the centrifuge, fetching food from the galley and walking around the drum to join Poole at the dining table. For this shot Lockwood was strapped onto the couch, hanging almost upside-down until the rotation of the set brought him back down again to meet Dullea, treading steadily at the bottom of the wheel. The attachment harness under Lockwood's costume was carefully concealed, and his meal tray was glued to the table.

The number of personnel in the drum had to be kept to a minimum. According to Dullea, "There were certain shots when we would lean forward and turn on the camera ourselves, because there was nowhere safe for the cameraman to go, or he'd be in the frame. Then we'd get into position and they would start up the wheel, and you'd have an everlasting tracking shot. You would just walk and walk—or run—and the wheel would revolve around you." Kubrick, working from within the safety of a room-sized wire mesh box adjacent to the set, with Unsworth by his side, directed using closed-circuit TV, relaying his instructions via walkie-talkie to the actors inside the drum. A half-silvered mirror and small TV camera mounted at a slant in front of the film camera fed a monochrome version of the scene to a video monitor on Kubrick's desk. A bulky videotape machine provided instant, if rather hazy, playback: a pioneering use of a technique now in common use.

The rim of the drum was calibrated like the dial of a giant compass. These markings tallied with the various areas of the set inside. Operators on the stage floor obeyed specific instructions to rotate the drum from one registered point to another, then halt it. Meanwhile the actors inside hit their marks too, using the internal furnishings around them as their guide. This system was designed to avoid the dangers of an actor reaching his mark, only to find that the drum was still rolling. There nearly was a catastrophe at one point. Marvin Minsky, cofounder of the Artificial Intelligence Laboratory at the Massachusetts

The centrifuge is lit up and spun for a "take." The thick pipes leading from the wheel's axis to the top right of these images were part of the air-conditioning system.

Institute of Technology (MIT), was visiting the set one day, when "a big heavy wrench fell down from the 12 o'clock position and got buried in the ground a few feet from me. I could have been killed. Kubrick was livid and quite shaken and fired a stagehand on the spot." This did not spoil Minsky's appreciation. He found the wheel "a technical marvel."[1]

There were other marvels, too. The Vickers drum was the largest of three sets constructed on mechanical moving frames. Audiences also see how the *Discovery* astronauts gain access to the centrifuge from the nonrotating, weightless control deck of their ship.

1 Stork, HAL's Legacy

Reference photographs of the centrifuge interior, showing the hibernation units, the sunbed lounger, and a functioning washroom. The groove for the bladelike steel camera mounting can be discerned as a slightly thickened line between the floor mats.

Dullea and Lockwood walk along a cylindrical corridor and step smoothly onto a "hublink" at the axis of the centrifuge. The two men accommodate themselves to the hublink's slow spin, as if caught in an oversized tumble dryer. The camera was mounted onto the front half of the set, while the background half was rotated by stagehands. As soon as the actors reached the far compartment, its spinning was brought to a halt, and the foreground was rotated, along with the camera. The audience only sees what the camera saw. The illusion is created that the foreground padded section is always stationary, while the hublink at the far end seems always to be rotating.

The famous scene in which stewardess Edwina Carroll walks around the walls of the *Aries* kitchen was achieved in a similar way. The set was rotated, while Carroll walked in place somewhat like a hamster at the bottom of an exercise wheel. She conveyed the impression of pushing her "grip shoes" onto the black fabric walkway, cautiously moving one foot only when the other was secured. Similar illusions (minus the grip shoes) were exploited by dance star Fred Astaire and film director Stanley Donen for the musical *Royal*

Wedding (1951), in which Astaire tap-dances his way up the walls and across the ceiling of his hotel room. A disorienting fight in a hotel corridor staged for Christopher Nolan's 2010 thriller *Inception* was inspired by the same idea. The viewpoint of the camera sets the frame of reference. Ingenious filmmakers know how to exploit this.

Clarke was thrilled when real life caught up with Kubrick's effects just a few years after the film's release: "NASA's first space station was Skylab in the early 1970s. It was converted from one of the huge cylindrical fuel tanks of a Saturn rocket. The astronauts did exactly the same thing, running round the walls fast enough to generate a centrifugal effect. They deliberately reproduced the scenes from *2001* in an actual spacecraft."

Kubrick's film editor, Ray Lovejoy, thought of all this as "movie-making at its most romantic, with big sets, big stages, lots of activity, massive lighting rigs, tracking shots—just completely sensational. Today, obviously a lot of that wouldn't exist. There'd be computer-generated backgrounds, and you'd sit at a table and punch a few buttons and away it goes. It's not the same, and not so convincing on screen. You can always tell it's not real. In *2001* you are absolutely convinced, because, in a sense, it *was* real. Everything was right there in front of the cameras."

Doug Trumbull and his colleagues in the special-effects department enjoyed this kind of attention, wherever possible, to tangible physical processes. "Special effects now are almost entirely based on computer graphics," Trumbull mourns. "We've moved completely away from miniatures, paint and sawdust and plywood and rubber and motors, and it's a vanished art. I think a lot of aesthetic depth and detail has been lost in the process."

Shots of Bowman clambering out the rear hatch of his space pod and then appearing to float freely away from it were achieved by positioning all the elements in line above the camera. A full-scale pod was suspended from the velvet-swathed ceiling of the studio, with its rear facing down, while the camera pointed upward from its mounting on the studio floor. Stunt performer Bill Weston was suspended on a wire that disappeared inside the pod. From the camera's point of view, he seemed to crawl out horizontally. Audiences already familiar with the layout of the pod accepted its apparent "right-way-up" attitude as their visual cue. For other space-walking scenes, Weston's orientation in the harness could be altered by wiring him up in different ways, just so long as the attachment point on the suit lay precisely above his natural center of gravity, so that his body did not tumble out of control. The bulk of his body always concealed the wires behind him.

The sequence showing Bowman's attempt to rescue Poole was particularly challenging for Weston. He had to pretend to be a dead body, drifting helplessly in the punctured

Dullea poses alongside the food dispenser, a supposedly perfect machine that delivers food slightly too hot for comfort.

▿ Another view of the galley area, showing one of the removable panels on the rim of the centrifuge.

The camera is pushed awkwardly against a wall as photography gets under way for Bowman and Poole's tense discussion with HAL inside the centrifuge.

△ Gary Lockwood discovered that he could make suggestions to Kubrick, who welcomed fresh ideas from his actors. The lip-reading scene was Lockwood's idea.

▷ From within the safety of an adjacent wire cage, Kubrick monitors centrifuge photography using a closed-circuit TV camera mounted close to the lens of the film camera inside the set. The TV pickup shared the main camera's perspective via a half-silvered mirror box.

Kubrick gives instructions through a hatch at the "bottom" of the centrifuge, as Dullea and Lockwood prepare for a scene.

yellow pressure suit. His support wires were suspended from a movable track rig on the ceiling. The camera underneath him was also on tracks, and moved along with him to keep the all-important vertical alignment intact. Weston was pulled toward the pod, which was motionless apart from the shifting of its arm and claw mechanisms. Subsequent manipulation of the drifting star field by the special-effects team gave the illusion that the pod approaches the lifeless Poole, rather than the other way around. On screen the final contact between body and pod looks weightlessly sedate. In fact, Weston's collision with the pod arms was faster than it appears on screen: sufficiently energetic to chip a fleck of paint from his helmet. The flying fragment can be seen in the film. The camera was running at high speed. The subsequent footage, replayed at the standard frame rate, appears slowed down.

Certain weightless scenes called for the relevant actor to be identifiable in his space helmet, such as the moment where Bowman penetrates HAL's inner chamber to dismantle him. Dullea was not a stuntman, but readily agreed to enduring the discomfort of the wire harness: "Stanley could get you to do things that you wouldn't do for any other director, because it could have been dangerous. Somehow I completely trusted him. I didn't think anything was ever going to go wrong. The scene where I climb up a ladder toward the HAL brain room was hand-held by Stanley himself."

The emergency airlock set was built vertically with its open door at the top, and the camera pointing straight up from its position on the studio floor. Dullea was "hunkered at the top of that set, waiting to fall through a trap door, so to speak. I had a harness and a thin wire, which is the length that actually got into the set. Way above that, out of sight from the camera, the wire was attached to a thick rope, knotted at intervals, and these circus roustabouts with gloved hands grabbed the rope and cinched it at certain places, hauling me up and down at the right moments, without dropping me to the floor or dragging me back out through the top hatch. I had no helmet, so I didn't want to do too many takes. That's the only dangerous thing I did on *2001*." In the HAL brain room, Dullea was upside-down for certain shots: "The blood was rushing to my head. It wasn't being suspended that was difficult, so much as the heat that would build up inside the suit. That was really rough, even though they had a compressed air hose coming in." (The roustabouts were provided by Eugene's Flying Ballets, an acrobatic troupe accustomed to aerial wire work.)

An earlier scene, immediately after HAL's murderous attack, shows Poole's body tumbling into the void, accompanied by a similarly lifeless pod. Even the tallest shooting studios at Borehamwood lacked sufficient room to accommodate this scale of relative movement between the stuntman and the camera. Footage of Weston was processed into a positive color film reel, then projected onto a small square of reflective white card set up on a darkened stage. A special-effects camera rephotographed this miniature film show, while backing steadily away from the card. Reversing the copy camera by just a few feet created the impression of opening up a far greater distance. In the completed scene, the addition of a star backing at constant scale persuades the audience that the astronaut is vanishing into the depths of space. The rocky asteroids drifting across *Discovery*'s path were among a number of similar effects achieved by rephotographing projections on cards.

A rare surviving blueprint shows the air vents and central axis of the centrifuge.

▹ Wherever possible, lighting for a set was incorporated into the physical architecture, as seen in this Widelux camera view of the pod bay.

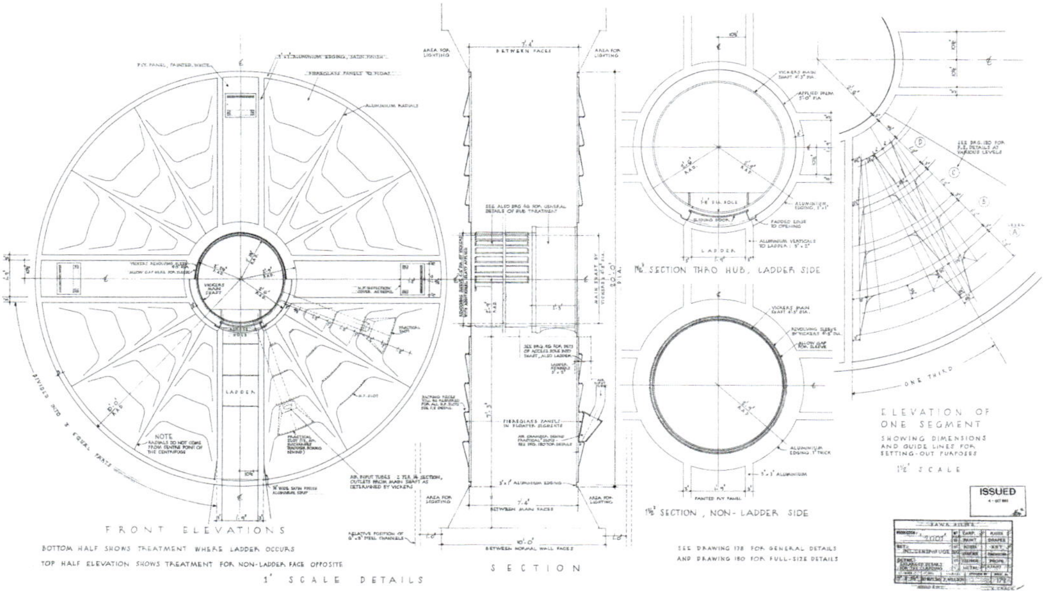
FRONT ELEVATIONS
BOTTOM HALF SHOWS TREATMENT WHERE LADDER OCCURS
TOP HALF ELEVATION SHOWS TREATMENT FOR NON-LADDER FACE OPPOSITE
1" SCALE DETAILS
SECTION
1½" SECTION THRO HUB, LADDER SIDE
1½" SECTION, NON-LADDER SIDE
SEE DRAWING 178 FOR GENERAL DETAILS
AND DRAWING 180 FOR FULL-SIZE DETAILS
ELEVATION OF ONE SEGMENT
SHOWING DIMENSIONS AND GUIDE LINES FOR SETTING-OUT PURPOSES
1½" SCALE
ISSUED

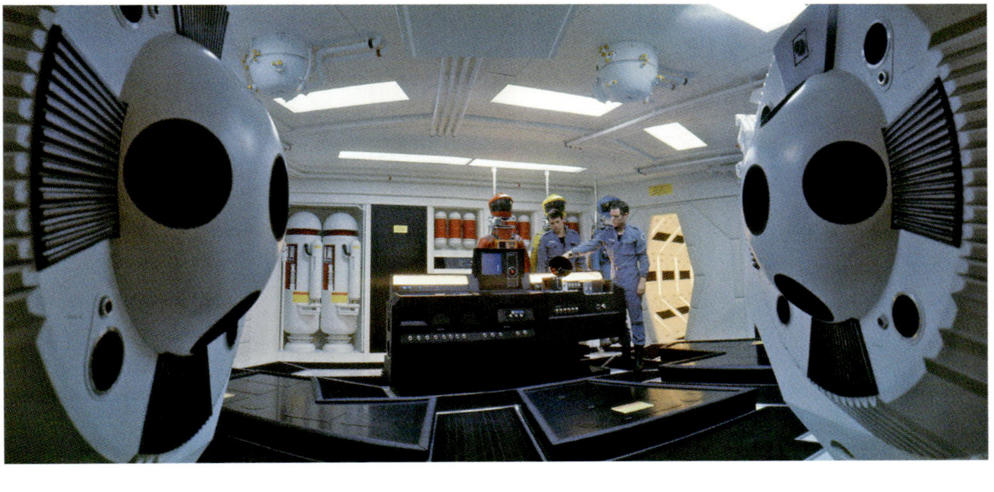

Stunt artist Bill Weston slams into the pod arms for a scene that appears deceptively slow and sedate in the finished film.

▹ 180 Dullea and Lockwood in a publicity shot taken by Dmitri Kessel for Life magazine.

▹ 180 Fine artist Damian Loeb's oil on linen painting, completed in 2003, is entitled *Good Afternoon Mr. Amer*. Loeb interpreted a selection of film frames to produce this widened view of HAL's main display area in the centrifuge.

▹ 181 A full-sized space pod and the mechanism for extending it through the *Discovery*'s hatch are tested prior to a shoot, in one of countless scenes requiring mechanical systems to function smoothly.

CAUTION
CAUTION

VEH
NAV
GDE

Keir Dullea inside the pod, photographed with and without his helmet: a distinction exploited by HAL.

Dullea rehearses his entry into the antechamber leading to HAL's brain room, surrounded by banks of circuit breakers.

◃ Kubrick insisted that the labels and instruction plaques on all items of hardware should be realistic, just in case his camera happened to close in on such details. These are fuel storage modules in the pod bay.

GRAPHIC FILMS

Con Pederson was drafted into the U.S. Army in 1956 at the age of 22. Fortunately for this peace-loving young man, his recruiters were impressed by his drawing skills, and sent him to Huntsville, Alabama, where the German-born rocket pioneer Wernher von Braun was working at the Army Ballistic Missile Agency (ABMA) on short-range rocket weapons, while trying to convince anyone who would listen that the same technology, somewhat scaled up, could be used for the peaceful exploration of space. The prospect of launching anything into orbit atop a machine designed by the creator of the notorious V-2 rocket bomb did not appeal to President Eisenhower, and von Braun was specifically banned from making any such attempt. Von Braun, dedicated as he was to the idea of space travel, was determined to change America's opinion of him, and set about this task using a classically American tool: public relations.

One of his most important presentations was a series of articles for *Collier's*, a popular illustrated magazine. Between 1952 and 1954 seven major features on space were published, including descriptions of a lunar colony and a mission to Mars, based intimately on his technical engineering descriptions, yet phrased in a language anyone could understand. The hardware was brought vividly to life by illustrators Chesley Bonestell, Rolf Klep, and Fred Freeman. There was a giant wheel-shaped space station gently turning on its axis: a concept destined to become associated with *2001: A Space Odyssey*. A painting by Bonestell showed the station attended by winged rockets, while in the foreground three huge landing ships are prepared for their trip to the Moon "within the next 25 years." Most of these dreams had been familiar to rocket visionaries and science-fiction enthusiasts since the 1930s, but the *Collier's* articles represented perhaps the first time that the general public had been asked seriously to consider rocket ships and space stations and trips to the Moon as serious elements of national policy. The magazine sold 3 million copies a month. As a family title, it would have been read by perhaps 15 million people.

There followed a succession of popular books and television shows, including three television films from Walt Disney, in which von Braun himself featured. The first, *Man in Space*, aired on the ABC television network on March 9, 1955. The second, *Man and the Moon*, was broadcast the same year. The final film, *Mars and Beyond*, came out in late 1957, just a few weeks after Sputnik had made such dreams seem that much closer, especially now that the White House had reconsidered its attitude to von Braun and unleashed his talents in response to the Soviet affront. Pederson was in the right place at the right time:

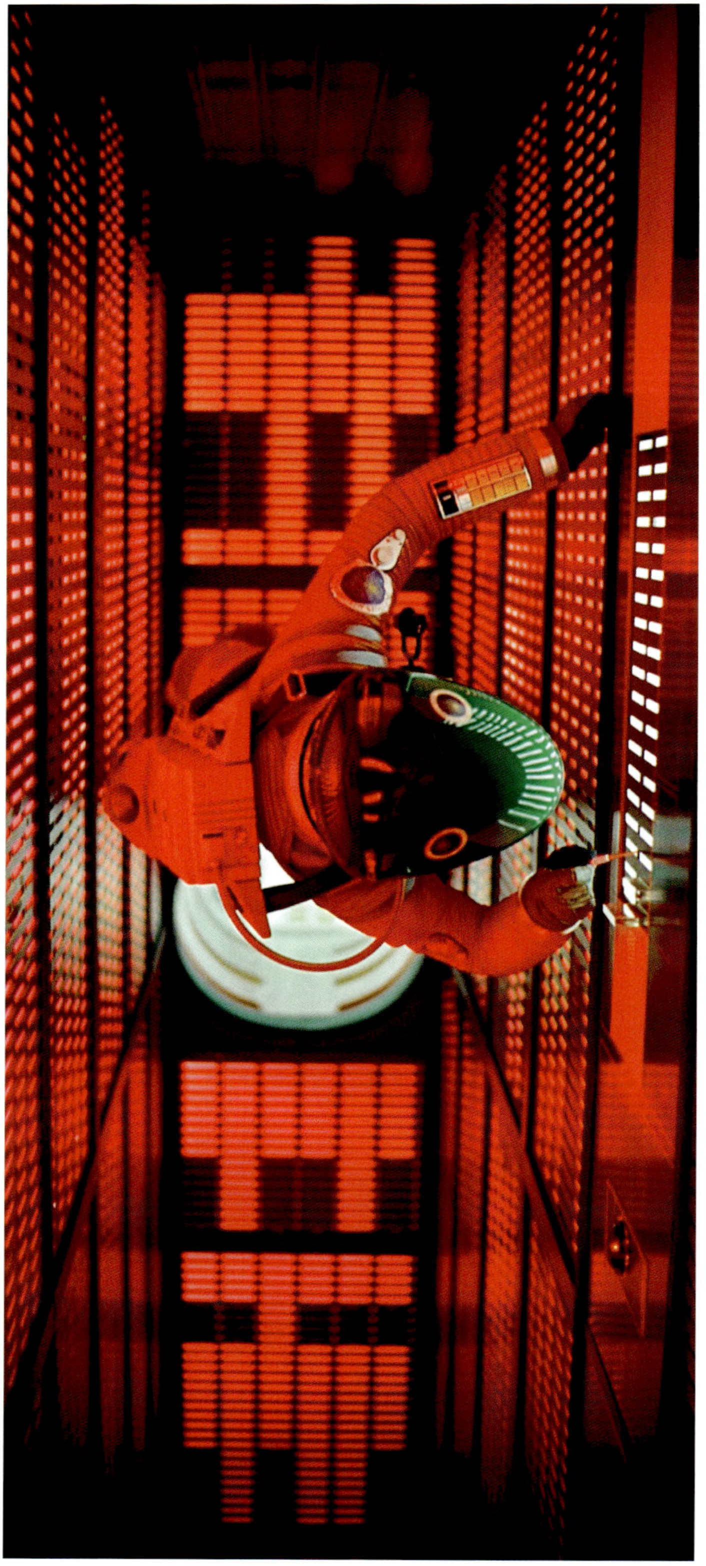

Dullea is helped into position, suspended upside down by a wire. He performed most of the stunt work inside the HAL chamber because his face needed to be visible through his helmet visor.

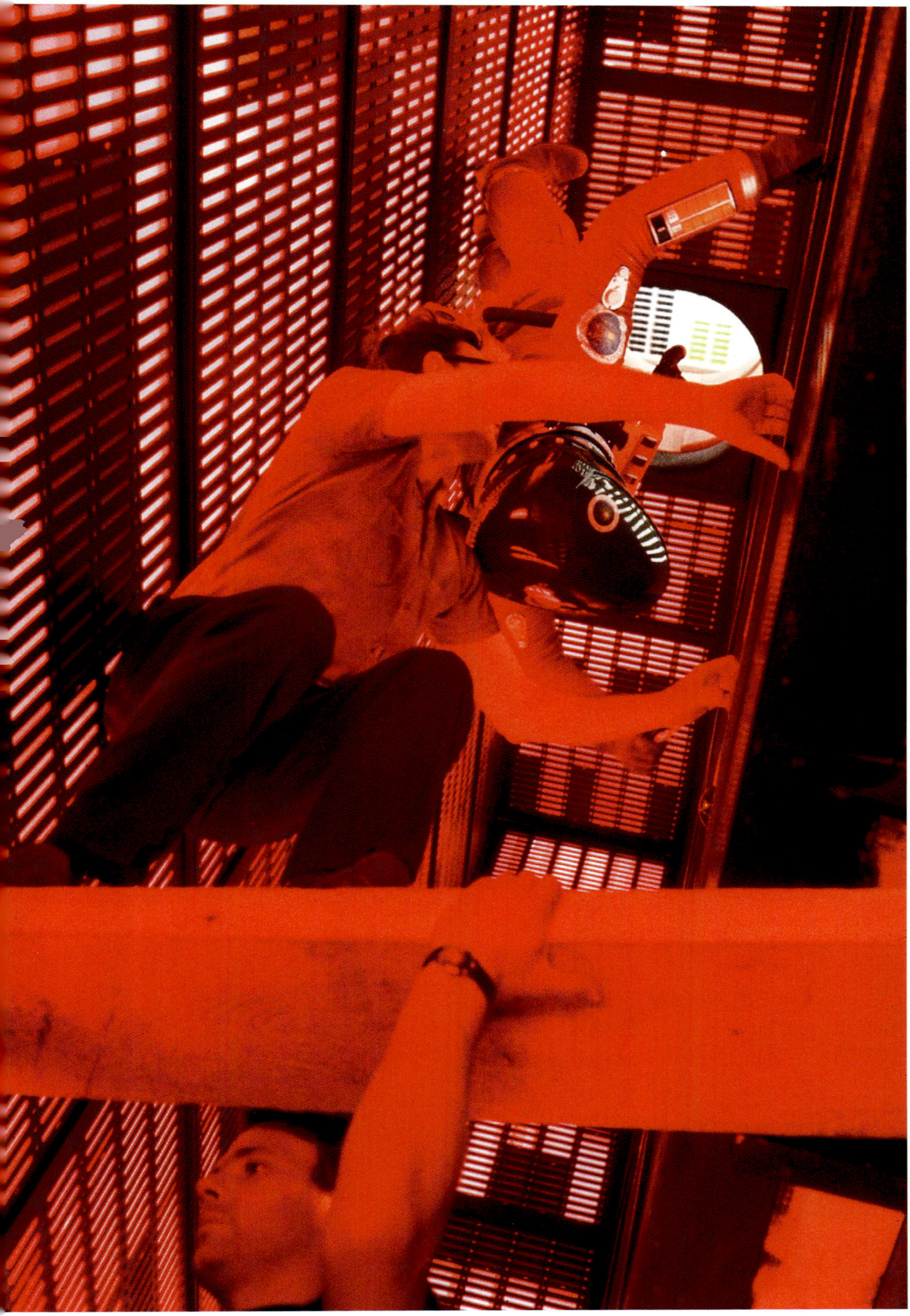

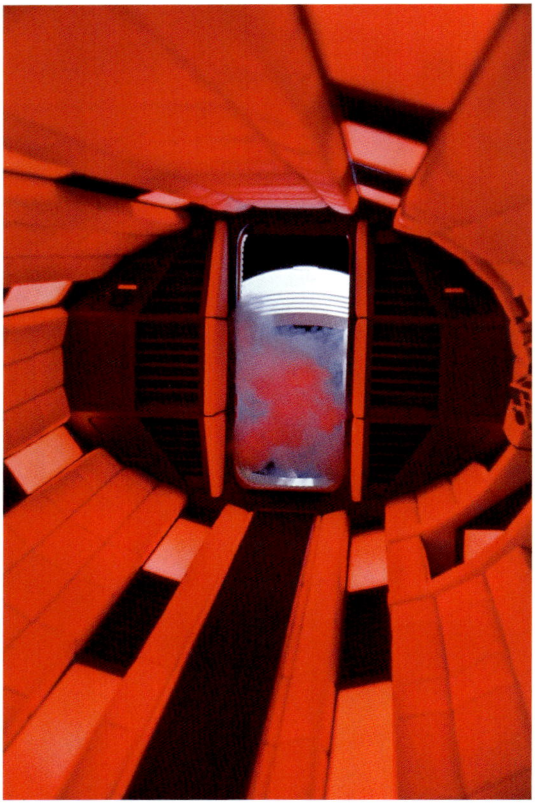

A circus troupe, Eugene's Flying Ballet, devised and operated the system of ropes and roustabouts that controlled Dullea's "fall" through the emergency hatch. The set was positioned vertically for shooting, but seems horizontal on screen.

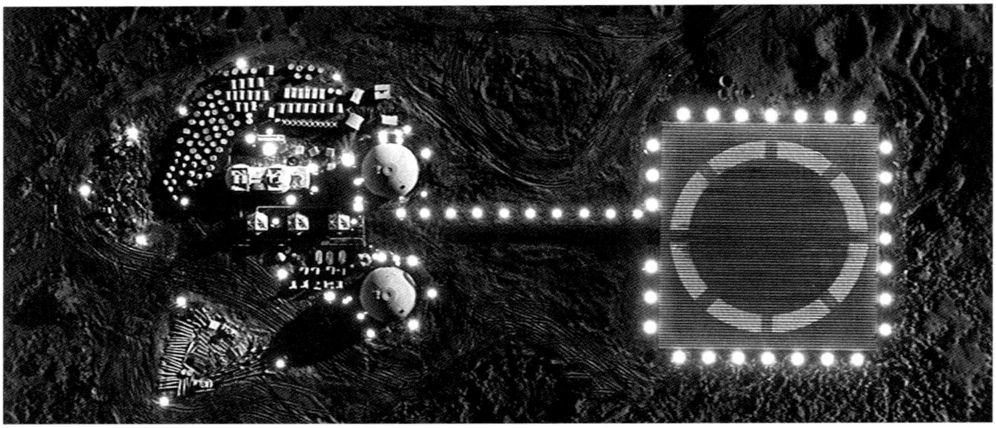

"Walt Disney personally had me transferred to von Braun's set-up at the Redstone Arsenal in Huntsville, where I found that they had an animation camera, and didn't know how to use it." Most of the workload consisted of short briefing films for Congress, in which secret and chilling aspects of Cold War preparedness for nuclear war were explained. In addition to these darker themes, there were presentations of ideas for peaceful space flight and lunar exploration. Pederson received "a very nice letter from von Braun complimenting me on a painting I made of a Moon landing."

In 1959 Pederson took up a contract with Graphic Films, a modestly scaled Los Angeles company founded by Lester Novros, a former Disney animator. A hopeful 20-year-old graphic artist from Los Angeles arrived in 1962, looking for work. Despite the applicant's lack of experience in the animation business, Pederson was impressed: "This was Doug Trumbull, and he had a portfolio of airbrush paintings, so I gave him a space satellite to do. He made a gorgeous job of it, and we hired him on the spot. We were making educational films for the Air Force about space and other advanced projects." In particular, Graphic Films was developing *To the Moon and Beyond*, a project commissioned by KLM Royal Dutch Airlines and the Cinerama Corporation for the 1964 New York World's Fair in Flushing Meadows Park. A contemporary report on the fair in *Business Screen* magazine describes what must have been a fascinating film:

> *Speeding up the events known to astronomers, the picture shows (through animation) how clouds of gas whirl into great galaxies, expanding outward from one another, with old generations of stars exploding to distribute the gaseous components of subsequent stellar generations. Returning to Earth, the film takes us to the middle of a great forest and to the bottom of the sea… The intricate*

workings of molecular and atomic space are the film's true goal... The incredible complexity of living forms is revealed.

Pederson and his colleagues worked fast to accomplish this astonishing breadth of material: "We made the film in about five months. It was in 70 mm format, and we projected it through a fish-eye lens onto the curved inner surface of a planetarium-style dome that was already built for the Travel and Transportation pavilion at the fair. They didn't have anything ready, and we foolishly stepped into the breach. And it just so happened that Kubrick saw the film in 1964, while it was still showing, and contacted us."

Pederson, Trumbull, and other artists began a long-distance dialogue with Kubrick, sending artworks and ideas on thin airmail paper to his Polaris Productions offices in New York. When *2001*'s small preproduction team began packing up for the move to England, this seemed no longer practical, and Kubrick reluctantly called a halt to the relationship with Graphic. The pace of work slackened across the board, and Trumbull decided to try his luck with Kubrick in England: "He was incredibly cordial and friendly, and he even helped me buy the airfare. My wife and I moved over there, lock, stock, and barrel, thinking that I'd be working on Kubrick's movie for eight months. In the end, it was almost three years," he recalls.

When Trumbull first walked through the gates of MGM at Borehamwood, jauntily dressed in cowboy boots and a hat, his optimism faltered: "Tony Masters was there, and his assistant John Hoesli," he remembers. "Most of the production crew was already in place, building sets. They had beautiful models of concepts for the weightlessness effects and the upside-down shots and the rotating sets. I was just blown away. I thought this was nirvana. It was beyond Disneyland—an extraordinary playground. My only concern was that I had arrived much too late." He needn't have worried. With his background in illustration and animation, Trumbull's first priority was to create interesting readout displays for HAL 9000 and the various spacecraft control panels. "In those days, there were

Douglas Trumbull works on a model of lunar terrain, in which the landing lights and touch-down pad for the Moonbus are incorporated.

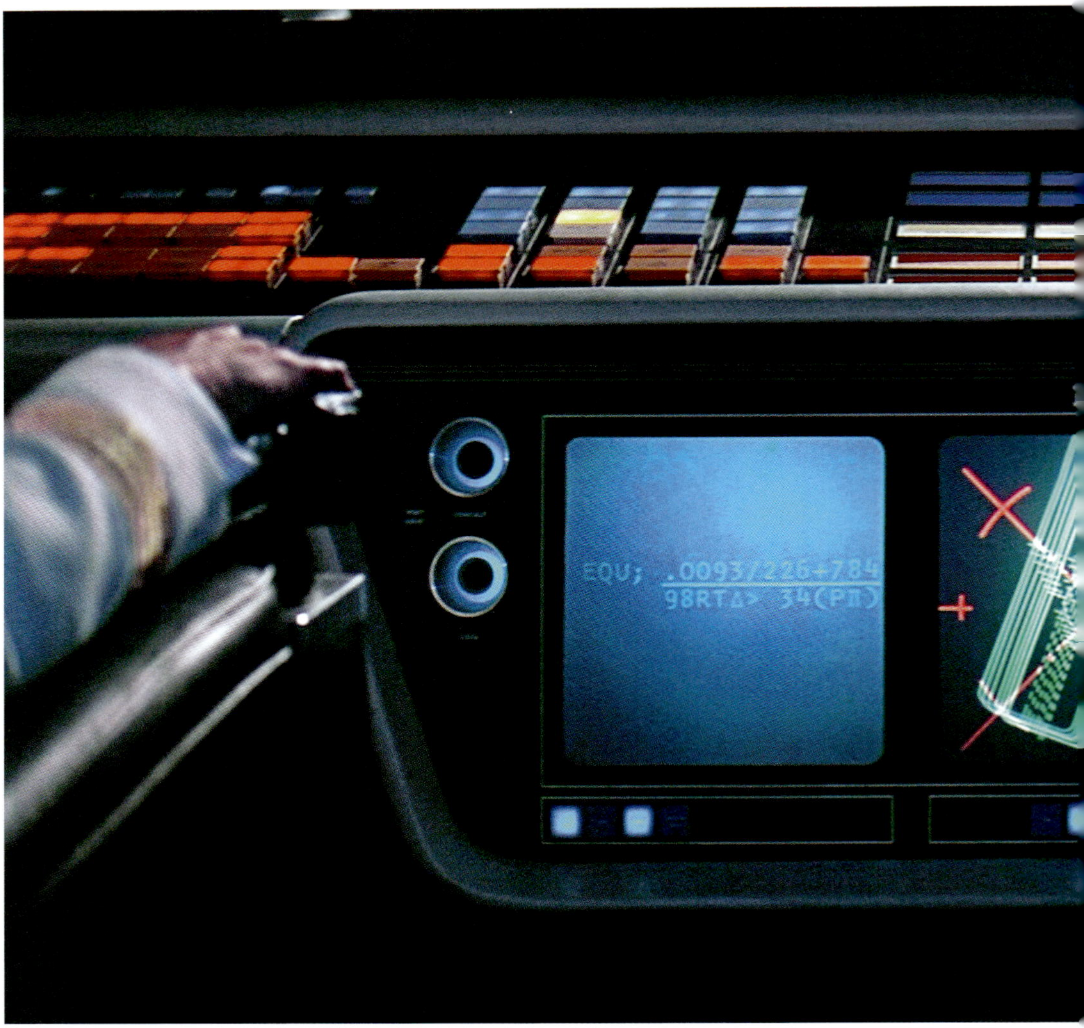

A graphical representation of the docking area at the hub of the space station is displayed in the cockpit of the *Orion* space shuttle.

▽▷ For the AE35 checking procedure, fake graphics were combined with genuine X-ray photographs of a real gyroscopic component.

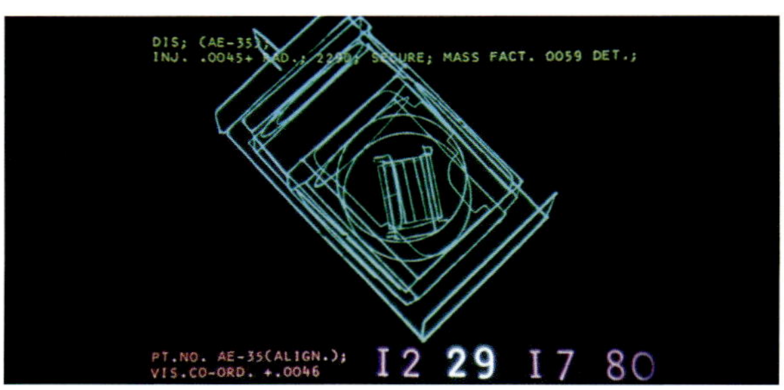

◁▷ 194–197 Countless reels of 16 mm footage simulated the apparent display of scientific or navigational data on screens built into in all the spacecraft sets.

△ A rotational view of the antenna was created by building a physical wire-frame model, painting it white, then photographing it from all angles and animating the results.

no computer-generated images. It was an idea that was really not fulfilled yet. So we had to make something that looked like computer graphics by using conventional film and animation techniques."

Actually, computer graphics did exist in the mid-1960s. Prior to coming over to England, Kubrick paid a visit to Marvin Minsky at MIT. His ideas would feed into the creation of HAL 9000. Additionally, on the graphics front, he had a couple of intriguing samples to offer, based on fractal patterns: "Stanley came to my lab to find out how to do it. We had some really good stuff. I was very impressed with him. He knew all the graphics work I had ever heard of." But there were problems. First, Kubrick could not easily gain access to the type of giant computers that were required, in those days, to produce even the simplest graphics; and second, the best screen resolution was 512 pixels across. Even Minsky knew that "this was too coarse for film audiences, and more importantly, far too coarse for what we all knew would be available by the year 2001. Kubrick was quite secretive, however, and I never really knew what he would or wouldn't be using from MIT."[2]

2 Ibid.

Kubrick opted for the finer resolution of film fakery. Trumbull, along with another young animator, Bruce Logan, devised a graphics system. Hundreds of technical illustrations, charts, and diagrams from science journals and technical magazines were copied onto high-contrast monochrome negative film, through which light could be shone. The ink-black letters, numbers, and graphs on the original magazine pages now took the form of clear white lettering against a black background. These semitransparent elements were mounted in various combinations onto a pane of glass resting on large ball bearings, so that the glass could be moved smoothly from side to side. An improvised animation camera was mounted on steel poles, with its lens pointing down toward the glass. An evenly diffused light source was positioned underneath the rig. Lateral movements of the glass, combined with colored transparent filters and gradual zoom-lens alterations on the camera, created interesting effects, as sheet after sheet of graphic elements were photographed like individual cels in a traditional cartoon animation. Finally the results were transferred to 16 mm film for projection into each of the rectangular readouts in the various spacecraft sets. Trumbull "started coming up with ways of doing multiple exposures and rather

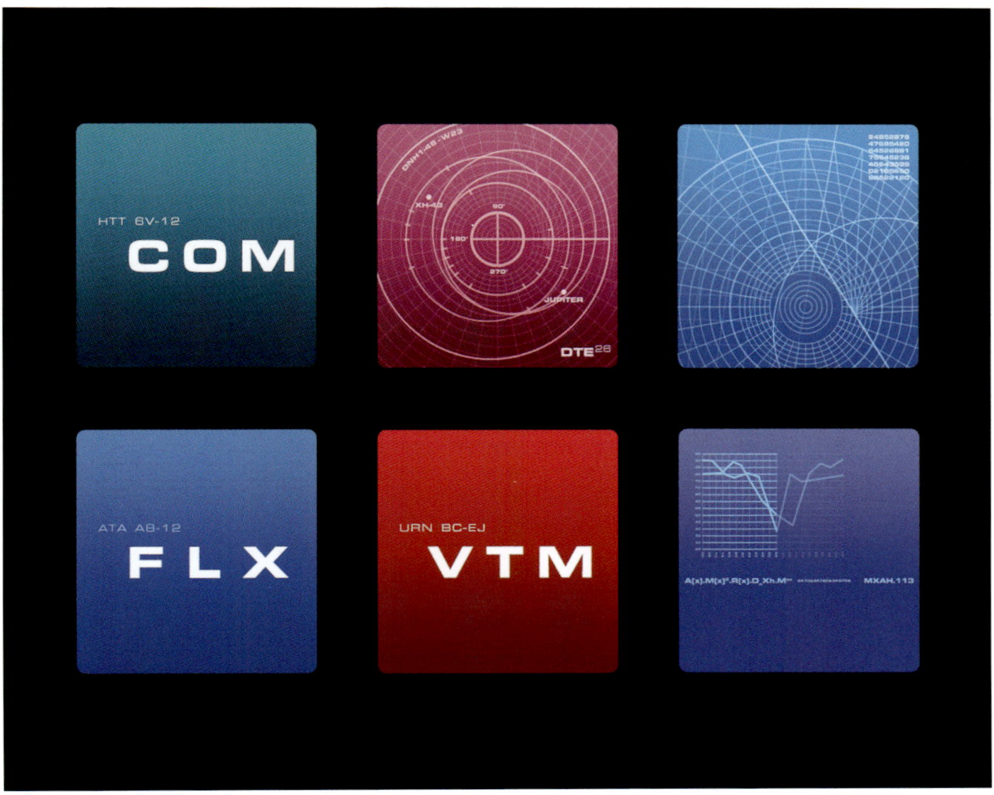

▹ 201 Kubrick and a small team experimented with paints, food dyes, and other chemicals at an abandoned corset factory in Manhattan. Some of these early tests made it into the final cut of the film.

HIB
LIF
ATM
COM
NUC

complicated readouts that were more three-dimensional in appearance. I was just finding my way, really, because my father was an engineer, my mother an artist, and I had these two genetic traits of solving technical problems and creative visual problems at the same time."

If all the graphic effects had been accomplished by hand, laboriously tweaking the illuminated artwork arrangements from one frame to the next, the animations for the readouts would have occupied the team for years, rather than the many months they actually did spend on the problem. Tens of thousands of feet of completed footage were needed for the cockpit displays in the *Orion* shuttle flight deck, the *Aries* Moonship, and the Moonbus. The *Discovery* sets alone required up to a dozen screens to function simultaneously for some shots. The effects team built mechanized, electrically powered rigs that could automate at least some of the processes required for the many animations. The camera controls and the rig motions were driven by an array of self-synchronizing ("selsyn") electric motors wired to banks of electrical switches and timers nearby. Each motor operated in synchrony with the others, thereby enabling precisely controlled incremental changes in the set-up ahead of each new frame exposure. One particularly important graphic of the *Discovery*'s antenna was achieved by building an actual wire frame model of the dish and its mounting, painting the wires white, and photographing this spidery structure on high-contrast film, rotating the model slightly between each exposure. HAL shows this as a supposedly computerized rendering when he announces, falsely, that the antenna control unit is about to fail.

THE UNIVERSE IN A CUP OF COFFEE

In addition to the Graphic Films presentation for the New York World's Fair, Kubrick was impressed by a short documentary released in 1960 by the National Film Board of Canada (NFBC). In *Universe*, directed by Roman Kroitor and Colin Low, an astronomer sets up a telescope at the David Dunlap Observatory in Richmond Hill, Ontario. As the observatory's protective dome opens to reveal the night sky, the audience is treated to an imaginary journey away from the Earth and into the farthest reaches of space. Supernova explosions, nebulous gas clouds, and colliding galaxies are depicted with exceptional realism and drama. While tremendous cosmic cataclysms unfold, a calm and reassuringly authoritative voice explains what is happening. The film's narrator was a Canadian actor, Douglas Rain. Kubrick thought that his might be an appropriate voice for *2001*'s prologue: a 10-minute documentary, filmed in monochrome, in which prominent scientists would set the tone

for the main feature to come. Roger Caras filmed extensive interviews with some of the greatest scientists of the 20th century, in the expectation that the basics of space flight and the possibilities of extraterrestrial intelligence would have to be explained to audiences unfamiliar with such material. By the time that *2001* was released, the many press and TV reports about NASA's exploits had helped the public into understanding as much as it needed to about orbital dockings, the vacuum of space, and the possibility of travel to other planets. The prologue idea was eventually dropped, as Kubrick edged away from such literal explanations and toward the more challenging and ambiguous audio-visual experience that *2001* eventually became. We can be grateful to Kubrick's longtime assistant Tony Frewin that the fascinating interview transcripts have survived.

Back in 1964, Kubrick's more urgent concern was with the technical achievements of *Universe*. Pederson remembers him "screening it repeatedly until the sprockets wore out, while he tried to figure out how they'd done it." Trumbull, too, was fascinated: "There was this incredible God's-eye view of the rotating of galaxies and the slow transits of stars. Even on *2001* we never achieved some of the stuff in *Universe*."

The man primarily responsible was Wally Gentleman, who had worked with the J. Arthur Rank company at Pinewood Studios and with MGM before joining the NFBC as director of special effects in 1957. He proved that the effects procedures normally associated with major 35 mm film productions could be applied to projects photographed in the smaller 16 mm format: something that the budget-conscious NFBC welcomed. One day, relaxing over a cup of coffee, he had noticed sunlight reflecting from the hot, swirling surface of his drink, and when he poured in some cream, the reflections created spirals of light on the ceiling above him. He recreated this lucky accident by pouring nonmixable oils and paints onto a gently rotating drum of water. While the incompatible substances swirled and reshaped themselves on the surface, Gentleman bounced a beam of light off them, and onto a nearby screen, which he then photographed. For other effects, he would shoot through semitransparent liquids, with inks, dyes, and paints slowly dispersing. In extreme close-up, they looked like nebulous gas clouds.

Universe inspired Mr. and Mrs. Kubrick to make similar experiments while still in New York. In Christiane's studio room at their 84th Street apartment, dishes of inky black water and trays were deployed in a bid to create the illusion of stars and galaxies inside a glass container the size of a cigarette pack. According to Christiane, "When you dropped the various paints onto the black water, each one—acrylic, watercolor, oils, and so on—had a slightly different way of spreading. If you had a cadmium color, it would actually shrink back. It occurred to us that the physical laws working in that small dish were the same as the laws that governed the universe, only much smaller." Kubrick confounded the problem of scale by setting up a macro lens and running his camera at a fast frame rate, capturing the slightest, eerie details of the reactions, lending the impression of gaseous events happening at cosmic scales. Christiane shared her husband's frustration when "the strong lights cooked the water, which turned to steam, fogged the lens, and ruined everything." An abandoned corset factory on Broadway and 72nd Street was hired for further, secret experimentation. Christiane attended some sessions there: "It took enormous patience. Stanley and a small crew made hundreds of tests and experiments. It was filthy work, and the fumes were disgusting. He would come home with red-rimmed, swollen eyes, and sniffles, because he'd inhaled this crap all day long. I always admired his courage to hang on and work long, long hours of it not working. But some of it did work, and would appear in the finished film four years later."

OLD HANDS VERSUS NEW

Kubrick's senior special-effects talent was recruited from closer to home. Wally Veevers made the model bomber "fly" for *Dr. Strangelove*, and rigged the huge tactical display screens in the War Room, delivering the impression of graphic displays by the use of lights attached to mechanical arms behind the translucent screens.

Keith Hamshere, a former child actor (he was the lead in the first stage performances of the musical *Oliver!* in 1960), joined the *2001* production as a stills photographer, and was pulled into the special-effects work. The thrill is easy to recall, even after so many years: "If someone said, 'This is your studio, you can do whatever you want, you can have all the toys you want. Now start playing,' you'd think this was your dream come true. I was 21 years old, with an entire studio at Borehamwood, all the camera gear I needed, and about five darkrooms to process and print up my shots, and four people working for me. It was the happiest two years of my working life." Hamshere's first impression of Veevers was that of "a quite large, very rotund, softly spoken character. His background was engineering, and he was also extremely artistic. He was a precise man, very creative, but also sensitive. He sometimes found it hard to put into words what he was trying to achieve. He and Stanley certainly respected each other, but of all the people on the film, I think there was probably more friction between him and Stanley than anyone else."

Veevers's principal frustration stemmed from Kubrick's insistence that special-effects materials should be accumulated into a stock library of different shots, so that he could pick and choose later, at the editing stage, just as he might select the best takes from live-action footage. This was not the normal way of proceeding, because of the great costs and complexities usually associated with effects work. Veevers assumed that individual spacecraft shots would be created according to pre-agreed storyboards: rough sketches showing the positions of the various elements, each based on the necessities of the script. McKenna, Carnon, Masters, Pederson, and Trumbull were adept at storyboarding, and Kubrick found their countless iterations useful, up to a point. What he really wanted was not to be constrained in the editing process by a predetermined lack of choice.

Sometimes Kubrick deliberately encouraged strife between the younger effects artists and their supposedly more experienced elders. For instance, Brian Johnson helped Veevers to set up the 16 mm film projectors that beamed HAL's computer displays onto the centrifuge control panels. Johnson recalls, "Wally had this elaborate system with different focal-length lenses on different projectors, because we couldn't stack them as close to each other as the HAL readouts actually appear in the film. Anyway, I said, 'Why don't we bolt pairs of projectors base to base, to keep them arranged as tightly as possible? That way, their lenses will be close together, and we can use the same length of lens on all the machines.' Wally said we couldn't operate projectors upside-down because the fragile bulbs would blow out. They all had to be upright, and that was that. Later, I thought, 'Wait a minute! The rotation of the centrifuge will spin them upside-down at some point anyway, and the bulbs are going to have to be replaced all the time whatever happens, so what difference does it make?' So I took that idea to Stanley, and he went with my idea. Wally didn't speak to me for days." Veevers certainly was not wrong in all of his assumptions. The bulbs did indeed last about three minutes apiece, although it was the centrifuge's noisy vibration that caused the problem, rather than the projectors' orientation.

A BRIEF HISTORY OF THE MATTE SHOT

Victor Lyndon's thick sheaf of production notes, compiled in June 1965, specify the live-action photography in painstaking detail. The book-sized document becomes a little vague whenever it touches on the exterior spacecraft effects and planetary scenes. In what now seems a telling understatement, the beautiful ballet of the winged shuttle docking with the space station is summarized in one short paragraph, with a note that "this is a special effects sequence with star backing." For other scenes, the notes specify only that "process photography may be required." The optical effects created for *2001* were the forebears of methods that prevail today. Modern effects still involve the same old problem: how to combine many different elements at different scales, shot at different times, in the same final image.

Here is an apparent paradox. In crafting *2001: A Space Odyssey* Stanley Kubrick initiated some of the most complex and advanced optical techniques in the history of cinema, many of which left the best capabilities of the 1960s film industry far behind. Or: to achieve technical excellence, Kubrick made use of some of the simplest and most basic procedures in the history of cinema, many of which stretched back to the first experiments with hand-cranked cameras in the early 1900s. Both statements are true.

The simplest special effect is to expose a piece of film more than once, superimposing one image on top of another. In the 1860s an opportunistic American photographer, William Mumler, made an accidental double exposure while taking a portrait. The first image was correctly exposed. Some while later, before the shot had been processed, a second and different image (supposedly of a cousin) was inadvertently overlaid onto the same plate. This was not so sharply captured as the first. When Mumler processed the plate, he saw what looked like a vague, wraithlike figure hovering over his main subject. Today we would dismiss such a thing as an obvious error in the technical process. A hundred and fifty years ago, photography was a young art and its secrets were unfamiliar to the general public. Mumler founded a new and fraudulent industry, known as spirit photography. In the shocked aftermath of the American Civil War, countless grieving clients were gulled into believing that the ghosts of dead loved ones could be revealed by a camera in the hands of a sufficiently sensitive expert.

After a decade of success, Mumler was revealed as a fraud. He died, penniless and disgraced, in 1884. Nevertheless, spirit photography retained its market. After the First World War many young widows and forlorn parents of lost soldiers were susceptible to new and more sophisticated versions of Mumler's trick. Even Sir Arthur Conan Doyle, creator of the relentlessly forensic detective Sherlock Holmes, was fooled for a while into believing some of them. The art of special effects was born with an attendant whiff of chicanery and superstition.

A more subtle variation on the ghost trick came into play when "ghost" sitters were photographed against a backdrop of black velvet drapes, masking off the rest of the studio and any props, such as fireplaces, vases, and even the chair upon which the unsuspecting primary subjects had been sitting earlier. Film does not "see" black, because the chemistry in the emulsion is only affected by light. Only the ghost stand-ins registered in the second exposure. This was the beginning of what is now universally known as the "matte" process, where unwanted objects in the first exposure are masked in some way and prevented from

The *Aries* lunar ferry cockpit photographed in normal light. The relative simplicity of the displays and lack of dials and levers suggests a vehicle controlled mainly by unseen electronic computers.

Kubrick chats with his actors as the *Aries* cockpit is red-lit for shooting. The actors work against a cockpit window shrouded in black velvet. Footage of the lunar surface, seen through the windows, was added later.

registering on film during the second. The term came into common use when the "matte box" became a familiar fixture on the front of a camera's lens barrel. A flat black sheet was used to mask off a selected area of the field of view: say, from the top of the frame to the horizon, where a dull sky meets a field of grass. The camera operator could expose the field, then wait for the weather to produce a more dramatic cloudscape, at which point he swapped his mask from the top to the bottom of the matte-box frame and photographed this more impressive sky onto the same sheet of film. Although he had double-exposed his film, the separate elements did not interfere with each other.

With careful planning, a scene-setting shot, known as a background plate, could be exposed and stored away unprocessed, in a cool dark place, waiting to be reloaded into the camera so that additional elements could be added at a later date. A tracing of the original horizon line in the large glass viewfinder of a plate camera could form the basis for a matte mask, ensuring that multiple exposures "married up" properly. Elements from different film negatives could be manipulated and merged in the controlled environment of the processing darkroom.

As the aptly named motion picture industry came into being in the early 20th century, "matte paintings" on glass sheets directly in front of the camera allowed nonexistent scenery, such as futuristic cityscapes or ancient Egyptian palaces, to be added to a live-action scene. In the 1907 film *Missions of California*, Los Angeles cameraman Norman Dawn documented church buildings and old mission houses that had fallen into disrepair. He interposed glass paintings over the more unsightly damaged areas, such as collapsed roofs and broken windows. His final shots appeared to show the buildings in their glorious heyday. This technique only worked for static scenes. What if the director wanted to pan or tilt the camera? In that case, any live-action elements would appear to slide across the frame while the matte painting stayed stubbornly motionless, and the effect would be ruined. The solution was a "traveling matte," a mask that changed its position in the frame, and its shape and perspective, in lockstep with any moving objects it was supposed to block.

This problem was considered as early as 1916. In *The Flight of the Duchess*, a gallery in an eerie house displays pictures of long-dead family scions. As the camera tracks along, ghosts seem to step out of the picture frames. Camera operator Otto Brautigan first shot the gallery set with all the paintings and fixtures, keeping a record of exactly how many

seconds it took to move the camera between each pair of pictures. His camera was attached to a wheeled dolly running along a 70-foot length of track. A winch drum at the farthest end of the track pulled the dolly along, and the cable between the winch and the dolly was marked with knotted distance indicators. Brautigan swathed the entire set in black velvet and removed the pictures to expose rectangular holes in the wall, from which his ghost-actors could climb out. Then he wound the film in the camera back to its starting position, pushed the dolly to its starting point on the track, and repeated the earlier camera move, using his stopwatch data and the cable markings to match the speed and fluidity of the first shot. The result was an impressively smooth sequence in which the background of the gallery and paintings matched with the ethereal ghosts clambering out of the picture frames.

How much easier it would be if only the matte could be generated automatically, no matter how varied the action in front of the camera. Throughout the mid-20th century, filmmakers searched for ever better means of automating the process, and the "blue screen" technique became a standard. Color film stock contains layers of emulsion, each sensitive to a different color. By using filters in front of a camera, certain layers can be blocked from seeing light. A red filter, for instance, will prevent blue and green light from entering the lens, and the film will process as dark where the blue or green tones would normally register. Shooting the primary subject (an action hero or a spaceship model) against a blue or green screen, then manipulating the positive film images with their negative counterparts,

allows—by an extremely tortuous route—the eventual substitution of blank screen areas for a background plate: a cityscape, for instance, or a field of stars in space.

When *2001* entered production, there were several methods for blue-screen shooting, and various combinations of film stock and filtration that could be used. The drawbacks were never quite eliminated: multiple copying and "sandwiching" of different film layers inside optical printing machines almost always led to some degradation in the final image quality. Color films for live action did not always match the warmth, graininess, and other characteristics of the film used to shoot the background elements; and the complexity of the process was such that a dozen different strips of film were often required to achieve a single matte effect. The results were seldom perfect. A characteristic fuzzy blue fringe can be seen around most early targets of the process. *The Thief of Bagdad* was stunning by the standards of 1940, and can still delight us today, but look closely, and the blue fringing can be seen in the shots where Sabu, the young hero, interacts with a genie, or steals a magic flying carpet. Despite many technical advances over the subsequent two decades, Kubrick decided that *2001*'s special effects needed to look flawless. The byzantine business of the blue-screen process was not an option. Crisp, clean traveling mattes for *2001* would have to be generated very simply, one frame at a time, and entirely by human hand. In order to accomplish this, the effects team turned to a process pioneered nearly half a century earlier.

◃ 210/211 Many shots required window action to be added later via the matte process. Sasco cards kept a log of progress, and reminded the effects team of the original live-action compositions.

▿▹ The "Sausage Factory" composited footage of the lunar background with the Moonbus model and a carefully matched view of actors at work in the cockpit.

THE "BLOBBING" DEPARTMENT

Max Fleischer, creator of *Betty Boop* and *Popeye* cartoons, realized that most of the individually hand-drawn frames in a cartoon are almost exactly like the previous frames, and similarly close to the ones that come next. It is only the small doses of apparent movement added to each frame that make any difference when cumulatively viewed on screen at 24 frames per second. In October 1917 he patented what became known as the Rotoscope, a machine that projects finished drawings onto a baseboard. Animators could simply trace over an earlier outline, thus saving themselves the usual tiresome flicking between one drawing sheet and the next. By working with transparent acetate "cels," they could overlay several frames at once and easily assess the cumulative effect of their drawings.

The traveling mattes that prevented star backdrops from exposing through the *2001* spacecraft were based on this principle. Processed copies of the spacecraft footage (shot against pure black velvet) were projected, one frame at a time, onto acetate sheets. Twenty hapless young artists, known by their colleagues as "blobbers," traced each spacecraft outline. Brian Johnson didn't envy them: "We had all these boys and girls in tight cubicles, breathing heavy industrial solvents from the blacking fluids, and all painting these things out frame by frame. It was an incredible job. It went on for pretty much an entire year. There were thousands and thousands of frames that had to be done." The traced areas were filled in with opaque black ink. Then the finished acetate sheets, all in the correct order, were transferred to an animation room, where they were photographed onto 65 mm monochrome film. The negative footage derived from this consisted of pure black frames with transparent (white) "holes" shaped exactly like the spacecraft. Printing this negative onto another strip of similar film produced a positive image: a black spacecraft-shaped silhouette against a clear background. The laborious but fairly simple process delivered one matte mask that would prevent spacecraft images from ruining a background of stars and planets, and an opposing matte to prevent stars from burning through the images of spacecraft.

The next step took place in a Mitchell 65 mm camera whose magazines and drive mechanisms were adapted to handle a double (bi-pack) thickness of film. The topmost film was one of the processed mattes, the black silhouette of the spacecraft against a blank surround. The underlying strip of film was raw, unexposed stock. Footage of a star-speckled background was projected through the blank areas in the holdout matte. In principle, the underlying film now held an image of a star field, across which a spaceship-shaped "black

The space-station model, and one of many thousands of the relevant mattes traced and blackened by the "blobbing department."

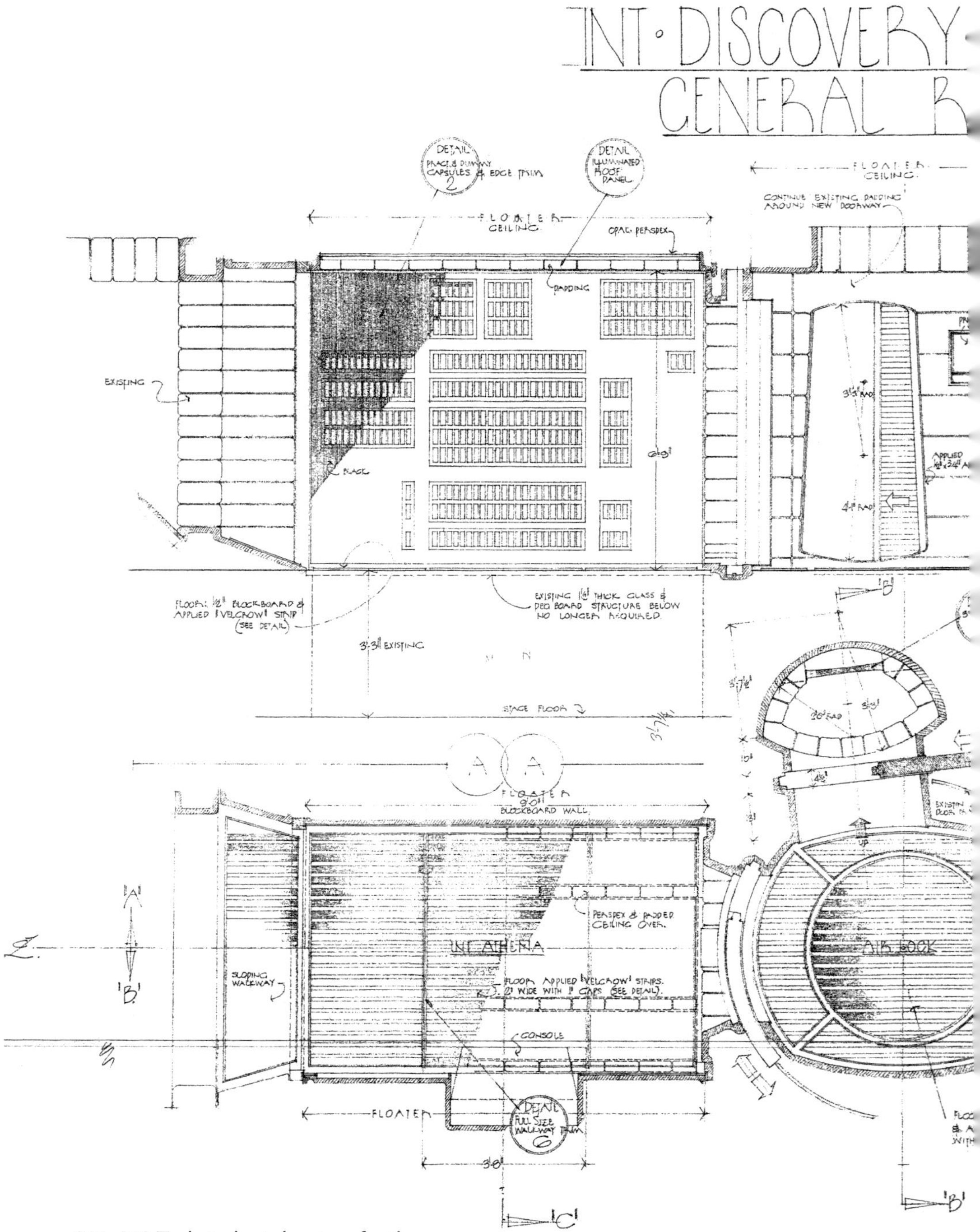

⊲⊳ 216–219 Technical set drawings for the switch room corridor at the rear of *Discovery*'s command deck, and the window and seating arrangements.

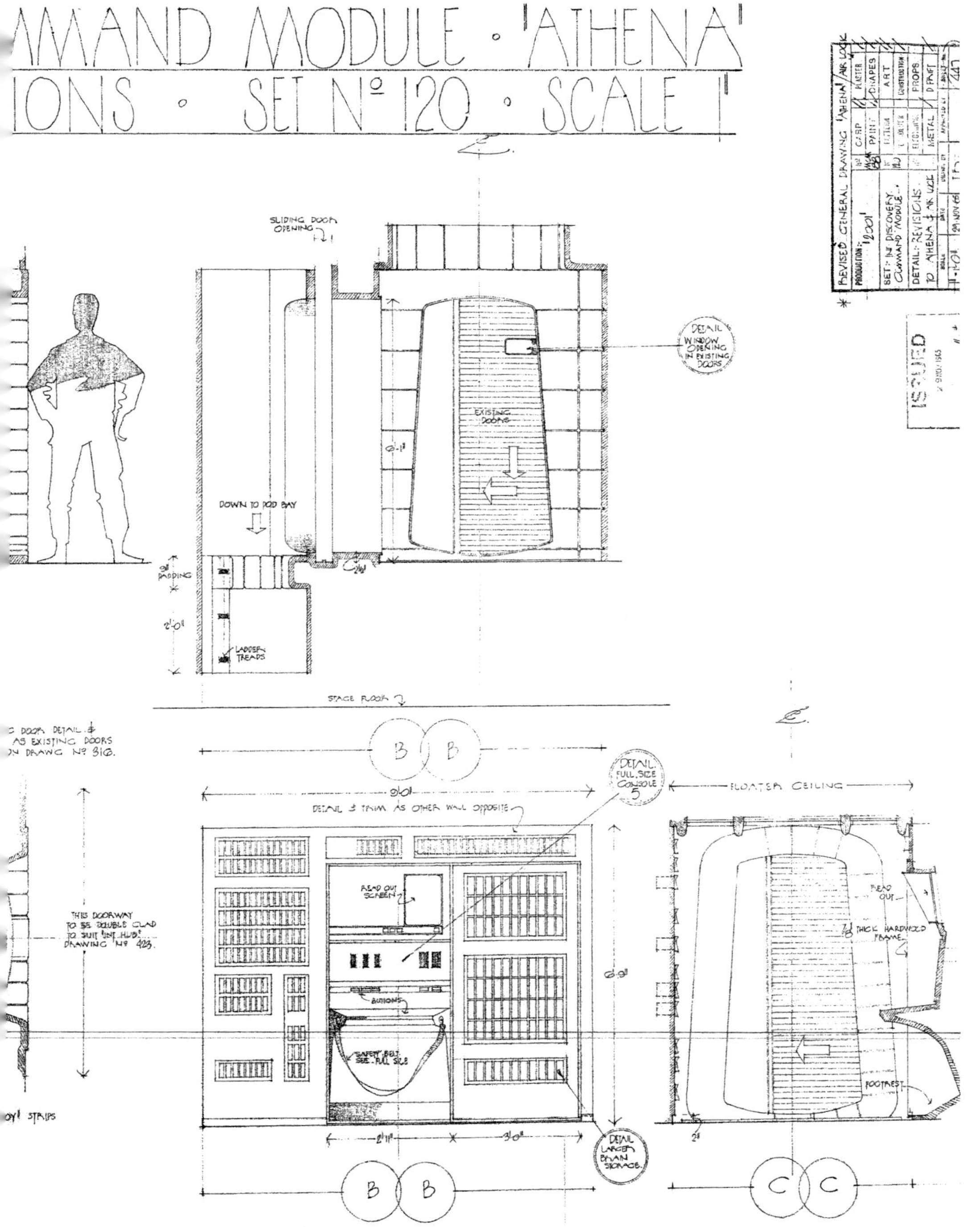

MMAND MODULE · 'ATHENA'
IONS · SET Nº 120 · SCALE 1"
REVISED GENERAL DRAWING 'ATHENA'/AIR LOCK
PRODUCTION: '2001'
SET: INT DISCOVERY. COMMAND MODULE.
DETAIL: REVISIONS TO ATHENA & AIR LOCK
CARP
PLASTER
PAINT
DRAPES
ART
CONSTRUCTION
PROPS
METAL
D'RAFT
ISSUED
SLIDING DOOR OPENING
DETAIL WINDOW OPENING IN EXISTING DOORS
EXISTING DOORS
6'-1"
DOWN TO POD BAY
9" PADDING
2'-0"
LADDER TREADS
STAGE FLOOR
DOOR DETAIL & AS EXISTING DOORS ON DRAWG Nº 316.
B B
DETAIL FULL SIZE CONSOLE 5
9'-0"
DETAIL & TRIM AS OTHER WALL OPPOSITE
FLOATER CEILING
READ OUT SCREEN
THIS DOORWAY TO BE DOUBLE CLAD TO SUIT 'INT HUB' DRAWING Nº 423.
BUTTONS
SAFETY BELT SEE FULL SIZE
6'-9"
READ OUT
7/8 THICK HARDWOOD FRAME
FOOTREST
2"
STRIPS
2'-11"
3'-0"
DETAIL LARGER BRAN STORAGE
B B
C C

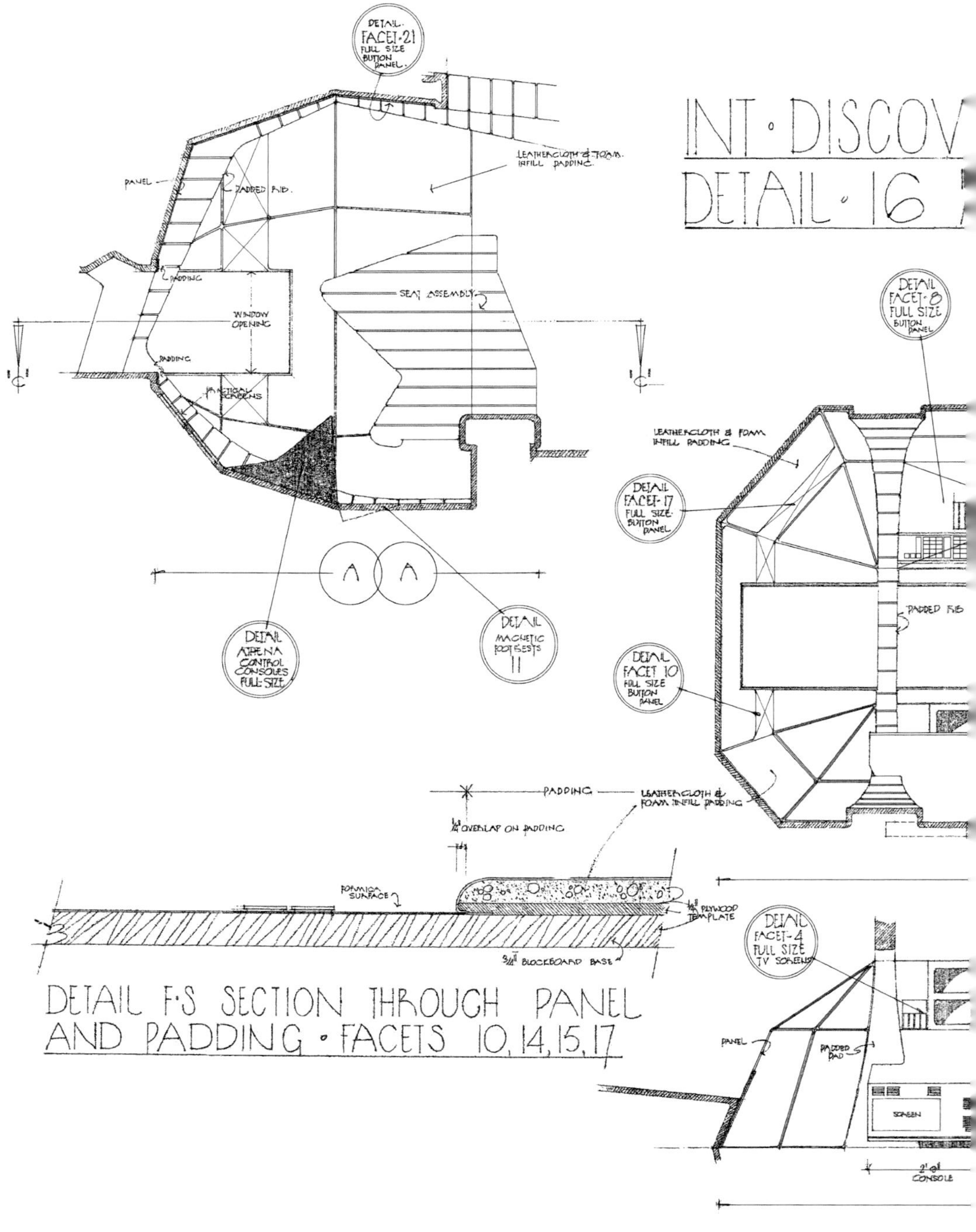
INT · DISCOV
DETAIL · 16
DETAIL FACET·21 FULL SIZE BUTTON PANEL.
LEATHERCLOTH & FOAM INFILL PADDING.
PANEL
PADDED RIB.
PADDING
WINDOW OPENING
SEAT ASSEMBLY
PADDING
VERTICAL SCREENS
DETAIL ARENA CONTROL CONSOLES FULL SIZE
DETAIL MAGNETIC FOOTRESTS 11
DETAIL FACET·8 FULL SIZE BUTTON PANEL
LEATHERCLOTH & FOAM INFILL PADDING
DETAIL FACET·17 FULL SIZE BUTTON PANEL
PADDED RIB
DETAIL FACET 10 FULL SIZE BUTTON PANEL
PADDING
LEATHERCLOTH & FOAM INFILL PADDING
¼" OVERLAP ON PADDING
FORMICA SURFACE
¼" PLYWOOD TEMPLATE
¾" BLOCKBOARD BASE
DETAIL F·S SECTION THROUGH PANEL AND PADDING · FACETS 10, 14, 15, 17
DETAIL FACET·4 FULL SIZE TV SCREENS
PANEL
PADDED PAD
SCREEN
2' 0" CONSOLE

COMMAND MODULE ('A' CONTROL CONSOLE & FRONT FACET PADDING · 1" SCALE)

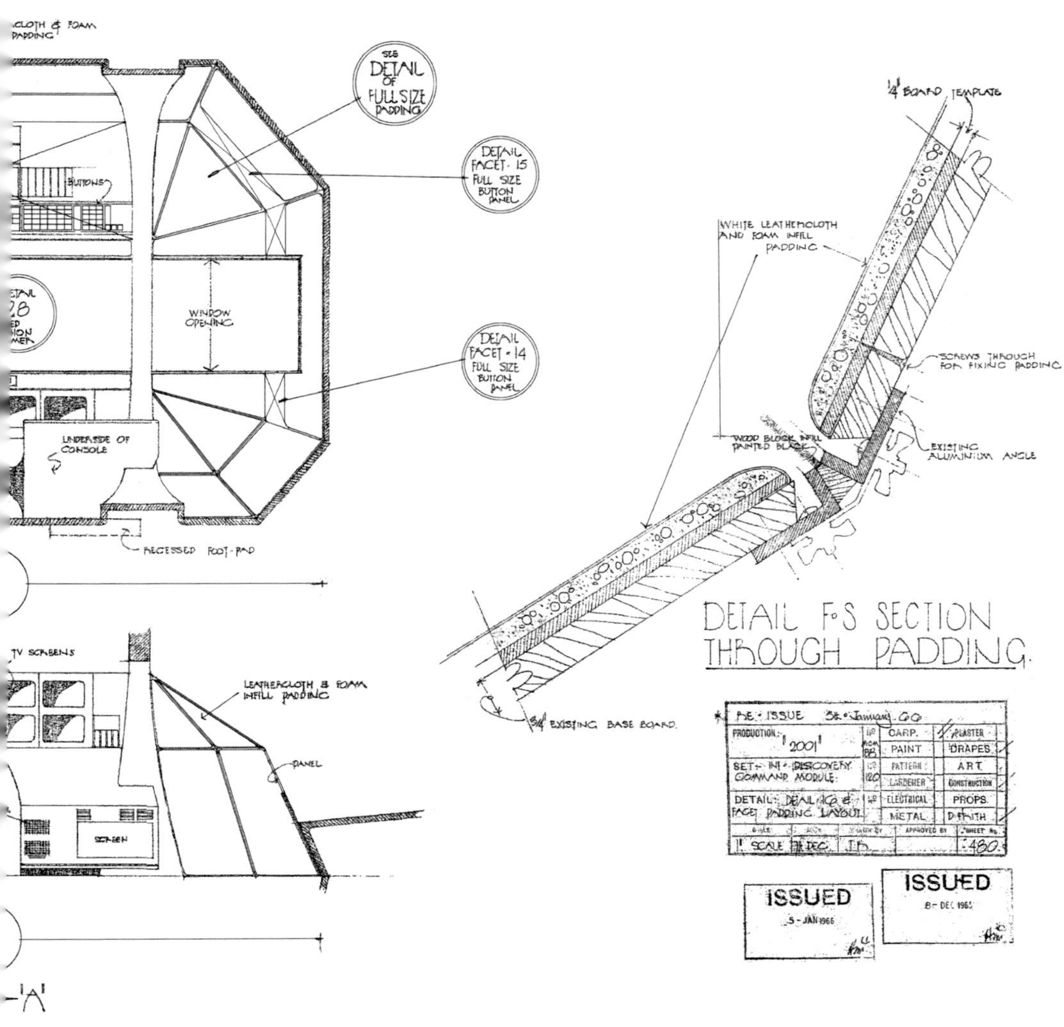

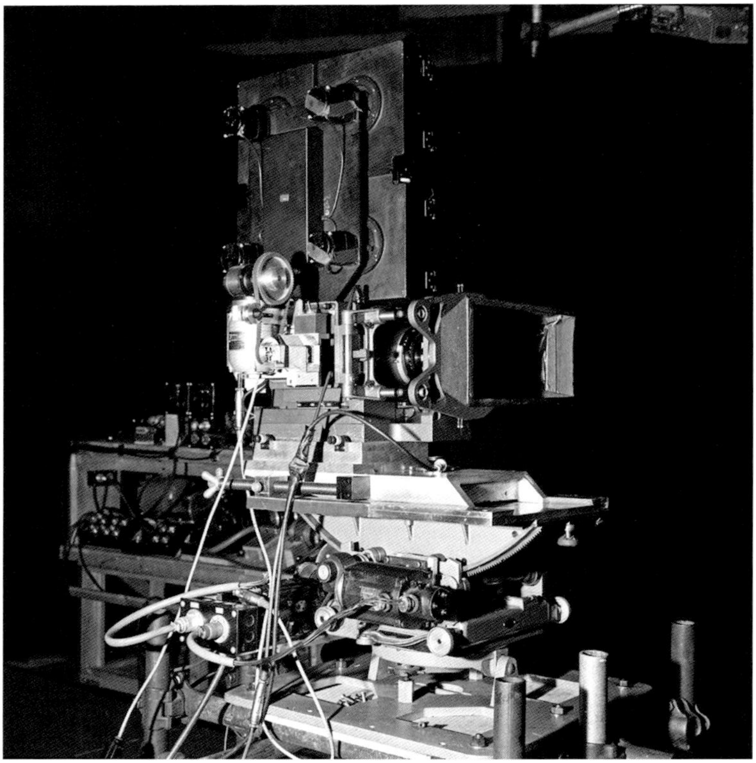

A hand-built control bench for the Sausage Factory simultaneously operated the film advance, the lens focus ring, and the drive mechanisms for the glass sheets and camera tracking.

▹ 222/223 Oliver Rennert's specially commissioned artwork demonstrates how the various interior sets for the *Discovery* would fit in to the habitation sphere if the ship were constructed at full scale.

hole" moved. This was, for now, a latent, unprocessed image. Both films were rewound to their starting points and the matte reels were swapped. Finally, the original color footage of the spacecraft was printed down through the counter-matte and into the spacecraft-shaped unexposed areas waiting for them on the as-yet-unprocessed film at the bottom of the sandwich. At last, when this final strip of film was processed, it yielded a color spacecraft sailing neatly across a field of stars.

Trumbull and his colleagues were learning as they went along: "Today, there's a million different ways to make a matte. We were babes in the woods back then, and we didn't know how to do it. We discovered that it didn't matter if a star 'switched off' a fraction before it hit the edge of a spacecraft, but if it blinked off a frame or two late, it was objectionable. So the blobs were always made a little bit fat."

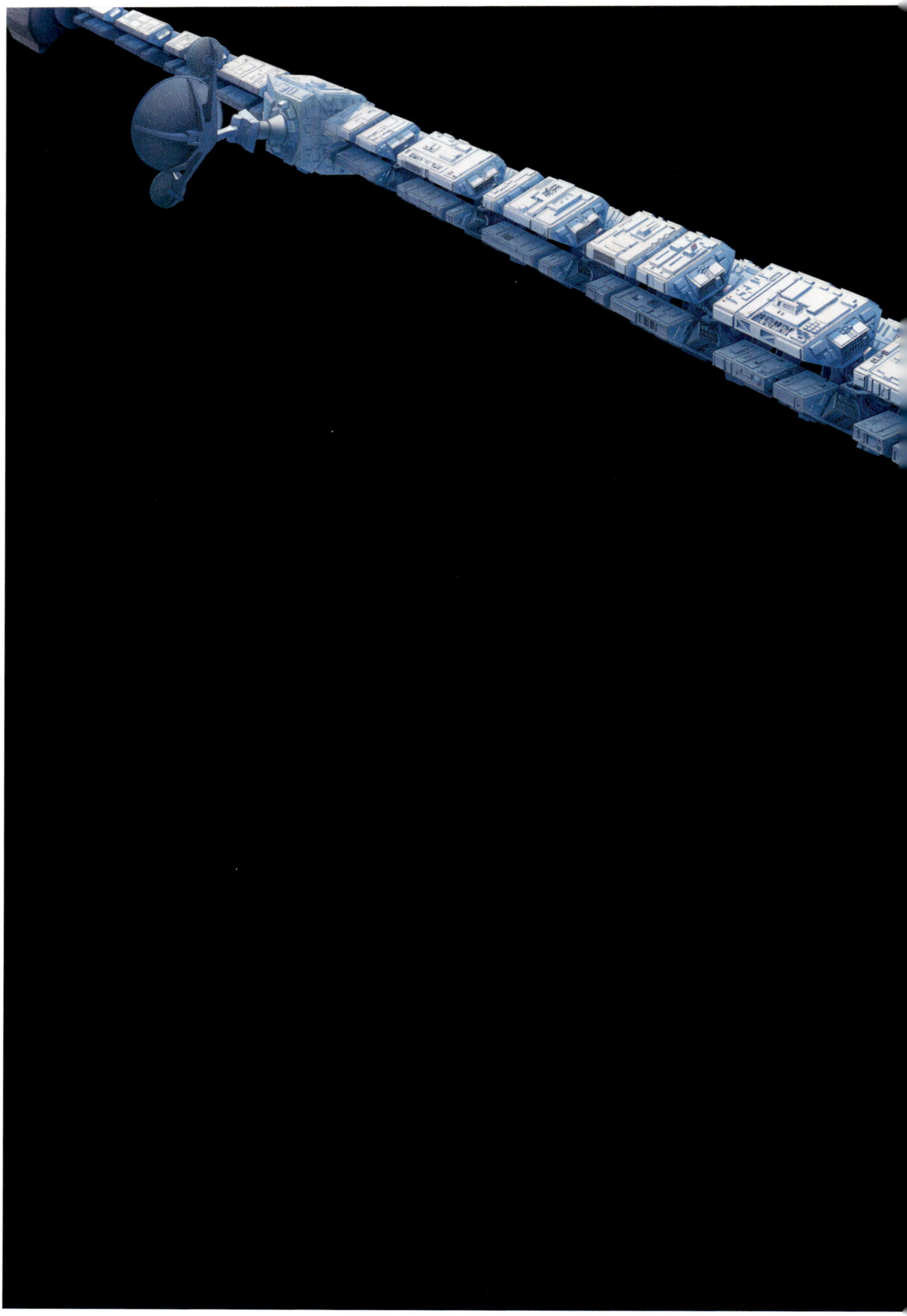

YCM SEPARATION MASTERS

A further complication for the *2001* effects team was that before anything was copied onto fresh film, an intermediate process was used to split the initial shots into three separate monochrome films, each of which stored the images filtered through one of three tinted filters: yellow (Y), cyan (C), and magenta (M), the three "subtractive" colors that make up a full-color image on film stock—or, similarly, the pages of a color printed book or magazine. These three reels of monochrome material were referred to as the "YCM masters." Mono film is inherently much sharper and less prone to fading than color stock, and the laborious process helped ensure that the quality of duplicated images was retained, especially on those occasions when a primary shot and its special-effect additions might be captured many months apart, necessitating careful storage of the separate film elements in the meantime.

Turning the three monochrome films back into a single color image required all three layers to be printed down onto fresh color film, using the relevant YCM filtration in the light sources in each case. Thus, many of the master shots were on three sets of film, not one (although star backgrounds only needed one reel, as they were always pure black and white anyway). The YCM masters also allowed consistent control of the color balance for all the spacecraft shots, and there are relatively few of the random jumps from warm tones to cold, or from fine grain to rough, that characterized effects sequences in almost every science-fiction film prior to *2001*. The key point is this: reconstituting any shot from the YCM masters created a perfect clone of the "first generation" color version. Nothing was copied from one color film to another color film, without first undergoing YCM transfers, because such a simplistic replication would have degraded the quality of the shots.

If all this sounds complicated, take a look at the establishing view of the Tycho excavation area. We see a group of astronauts approach the pit, which is clearly a live-action element. The horizon consists of dark lunar hills, while the black sky is adorned with stars, and one bright planet, the Earth. The live action was photographed over the first days of 1966. The other elements weren't added until two years later. Storing the live-action material as YCMs ensured that they could be retrieved and reconstructed at any time, and in pristine condition, prior to addition of other matted elements: the stars, the Earth, and the mountains. This technique, known as the "held take," predominated *2001*'s visual-effects workload. Similarly, the live action of the pod interiors, photographed in mid-1966, was "married up" with the appropriate view through the cockpit windows more than a year after Dullea and Lockwood's work was done. Over that long interval, the live footage had to be archived as YCMs.

The relevance of the YCM process persists even into the digital age. Modern museum conservators understand very well how to restore and display a 500-year-old pencil sketch from a Renaissance genius. They know, also, how to keep such treasures in excellent condition for the benefit of future generations. It is much more of a challenge to protect a 50-year-old color film. Merely transferring the visual information onto digital media does not constitute an act of preservation. The digital machinery eventually becomes obsolete: formats such as CD, Blu-ray, hard drive, or magnetic tape, are merely passing fashions in the technological landscape. The only absolute solution is to keep the original film in flawless condition. Early silent movies were photographed onto film stock with a frighteningly flammable nitrate film base. Many titles (and some unfortunate theater audiences, too) were lost decades ago. The film-base problems were solved as the silent era gave way to the "talkies." By the late 1930s another significant advance had been made: how to capture full color on these increasingly sophisticated film stocks. The problem was—and has been, ever since—that color footage eventually fades. Countless famous films are preserved in vaults in the form of YCM masters.

THE DAWN OF MOTION CONTROL

The 54-foot *Discovery* model was supported rigidly on steel stilts, which in turn were secured to heavy foundations. A less mobile spaceship one could never have found. The camera did all the moving. Alongside the intricate model a kind of mini "railway" ran, consisting of tracks about 150 feet long. The camera platform was pushed along the rails by a massive worm gear specially imported from a Detroit automobile plant. The camera had to be made to move smoothly along the track, so that when the resulting footage was projected it would show *Discovery* gliding rather than shuddering across screen. Witnessing a shoot gave the impression that nothing much was happening. Kubrick described the process as "like watching the hour hand of a clock." Because the camera motion was barely visible to human observers, the occasional jiggles didn't show up until the day's shooting was over and the film was processed. It was a painful business. *Discovery* demanded deep-focus photography to ensure that the model would remain pin-sharp from one end to the other. The camera lens had to be stopped down so that the aperture was little more than the size of a pinhole. This maintained deep focus, but the light levels filtering through the lens and onto the film were reduced almost to insignificance. Consequently, exposure times were several seconds per frame, rather than the more usual fractions of a second for live-action photography.

Every inch that the camera moved along the worm gearing had to be matched by an exact number of film frames exposed. If the mechanical gearing and the camera's frame rate fell out of phase, *Discovery*'s apparent rate of movement across screen would appear shaky in the processed footage. There needed to be some kind of communication between the motor that was driving the camera along the worm gearing, and the other motors that were firing the shutter and advancing the film onto new frames. The effects team built a system that could integrate the camera motors with the worm gearing drive by allowing them to cross-talk.

In theory at least, the worm gearing allowed for repeatability. The camera could be backtracked to its start position, the film rewound, and additional exposed elements, such as window action, placed onto the film in such a way that they kept pace with the earlier exposure of *Discovery*, apparently drifting from left to right across the field of view. The window footage was projected onto small reflective cards in the model's window slot, while the rest of the model was swathed in velvet to prevent it re-exposing onto the film. The modern art of "motion control" was conceived on the *2001* model stages. It was not an easy birth. Zoran Perisic, who slaved for many months at a time with an animation camera turning out star-field footage, thought that the best way of creating a traveling matte would have been to shoot the spacecraft models against the black velvet, then bring the camera back to its starting position, load another roll of film, and shoot the models again—this time in silhouette, against a pure white background: "It would have created the same mattes on an otherwise completely transparent strip of film, and we could have saved all that business with hand-painting them for every frame. Wally [Veevers] shot the models against black velvet, but he never shot them against white."

In a detailed 1968 article for *American Cinematographer*, Trumbull wrote that the hand-painting of the mattes, although laborious, "required only the simplest darkroom enlargers, and this freed up expensive animation cameras for other work." This may have been a slight tidying-up of history after the fact. For many months, crucial footage of the *Discovery* and other models against their black velvet backing lay in reserve in the form of "held take" YCM masters, while the effects department tried to work out how to put the stars in. At one point, Veevers and Kubrick thought they could create a star field from thin sheets of steel, painted black, and punctured with needlepoint holes illuminated from the rear. By placing these sheets behind the models, Veevers hoped to capture the spacecraft and the stars in one take. The results weren't a success. Hamshere recalls, "Every time you

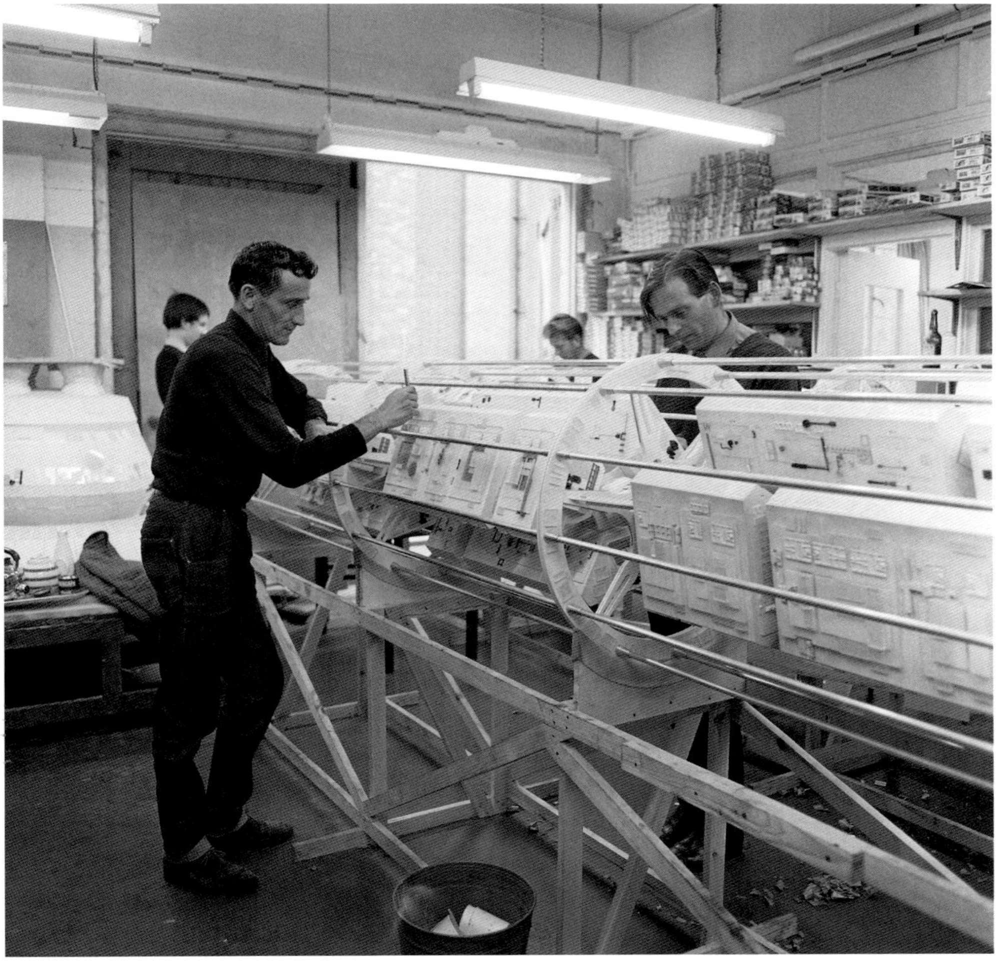

changed the camera lens, or the distance between it and the model, the stars looked a different size, or even went out of focus."

Would it have been easier to create the mattes by shooting the models against a white background? According to Zoran Perisic," getting precision duplicate passes is tricky enough today, with state-of-the-art computerized motion-control systems. On *2001* we

Kubrick banned any casual photography of the 50-foot *Discovery* model. This rare photo shows model makers detailing parts of the segmented boom.

▷ 228/229 The small (15-foot) *Discovery* model, mounted on steel pylons, and surrounded by black velvet.

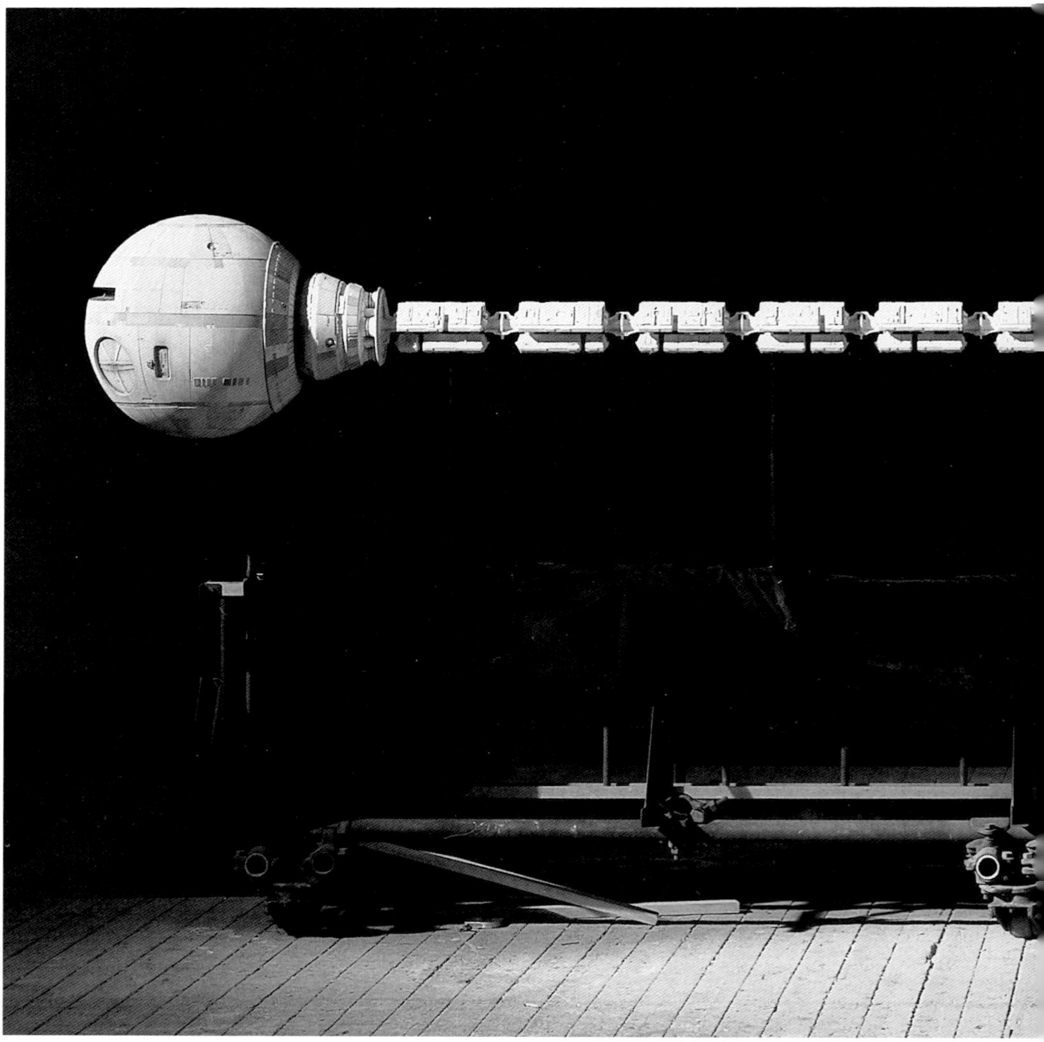

had enough trouble getting one smooth pass, let alone two." Pederson was happy just to get any decent passes: "That smoothness—the absolute perfection of movement as the spacecraft drifts from one side of the screen to the opposite side—that was Wally's triumph, with all his massive gears. Trying to repeat the passes too many times probably would have broken us." Trumbull came up with the idea of hand-painting the matte masks. If they could have done it another way, they would have.

Veevers and Gentleman persuaded Kubrick to take over a partially disused film-processing laboratory on the lot. MGM's gradual decline was illustrated by the fact that this

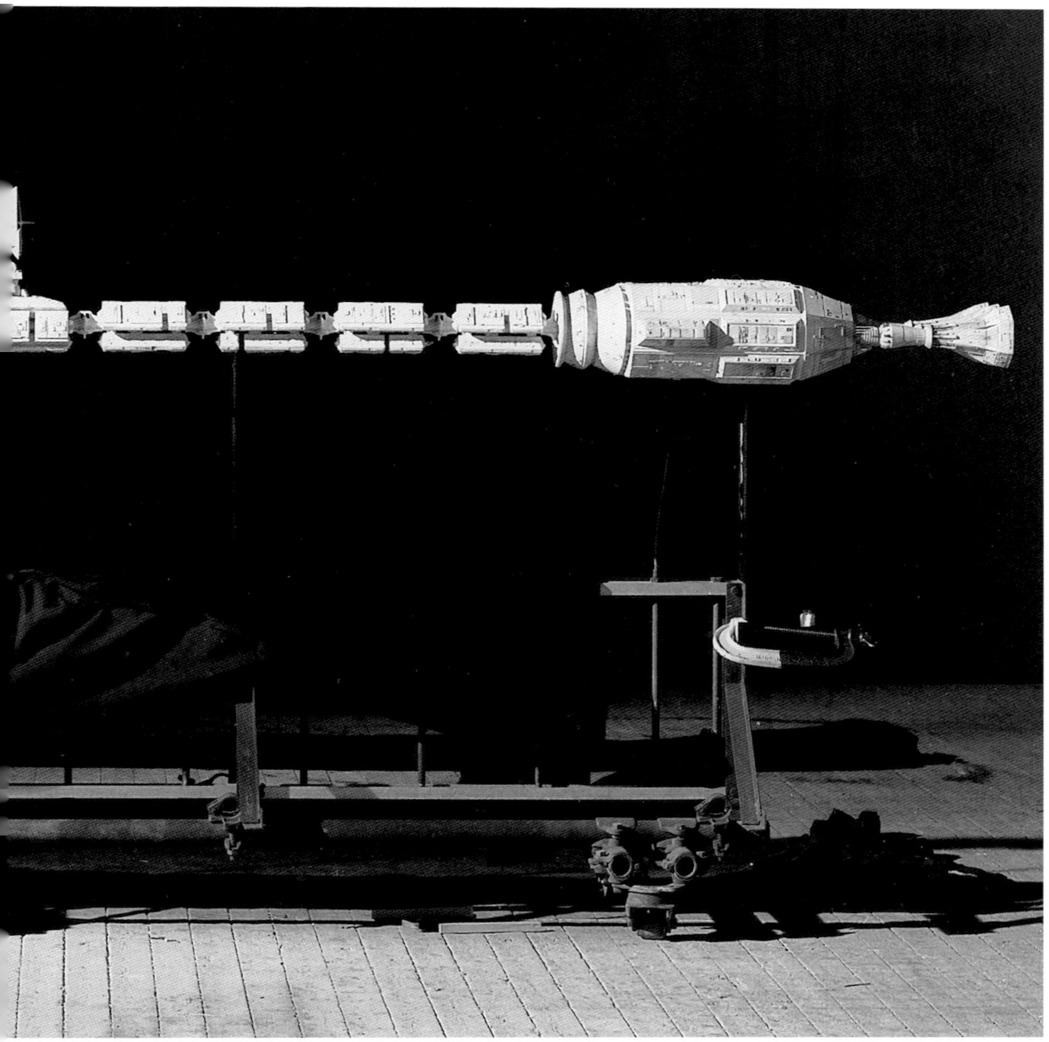

once busy department could no longer justify keeping its doors open. The rooms were vacant, and best of all, extremely clean, and with air-conditioning filters still operational. Some of the optical printers and other visual-effects equipment that were particularly sensitive to dirt, or motes of dust floating in beams of light, were transferred from the large shooting studios and into the abandoned labs.

Despite the seemingly imperturbable tonnage of gears, one reel of space station material came out shakier than anyone had expected. The station, rotating about its axis in a delicate ballet, suddenly lurched from one side of the screen to another. "What the hell was that?" Kubrick gasped when he saw the test footage. Had the massive worm gearings shredded at last? Had the camera mechanisms failed? Just for once, he wasn't able to think the problem through. Then someone took a closer look at the log sheets for the original model photography and found the answer to the mystery.

One sheet logged photography during the last Saturday of July 1966. Kubrick now remembered that many of his staffers hadn't been willing to work that day unless they could wheel a television into the shooting studio and look at it from time to time. It turned out that, as England and Germany went head to head in the World Cup football final, every last technician in the building was glued to that single screen. In the same instant, they'd all leaped up to applaud England's winning goal. Meanwhile, on its reinforced shooting stage, the space station had been turning gently for three hours, while the camera snapped doggedly away at six seconds exposure per frame, for 1500 frames: enough to generate about a minute's worth of footage. And for three frames somewhere about halfway through that 1500, the studio floor had shaken. At least the answer to the riddle was there, in the vast swathes of special-effects documentation.

Some space vehicles were shown tracking from one side of the screen to the other, or heading deep into the frame with no change in the orientation of the ship. A relatively simple animation rig was built to handle these shots. It was nicknamed the Sausage Factory, in the vain hope that it might be able to turn out completed scenes as easily as a meat-packing plant. The process began with a large-format positive paper print of a relevant vehicle model (typically photographed by Keith Hamshere). The lighting on the model was carefully tuned to match the expected lighting in the finished scene. The spacecraft was sliced out, extremely carefully, from the print, and mounted onto a sheet of glass positioned at the end of a typically ingenious and step-controlled piece of Veevers's engineering. Moving the glass sheet sideways, while tracking the camera forward or back, could produce a reasonable range of apparent motions, simultaneously across and into the depths of the frame. Audience members used to photographic techniques may spot the telltale lack of perspective change that betrays the essentially "flat" nature of the spaceship cutouts. The Sausage Factory compensated for its limitations by enabling window action to be projected from behind the glass sheets and into vacant slots in the appropriate areas of the spaceship cutouts. A three-foot *Aries*, for instance, looks much more substantial when one can see the pilots at work behind the windows.

Storyboards outlining requirements for the Moonbus scenes, including lunar terrain in the background, and live action of astronauts visible through the vehicle's windows.

2

15

3

15
52-1A A.C. 65

5

6

10

Fans of action-adventure films sometimes bemoan the sedate spaceship movements in *2001*. This has nothing to do with the "old-fashioned" special-effects procedures used in the pre-digital era. Kubrick's spaceships move sedately because, in space, and when seen from the perspective of astronauts or other ships nearby, this is what real spacecraft appear to do. Space machines are not airplanes. They do not dive or cartwheel. They obey Newton's laws of motion, and continue drifting through space in a particular direction (or trajectory) unless something causes them to stop.

THE SLIT-SCAN MACHINE

Arthur Clarke conceived the "Stargate" as a multidimensional wormhole in space, a portal by which to convey Bowman toward his ultimate encounter with an alien civilization. The final words of an early script treatment were, "In a moment of time, too short to be measured, space turned and twisted upon itself." This was a nice idea on paper. How was such a phenomenon to be filmed? Kubrick and Trumbull agreed that Bowman should "go through something," and that the audience should experience that "something" as if from the stunned astronaut's point of view.

While still in Los Angeles, Trumbull had been intrigued by the work of several abstract animators, such as the Texas filmmaker Mary Ellen Bute and German-American artist Oskar Fischinger. The unusually technological approach of fellow Californian John Whitney was a particular inspiration. Saul Bass's famous opening credits for Alfred Hitchcock's *Vertigo* (1958) include a characteristic Whitney effect of interlinked spirals and whorls of color, suggestive of the nausea induced in someone susceptible to heights. Whitney's techniques were derived from sinister sources: mechanical computers of World War Two vintage, whose original purpose was to aim antiaircraft cannons semi-automatically, or steer bomber aircraft in the final approach to a target and indicate the best moment of release for the bombs. Whitney recognized that the innards from surplus war matériel could be redirected into art rather than annihilation. He built an animation system that automatically altered the settings of a camera, such as its shutter speed and frame rate, at the same time as it manipulated specially mounted sheets of illuminated artwork, shifting them back and forth, spinning them around or tilting them in front of the lens. A 1961 Whitney film, *Catalog*, demonstrates all these capabilities.

Oliver Rennert's illustration demonstrates the basic principle of the slit-scan machine.

▷ The metal pipes, screw clamps, and other improvised components of the slit-scan machine.

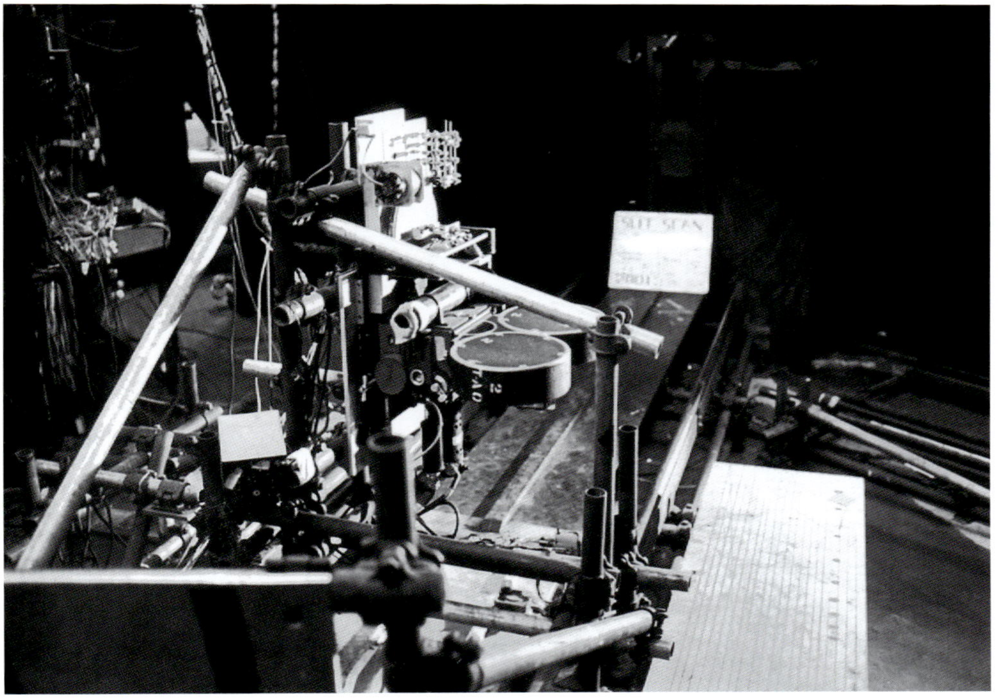

A striking forerunner of *2001*'s Stargate sequence was achieved by yet another Californian. Experimental filmmaker Jordan Belson employed a handmade assembly of plywood frames, salvaged X-ray camera stands, rotating tables, and variable speed motors. His short film *Re-entry* (1964) was inspired by Mercury astronaut John Glenn's fiery return to Earth two years earlier, at the conclusion of America's first orbital manned space flight. Belson strived to create a purely sensory and abstract fusion between music and moving images, resolutely devoid of dialogue or plotting, yet laden with a sense of cosmic mystery. In the late 1950s Belson collaborated with Whitney and sound artist Henry Jacobs on *Vortex*, a series of audio-visual concerts held at the Morrison Planetarium in San Francisco. Kubrick gravitated toward this abstract approach for *2001*, except that he was experimenting with a multimillion-dollar widescreen MGM release, rather than from within the safety of an avant-garde filmmaker's studio.

Trumbull, never at a loss for his own ambitious ideas, thought he could see the next step forward: "I had heard about something Whitney had attempted, involving a slit that moved across the frame while something moved behind it in a pattern that distorts in an odd way. I asked myself, 'Why couldn't that pattern move in depth, so to speak?' There seemed to be no reason why not, so I decided to try it." The *2001* special-effects log sheets for January 1967 record Trumbull and Zoran Perisic experimenting with single 65 mm frames shot on a vertical animation stand. They shifted the camera left to right, and rotated it clockwise and counterclockwise, with the shutter jammed in its open position, while photographing backlit artwork. Their significant advance over Whitney's experiments was to move the camera towards the artwork during each frame exposure, or pull it several feet back, creating the impression of motion blur into the depth of the frame as well as merely from side to side. Kubrick was intrigued, and authorized construction of yet another special-effects rig.[3]

Trumbull and his immediate colleagues went on a strange shopping expedition, as Pederson recalls: "For about $100, we found this huge Meccano construction kit, basically a toy, out of which you could build just about any kind of mock-up of a mechanical device. We played around with that, and eventually scaled it up with more solid gears and struts, and ended up using the same bug-eyed camera that we'd used for the New York World's Fair show. Doug built this enormous rig to do time-lapse controlled streak photography on a very large scale. He called it the 'slit-scan machine.' It took up a whole studio."

In any photograph or film frame, there is a marked difference between images that are blurred, or streaked, by motion, and images that are merely out of focus. The subject of a photo can be perfectly sharp without being distinct. The impression of speed is often conveyed by allowing a car, for instance, or a sprinting athlete, to streak from one side of

3 Lightman, Herb and Douglas Trumbull, "*Filming 2001: A Space Odyssey*," American Cinematographer, June 1968

the frame to the other before the camera's shutter has had time to complete the exposure. Although pictures in newspapers and magazines do not move, we are accustomed to interpreting the streaks as motion. Trumbull was interested in capturing and controlling just the streak alone, without any need for a conventional photographic subject. To get a sense of what this might mean, try to imagine a pencil torch held in the dark by a friend. A photo will reveal just that one spot of light in an otherwise dark scene. If the camera shutter is held open and the torch is waved from side to side, the single, moving dot of light will be recorded on film as a bright line. The slit-scan machine took this spatial trick one step further by photographing an illuminated slit and deliberately streaking its image across the field of view to create a bright plane, a "wall of light," on film. Trumbull's machine could generate what he described as "illusions that have perspective and appear to be solid, three-dimensional objects. But they have no physical structure at all, because they're created purely from light."

At one end of the rig was a sheet of glass, about five feet high and twelve feet across. Most of the glass was masked in black, with the exception of a narrow vertical slit cut into the middle of the masking sheet. At the other end of the rig was a camera, separated from the glass by a fifteen-foot-long tracking system driven by worm gearing. A bank of electrical switches, timers, and selsyn motors controlled the camera movements along the track. It could move up close to the glass until it was no more than four inches away, or reverse to the farthest end of the track. The worm gear, a heavy piece of engineering specially acquired from a Detroit automobile factory, ensured that the camera's back-and-forth movements could be repeated many times with exact precision. The electronic timers were also rigged into the camera controls, so that opening and closing the shutter, advancing the film, and so on could be kept in lockstep with the slit-scan machine's broader mechanical movements. The camera also incorporated a device that kept it automatically focused on the slit, no matter how close or how far away it moved along the track.

Behind the slit, yet more mechanisms drove sheets of transparent artwork, held steady by the large glass plate, and illuminated from behind. Geometric patterns would first be photographed on a large stills camera, in order to yield images as transparencies, or sometimes as negatives—just so long as a light could be shone through them. With overlays of transparent colored gels adding to the whole effect, backlighting made the artwork glow in a satisfactory way.

The camera would begin each exposure just four inches from the slit, then trundle back, allowing the slit to dwindle into the distance until there was nothing much more in shot than a narrow line. All the while (about one minute per exposure) the camera shutter remained open, and the camera panned slightly, streaking the image of the slit across half

Two frames from the dynamic Stargate sequence: an effect generated without the use of computers by carefully controlled streak photography. Despite advances in digital visual effects, this scene retains all its power today.

the film frame. Additionally, the illuminated glass plate behind the slit moved sideways. A simple slit of multicolored light on its own would have produced too-tidy walls. The sideways shifting of the illuminated artwork behind the slit produced dynamic and unpredictable effects: undulations and swirling patterns within the walls. At the end of each camera pass, the shutter would close and the next frame of film would be wound into position.[4]

The camera could just as easily begin its next run from the far end of the worm gear track and move in towards the slit, so long as the movements of the glass sheet corresponded properly. In the same way that a cartoon animator will repeat frames almost, but not quite, exactly, so as to add a tiny element of movement, the slit-scan machine automatically introduced controlled doses of difference to each exposed frame, thus building up a sense of rapid motion when processed footage was projected at 24 frames per second. Look at any frame of the Stargate sequence, and it becomes clear that there are, in fact, two walls of light. They are not simply mirror images or duplicates, but the result of separate scan procedures, each of which exposed half the film frame.

An additional, fascinating experiment with the slit-scan machine came close to suggesting an actual alien community, a "city of light." Trumbull replaced the backlit artwork with small lightbulbs controlled by timer switches. Unfortunately, he recalls, "There was some jiggle to the footage and Stanley rejected it, although, towards the end of production, he realized there were some good ideas going on here. But we were out of time. As far as I know, a single frame, reproduced in Jerome Agel's book [*The Making of Kubrick's 2001*, 1970], is all that remains of it."

One final adaptation of the slit-scan technique was known as the Jupiter Machine. No matter how hard *2001*'s many illustrators and airbrush experts tried, artwork of Jupiter's banded clouds and Great Red Spot storm system failed to deliver anything but a lifeless flat disc instead of something that looked like a planet. The solution was to project the artwork onto a rotating metal disc. The front and rear flat faces of the disc were covered in nonreflective black paint, while the whitened rim, just one-sixteenth of an inch wide, reflected the light from the projector. As the disc rotated through 180 degrees, the whitened edge scanned slowly through the darkened studio space, essentially streaking the artwork around a hemispherical screen.

The realism of planets in general was a hard quality to judge. Harry Lange and his colleagues in the art department pored over reams of NASA data. In those days of fuzzy monochrome images beamed back from early space probes. Lange was anxious, because "we had so few real images to go on. In particular, the Earth as seen from far off in space worried us a great deal. Stanley had all this scientific data about its exact albedo—its brightness relative to the absolute standard of the Sun's brightness. All the boffins said that

4 Trumbull, Douglas, "The Slit-Scan Process," *American Cinematographer*, October 1969

Earth would be very bright indeed when seen from the Moon. We went with that. How could we have known how deep blue it would really seem from the viewpoint of an Apollo Moonwalker in 1969, a year after our movie was finished?"

THE MONOLITH

Clarke's short story "The Sentinel" featured "a glittering, roughly pyramidal structure, twice as high as a man" resting on a leveled platform of lunar rock "like a gigantic, many-faceted jewel." By the time that he and Kubrick had settled on the basic narrative of the *Dawn of Man* sequences, the pyramid shape had been discarded, because no one wanted any inadvertent associations with the tombs of ancient Egypt. By October 1965 the device was scripted as "a cube about fifteen feet on a side, made of some completely transparent material; indeed, it is not easy to see except when the light of the sun glints on its edges." As the man-apes approach the strange object that has arrived in their midst, it presents a visual display of a potential and better future for its primitive audience:

> *A small wart-hog ambles past the group of browsing humanoids without giving them more than a glance, for they had never been the slightest danger to its species. But that happy state of affairs is about to end. The big male hominid suddenly bends down, picks up a heavy stone lying at his feet and hurls it upon the unfortunate pig. The stone descends upon its skull. The wart-hog gives one amazed, indignant squeal, and collapses in a motionless heap.*

As if taking into account the dullness of the man-ape mind, the lesson is repeated in slow motion, so that "every detail of the movement can be followed; the stone arches leisurely through the air, the pig crumples up and sinks to the ground. There the scene freezes for long moments, the slayer standing motionless above the slain, the first of all weapons in his hand." With the creation of this scene in mind, Kubrick asked Tony Masters to obtain a suitable transparent block. As Masters told Don Shay in 1977, he found a Perspex manufacturer at a trade show in London (Stanley Plastics) and commissioned a translucent slab of the material to be molded: "It took a month just for the slab to cool. It had to cool very slowly or it would shatter. After that, they had men polishing it for weeks to get every surface perfect. Then we brought it up to the studio, stood it up, and it looked magnificent." Kubrick inspected it and was disappointed by the slab's greenish, glasslike tinge. The experiment was abandoned. The Slovakian-born sculptor Arthur Fleischmann eventually

◁ 240/241 What we think of as "the" monolith was in fact several duplicates. The crisp edges and delicate paintwork of each one seldom survived more than a few takes.

△▷ Kubrick directs the lunar monolith scenes over the Christmas of 1965 at Shepperton, on Europe's second-largest shooting stage.

The challenge for any film director is to match external reality with an inner vision; not always easy, as demonstrated by these snaps of a frustrated Kubrick on the set of the *Aries* passenger cabin.

acquired the two-ton block and created an artwork, *Crystal Crown*, in commemoration of Queen Elizabeth II's Silver Jubilee. It was unveiled in June 1977 and is still on display at St. Katharine Docks, London, not far from Tower Bridge.

April 1966 was a turning point, not just for the alien artifact but also for Kubrick's perception of *2001: A Space Odyssey* as a whole. After many months of accumulating careful scientific justifications for everything that was to appear on screen, what was missing, he felt, was mystery. Armed with hundreds of pages of dialogue and exposition, he began slicing away at the literalism. In a note to Clarke he said that, "despite the fun of paralleling a television commercial, the specific visions in the Cube are not only unnecessary but harmful. I propose that the specific contents of the lesson are not known to the audience. We see only the spellbound faces of the man-apes as they watch."

Even the Honeywell Systems company expressed doubts about Clarke's teaching machine in their specially bound volume of briefing papers for Ordway, *A Prospectus for 2001 Interplanetary Flight*. The alien crystal's indoctrination method was "an essentially passive process," their experts argued. Rather than simply showing the man-apes what to do, as if in a school's educational film, they should be actively rewarded for learning their lessons: "The efficacy of having something pleasant happen to the learner cannot be denied." Honeywell's list of potential incentives included "drugs, potions, elixirs, hypnosis, incantation, and revelation."

Drugs and potions aside, Kubrick agreed with Honeywell, and also cautioned Clarke against a similar excess of literalism in the film's finale. A more oblique narrative style would "prevent a kind of silly simplicity of which I think we are presently in danger." A subsequent comment in his personal notebooks shows Kubrick reaching, at last, toward *2001*'s famous ambiguities: "Essential to remember all psychological explanations are speculative, poetic. Never try to be too airtight."

The alien slab became a tall, black monolith crafted from wood and painted black. Harry Lange remembered a graphite mix being added to the paint in order to lend a particularly smooth sheen. Touching the immaculate surface on set with greasy fingers was forbidden. Between scenes, the 12-foot-high monolith was swaddled in thick layers of plastic sheeting. According to Masters, "Keeping it clean was a nightmare. For one reason or another, it attracted dust. You'd put it on stage, and—foomp! It would be covered in dust. You'd think, 'Oh, Christ! I wonder if Stanley will see that?' And if anyone put their hand on it—'Stop the shooting! Back to the paint shop for a respray!' It was unbelievable, what went on to protect that thing." In fact, several monoliths were constructed, because the heat from the lights tended to warp the wood or blister the paint, ruining their supposed alien perfection.

Throughout the production of *2001* Kubrick wrestled with the possibilities of showing the aliens themselves, unwilling to surrender this most tantalizing filmic possibility. Quite apart from Trumbull's "city of light" effect, generated with the slit-scan machine, Christiane Kubrick and other artists worked up a few alien creatures in a bid to satisfy Stanley's half-humorous request. "He said, 'I want you to do something in a shape that doesn't remind you of anything, in a color that doesn't exist.' Each time, we thought we'd done something nobody had ever seen, and it turned out to be something *everybody* had seen. By making such a mess of this, we all knew the best alien is the one you don't see, and can only imagine. The minute you try to make one, you show your cultural background, or your interests in biology and zoology. You cannot make a shape that doesn't remind you of something. In the end, Stanley liked the Stargate because it was based on hidden mathematical and geometric concepts."

Man-ape troupe leader Dan Richter's final duty for *2001* was a last-ditch attempt, during September 1967, to conjure an alien, with help from makeup artist Stuart Freeborn:

"At one point Stanley had me made up with thousands of polka dots and then photographed me on high contrast film against a similarly dotted background. It was like a Pop Art experiment, and I just disappeared into the background. It was fun and utterly useless." Freeborn thought the results were better than useless: "It was stunning. Standing still, he would disappear, but when he moved, you could just make out his shape. It was an amazingly weird effect, but I don't think it really fit in the movie."[5]

Trumbull experimented with video feedback, too. Pointing a TV camera at its own monitor's output creates something like an infinite hall of mirrors. A shimmering, ghostly apparition in approximately alien-humanoid outline was easy to generate. Unfortunately, it matched everyone's expectations for just such a thing: a shimmering, ghostly apparition. Kubrick turned, at last, to Clarke's favorite idea from the fall of 1965: "Bowman will regress to infancy, and we'll see him at the end as a baby in orbit. It's his image of himself at this stage of his development."

The final images of *2001* are perhaps the most powerful of all: that moment when Bowman is reborn as a glowing "Starchild." The internal luminescence of this bright creature was generated by powerful backlighting. When the baby turns his head towards the audience for that final awe-inspiring gaze, we register his direct eye contact with us for a brief, heart-stopping moment. The 10 seconds that it takes for the baby to turn its head toward us took eight hours to film. The light shining into the back of the resin sculpture made the semitranslucent materials appear to glow after a long exposure for each frame of film. The child's enveloping aura was a superimposed piece of airbrushed artwork, subsequently double-exposed around the footage.

The Starchild was sculpted by Liz Moore, the same artist who created the sexually suggestive girl-shaped white furniture for the "milk bar" in Kubrick's subsequent film, *A Clockwork Orange*. A few years later she was killed in a car crash while working on Richard Attenborough's *A Bridge Too Far* (1977). Her principal creative legacy is a few seconds at the end of *2001*. But those seconds convey one of the most stirring, perplexing, and memorable images in all of modern cinema.

5 Interview with Don Shay

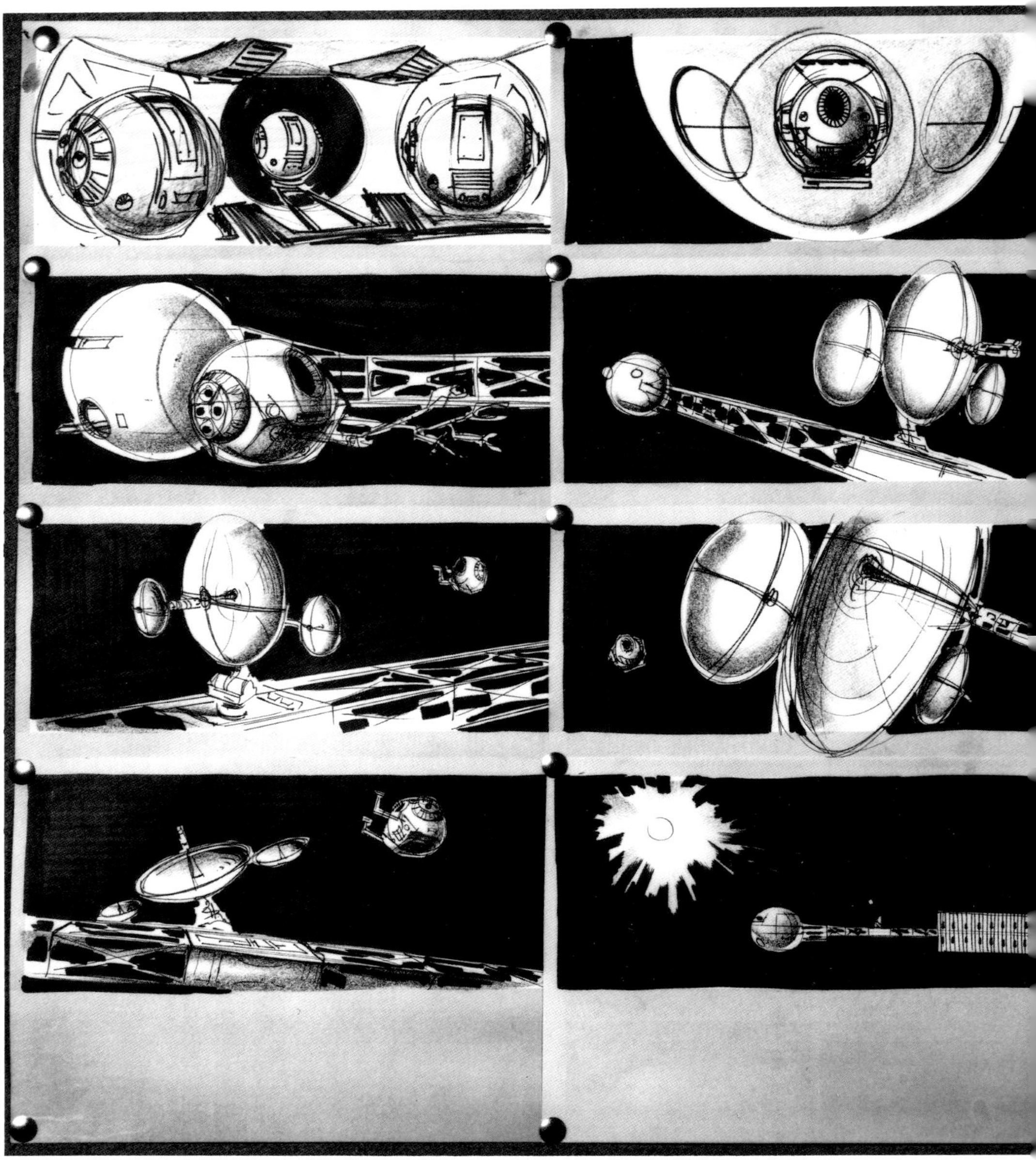

A storyboard showing the use of a space pod to access the antenna unit.

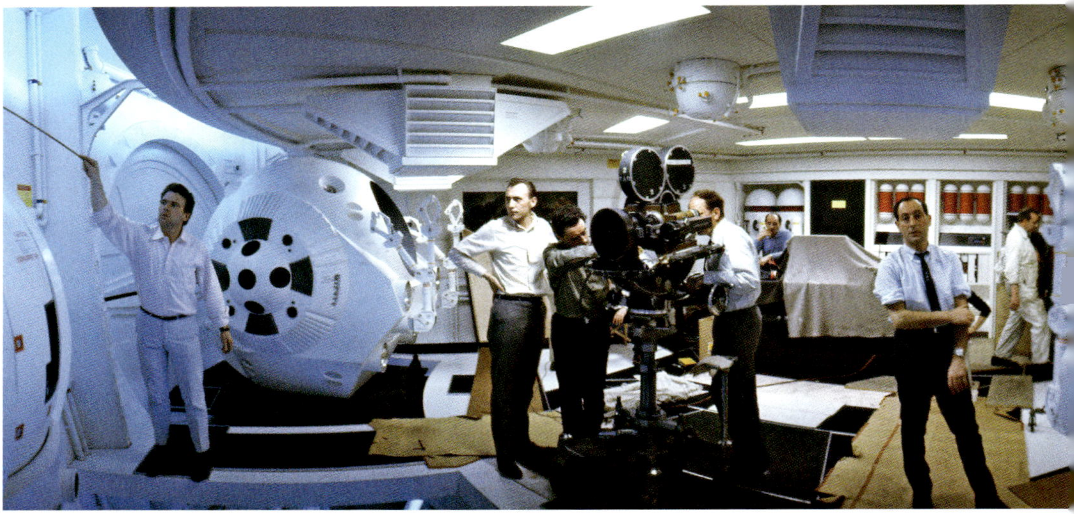

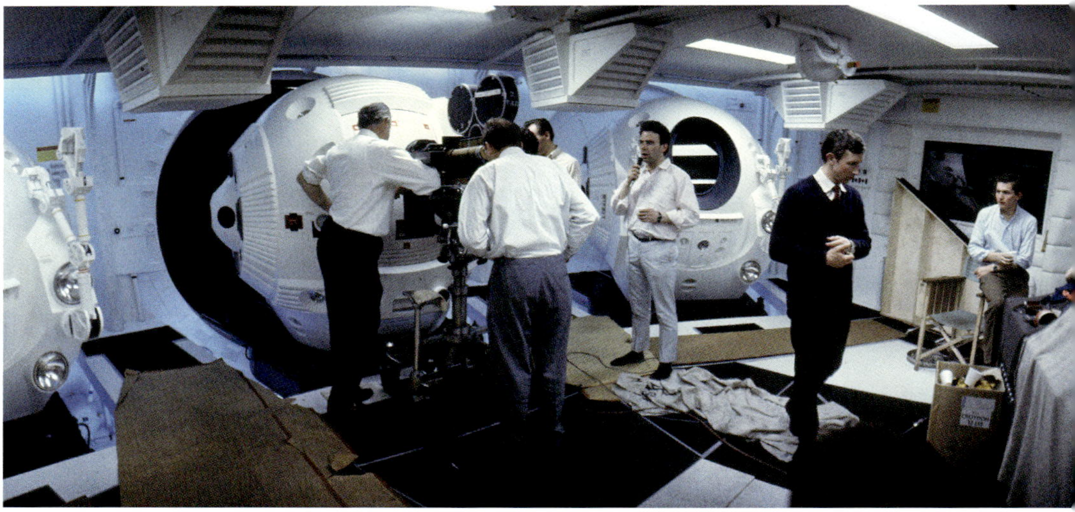

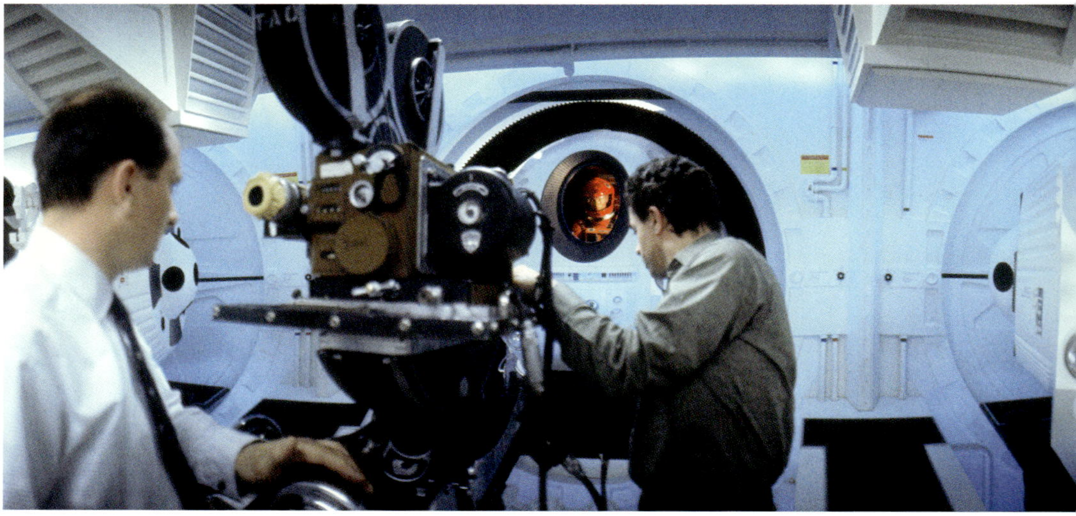

REACHING THE END

The making of *2001: A Space Odyssey* was exhilarating—until the point was reached when it became just sheer, hard work, seemingly without end. According to Trumbull, "everything had to be absolutely, spotlessly perfect. There wasn't a fleck of dust on any of the artwork. There were never any technical flaws, or jiggles to the movement, or bad lighting. And we had to shoot over and over until everything was perfect in all respects. It was grueling." After two-and-a-half years of nonstop work, the crew was beginning to show the strain. "Towards the end of the film, in the last few months and weeks, there was a lot of anxiety and antagonism. People were saying they were tired of it—that it had gone on too long, that it was too agonizing, too difficult."

Wally Gentleman from the National Film Board of Canada, the man whose effects for the film *Universe* had so much impressed Kubrick, was among several senior figures to resign outright from the production. Even Pederson, among the most enthusiastic of Kubrick's collaborators, was relieved when the thing finally came to an end: "I was worn out. At the beginning of '68 I went back to California and took a couple of years off from the movie business. I got to know the High Sierras like the back of my hand." Hamshere also left the production fairly exhausted: "Stanley could drive you absolutely nuts, but when you saw the completed footage you just thought, 'Wow! That's fantastic!' It was worth all the pain and heartache." Brian Johnson's mood was similar: "We all knew we were working on something truly significant—something that would make all the strains worthwhile."

Almost alone now, in the semi-abandoned special-effects department, animation cameraman Bruce Logan was assigned one last, monotonous job just before the film's release: "Our effects shots were as close to first-generation as possible in every instance. The problem was that, for foreign releases of the film, the *2001: A Space Odyssey* title card in the first few frames obviously had to be translated into the relevant languages. Stanley ordered us to create the background sunrise effect as fresh footage for every translation, so that it wouldn't simply be copied and recopied every time the film went to a different country. Long after everyone else had packed up and gone home, I was shooting seven

The camera crew lines up shots of the space pod's rear hatch, and works on a scene, ultimately deleted, showing Bowman returning from his repair expedition.

exactly similar versions of that opening, each one onto fresh film, using the original hold-out mattes, planet artworks, light sources, and so on. It damned near killed me," Logan remembers.

Minor tensions emerged after release. At the 1969 Oscar ceremonies, Kubrick collected the statuette for Best Visual Effects on behalf of all the effects supervisors. According to the Oscar rules in place at that time, a maximum of three effects artists could be nominated per film. Kubrick collected the statuette as a "solution" to nominating too many colleagues. Trumbull's view was that "the effects weren't designed just by Stanley. They were *directed* by him. I think it was one of the rare times in movie history when a director was so integrally involved in the effects, but it was a collaborative process involving a lot of people." Pederson was more sure of Kubrick's centrality to the process: "He directed all the effects on the film. There should never be any question about that."

Trumbull lost contact with Kubrick during the 1970s, though he never once wavered in his gratitude to him: "I did not, at any time, claim to be the only guy who worked on *2001*. The press always simplifies things. 'Doug Trumbull, who did the effects for *2001*.' Well, Stanley would read these articles and he'd write, or phone me up, and he'd say, 'What are you doing, going round claiming to be the only guy who did the special effects?' And I'd have to tell him, over and over, that I'd never said that." Of all people in the world, Stanley should have been in a good position to know how the media tend to simplify the truth. When it comes to the making of *2001: A Space Odyssey*, the complicated story of its production cannot easily be simplified into easy sound bites.

A flexible pipe sends cool air into the hotel-room set, while Kubrick shoots through a screen to prevent the camera from appearing as a reflection in Dullea's helmet.

Gary Lockwood acts out preparations for Frank Poole's fatal space walk.

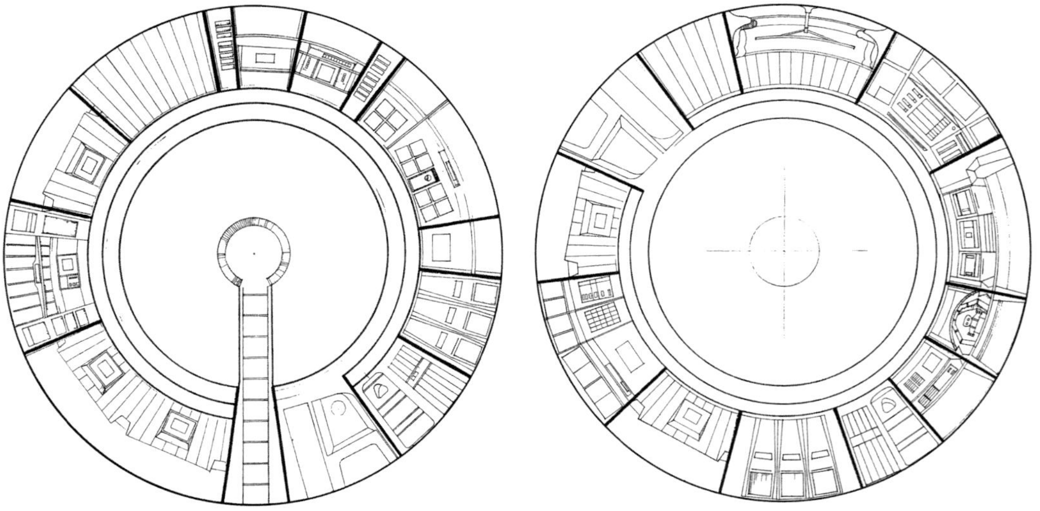

IN SEARCH OF THE LOST PROPS

So, where did everything go—all those incredibly real-looking space pods, the *Discovery*, the hibernation units and space suits, the Pan Am rocket plane, the lunar shuttle? Modern auction houses like nothing more than to put on sale relics from famous films. Items from *2001* are especially valued because they so rarely emerge. In 1971 a sharp-eyed young man, Chris Randall, found a HAL 9000 face plate and lens in a north London junk shop, on sale for a few shillings. Twenty years later it was in the possession of Dr. David Stork, a computing expert at the Ricoh Research Laboratory in California. Stork's keepsake inspired *HAL's Legacy* (1997), his much-praised book on the current state of play in artificial-intelligence research, with essays from leaders in the field. One can hardly blame Stork for succumbing, eventually, to temptation and parting with his precious relic. Christie's auction house in London sold the plate in November 2010 for $27,600. Californian aerospace engineer and pressure-suit historian Dennis Gilliam obtained, and painstakingly restored, Bowman's red helmet. To hold it in one's hands is to appreciate the extraordinary quality of its construction. This is not a simple plastic mock-up intended to fool the eye for a few moments. It is at once a beautifully crafted work of art and a precision-engineered product of scientific research.

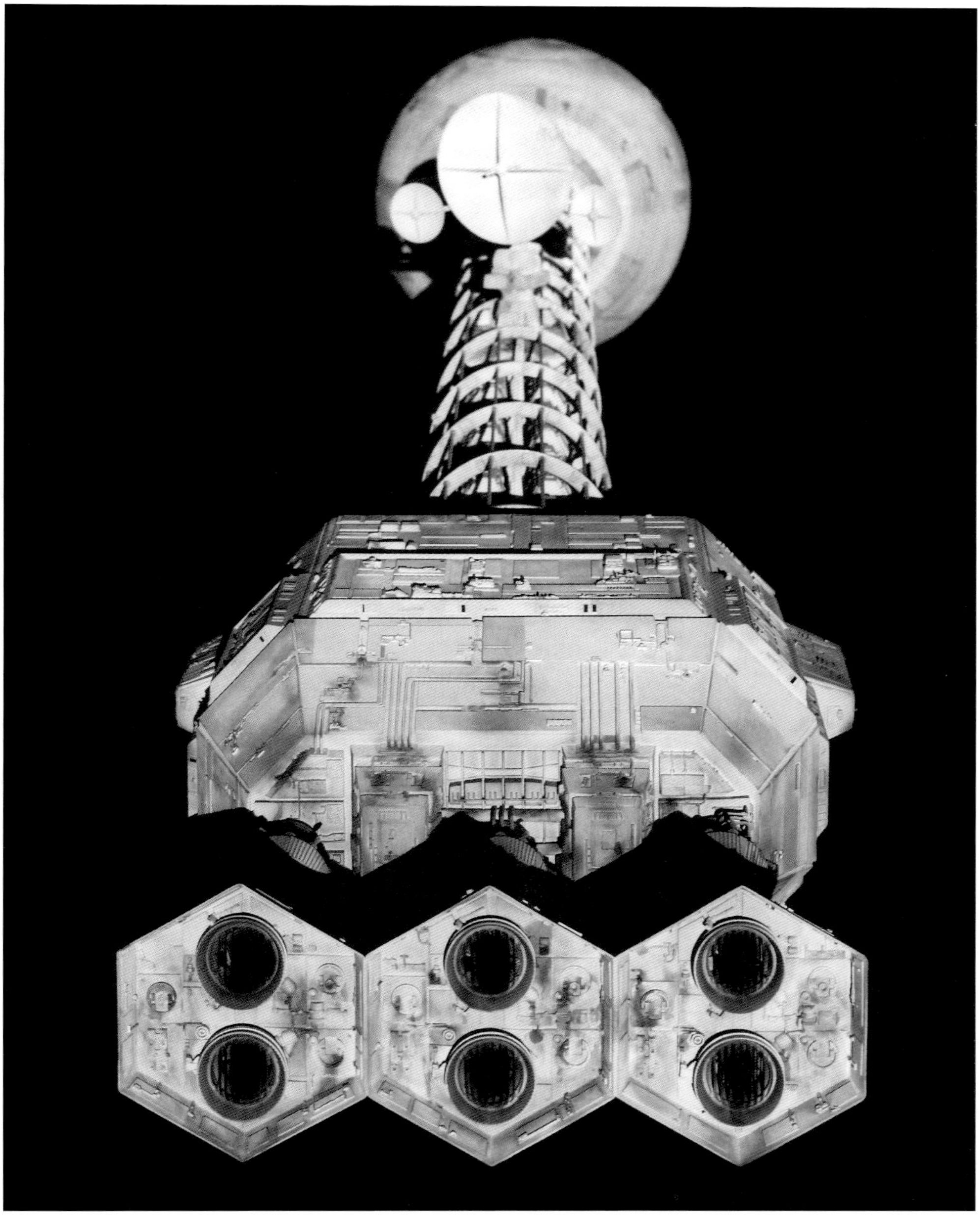

Reference drawings showing the main centrifuge set dressing panels.

△ The engine section of the smaller *Discovery* model. Notice the ribbed cladding of the boom, which was stripped away in one last design revision.

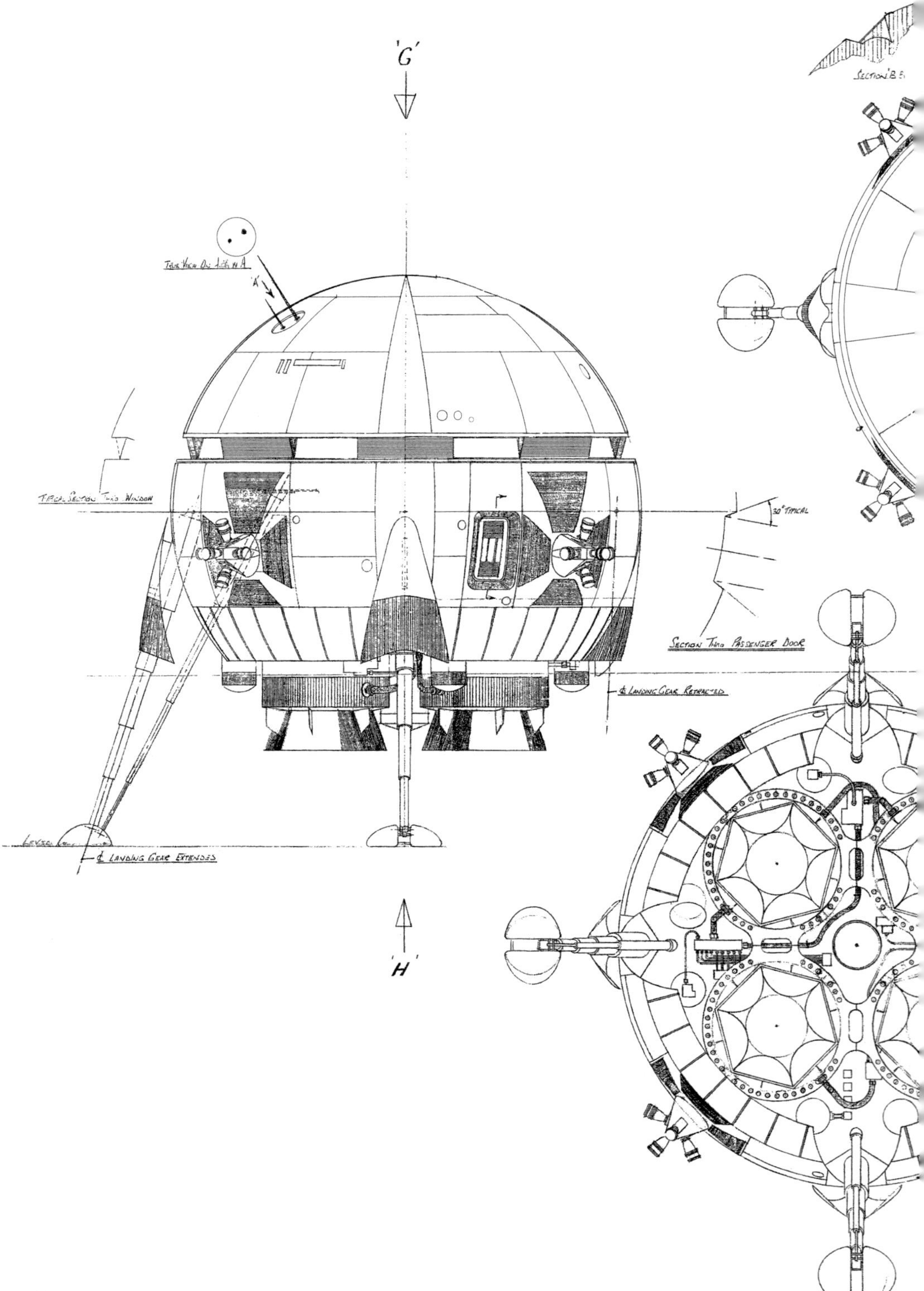
'G'
'A'
TYPICAL SECTION THRO WINDOW
30° TYPICAL
SECTION THRO PASSENGER DOOR
℄ LANDING GEAR RETRACTED
℄ LANDING GEAR EXTENDED
'H'

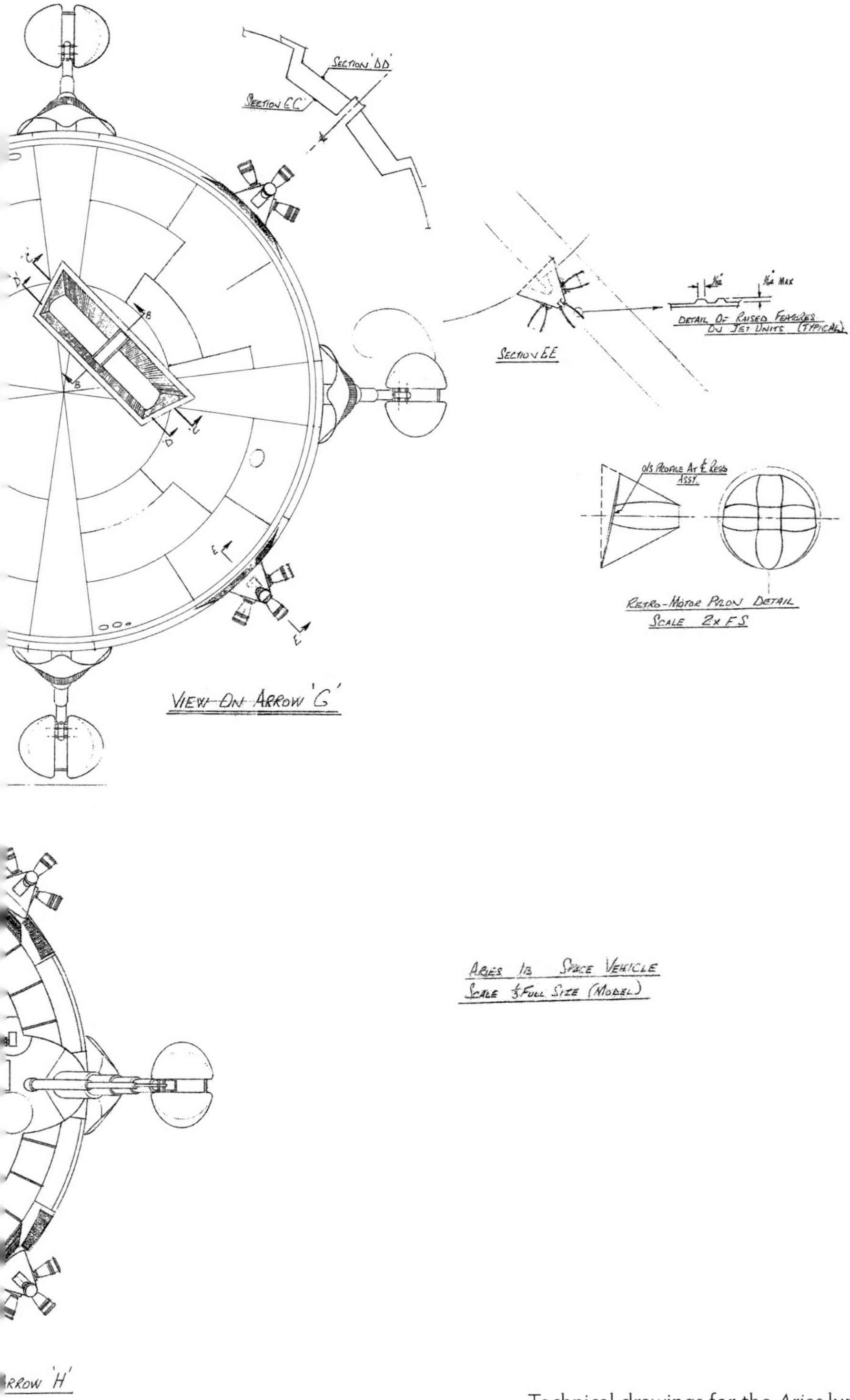

Technical drawings for the *Aries* lunar shuttle.

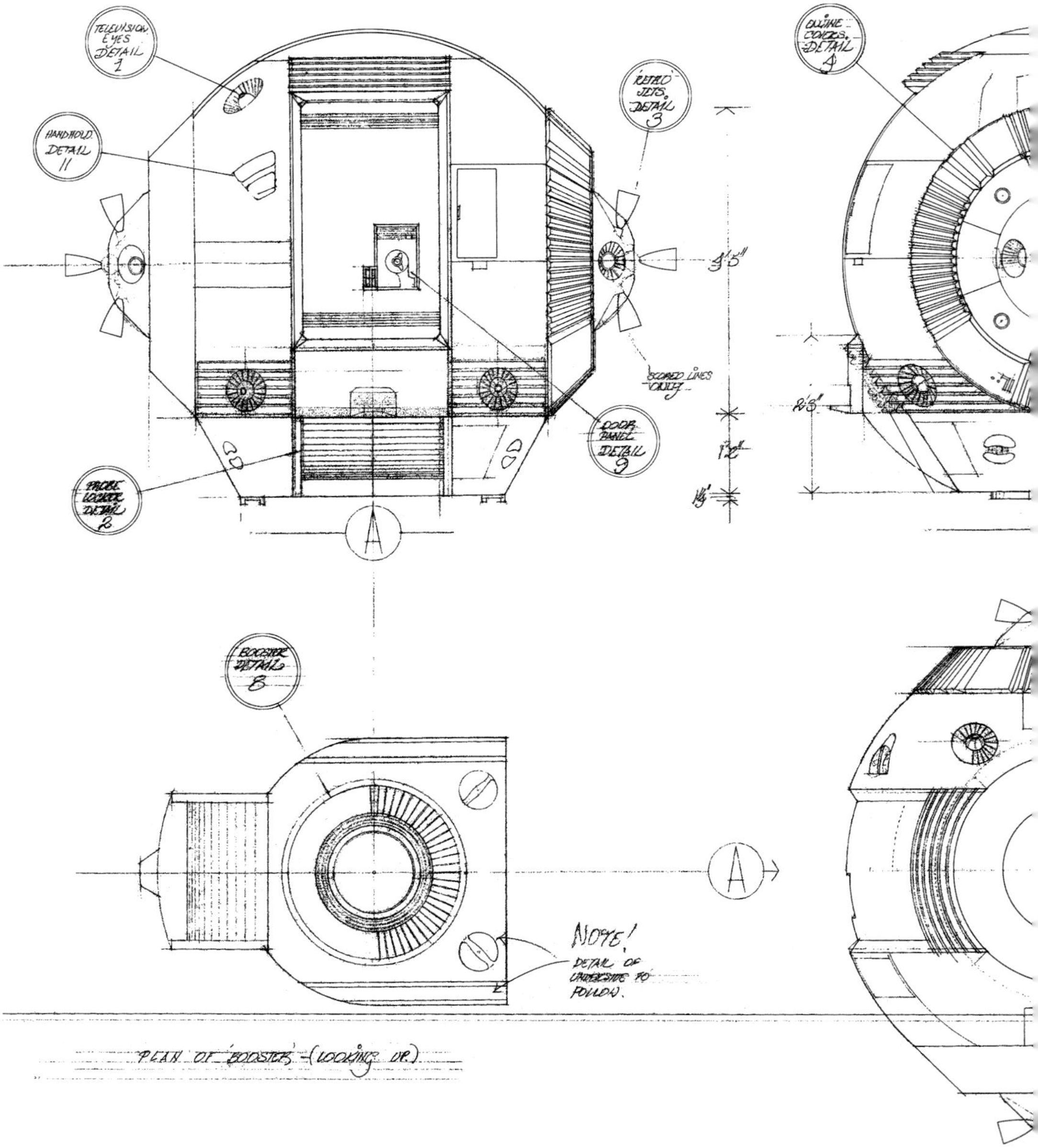

Construction plans for the space pod, prior to the addition of flood lights on the front face, and adaptations to the robotic arms.

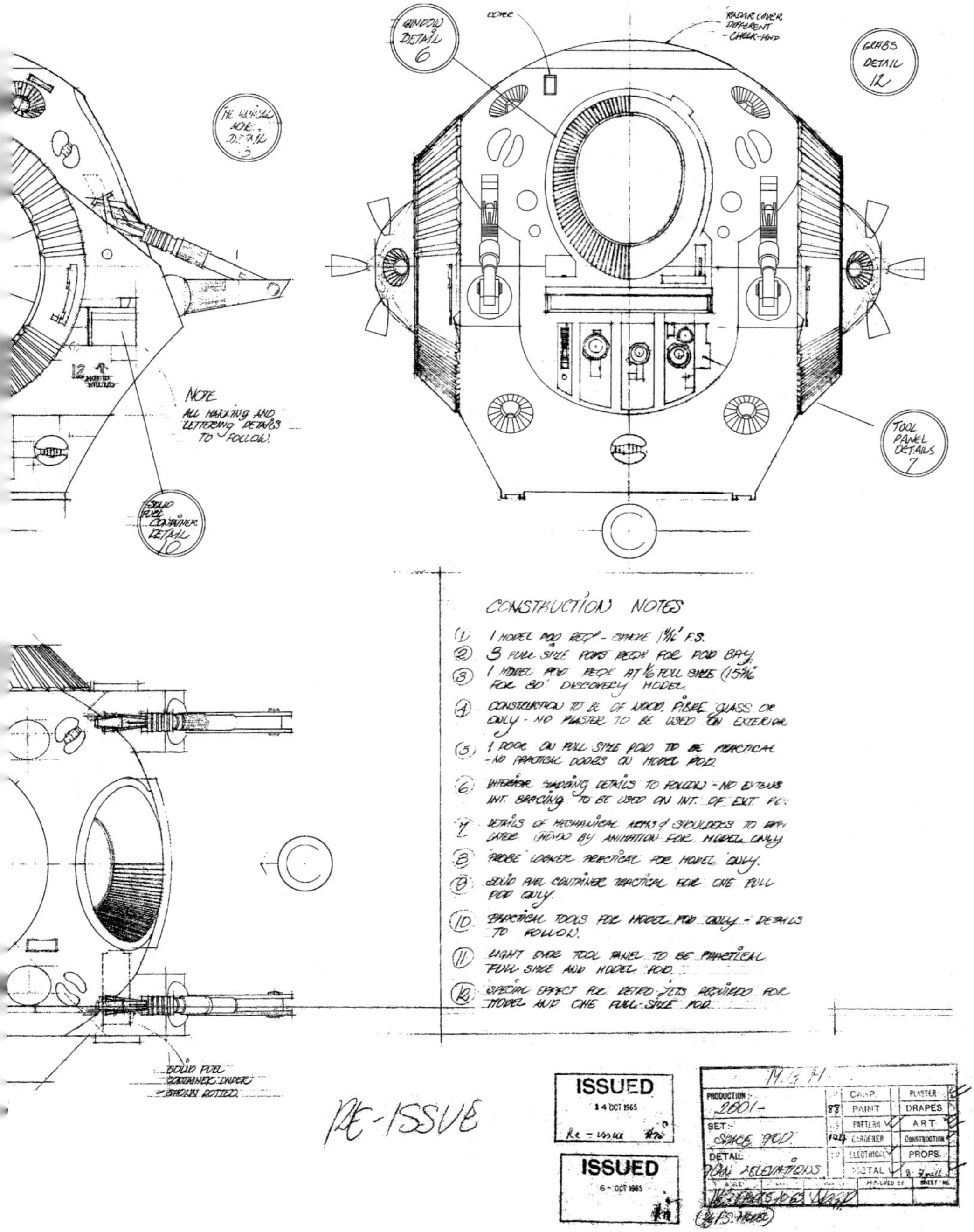
WINDOW DETAIL 6
RADAR COVER DIFFERENT - CHECK-AND
GRABS DETAIL 12
NOTE
ALL MARKING AND LETTERING DETAILS TO FOLLOW.
TOOL PANEL DETAILS 7
SOLID FUEL CONTAINER DETAIL 10
CONSTRUCTION NOTES
(1) 1 MODEL POD REQ'D - SCALE 1 1/16" F.S.
(2) 3 FULL SIZE PODS REQ'D FOR POD BAY.
(3) 1 MODEL POD REQ'D AT 1/6 FULL SIZE (15 3/16" FOR 80' DISCOVERY MODEL.
(4) CONSTRUCTION TO BE OF WOOD, FIBRE GLASS OR ONLY - NO PLASTER TO BE USED ON EXTERIOR
(5) 1 DOOR ON FULL SIZE POD TO BE PRACTICAL - NO PRACTICAL DOORS ON MODEL POD.
(6) INTERIOR SHADING DETAILS TO FOLLOW - NO EXTERNAL INT. BRACING TO BE USED ON INT. OF EXT. POD
(7) DETAILS OF MECHANICAL ARMS & SHOULDERS TO FOLLOW LATER (MOVED BY ANIMATION FOR MODEL ONLY
(8) PROBE LOCKER PRACTICAL FOR MODEL ONLY.
(9) SOLID FUEL CONTAINER PRACTICAL FOR ONE FULL POD ONLY.
(10) PRACTICAL TOOLS FOR MODEL POD ONLY - DETAILS TO FOLLOW.
(11) LIGHT OVER TOOL PANEL TO BE PRACTICAL FULL SIZE AND MODEL POD.
(12) SPECIAL EFFECT FOR RETRO JETS REQUIRED FOR MODEL AND ONE FULL-SIZE POD.
SOLID FUEL CONTAINER UNDER - SHOWN DOTTED.
RE-ISSUE
ISSUED
14 OCT 1965
Re - issue
ISSUED
6 - OCT 1965
M.G.M.
PRODUCTION: 2001-
SET: SPACE POD.
DETAIL: POD ELEVATIONS
CARP.
PLASTER
PAINT
DRAPES
PATTERN
ART
GARDENER
CONSTRUCTION
ELECTRICAL
PROPS.
METAL
(1/6 F.S. MODEL)

Fred Ordway, *2001*'s tireless technical advisor, tried his best to salvage the centrifuge, the spacecraft models, and other props, knowing that people would flock to see them if only they could. He and Kubrick came close to agreeing on terms. Crates of dismantled materials were to be shipped off to America for reassembly at a venue to be known as the International Space Museum. In the event, the scheme became impractical.

The closure of MGM's Borehamwood studios in 1970 was something of a shambles. Vast amounts of material from many productions, famous and bscure alike, were dumped into skips as developers moved in with an eye to turning the place into a huge food-freezer compound. Around that time, a fire destroyed several buildings. It was never Kubrick's intention to lose everything from *2001*. Christiane recalls her husband's dismay when he learned that the contents of entire storerooms had been arbitrarily trashed. Nevertheless, he did wish to see certain items disposed of. Pederson understood why: "One day Stanley and I were walking towards Stage Three at Borehamwood, and we saw this large airplane model that someone was planning to use on some other movie. Stanley said, 'Oh, my God! That looks just like the bomber in *Dr. Strangelove*!' He freaked, and from that point on he had this slash-and-burn policy of destroying sets and models so that they couldn't be used in other movies. Today I guess those props would be celebrities in their own right, but at the time we didn't think about preserving them. He was just trying to stop them turning up later in some vastly inferior movie."

The *Aries* miniature, seen here during modifications to add greater detail, was 27 inches in diameter. Very few props from *2001* survive today, but this one is a rare exception. In March 2015 it was acquired by auction, from a private owner, by the Academy Museum of Motion Picture Arts and Sciences for over $340,000.

▹ 263–265 Detailed photographs of the *Aries* prior to Sausage Factory animation. Kubrick preferred the lighting to match the harsh contrast of outer space. His colleagues persuaded him that some slight shadow fill was needed.

Perhaps the saddest tale is told by Trevor Parsons, who was studying to be a graphic artist at a college in Stevenage, a half hour's drive away from Borehamwood, when he stumbled, briefly, across a doomed treasure: "Our studio faced the entrance to the local dump. One afternoon in 1974 a truck turned up after the dump was closed and left some crates in the entrance way." Parsons heard that the boxes contained some of the props from *2001*, including the eight-foot-diameter space station. By the time he went on site to investigate the rumors, the station had been clumsily uncrated and tipped into a field. He took photographs of the still-recognizable wreckage. "I desperately wanted to take it home. I only had a motor bike, so it wasn't really workable." When he returned a day or two later to see what might be done by way of a salvage operation, he found that it had been "smashed up by kids." Perhaps this is for the best. Today there is no trace of the scuffed and abused eight-foot model, betraying its secrets of glue and artifice. What's left is what we see on screen: a space station, obviously hundreds of feet across, its many windows alive with light, waltzing gracefully in orbit high above the blue Earth.

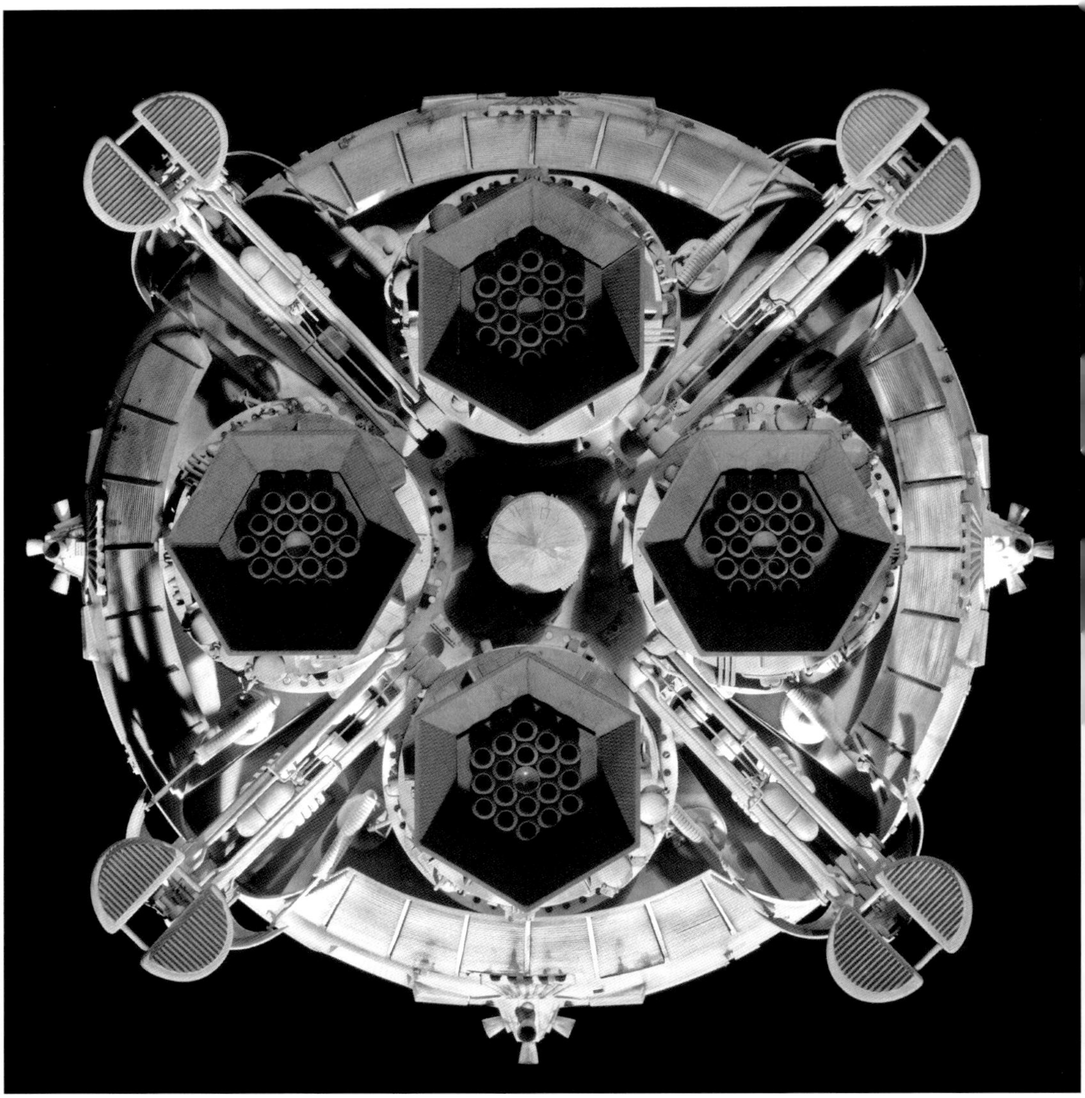

Small pipes hidden in the *Aries* engines pumped out compressed air to stir up chalk powder on the landing pad, simulating the disturbance of lunar dust by the exhaust plumes.

▹ The Moonbus was three feet long, and was one of the first models to be super-detailed with extra components from plastic kits, with a "dirty" paint scheme to finish.

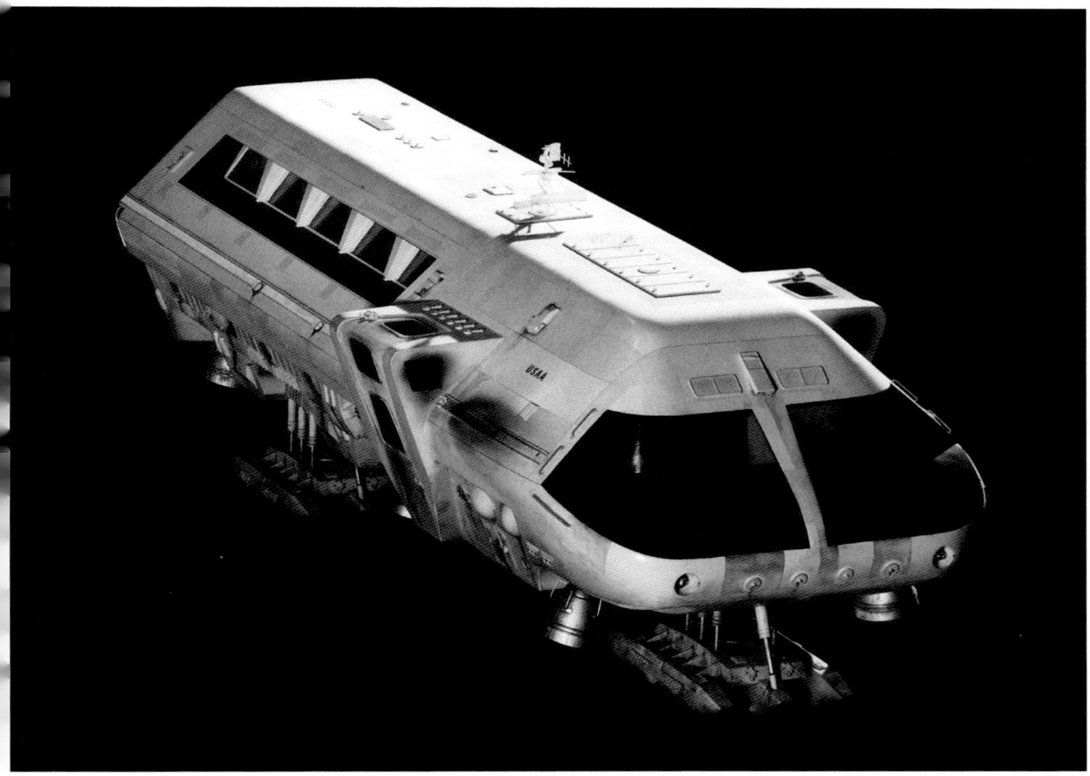
USAA

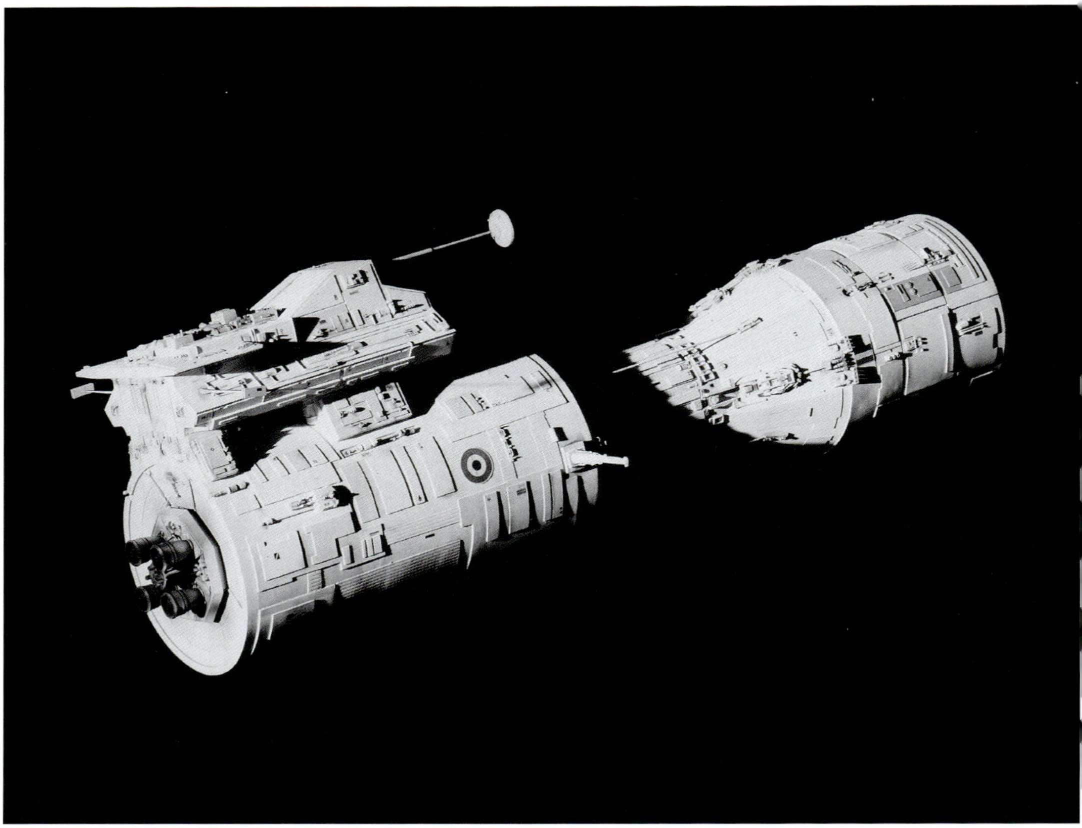

A test photograph of an orbiting space bomb.
A French military roundel can be seen at middle left.

A large-format photograph, derived from fine-grained Polaroid negative film, showing the completed space-station model, which was eight feet in diameter.

IV

"The only thing we're sure of is,
it was buried four million years ago."

THE DAWN OF MAN

Connecticut-born Dan Richter developed a passion for mime as a drama student in New York, after which he spent four years touring with the American Mime Theatre as its lead performer. In the early 1960s he came to London and set up as a mime coach, while running his small literary magazine, *Residu*. In October 1966 his stage skills came to the attention of scuba-diving enthusiast Mike Wilson, a close friend of Arthur Clarke. Wilson knew that the *Dawn of Man* prologue had yet to be photographed, and that Kubrick was still unsure about the casting of the man-ape actors. Perhaps mime artists would be better candidates than conventional performers, especially given the lack of dialogue in those scenes? Richter, in his own estimation "a 28-year-old starving mime teacher and editor of an avant-garde poetry review," was summoned to Borehamwood for a discussion on October 21. Passing through the main gate he encountered something like a small town, or a military base, with an odd mix of buildings: some in ornate 1940s deco style, including the white stucco clock tower, and others, featureless and vast, with windowless brick walls and huge doors. These were the main shooting stages. As if to offset their inhuman scale, the stages were linked by glass-lined walkways that kept the rain off people and props as they moved to and fro. Peppered across the site were utilitarian single-story prefabricated buildings. In one of these, Building 53, was Kubrick's British production office, Hawk Films. Richter's initial impression was that it didn't look like the inner sanctum of a great Hollywood director. It was more like the site office of "an insanely busy" building contractor. Kubrick seemed "so unpretentious and genuine that I was immediately at ease."

Relaxed though the meeting was, Kubrick lost no time explaining the nature of his problem: "Dan, they can't look like men in monkey suits." Richter suggested that great actors sometimes cannot move in the right ways, while stuntmen might be able to perform the moves, but not all of them can act. On the other hand, as a mime, he could do both, using movement and gesture alone to convey narrative and emotion. "Stanley listened to what I had to say and he said, 'Well, this all sounds very good. How do I know that what you're saying is true?' And I told him that if he could give me half an hour, a black leotard and some towels and a stage, I could show him." A modest photographic studio on the lot was the venue for Richter's first attempt to portray one of our primate ancestors, a creature more than an ape, yet still a long way from human. "The wardrobe department came up with a tattered leotard that was good enough to meet my purposes, and I put towels in it to change the shape of my body. Then I did what we would call at the mime theater 'forum walks,' where I walked in character, extending the expressions with large movements."

Lacking any deep knowledge of primate behavior, Richter played a brutish, slow-witted, inarticulate man, swift to take fright or rise up in defensive anger, yet also inquisitive and childlike. Kubrick was sufficiently impressed to lay down his next challenge. If Richter

Roy Carnon's depiction of the man-ape's environment. A transparent monolith is visible in the cleft between the rock formations.

▷ During production, Kubrick was intensely secretive about many of the filming techniques used for *2001*. This rare Polaroid photo shows the controllable lighting array above the *Dawn of Man* stage set. The mountains and clouds in the background are projected.

could turn himself into one man-ape character, could he find and prepare a team of 20 or 30 more? Did he have any ideas about costumes? Did he think he could be ready to shoot in Andalusia, Spain, starting in the next 10 weeks? Richter tactfully explained to Kubrick that simply finding another two dozen mime artists would take more time than that, let alone researching ape behavior and training the troupe of performers. He would need months, not weeks. Far from feeling nervous, he saw that Kubrick "was very intrigued by the fact that I wasn't just agreeing with him. He hated sloppy thinking, but if you had real ideas and real reasons for what you felt and thought, he wanted to hear it."[1]

This encounter took place on a Friday. By the following Monday, Richter had an office on the MGM lot, a salary, and an official job description: choreographer for the *Dawn of Man*. He had decided to invent a naturalistic mime technique, far removed from the tragicomic traditions of Marcel Marceau and other practitioners: "You couldn't just have dancers making up the movements as they went along. I saw this essentially as an acting

1 Richter, Daniel, *Moonwatcher's Memoir: A Diary of 2001: A Space Odyssey*, 2002

problem. You had to make the performers think and feel like man-apes. Method acting isn't something that you'd associate with Stanley, but when I put these ideas to him, he was immediately impressed." Richter had even convinced himself, until he was granted access, for the first time, to pages from the *Dawn of Man* treatment and sensed the enormity of the challenge ahead.

> *Among his kind, "Moonwatcher" is almost a giant. He is nearly five feet high, and though badly undernourished, weighs over a hundred pounds. His forehead is low, and there are great ridges over the eye sockets, yet he unmistakably holds in his genes the promise of humanity. In those dark, deep-set eyes is a dawning awareness—the first intimations of an intelligence which would not fulfill itself for another two million years...*

The basic principle of the front projection system, illustrated here by Oliver Rennert. As Dan Richter explores the pile of bones, he masks his own shadow on the huge reflective screen.

▹ The front projection rig, showing the projector and its powerful lamp housing, and the half-silvered mirror positioned at 45 degrees in front of the camera lens. Kubrick and his team scaled up a technique devised originally by Philip Palmquist at the 3M company.

Kubrick's young assistant Tony Frewin showed Richter around. Slipping quietly into Stage 4 through one of its smaller side doors, Richter felt as if he were entering a cathedral with a limitlessly high roof. Immense black velvet curtains blocked out stray light. High above his head a stuntman in a space suit (Bill Weston) twirled slowly on the end of a thin wire, with a complicated camera and its attendant crew looking up at him. Models of spaceships and strange, egg-shaped pods with claws were scattered about the stage floor. Richter "had trouble breathing. It was stunning."[2]

He was taken to another building, near the far end of the lot, where make-up artist Stuart Freeborn, his wife Kathleen, son Graham, and assistant Charlie Parker were already at work on man-ape costumes. Their workshop was on the top floor of an old converted studio. Huge skylights stretched across the roof. Freeborn had worked with Kubrick on *Dr. Strangelove*, and was responsible for turning Peter Sellers into his three distinct and memorable characters: the mustached British officer Lionel Mandrake (one of the few sane people in the film); the distressed American president, bald-pated Merkin Muffley; and the blond-haired, pallid-faced maniac, Dr. Strangelove himself. Richter looked in awe at Freeborn's preliminary masks and prosthetics, and expressed his admiration for the craftsmanship and artistry on show. Then, wondering how he—an inexperienced brat from a mime theater—could have the nerve to say anything, he tried to explain to the veteran movie expert why his man-ape ideas wouldn't work. Despite the realism of the masks, they lacked the flexibility and expressiveness that Richter felt he needed: "It would be like wearing a bag over my head. I couldn't express myself." Much to his surprise, Freeborn listened attentively.

ACTING AS ANTHROPOLOGY

Richter familiarized himself with the broader context for the *Dawn of Man*, "extrapolating from the Robert Ardrey materials that Arthur Clarke had found. The aliens put the idea in my head to kill, and once we start killing, we have all this food and we can start beating up our neighbors. And eventually, four million years later, we will be able to communicate with the aliens." He studied everything he could find on anthropology and human evolution.

2 Ibid.

These large-format transparencies were among many hundreds of background plate photographs brought back from the Namibian desert.

"There was a debate about how much these creatures should look like apes, or men. In the mid-1960s, we didn't know anything like as much as we do today about human origins. A lot of it was inspired guesswork."

Kubrick decided that an overseas location shoot for a troupe of actors in heavy costumes was out of the question on grounds of the cost, the scheduling complexities, and the safety of the performers, who would have suffered heat stroke in their man-ape costumes and latex masks. Almost everything would have to be photographed on set. While his production team planned the necessary staging and equipment to create prehistoric Africa in a London suburban studio, Richter was installed in his own rehearsal space. What he and Stanley needed now was a couple dozen suitable performers. Journalist Victor Davis takes up the story in the *Daily Express*, April 18, 1968:

> *Research suggested that the creatures should be more man than ape—a nude with a sparse covering of hair. The hard-pressed make-up department presented 75 examples for Kubrick's inspection. He blanched. The cavorting actors presented a fair facsimile of a Mau-Mau orgy in progress. Kubrick solved the nudity problem by putting the actors into monkey suits. But he also decided that the performers should not be more than five feet tall, and should have long upper lips to carry the simian make-up. He mused, "The Irish have long upper lips. Get me 50 five-foot Irish actors with long upper lips." The Dublin agencies were combed, but most of the mini-apemen were found nearer home. The first was diminutive Ronnie Corbett, the TV comedian, then a relatively unknown entertainer.*

Apparently, Corbett was interviewed by Kubrick: "I want you for a major part in my film. You will be the first man. It's a most tender and moving role." The comedian submitted to a series of tests in which he donned rough mock-up costumes "like hairy combinations." According to Davis, the production secretaries screamed at the sight of Corbett, and he was released from any further obligations. Kubrick wrote to Davis, thanking him for his many stories about *2001*, "despite their great inaccuracy." Even so, the Corbett incident suggests the tremendous—and at times, ridiculous—problems encountered as Freeborn developed the man-ape costumes.

Keir Dullea shakes the hand of an "ancestor" during an unsuccessful make-up test. Prehistoric human skin wasn't sufficiently hairy to hide the genitals. Man-apes from an even earlier epoch were chosen because of their hairy pelts.

A portrait of a man-ape, showing the intricate layers of wool, yak hair, and other fibers that lent realism to the thick, matted pelt.

An unsuccessful attempt at portraying a prehistoric human. Everyone agreed that a hairier creature was required.

Arthur Clarke's story "Encounter in the Dawn" features hominids living in a village protected by a primitive wooden palisade. Clindar, an alien from a possibly doomed far-off world, leaves behind some tools that, he thinks, the hominids might find useful. A slight problem with the story is that the very existence of a "village" implies that the hominids must possess tools already. As Kubrick and Clarke dissected these ideas, it seemed best to go back further in evolutionary time, to a point just before the supposed invention of the first tools. Around 300,000 years ago, Neanderthal hominids ranged far and wide across the land masses that we now call Europe and Asia. The story of human evolution is complex and tangled. Where Neanderthals were once thought to be our ancestors, it now seems that they were either killed off by more intelligent competitors from a different branch of the hominid evolutionary tree, or else interbred with them. Kubrick, anyway, thought that something approximately Neanderthal might work as a prehuman ancestor for the *Dawn of Man* sequences.

The problem, as Freeborn quickly discovered, was that "although the Neanderthals had body hair, it would have been rather sparse, covering only certain parts of their bodies. Essentially they would have been totally nude—which would have made them difficult to shoot." Kubrick proposed photographing them from the waist up, or in long-shot. Freeborn conducted a test, "trying to cover up crotches, male and female, with short hair in such a way that you wouldn't notice anything. We cast the performers' crotches and made plastic coverings, and added hair to them. The characters looked completely neutered." The only sensible solution was "to go back another million years or so. That way, they could be entirely covered with hair."[3]

The target range was within a genus known as the Australopithecenes, described by Robert Ardrey as "a zoological group of small-brained erect-running creatures, hesitating between the roles of ape and man, who haunted the high African savannah a million or two years ago." Popular and academic journals of the time gave extensive coverage to hominid fossil fragments discovered in Tanzania, East Africa, between 1962 and 1964. The bones were two million years old, and came from an Australopithecene species named Homo habilis, or "Handy man," so-called because of the deliberately shaped stone tools found in association with some of the fossils. The shards were on the borderline between the random shatterings of nature and the conscious crafting that prehuman hands might have accomplished. When Freeborn's Neanderthal experiments became unworkable, the *2001* team decided there was sufficient evidence from Homo habilis to place the first use of tools several million, rather than mere hundreds of thousands of, years in the past.

Freeborn and Richter explored this possibility, and took advice from anthropologists Jane Goodall and Louis Leakey. It became obvious that the body forms and skull shapes of such early hominids were very different from those found in modern humans. The head makeup for the *Dawn of Man* performers would have to include pronounced eyebrow ridges, a shortened nose on a long, broad snout, and large teeth with pronounced canines, along with other subtle details such as a longer arm length in comparison to the torso.

Neanderthals, with their more or less recognizable human shape, would have called for subtle prosthetic additions to the performers' faces, each requiring several hours to apply. Freeborn was quite relieved that the jump back in time allowed for a completely different skull shape: "The idea was to make an entire head that could be put on, or taken off, in seconds. Up until then, whatever you had put on had to *stay* on all day. This was a tremendous breakthrough."

3 Interview with Don Shay

BONDING THE TROUPE

Richter acquired a team of suitable man-apes tempted away from dance troupes, mime theaters, and the world of horse racing. The man-apes had to appear thin and underfed, even when bulked up by their costumes. The performers had to be fit, yet shortish and very thin. A couple of horse enthusiasts fit the bill. Dancer Simon Davis had wanted to become a jockey, while Brian Hawley actually was one. A lucky discovery was a trio of dancers in their early 20s whose youthful demeanor and small frames (David Charkham, Danny Grover, and Andy Wallace) allowed them to pass as teens in the Young Generation, a popular television dance group of the time. Richter was pleased to find that "they were already pretty fit. They just needed toughening up. In the end, I just put 'em all through a process like an army boot camp."

A real band of apes would be tight-knit and protective, Richter knew. He worked to establish a similar mood among his humans: "I gave them awkward method exercises, where you have to pick the person you hate the most, and tell them you love them, and all that kind of stuff. They thought I was crazy, but that was the point. They *all* thought I was crazy, and this helped to unite them. Also, they developed a betting pool. We had some jockeys playing the females, and they were betting all the time. I encouraged anything that brought the group together—going to the pub, all of that. We did everything together. Always together."

After physical exercises at Borehamwood in the morning, the squad would spend afternoons at London Zoo in Regent's Park, studying the chimpanzees and other primates in the collection. Richter took careful note of every gesture and grimace he saw: "Guy was my inspiration and mentor, you might say." Guy, a lowland central African gorilla, was brought to London Zoo in 1947 as a youngster and became one of the most popular attractions. A gentle giant, he would allow small birds to perch on his hands. His death from heart failure in 1978 at the age of 32 was a cause of national mourning. Despite what we might now regard as the dubious origins and cruel nature of his captivity, he was a peaceable and popular presence at the zoo, and seemed just as curious about his human visitors as they were about him. Nevertheless, Richter was disturbed that such a fine and intelligent creature should have to live in a cage: "I couldn't help feeling that Guy was like an innocent man in jail for something he hadn't done, with no idea what he'd been charged with."

Richter tutored his band of actors, day after day, until they hardly knew the difference any more between human and animal ways of behavior. He recalls, "It took about three

Stuart Freeborn in his studio, and "playing" with members of Dan Richter's specially trained and costumed man-ape troupe.

months, and by the end of it, you could have picked up all these fellows and dropped them in the middle of town, and they would have gone right on functioning—stealing food from passers-by, fighting among themselves. I didn't choreograph them, I created an actual tribe, with relationships, a social order, and a prehuman way of thinking. They really bonded. They thought I was a little bit aloof from them, and that was deliberate."

Fellow man-ape Simon Willis tried not to be offended: "Dan kept himself to himself, and his approach really worked. We would get up from the table after a meal, and we constantly found ourselves pushing against the tabletop with our knuckles. It came so naturally to us, it was quite scary. We even had our backs arched like apes, without even thinking about it."

AN ENGLISH SAHARA?

If Doug Trumbull was the driven young man of the special-effects department, he more than found his match in Andrew Birkin, one of Kubrick's several young assistants. Brother to actress Jane Birkin, Andrew was an experienced movie set runner by the time he entered the world of *2001: A Space Odyssey* at the age of 19: "A friend of mine got me a job as assistant and teaboy for the princely sum of eight pounds per week. For about six weeks, I operated a photostat machine, and that was about it. I was going mad with boredom, and I was ready to quit. I hadn't even met the great Kubrick. All I'd done so far was wind the clock in his office when he wasn't there."

At the close of each day's shooting Birkin wandered around *2001*'s huge spacecraft sets. He wasn't allowed anywhere near them in working hours, because he had few useful functions to perform on the studio stages apart from delivering tea and call sheets. Worse still, he had no union card. He was fascinated by what he saw, but his prospects in the movie business were not improved when he accidentally sealed himself into a space pod during one of his illegal visits. One day during February 1966 he was delivering yet more tea to one of the stages where, for some reason not immediately apparent to him, a new set had been constructed with a giant artwork of rocks and desert for a background. It looked like an inhospitable patch of African scrubland. Production designer Tony Masters, art director John Hoesli, and construction manager Cliff Brandon had spent a small fortune building the thing. Kubrick arrived for a first inspection and was unimpressed: "Forget it. This won't work. There must be a location somewhere that we could use instead of this? Does anyone know, are there any desert-type terrains in England? I'm not asking for the Sahara, just some sand dunes." His disconsolate designers shrugged their shoulders. Almost without thinking, Birkin began to speak. "To this day I don't know why I did it, but I shouted, 'Yes! There is somewhere we can go.' And Stanley asked, 'Where?' And I said that I could look up the information at home," he remembers.

With approval from Kubrick, Birkin caught an early morning train so that he could investigate an industrial site outside Liverpool, which by chance he had remembered seeing in one of his old school geography textbooks. Using a borrowed Polaroid camera, he snapped the site, a mixture of shallow scrub and dunes of sand, albeit with an unsightly oil-processing complex in the background. That night, in his Liverpool hotel, he glued his shots to a board in the form of a panorama, and compiled a set of notes to explain the composite scene. He caught the "milk train" in the small hours of the morning and arrived

A test photograph of a man-ape trio silhouetted against the yellow dusk of a background projection plate.

back in London at five o'clock in the pre-dawn darkness. Risking the wrath of the accounts department, he took a taxi to Borehamwood, where a friendly gate guard allowed him to deposit his neatly wrapped package on Kubrick's desk. Then, at last, he went home to get some sleep. No sooner had he shrugged out of his coat, than Victor Lyndon was on the phone: "I don't know what you've been up to, but Stanley says we should give you a union card and triple your salary."

Reporting for work next morning, Birkin was summoned into the privileged world of the art department, where Kubrick was playing a little game with his designers: "I don't know, guys. It's taken you five months and 10,000 pounds to come up with nothing. Then the teaboy gives me an answer in one day, for seven pounds and change." Kubrick knew he was being mischievous. Birkin's location was useless. Nevertheless, after he'd had his fun with his poor designers, Kubrick took the young man aside. He asked, "Do you know how to use a real camera? Do you know about different film stocks? Emulsions? Processing? I'll send you over to the Technicolor lab for a couple of days. They'll teach you."

Birkin was now an official Kubrick protégé. The crew immediately began to take him more seriously, and he learned from them at a ferocious pace, with a hunger that surprised him as much as any of his colleagues. With his union card approved, and empowered by

Kubrick's Widelux camera captured this image of the lunar lobby set. The footage of an art lesson was abandoned, and nothing of these scenes was retained in the finished film.

B1
B2

B1
B2
RECEPTION
C2

This production sketch by Tony Masters shows artificial grass and a small pond in the lunar base.

the new rank of third assistant director, his first task was helping to log *2001*'s special effects. Perhaps for the first time in his life, he says, "I wanted to accept responsibility for something that was much bigger than myself." Another duty was to continue scouting potential locations within Britain that might suit Kubrick's requirements. Birkin traveled to Bangor in North Wales, armed with 50 packs of Polaroid film, looking for that elusive desert.

Birkin also scouted several country houses. For the Moon base scenes, Kubrick was interested in showing the family life of lunar colonists (following from the theme of a future generation born off the Earth in Clarke's story "Out of the Cradle, Endlessly Orbiting") and wondered how future space planners might create pleasant living and communal areas, slightly different in tone from the mechanistic control rooms and docking bays. Roy Carnon and Tony Masters worked up a design for a spacious lobby and reception area with a pond and an artificial lawn, where children would be seen attending an art class. On September 27, 1966, actor William Sylvester, a dozen extras, and seven children (including Kubrick's daughters) arranged themselves in front of Luton Hoo country house in Bedfordshire, where there happened to be a pond that met with Kubrick's approval. At the top of the steps leading up to the house, riggers built a section of the base interior, including a lift doorway and a wall panel. Wally Veevers was on hand to ensure that the footage of the pond, with the lift in the background, would eventually marry up with the larger interior sets at Borehamwood. Luton Hoo's real pond, with its ancient scuffed stonework and lichen patches, proved unsatisfactory. The entire scene was rephotographed again at Borehamwood on a large lobby set, equipped with a clean artificial pond and similarly neat grass. In the event, none of this material was incorporated into the finished film.

Christiane Kubrick was assigned to play an art teacher tending a group of little students. She recalls, "Arthur was fascinated by how homesick we would be on the Moon. It would be much worse than just being in a foreign country, and so much more frightening, psychologically. How was Stanley supposed to show such an abstract emotion?" A group of children from a theater school turned up for audition. Christiane and two of her girls joined the other kids—not all of whom could act. "Stanley said, 'Oh my god, I can't send any of them home. They look so sad. They just start to cry.' So he hired them all, and he was stuck with all these children. He just had to laugh—it was going so wrong. This was all the result of Arthur's fascination. Yes, we want to leave the cradle. We want to go places, but it would be so hard! The things you would miss! Anyone on a long trip knows the depression that comes over you when home seems so far away. Putting this into pictures on the screen was not so easy, so these scenes were never used."

▹ 290 Test photographs of man-ape costumes. Notice the varied textures, the unhygienic yellow teeth, and deliberate incorporation of dirt and dust in the pelt fibers. The skin around the actors' eyes was blackened to help their eye sockets merge seamlessly with the costumes. Ape-like eye coloration was achieved with uncomfortable contact lenses.

▹ 291 Dan Richter in bodysuit and "polka dot" makeup, during attempts to create an alien entity. Kubrick eventually decided not to show the aliens themselves.

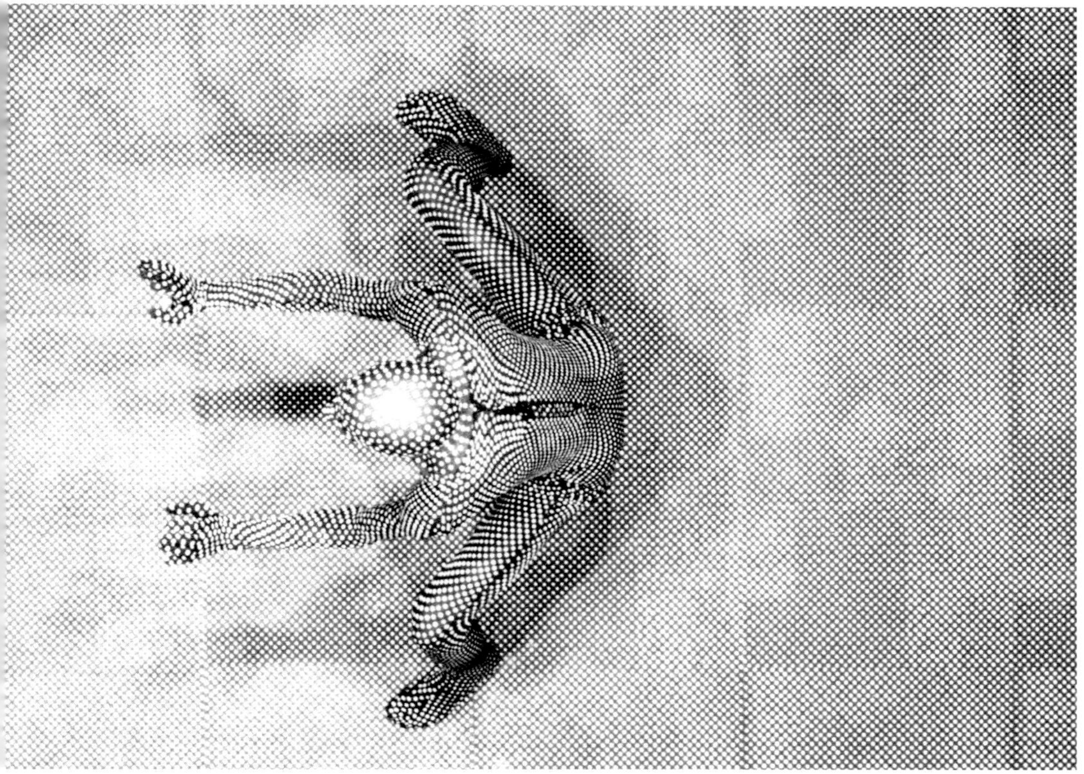

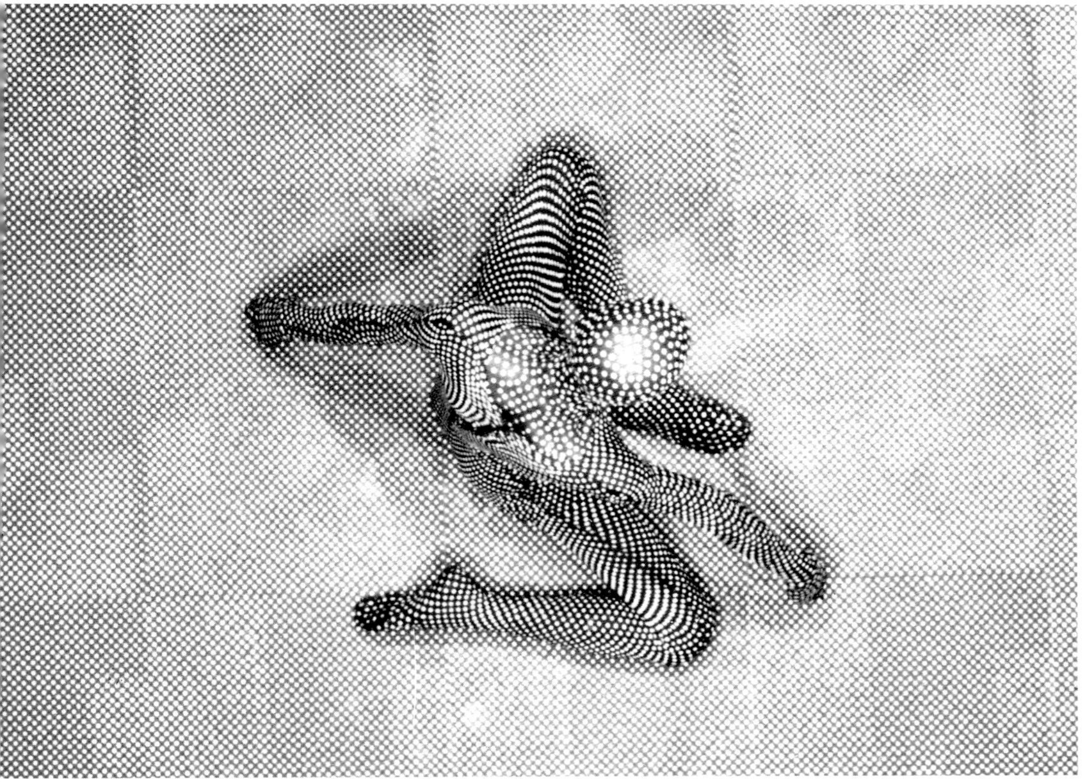

BRINGING AFRICA TO BOREHAMWOOD

Birkin's location scouting for *2001* had only just begun. In late 1966 he encountered Bryan Loftus, one of the senior effects technicians, playing with the YCM film negative separations, deliberately printing them back onto fresh film through the wrong filters to create distorted colors in the positive prints. (He was experimenting with an idea first proposed by Wally Gentleman, who had left the production early.) Birkin persuaded Loftus to take the test prints to Kubrick, who liked what he saw. By the end of November 1966, Birkin was shooting aerial footage of the Outer Hebrides islands for what became known as the Purple Heart sequence during Dave Bowman's mind-warping trip to the hotel room. Birkin recalls, "Suddenly I had a budget for three days in a helicopter, a camera operator to boss about, and all this responsibility. For two days, the weather was terrible and we couldn't fly. On the third day I told the pilot, 'Fly anyway.' I was determined to get the shots. Everyone kept asking me, 'Andrew, do you have kids?' And I said, no, I didn't. And they said, 'Well, why are you risking your neck in a helicopter in rotten weather just for a film?' I didn't worry, because I was determined to get my job done." He brought the shots home, and the effects department applied Loftus's deliberate color-processing misalignments to the footage, creating the effect of an eerie alien landscape.

Additional aerial shots of Monument Valley and other arid landscapes in northern Arizona were captured by Bob Gaffney, whose second unit photography of American exteriors and road scenes for *Lolita* had melded successfully with the rest of the film, which Kubrick had shot in Britain. Gaffney sat in the passenger seat of a Cessna 210 airplane with a film camera mounted under the wing. The desert air turned out to be unpredictable, and the Cessna's owner complained to Gaffney in fruitier language than Birkin had encountered from his polite British chopper pilots: "I knew you were going to get me killed one of these days, you stupid son-of-a-bitch!"[4]

On January 31, 1967 Birkin and production designer Ernie Archer were dispatched on safari with Paris-based *Life* photojournalist Pierre Boulat, charged with acquiring large-format transparency photographs of skies and landscapes from specially selected areas of the Namibian Desert in southwest Africa, which Kubrick now intended to use as a new and more convincing backdrop for the *Dawn of Man* sets at Borehamwood. Birkin wired Victor Lyndon: "ARRIVED SAFELY JOHANNESBURG THOROUGH BODY SEARCH AT CUSTOMS CAUSED TWO HOUR DELAY." Lyndon, stuck in Borehamwood in the middle

4 LoBrutto, Vincent, *Stanley Kubrick: A Biography*, 1997

of a cold, dark British winter in the first days of February, replied by airmail to Birkin, who had flown on to the Namibian capital, Windhoek, where he was waiting to rendezvous with Boulat and his obviously lovely assistant, Catherine Gire, a staffer from the French version of *Life* magazine. "Stanley says, do not let Pierre read the entire script," Lyndon warned, before spinning off into his own fantasy:

> *Apparently "Life" is keen to get information about the film, so let caution be your watchword, and beware of attractive Frenchwomen! What a classic situation: one beautiful woman and a group of sex-starved film technicians in the savage, burning heat of the desert. Who will win her love? The suave, sophisticated Frenchman or the handsome young English aristocrat? They knew that only one could get out of that hell-hole alive with the photographs that meant survival or extinction for Western civilization. Could they trust Schmitt, the agent in Johannesburg, or was he in the pay of… "Them?" Look after yourself. Yours, Victor.*

As if to highlight the difficulties of location shooting that Kubrick was habitually so keen to avoid, Boulat broke both legs when his Land Rover ran head-on into another truck, deep in the heart of the desert. The two vehicles involved were the only motorized transport for many miles around. "If anything can go wrong, it will," was a Kubrick motto. "Don't save the day. Anticipate it." Birkin saved and anticipated as best he could, far from home. He had been assigned responsibility for transportation, equipment, the camping gear, and the budget—practically everything on the shoot except taking the photographs. The sheets of film had to be kept cool, and zealous customs authorities at every stage of the air-freight route between London and Africa prevented, somehow, from opening the film boxes and fogging the contents. His crew had to sleep rough most of the time; the food was poor; funds weren't getting through from London on time because MGM had no formal banking relationships out here. From back home, *2001*'s production accountant, Ron Phipps, quibbled, by airmail, about Birkin's expenses.

> *We were horrified at the cost of your taxi from Chelsea to MGM and to London Airport, for which you have claimed £10, but have not provided a receipt. This item should be explained. We could have had a Rolls Royce for this money.*

More urgently, Birkin had lost his stills photographer. John Cowan, whose fashionable London studio featured in Antonioni's film *Blow-Up*, arrived after a few days to replace Boulat. His relationship with Birkin and Archer was not a success. Kubrick and Lyndon politely fired him by airmail ("we understand that other urgent commitments prevent you from working with us further") and sent the reliable *2001* unit photographer, Keith Hamshere, to replace him. At last, events moved Birkin's way. A comprehensive range of ten-by-eight-inch transparencies was dispatched to Kubrick in England, to his eventual satisfaction. Archer, Birkin, and Hamshere returned to London at the end of May 1967, exhausted, but satisfied that they had done the job.

For Birkin, this African adventure was the beginning of a successful career in films as a scriptwriter and director. He reflects, "That was Stanley's knack—to give you a break if you were halfway interested in accepting the challenge, or if you showed any kind of willingness or curiosity to participate in what he was doing. After *2001*, I never looked back, and I owe the start of my real career to him." Birkin's direct involvement with *2001* came to an end in June 1967, when he received a note from Kubrick's post-production manager, Ronnie Bear, acknowledging "the way in which you handled a difficult and arduous location in South Africa under, to say the least, very difficult conditions."

In the first days of *2001*'s release in Europe, Kubrick arranged for Birkin to slip into the major theaters and photograph their screens while the film was playing, just to be absolutely sure that the projection systems were up to scratch. Significantly, the only time Birkin ever blotted his copybook was when he rescued an early draft of *2001*'s script, complete with the director's handwritten notes, from a wastebasket. Some years later, he gave it to the British Film Institute, whose in-house magazine *Sight & Sound* announced how proud the institute was to have received such a fascinating item into their collection. Kubrick called Birkin: "One day, I'm sure you will become a great director or a writer. And then you'll realize you don't want people seeing your first drafts."

OUTFITS FOR AUSTRALOPITHECINES

The troupe of man-ape performers came into Freeborn's den so that casts could be made of each man's face. Around these templates, he built individual urethane undermasks that fitted snugly, without suffocating the wearer. A foam overlay with more specific man-ape character details was placed on top of the urethane. Freeborn made sure to match the age and personality of each man-ape mask with the character and build of the human performer underneath. Only the performer's eyes were visible from behind the prosthetics. Soft glue held the foam in place around the eye sockets. Black makeup around the eyes helped blur the distinction between man and mask. Blue or green eyes required additional masking with brown contact lenses, made from thick glass, and fearsomely uncomfortable.

Kubrick confers with John Alcott, who took over as principal cinematographer after Unsworth's departure.

The lower part of a mask's protruding jaw could be pushed open by the performer's real jaw. Freeborn knew that a simple up-and-down hinge movement would look terribly unconvincing: "These characters were going to be eating, and they had to chew sideways, not just up and down." He solved this problem, only to encounter a new frustration. Once opened, the jaws would not close properly. He tried spring-loaded mechanisms, which proved too loud and intrusive, and settled instead for elastic, which lost some of its pulling power after a few cycles. The foam masking around the jaw tended to stretch, preventing the upper and lower parts of the skin and lips from matching up again. Magnets hidden in the prosthetic teeth eliminated most of these issues by introducing a new snag: the jaws became impossible to open because the magnets were too strong. The upper and lower magnets were adjusted to meet at an angle, reducing their connective pull to the point where human jaw strength could overcome it.

Freeborn, a sprightly man in his mid-50s with a mischievous energy and sense of fun, relished Kubrick's incessant demands for improvements: "What I liked about Stanley was that if it seemed you had accomplished something easily or quickly, he would always ask for more. So, he came back, after looking at our apes, and said, 'Right—I've been thinking about this. Now I want to see them snarl with their jaws and teeth closed.' I thought, 'How the hell am I going to do that?'" The solution was a system of toggles on the inner surface of each mask, activated by the performer's tongue. The upper lip could be raised, revealing the teeth. Once Kubrick was happy with the snarl, he imposed a messier challenge, a scene in which the man-apes eat fresh meat. Special-effects substitutes were ruled out. Only real meat could be used, he insisted. Freeborn knew that the fat and grease would destroy the rubber components inside the masks, which would become smelly and unwearable no matter how carefully they were cleaned. There was no alternative except to set up a production line, "mixing the foam rubber, pouring it into the molds, cooking it in the oven." He ran "three crews working eight-hour sessions, day and night" to satisfy the demand.

The bodysuits had to be made from something thin that wouldn't bulk out the performers' bodies. The *Dawn of Man* called for creatures on the brink of starvation, not yet capable of living off the fat of the land. Freeborn made a lightweight undergarment from fine wool, back-combed to ruffle its surface and hide any seams. Hair from different animals (horse, yak, and human) was woven through the fibers of the soft woolen fabric. Short, fine strands gave the impression of an inner pelt near the skin. Longer, coarser hairs added bulk. Professional wig-makers pronounced the task impossible. Freeborn and his assistants did it anyway. The undergarments fitted snugly without creasing; they were lightweight and did not hinder the performers' movements. Having determined that the man-apes needed to look hungry, there were certain areas around the shoulders and on the upper torso that did need to be bulked out with foam padding to create a realistically simian anatomy. The longer arm length was achieved with gauntlets, and by lengthening the hands and fingers. The performers' actual fingers came up to just past the middle set of knuckles. This was sufficient to enable grasping movements from within the costumed hands.

Kubrick's most peculiar request was that one of the man-ape suits, fashioned in the guise of a mother-ape, should feature functioning breasts capable of exuding real milk. He hoped that this would tempt a baby chimpanzee to suckle. The Chipperfield's circus company loaned a couple of chimps, Johnny and Timmy, whose ears were painlessly augmented with prosthetics to make them seem more like ancestral prehumans. Mary Chipperfield assured Freeborn that her youngest chimps were still at the milk-drinking stage of their lives, although she did warn him that they only knew how to drink from plastic cups. A tender sequence of mother feeding child was photographed with mixed and messy results. The suckling experiment was abandoned. Keith Denny (working at that time under his stage name, Simon Davis) acted the role of mother to one of the chimps: he recalls,"The funny thing was, we got so used to being apes, and wearing those costumes. For a good while afterwards, you felt lost without it. After all those incredibly hot, uncomfortable months, we missed them. Stanley knew us all, even with our head masks and costumes on."

Stanley also discovered Dan Richter's terrible secret, one that haunted the young mime artist every day as he went through the gates of MGM. He and his wife, Jill, were serious heroin addicts. In mid-1960s London it was possible to obtain heroin from officially sanctioned doctors. A certain Lady Frankau ran a clinic in Wimpole Street. The Richters were regular visitors to her consulting room, which looked like something out of Sherlock Holmes. Fashionable victims of addiction depended on her kind and well-meaning administrations. Professionally qualified in psychiatry, she had written in the sober pages of the *Lancet* medical journal that government-monitored access to drugs might "prevent addicts from returning to the black market, which could mean a return to the degradation and humiliation of buying from criminal dealers." By decade's end, the British authorities realized, with something of a shock, that Frankau and her colleagues ("society doctors," as they were known) had created a surge in the volume of heroin coming into the country.

Just because Richter's habit was known to the health authorities did not, he feared, make it a virtue on the MGM lot. Having confessed all to Kubrick, he expected to be sacked from *2001*. Instead, Kubrick expressed his usual curiosity. Why had Dan become a drug addict? What were the effects? What was the treatment regime, and so on. He made no simplistic moral judgments, and concluded that if Richter had not done anything illegal, he should stay on and continue with the *Dawn of Man*. Richter was overwhelmed with gratitude, and went back to work determined to conjure up something brilliant for his mentor.

Man-ape rehearsals called for arduous squatting and jumping, and only very rarely a fully erect bipedal stance. It was painful and demanding on human muscles that had long since evolved out of those postures. Richter also insisted on constant energy from his troupe: "It was essential for the audience to believe in them in the first few minutes. I thought the way to solve the problem was to give them the same kind of restlessness and perpetual movement that you find in real animals when they're awake. Compared to animals, humans walking down the street hardly move at all." While Richter taught his performers to act like animals, Kubrick searched for animals who could perform like actors. Victor Lyndon's production notes called for "a leopard or lioness to do the following tricks: prowl, snarl, leap and, if possible, fight with a man-ape. Grazing animals to mix with our man-apes in the field. Four warthogs to be trained."

Tapirs were eventually awarded the grazing contract. Kubrick did not seem unduly concerned about this strange version of prehistory, where African leopards were supposed to coexist with creatures from South America. Terry Duggan, an expert animal trainer, joined Richter's department, and had the distinction of playing the first of *2001*'s eight murder victims. Duggan brought with him a handsome young leopard whose main task was to leap off a promontory and "kill" him as prey. Richter was more worried about Duggan's body shape than his safety: "That scene had to be kept very short in the final cut. It wasn't because of any danger from the leopard. He was happy to roll around chewing on Terry all afternoon, just play fighting. He knew he wasn't supposed to chew too hard. Our problem was that Terry had a stocky build, and he didn't look quite right in his man-ape costume."

Kubrick's *Notes on Special Effects*, delivered as part of his 1969 Academy Award submission, explain that Duggan and the leopard were supposed to be entirely alone on stage during the shoot, just in case the playful predator made a move for one of the other actors. Background performers were to be added later, after the hand-drawn matte technique had been applied to Duggan and the leaping leopard. Richter's recollection is that the background boys simply had to take their chances with the leopard, whose other, more sedate job was to sit next to a horse carcass, painted up as a zebra, as if he had killed it. By a stroke of luck, when he stared directly towards the front projector beam, the retinal cells at the back of his eyes demonstrated the same kind of reflectivity as the glass beads in the screen behind him. Literally, he had "cat's eyes." He looked impressive looming in the twilight over his victim, with his eyes seemingly ablaze. In truth, he was restless because the dead horse was past its prime.

Another significant animal shot came about by accident, after a nervy tapir ran off the edge of the stage during a camera test session and was killed. The animal's misfortune was an opportunity for Kubrick, who had the body frozen. Eventually it was thawed out, propped up on stage again and allowed to slump, as if killed by something more aggressive than mere accident.

FRONT PROJECTION

Audiences never knew at the time that the vast landscapes, distant horizons, and blazing skies of *2001*'s opening scenes were realized deep within the confines of a studio. In the process of large-scale "front projection" pioneered for the *Dawn of Man*, the man-ape performers were photographed in front of a huge screen, 40 feet high and 90 feet wide, consisting of millions of microscopic glass beads, which absorbed light, bent it, and then hurled it back out again along exactly the same path as it first arrived, with negligible loss of brightness. Kubrick's alert technical researchers had come across a suitable material, Scotchlite,manufactured by the 3M company for use on reflective road signs and safety vests. For initial experiments, several rolls were pasted onto the screen in parallel 40-foot lengths. Slight variations in manufacturing tolerance between one batch and the next produced an uneven, stripy effect, much to Kubrick's dismay. According to man-ape performer Simon Davis, "Stanley came in really early one morning with a flask and a box of sandwiches, and he just sat looking at that screen without saying a word, trying to figure out a solution. Next thing we knew, the whole lot—all the reflective material—was torn down." Then it was cut into random, jagged shapes and glued back onto the screen as an intermingled patchwork to achieve a more consistent blend.

A transparency of an appropriate backdrop was projected onto this glassy surface, just as with a home slide projector, except that *2001*'s front-projection machine bore the same relation to a domestic system as a flamethrower to a candle. Kubrick and Tom Howard, director of the MGM's in-house special-effects department at Borehamwood, designed a projector to take the high-definition ten-by-eight-inch Ektachrome transparencies from Namibia. Howard had worked on *The Thief of Bagdad* (1940) and dozens of other complex projects, including several of George Pal's fantasy and science-fiction pictures. He won his first Oscar for conjuring the sprightly ghost in *Blithe Spirit* (David Lean's 1945 adaptation of the Noël Coward stage play) and a second for Pal's *Tom Thumb* in 1958.

Only by beaming transparencies more or less the size of the page you are reading now could Kubrick hope to avoid grain and blur. Illumination was derived from a powerful carbon arc lamp similar to the kind found in an antiaircraft searchlight. The projector's lamp threw out an intense blast of heat as well as light. Cooling systems protected the projector's lenses from cracking. Reserve copies of favored transparencies had to be on standby before they could be risked in the projector itself, in case their emulsion layers melted or the glass mountings broke. Once the machine was powered up, the slightest change in ambient temperature could create havoc. On one occasion the door to the shooting studio was opened by mistake, and a blast of cool morning air swept past the hot machinery. A glass plate immediately shattered, just as an expensive crystal wine glass washed in hot water will splinter if unwisely rinsed under a cold faucet.

Just as fragile was the slanted mirror in front of the Mitchell 65 mm camera lens, which bounced the projector beam so that it fired along exactly the same axis as the camera lens was pointing. This mirror was half-silvered, so that the camera could see through it. From the camera's point of view, the *Dawn of Man* performers masked their own shadows on the reflective screen—while, around the man-apes, the Namibian landscape images, reflected by the screen, remained visible to the camera. The dark, hairy costumes were not reflective. Unless one happened to look exactly along the camera's axis, there was no sign of the front-projected Namibian landscape. When viewed obliquely, the screen looked like a blank gray wall. As a final touch, the foreground lighting on the set was arranged to match the original sun angle and daylighting conditions in the projected background plates.[5]

Geoffrey Unsworth had completed his work on the production by the time these sequences were ready for filming. He had shot solidly from Christmas 1965 through July 1966, and was now required by other productions. Unsworth's assistant cameraman, John Alcott, stayed to oversee the *Dawn of Man* photography. This was the beginning of a long working relationship between Alcott and Kubrick. Ernie Archer built the physical sets of rocks, muddy pools, and caves on a 90-foot-diameter rotating platform, so that different foreground scenery could be positioned in front of the reflective screen without having to move the delicate yet massively heavy front projection rig between setups. Alcott and Kubrick decided to build a ceiling array of hundreds of individual lamps with semitranslucent diffusers, in imitation of a wide, white sky. Every time a fresh section of Archer's set was rotated into position in front of the camera, a different configuration of high ground reached upward, too close to the lights, threatening the scenery at those points with overexposure. The only solution was to wire each lamp onto an individual switch controller so that the entire array could be tuned to suit the scenery beneath. Eight miles of electrical cable were used to rig the connections. Another memorable scene in *2001*, depicting astronauts walking on the lunar surface with their base in the background, was also achieved with front projection.

5 *American Cinematographer*, October 1969

▹ 301–303 The jump cut from ancient bone weapon to futuristic space machine is one of *2001*'s most celebrated moments. Violence is an underlying theme in *2001*. In this seemingly languid film, at least eight deliberate killings occur.

PART IV

THE LEAP OF IMAGINATION

An uninterrupted month of principal photography for the *Dawn of Man* got under way in August 1967. Richter realized something odd. He had "spoken with Stanley almost every day for a year, and talked in detail about the minutest parts of the picture. On reflection, I realized we had rarely talked about the larger themes of the plot and the story." For instance, Kubrick had not shown him any of the shots from the lunar excavation, photographed many months ago, over the Christmas of 1965, where Floyd reverently touches the monolith with his gloved hand. Kubrick simply asked Richter and the other man-apes to act as if entranced by the dark alien slab appearing in their midst. Only later did he explain the connection between the two scenes, set millions of years apart. Richter wishes that Kubrick was still around, "so that I could ask him how his mind was working."

The mime artist turned man-ape choreographer played each moment according to his instincts: "At the outset, the famous throwing of the bone into the air so that it becomes a spaceship was not planned. We all thought that smashing the skull on the ground was the important moment. I'm supposed to be shuffling along, just going after roots and whatnot, and suddenly it occurs to me to pick up a bone. I decided I was going to play it slow, take my time. I'm in a big frame, a tight shot. Too much movement would look bad on a Cinerama screen. I decided to cock my head slightly—a very small move. That was enough to convey that an idea comes into my head. Then I made a small movement forward, from deep in the center of my body. And it worked. You had a sense of moving *forward* into something—and then, the wonder of it."

Kubrick was thrilled. All he wanted now was an upward shot of Richter's snarling, mask-clad head and furry torso, making him appear monumental and fearsome against the sky. The reflective backdrop for the front projection stage only worked for horizontal framing. This next shot would have to be accomplished against a real sky, almost directly overhead.

Arthur Clarke visited Borehamwood on the first day of September 1967. On a back area of the lot, "Dan was on a platform, wearing his ape suit and banging away with his bone at the skeleton. It may have been the remnants of that poor horse who played the dead zebra supposedly 'killed' by our tame leopard, or maybe a tapir. Anyway, the camera was shooting up. If it had pointed a little bit lower, it would have shown London buses in the background, which would rather have spoilt the illusion. After this was shot, Stanley was walking back to his office, and he had a broomstick, and he was throwing it up in the air.

I was quite worried it might come down on him. And I think that's when he got the idea of this transition, which, of course, is what happened. The bone goes up and turns into what is supposed to be an orbiting bomb, a weapon in space."

Man-ape Simon Davis thought that the two genuine apes working among the gang of human impostors may have been an inspiration: "Once, when they were relighting the front projection area, it was still dressed and ready for a shoot, and a baby chimp started playing with a pile of small bones. Chimps flail their arms sometimes when they're playing. She picked up a bone and threw it in the air. Stanley watched her with great interest, but you could never tell what might be going through his mind."

Today we know the director was laying the groundwork for the most famous jump cut in cinema history. Kubrick's friend, second unit cameraman Bob Gaffney, watched the final photography of the flying bone. As he recounted to Kubrick biographer Vincent LoBrutto, "They threw it to go end over end, so you'd follow it up and follow it down. The camera operator missed it three or four times. Stanley got behind the camera and did it the first time, and that's the shot that's in the picture."[6]

At the 1969 Oscar ceremonies, 20th Century Fox's *Planet of the Apes* won an award for its gorilla masks. This was an unexpected shock. Although John Chambers's costumes for *Planet* were fine in that they allowed the personalities and mannerisms of the well-known actors underneath to shine out, they could not be compared with Freeborn's more subtle and realistic accomplishments. According to Richter, "There was a lot of paranoia while we were preparing the *Dawn of Man*. We didn't know for sure, but we thought we were being watched by the *Planet of the Apes* people. Parts of our costumes did go missing, and Stanley went ballistic. Once a helicopter flew over us while we were in the open, and we all dived for cover." The Academy's award to Chambers seemed a genuine injustice. After the ceremony, Arthur Clarke went round muttering his dissatisfaction as loudly as he could: "What did they think we used? Real apes?"

6 LoBrutto, *Kubrick*

▹ 306/307 Test photograph of the first spacecraft seen in *2001*, supposedly an orbiting American bomb platform. Shows the angle and lighting actually used in the film.

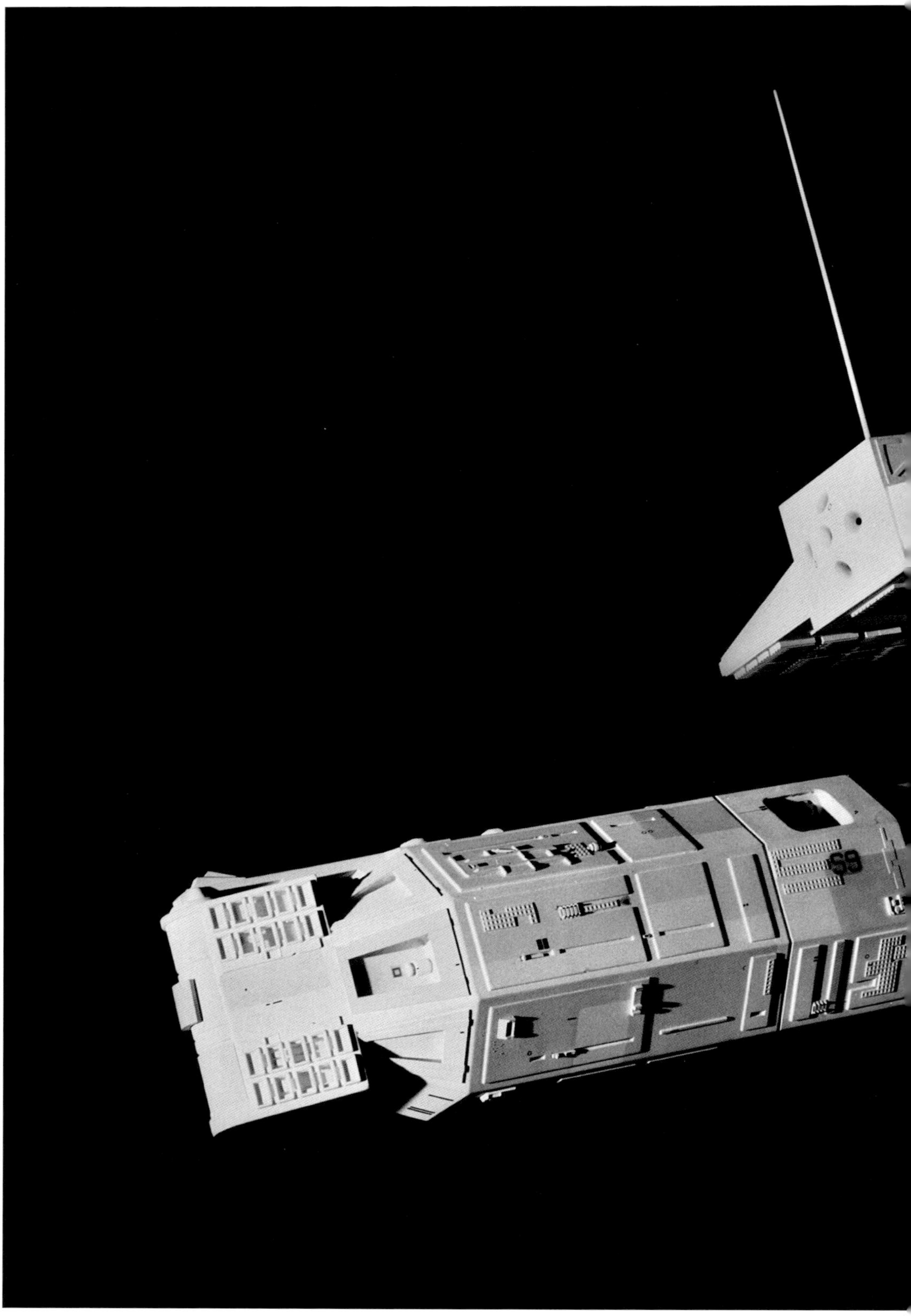

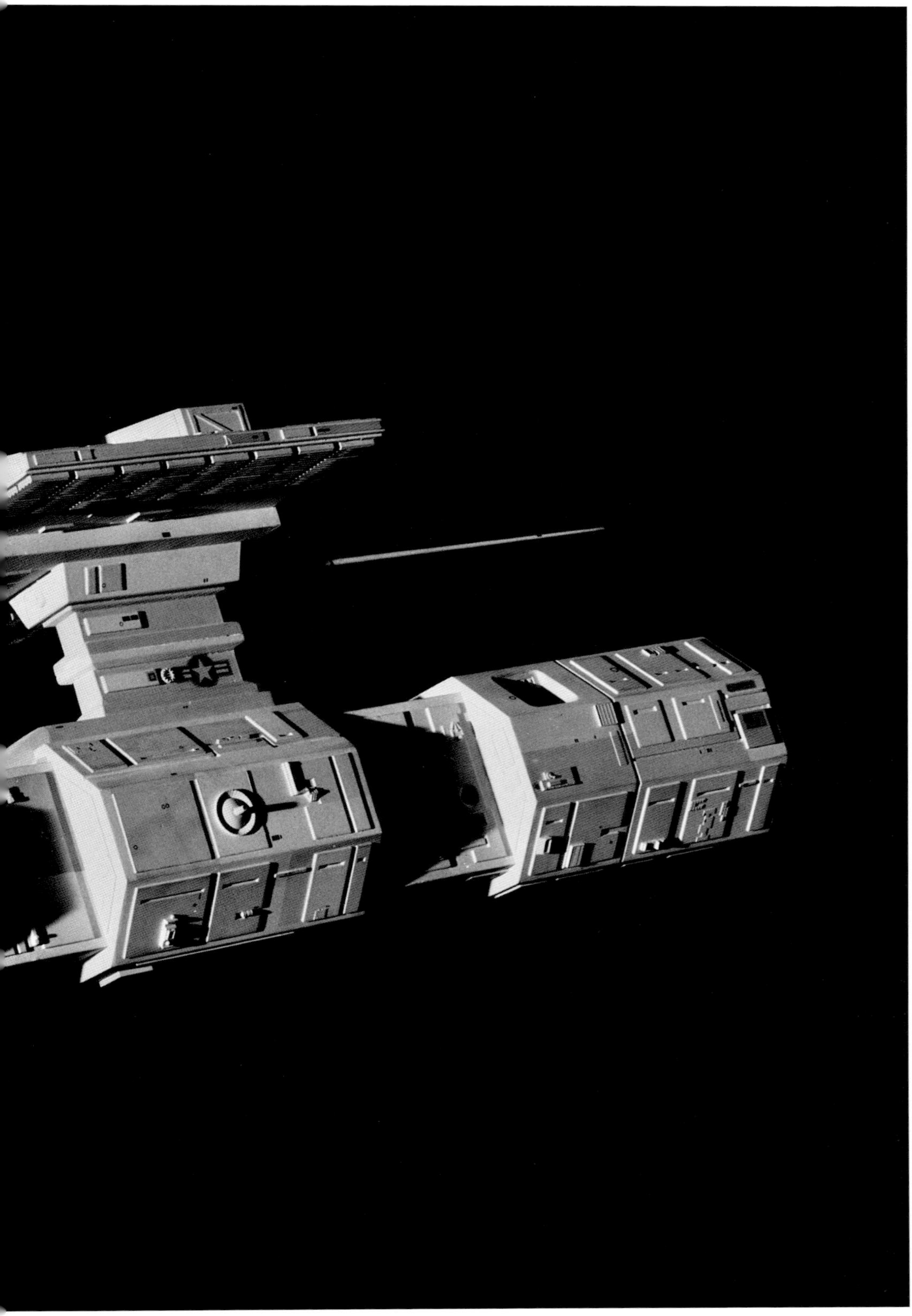

V

"I am putting myself to the fullest possible use, which is all, I think, that any conscious entity can ever hope to do."

STANLEY ON SET

WORKING WITH ACTORS

Actors fell into two groups: those who could figure things out on their own, and those who needed to be told exactly what to do, and were alarmed when no such instructions came. Kubrick's attitude to his performers was that of a film director, not a theater manager. He expected actors to contribute their acting skills, because that was their job, while his was to shoot the film. According to Christiane, "The only time Stanley was impatient was if actors didn't know their lines. He hated, on screen, to see them fishing to remember their lines. At the same time, if they were prepared, and then made changes, or invented things that they thought would be interesting, he was very responsive, because now they were collaborating, coming up with new ideas." Some performers thought Kubrick uninterested in them, or unwilling to lead them into giving their best. After a particularly frustrating failure to connect with one actor, Kubrick told Bruce Logan, "how great it would be if he could make films without having to use people. I think he was 90 percent serious."

The best performers—those whom the director most enjoyed working with—felt themselves free to explore a scene, try things out, generate intriguing diversions, and run on instinct (Peter Sellers in *Strangelove*, for instance, routinely throwing away chunks of scripted dialogue and inventing superb comedy on the spot, while Kubrick chewed on a handkerchief to stop his laughter from ruining the take). Dullea found Kubrick "immensely supportive. I loved working with him. People say he wasn't an actor's director. That doesn't make sense. When actors just don't get it, I suppose that's when conflict arises, but I believe that, as a performer, you had an obligation to try and understand what he wanted, and then deliver it."

Lockwood was completely at ease on a set where, despite many months of preplanning, the best moments often were made up on the spot: "Stanley was simply much more intelligent than other directors, and in a nonlinear way. You found that anything could happen at almost any time. Despite all the careful preparations, he designed *2001* with an air of flexibility, and that's what made the picture brilliant. Directing is all about management of human relations, logistics, details, and so on. On top of all that, Stanley still found room for a kind of danger—even a kind of bravery or recklessness. He was always trying things where there was a high risk of failure. He wasn't this obstinate solitary genius of popular imagination. He needed people to bounce off, and he would often turn around and ask if he was doing the right thing." It was Lockwood who suggested that the best way for HAL to learn of the astronauts' plans to disconnect him was to lip-read their conversation through a pod window.

Nothing was more exciting for the younger actors on *2001* than to come up with an idea, then have Kubrick use it. According to Richter, Kubrick "was great to be around. He loved to look at every possibility, to try things countless different ways. You'd have one idea, and he'd bounce off you and come up with a hundred more. The older movie professionals found his approach difficult, because they were fixed in their ways. They thought they knew how certain things were supposed to be done. The only time I ever saw him get angry was with people whose minds were closed. That's another reason why young people did the lion's share of the work on *2001*."

Dullea thought of Kubrick as "a benevolent con man in the sense that we ended up doing exactly what he wanted, but he made us feel as if we were discovering those things ourselves." This benevolence was not so obvious to Heather Downham, who played the flight attendant on board the *Orion* space plane. When she first came to Borehamwood on a casting call, she encountered "about 250 people waiting there, all in their black leotards and tights. I was suffering from toothache, so I wasn't in the best of moods. When my turn came, Stanley wanted me to walk as if in a zero-gravity spaceship. I didn't really know what he was driving at, but I gave it a go. Then he asked me to do it again, and I said, 'No, I've

On the giant Shepperton stage, Kubrick lines up a shot of the monolith as the astronauts prepare to approach it for a closer look.

done it once, that's all you're getting.' I went home, not expecting to hear from him ever again. Next day my agent rang and told me, 'Kubrick says he absolutely has to have you!' So, he didn't like it if anybody showed they were frightened of him, and you had to push back as far as you could, without being rude to the director, of course."

Downham never felt as close to her director as she would have liked: "I think Stanley's method of working was to make everybody feel as if you were never getting it right, because then you would pull out all the stops to try and find what he was looking for. This was his way of getting the best performances out of everybody, and to see if they had any creative ideas that maybe he hadn't thought of first. Everything he did was done towards improving the picture and getting the best creativity out of us. It's just that, in my opinion, this didn't always make for a very comfortable working life."

Much of Downham's discomfort arose from Kubrick's concerns for security. He hated the idea of *2001*'s story details being leaked to the press. As a consequence only his most important players were told, for instance, about the monolith, or the hidden agenda behind *Discovery*'s mission. Downham's function was to be an unknowing stewardess on a shuttle, and nothing more. Consequently, she only saw those few pages of the script that were relevant to her part. She recalls, "I had no idea what I was meant to be doing, and nobody was going to give me any clue. I was the prisoner of Stanley's imagination." At the same time as she fretted about this, Downham knew that she was, at least, taking part in a worthwhile project: "It wasn't like it would be nowadays, faked up with computer graphics. The sets actually were vast, and you just stood there and thought, 'Good heavens! This is totally amazing!' I think everybody realized they were working on something big, and I think Stanley by this time was working on another plane of existence altogether. He was living in his head and his imagination, and was totally obsessed by this film he was making."

Canadian actor Douglas Rain, narrator of the *Universe* documentary that had caught Kubrick's eye in 1964, was hired for a fortnight to record HAL's lines, and completed his entire workload over a single long weekend. He never got to see where his lines fitted into the greater scheme until he saw the film on its release. As it turned out, his voice was perfect for the part. Kubrick recorded some experimental HAL dialogue using the voice of Martin Balsam (one of the jurors in *Twelve Angry Men*). He seemed too emotional. A well-spoken British actor, Nigel Davenport, was also tested. On set, Dullea and Lockwood usually responded to the broad Cockney accent of Kubrick's assistant director, Derek Cracknell, shouting HAL's lines from somewhere off camera.

It was the actors in smaller, briefer roles who found *2001* an awe-inspiring yet ultimately frustrating experience. Everywhere were signs and wonders, fabulous machines and huge, exotic props, but the man at the very heart of the project simply refused to let them in on what it was all about. The lesser players were only given brief fragments of the script. Ed Bishop played the captain of the *Aries* lunar ship: "I was the kind of actor who liked to be told what we're doing, and I think Kubrick locked in—probably early in his career, and whether consciously or not I don't know—to the supreme vulnerability of actors. From my point of view, he played his cards so close to his chest, he never revealed himself. You never knew where you were going." Bishop worried about the number of takes Kubrick put him through: "We're not talking Greek tragedy here. I was the pilot who wanted to know why Floyd was going to Clavius. He didn't want to tell me, and that was the scene. You could have a little fun with that. But the extent to which Stanley ground the sausage was, I thought, a little excessive."

Christiane always was impatient with stories about her husband's supposedly endless numbers of takes: "There's a strange pride in so many films. 'Oh, we managed to get that shot in one take.' What's the big deal about that? You've spent months and months arranging a whole operation at vast cost, with lots of technicians, complicated locations, and fabulous sets, and then suddenly, when it comes to the point of what's actually going

Kubrick and his "lunar scientists" survey the Tycho excavation pit at Shepperton Studios on the morning of December 29, 1965, the first day of shooting.

to go on screen, you hurry up? Surely it should be the other way around? Stanley kept the production aspect as economical as possible—small offices, the smallest possible crew—so that he could spend all the time in the world on set with the actors."

Perfectionism is another quality associated with Kubrick. According to Hamshere, there was a well-worn joke doing the rounds at Borehamwood by late 1967: "In six days, God created the heavens and the Earth. On the seventh day, Stanley sent everything back for modifications." A photo of him was pinned on the wall of the art department, with a scribbled caption: "Okay, guys, what do we do on day eight?" After the Creation of any Kubrickean universe, there was always a "day eight." Second assistant director Richard Jenkins wasn't sure if he could stand another minute of stewardess Edwina Carroll walking the treadmill for the *Aries* galley scene. "We shot it time after time for a week, and every next morning Stanley would view the rushes, which always looked fantastic, except there'd always be something he didn't like that none of the rest of us even noticed. At last the day came when the scene was absolutely flawless. And Stanley said, 'That's it! That's great! We'll shoot it this afternoon.' It just went on and on." Harry Lange's wife, Daisy, and several other production-unit wives and girlfriends spent many days creating information panels and locker numbers from Letraset to embellish obscure pieces of the spacecraft sets. On camera, the tiny lettering would register as little more than a smudge, but Kubrick wanted realism at the smallest scale, just in case he happened to decide on a close-up.

Lovejoy's abiding memory of Kubrick was "not behind a camera. I see him in the editing room. You'd find him sitting in at the Steenbeck, running a piece of film backwards and forwards, backwards and forwards, looking for the quarter-second that, in his opinion, would make the difference. That would be Stanley. There would be a smile at the end—certainly not while he was concentrating, but definitely when he'd found what he was looking for."

When Downham saw the completed film after release, some of her experiences on set began to make more sense to her: "The performances that Stanley got from us probably mirrored the physical look of the film. Space is an icy cold concept, and we were supposed to be cold and precise people as part of that scenery. When I thought about it afterwards, that was probably what he was aiming at."

Bishop also was stunned by the power of Kubrick's vision, even while he remained puzzled as to its broader aims: "The set for the Moon-bound ship was absolutely breathtaking. The levels of detail, the layer upon layer of attention that had been paid to everything, and all brought together, all coalesced, by one mind—it was like walking into a cathedral, where you gaze up at the ceiling, and you cannot help being amazed. I've never seen anything like it, before or since. But what it all meant, I never found out until I saw the movie. And even then, I still wasn't sure."

Dullea trusted Kubrick, and took physical risks for *2001* that he might not have considered if working for a less obviously fascinating director.

USA

In return for putting up with the long hours, the relentless workload, the countless takes, and Kubrick's incessant demands for improvements, those who could take the pace were in a privileged position, as Trumbull never forgot: "It's one of the things I thank Stanley for so much, because I know he took the brunt of the pressure. He must have had MGM breathing down his throat and making his life miserable over how much it was costing, how long it was taking. He protected us from all that." Conjuring the vastness of the universe inside the confines of brick-lined studios, Kubrick might have felt some affinity with Shakespeare's clever and restless prince Hamlet: "I could be bounded in a nutshell, and count myself a king of infinite space, were it not that I have bad dreams." There is nothing to suggest that Kubrick lost too much sleep at night, but certainly the shores of his domain were threatened, from time to time, by men in suits wondering where all their money had gone—and if they would ever get it back.

Ed Bishop was not alone in his confusion. When, at last, *2001: A Space Odyssey* was unveiled at a private screening at the end of March 1968, MGM executives were unsure if they had a masterpiece on their hands, or a costly disaster. Rock Hudson, a major star in those days, attended one of the previews, and rose from his seat in disgust as the lights came up. "Will somebody tell me what the hell *that* was all about?" he said.

Keir Dullea seated at an astrownomy unit inside the centrifuge: one of many complex pieces of set dressing that are barely glimpsed in the final cut of the film.

Edwina Carroll performs her famous treadmill routine inside the rotating *Aries* galley set.

▹ 320/321 Shooting the final scenes of *2001* in the faux-luxurious bedroom. The underfloor lighting made the room uncomfortably hot. Critics and audiences alike argue about the meaning of this room. Is it a comfortable cage constructed by the aliens, and based on their observations of Earth, or does the décor spring from Bowman's hallucinatory ideas of what an expensive hotel room should look like?

▹ 322–327 A *2001*-themed children's menu for Howard Johnson's hotel company: just one product of the production's close working ties with corporate America.

CINERAMA

HOWARD Johnson's
CHILDREN'S MENU
FEATURING
MGM PRESENTS A FILM BY STANLEY KUBRICK
2001
A SPACE ODYSSEY
DIRECTED AND PRODUCED BY STANLEY KUBRICK
SCREEN PLAY BY STANLEY KUBRICK AND ARTHUR C. CLARKE
in CINERAMA Super Panavision and Metrocolor
"A MYSTERIOUS ACCIDENT SENDS HIM ADRIFT IN THE VASTNESS OF OUTER SPACE!" ONE OF THE SPINE-TINGLING EPISODES IN THIS DRAMATIC FILM OF ADVENTURE IN SPACE.
Preview
EDITION
PRESENTED FOR YOUR ENJOYMENT BY HOWARD JOHNSON'S
HOST OF THE HIGHWAYS • COAST-TO-COAST.

©1968 AMUSE-A-MENU COMPANY, 456 LITTLE BUILDING, BOSTON, MASSACHUSETTS 02116 AND HOWARD JOHNSON'S. TEXT AND DRAWINGS APPROVED BY MGM AND STANLEY KUBRICK PRODUCTIONS, BASED ON THE CINERAMA® PRODUCTION IN SUPER PANAVISION® AND METROCOLOR.

TUNING IN ON THE SPACEMAN'S AUTOMATIC BEEPER, THE RESCUE POD SPEEDS DIRECTLY TO HIM. MECHANICAL CLAWS REACH OUT AND FIRMLY-BUT GENTLY-GRASP HIM...
BUT WILL IT GET HIM BACK SAFELY TO THE DISCOVERY IN TIME?
DEBBIE AND ROBIN WATCH GOGGLE-EYED AS THE AMAZING MOVIE ROLLS ON. THE REALISM OF THE SCENES OF LIFE ABOARD THE SPACE-SHIP ARE TRULY ASTOUNDING.
LOOK AT THAT STEWARDESS! SHE SEEMS TO BE ACTUALLY WALKING UP-SIDE DOWN!
ISN'T IT AMAZING?
THE "ARTIFICIAL GRAVITY" CAUSED BY THE GIANT DRUM'S SLOW ROTATION GIVES THE DISCOVERY'S CREW A FEELING OF NORMAL WEIGHT. THIS PREVENTS THEIR MUSCLES FROM BECOMING SOFT AND FLABBY DURING THE LONG VOYAGE. THE ENTIRE MOVIE OF THIS SPACE ODYSSEY IS CRAMMED WITH THE MOST REMARKABLE SCENES EVER CREATED. SPACE ENGINEERS AND SCIENTISTS PROVIDED THE MOST EXACTING AND AUTHENTIC DETAILS EVER FILMED.

THIS IS ONE OF THE CREW RUNNING AROUND THE CENTRIFUGE FOR EXERCISE. BUT WHAT ARE THOSE THINGS THAT LOOK LIKE MUMMIES?
THOSE ARE SCIENTISTS IN A STATE OF ARTIFICIAL SLEEP. THEIR HEART-BEAT AND BREATHING IS REDUCED TO NEARLY ZERO. THEY'LL BE AWAKENED WHEN THEY ARE NEEDED.
NOW THE DISCOVERY HAS PASSED SAFELY THROUGH THE ASTEROID BELT AND IS APPROACHING THE GIANT PLANET JUPITER...483.4 MILLION MILES FROM OUR SUN. HAS ITS STRANGE RED SPOT SOMETHING TO DO WITH THE MYSTERIOUS SIGNALS RECEIVED ON THE MOON?
JUPITER AS SEEN FROM ONE OF ITS 12 MOONS ABOUT 115,000 MILES AWAY.
WOW! WHAT A FINISH! I'D NEVER HAVE GUESSED THE WAY THIS MYSTERY IS SOLVED!
NOBODY WOULD. THAT'S WHY EVERYONE PROMISED NOT TO TELL THE ENDING...IT'S TOO SURPRISING!
WELL, HOW DID YOU LIKE "2001, A SPACE ODYSSEY"?
IT'S GREAT! I'VE NEVER SEEN ANYTHING LIKE IT. IT'S REALLY OUT OF THIS WORLD!
WAIT TILL WE TELL OUR FRIENDS ABOUT THIS UNBELIEVABLE MOVIE PREMIERE.
I CAN HARDLY WAIT FOR THE YEAR 2001 SO I CAN BE A SPACE STEWARDESS!
I'M GOING TO BE A SPACE PILOT.

HOWARD JOHNSON'S
EARTHLIGHT ROOM
HERE'S THE LOUNGE WHERE PASSENGERS WAIT FOR THE SHUTTLE NAMED ARIES THAT WILL TAKE THEM TO THE MOON!
LOOK! THEY'VE GOT A HOWARD JOHNSON'S EARTH-LIGHT ROOM UP THERE.
A BREATHTAKING VIEW OF EARTH AND THE STATION! EVERYTHING'S SO REAL!
THERE IT IS—THE LUNAR COLONY! THE ARIES IS ABOUT TO LAND. ITS RETROROCKETS SET IT DOWN AS GENTLY AS A FEATHER! THE LUNAR COLONY IS INSIDE THE 150-MILE-WIDE CRATER, CALLED CLAVIUS. THE RESEARCH STATION IS IN A SMALL CITY FAR UNDERGROUND.
THE MOONBUS TAKES PASSENGERS AND CARGO TO OTHER STATIONS ON THE MOON.
THE STARS AND THE MILKY WAY ARE VERY BRIGHT BECAUSE THERE'S NO ATMOSPHERE IN SPACE TO DIM THEM.

OOH! HERE'S THE PART WHERE THE MOON SCIENTISTS DISCOVER THAT THERE ARE OTHER INTELLIGENT BEINGS SOMEWHERE OUT IN SPACE!
AND THEY'RE GOING OUT IN THE ATOM-POWERED SPACESHIP, DISCOVERY TO SEARCH FOR THEM!
THE DISCOVERY ZOOMS FROM LUNAR COLONY TOWARD JUPITER—THE SOURCE OF THE MYSTERIOUS SIGNALS!
ONE OF THE DISCOVERY'S CREW CRAWLS OUTSIDE TO CHECK A FAULTY COMMUNICATIONS ANTENNA. THE SPACESHIP IS SPEEDING THROUGH SPACE AT A HUNDRED THOUSAND MILES PER HOUR...
JUST AS THE REPAIRMAN IS ABOUT TO RE-ENTER THE SPACESHIP HE SLIPS AND FLOATS AWAY!
ON BOARD, ALARMS RING OUT AND ONE OF THE RESCUE PODS IS QUICKLY LAUNCHED.
BY NOW THE VICTIM HAS DRIFTED FAR FROM THE SPACESHIP INTO THE COLD BLACKNESS.

William Sylvester takes a break from shooting the lunar conference, and shares smoking time with Kubrick.

▷ Kubrick took every opportunity to make a personal photographic record of the production. Here he uses a Nikon Photomic 35 mm camera. He also favored the latest Polaroid instant films, and a Widelux panoramic camera.

AVISION

SUPER PANAVISION

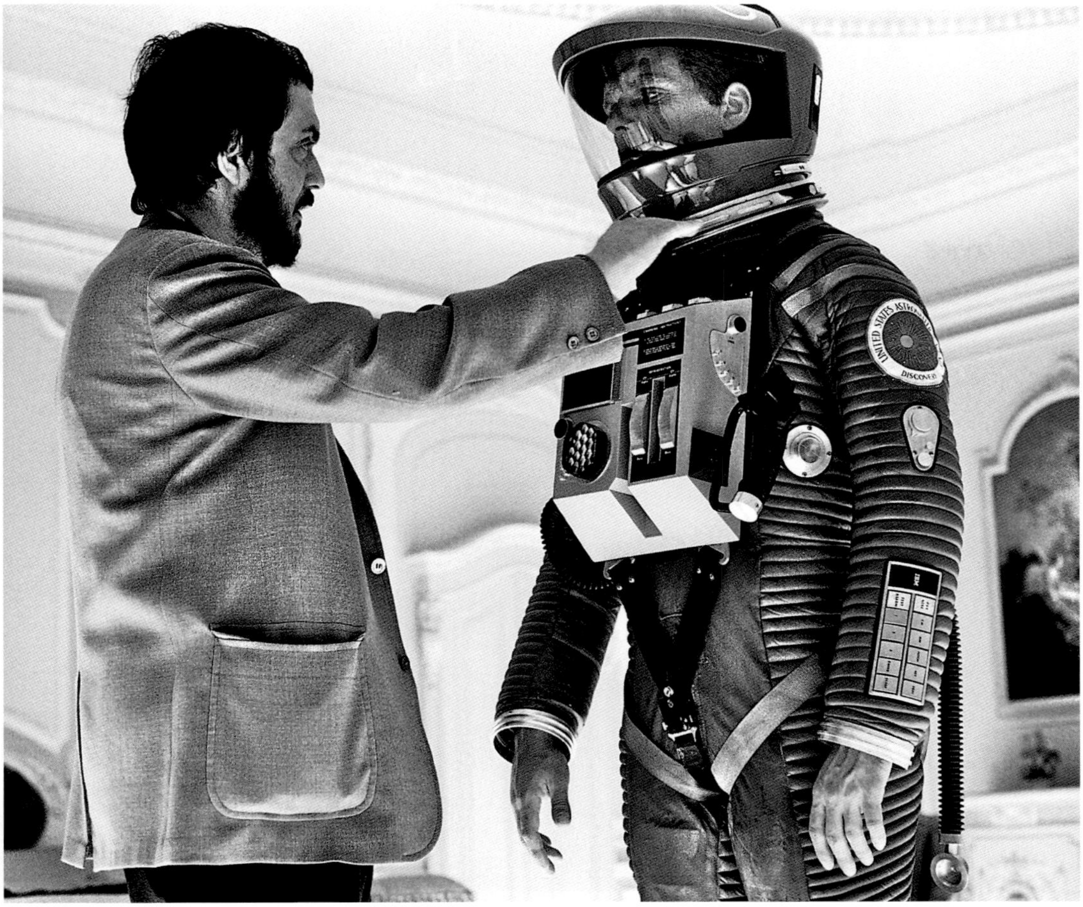

Kubrick with one of his many "occasional" smokes, all too often acquired from nearby colleagues. "You got a cigarette?" was a frequent starter to a conversation.

△ Actors who trusted Kubrick's judgment tended to get along with him very well. Dullea's relationship with him was excellent.

Bishop, as captain of the *Aries*, asks Floyd about the rumors of secrecy. Exerting his director's prerogative, Kubrick decided that this dialogue added nothing of consequence to Floyd's earlier scenes on the space station, and overlaid the Strauss music track instead.

▹ Bishops sucks on space food in the *Aries* flight deck. Pedants notice that Floyd's similarly packaged food slips back down the straw, which it would not do under weightless conditions. Like all movies ever made, *2001* yields up several insignificant "errors" if one chooses to search for them.

△ Margaret Tyzack and Leonard Rossiter chat with Kubrick on the space station. Whenever possible, Kubrick preferred to assume that his actors would know what to do, based on the contingencies of the script. Self-motivated performers, such as Rossiter, or Malcolm McDowell (*A Clockwork Orange*) and Peter Sellers (*Dr. Strangelove*), particularly thrilled him.

In a scene ultimately deleted from the final cut, Dullea retrieves a fresh AE35 control unit from the storage corridor and closes the locker door when the job is done. These are Widelux frames shot by Kubrick.

Dullea poses in the equipment storage corridor to one side of *Discovery*'s pod bay.

△▷ The convincing hardware, realistic space suits, and functioning control switches helped Lockwood and Dullea to believe in their roles. Here, Kubrick and Lockwood rehearse a scene in the space-pod cockpit. Sections of the wall have been removed to enable camera access.

VI

"I don't suppose you have any idea
what the damned thing is?"

THEY HATED IT, THEY LOVED IT

Space artist Robert McCall created this impression of an *Orion* space plane departing from the giant orbiting station. This was the most frequently used poster image.

On March 7, 1968, Kubrick and his family set out across the Atlantic aboard the ocean liner *Queen Elizabeth*. A separate cabin was equipped with an editing desk so that he could work on the film while at sea. March 31 was the deadline for the first of several private preview screenings at Loew's Capitol Theater, 1645 Broadway, one of MGM's favored venues for big releases. Other screenings were to be held in Washington and Los Angeles. The first couple of days in New York were critical, for here, studio executives and influential newspaper critics would see the completed film for the first time. No one knew at the time that *2001* was to be the last big show for the Capitol. Its parent company was about to disintegrate.

Christiane Kubrick never forgot the intense terror of that first night: "All the wives arrived in uniforms of mink stoles. Everyone was old, and truly not that thrilled to go to the cinema." As Kubrick checked the projection and focus, he was "flitting about, crazy with nerves." A junior secretary in the front row chattered throughout the opening scenes.

"Stanley was crazy with irritation. The audience seemed bored from the beginning. Sitting there as the person who's *made* this film, you soak up these failure moments. 'People aren't going for it. There are people walking out.' Halfway through, Stanley ran back to the projection booth. I could see he was very nervous and my heart sank. There was such an atmosphere of ill will in the room. For these people, science fiction was next to pornography. They thought it was an embarrassing subject. We slogged on until the intermission, and then, in the toilet, I heard someone say, 'I didn't know there was no air on the Moon,' and other really sad stuff. I remember thinking, 'This is the wrong audience. They're all over 50.' I felt nauseous with tension. The film had a really flat, bad reaction from these people. Stanley was silent. He almost lost the use of his voice, he was so upset."

Later that night, an MGM delegation arrived at the hotel where the Kubricks were staying. Christiane remembers them as "all glum, and I saw Stanley being killed by these people. They were so dismissive." Terry Southern was a much-needed ally, "one of the few people attending that night who kept the faith. He kept whispering at us, 'Would you talk to these people normally? No, you wouldn't, would you? They don't speak the same language. They don't read science fiction. They don't even keep up with the space program. They know nothing. They're not the people who are going to go and see this movie.' Terry kept reassuring us that everything would be okay. I really appreciated that."

A few days later, *Variety* quizzed Kubrick, wondering why MGM's reaction had been so negative. Were the studio chiefs, perhaps, taken by surprise by what they saw? Kubrick insisted this was untrue. "Bob O'Brien came over to London periodically to look at footage, and each time he went back to New York and argued for no budgetary compromise in the result. I have to give him tremendous credit. He never transferred on to me the pressure he must have felt." Choosing his words carefully, what he'd failed to stress was that the relatively short showreels presented to MGM in order to reassure them that something wonderful was shaping up didn't necessarily convey the abstract nature of the final film. Ivor Powell, who worked under Caras on the publicity and tie-in campaigns, often found Kubrick on the phone to MGM in America. "He'd tell them how wonderful everything was, and then he'd get off the phone and say to Victor Lyndon, 'Send them three minutes of centrifuge footage.' He fed them snippets of the film, piecemeal, to keep them distracted. It was always just enough so that they would see that something really good was happening,

A McCall poster image of men on the lunar surface, with their underground city in the background. One of them holds a tablet-style computer. Many people are puzzled that what seemed an obvious prospect for the near future did not come to pass. We do not have a base on the Moon.

An epic drama of adventure and exploration
Man's colony on the Moon...a whole new generation has been born and is living here...a quarter-million miles from Earth.
2001: a space odyssey
MGM PRESENTS A STANLEY KUBRICK PRODUCTION
Super Panavision® and Metrocolor
MGM

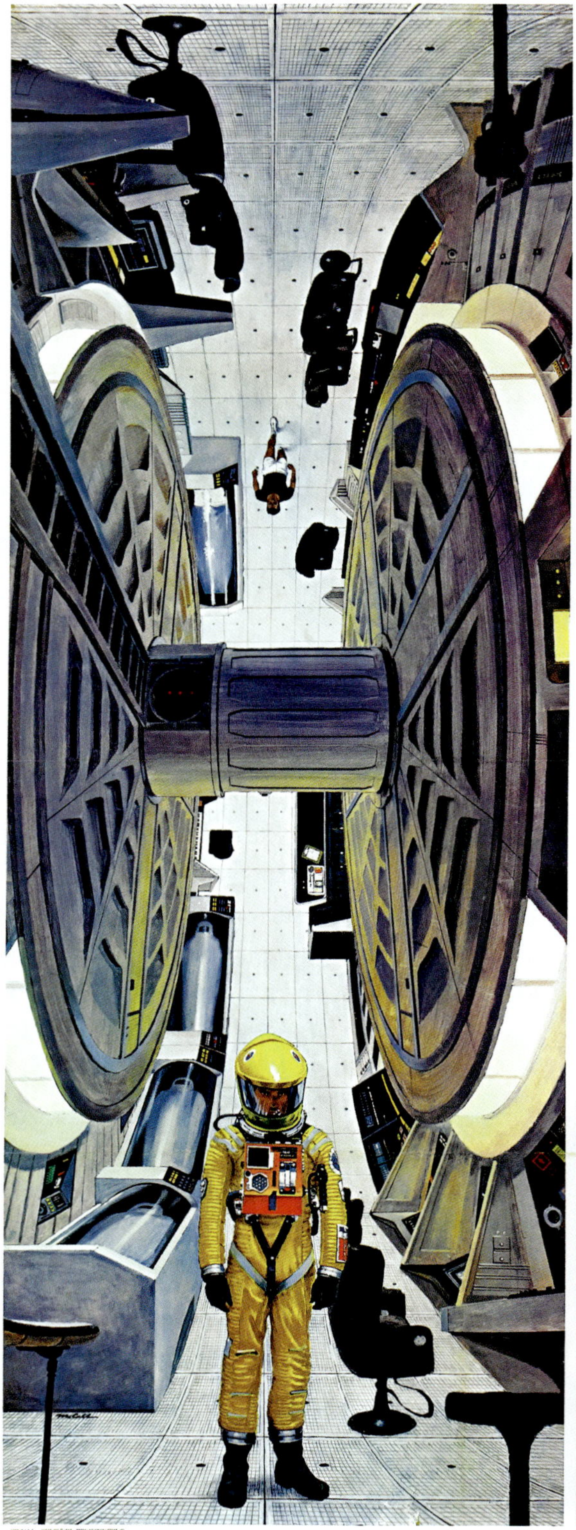

An epic drama of adventure and exploration

...taking you half a billion miles from Earth... further from home than any man in history. Destination: Jupiter.

MGM PRESENTS A STANLEY KUBRICK PRODUCTION

2001 a space odyssey

CINERAMA® Super Panavision® and Metrocolor

MGM

but never enough for them to understand how the movie as a whole was shaping up." (A decade later, Powell learned about studio pressure for himself as associate producer for Ridley Scott's *Alien* and *Blade Runner*.)

Of course MGM executives had occasionally turned up at Borehamwood with dark expressions on their faces. According to Arthur Clarke, "they muttered about Stanley perhaps being kind enough to let them have *2001* in time for a release in 2002." Warned of an impending visit, Kubrick summoned Powell and Birkin: "Guys, it's a raid! Make up some more charts and plans for the walls here. Let's blind 'em with science." Powell mocked up serious-looking material purporting to illustrate obscure administrative aspects of the production. Nervous in case MGM asked any questions, he wondered if the data should represent something real. Kubrick told him not to worry. So long as everything looked convincing, the studio visitors would be satisfied. Nevertheless, Powell played it safe. "The suits turned up, and of course they asked, 'What do all these charts mean?' Knowing Stanley as I did, I always had some kind of an answer prepared. He liked people who could anticipate the unexpected."

The "unexpected" that Kubrick himself failed to anticipate was the initial hostility of well-known movie critics. Press screenings in New York were extremely discouraging. Renata Adler of the *New York Times* judged *2001* "so completely absorbed in its own problems, its use of color and space, its fanatical devotion to science-fiction detail, that it is somewhere between hypnotic and immensely boring." She refused to buy into Kubrick's nonverbal means of expression. In her opinion the Stargate and hotel-room sequences needed extra scripting and explanation: "The all-purpose answer, 'relativity,' does not really serve unless it can be verbalized." Stanley Kauffmann at *The New Republic* magazine obviously wasn't the right man to watch anything set beyond the Earth's atmosphere: "Everywhere outside the spaceport, men are constricted and dehumanized. They cannot move without cumbersome suits and helmets. Despite the size of the starry firmament, the idea of space travel gives me claustrophobia." Charles Champlin at the *Los Angeles Times* seemed incapable of interpreting *2001* from its visual cues alone: "A spacecraft manned by Keir Dullea and Gary Lockwood, and a rather epicene talking computer, takes off for Jupiter. Whether they make it, I honestly don't know."

Almost everywhere one looked, from the ink-stained newspapers to the slick layouts of magazines, the initial critical response from the New York media was savage. The very airwaves seethed with indignation. David Goldman insisted on CBS Radio that Kubrick's

McCall invented a composition not featured in the film: a space-suited Poole standing in the centrifuge, at the same time as he performs his exercise routine in the background.

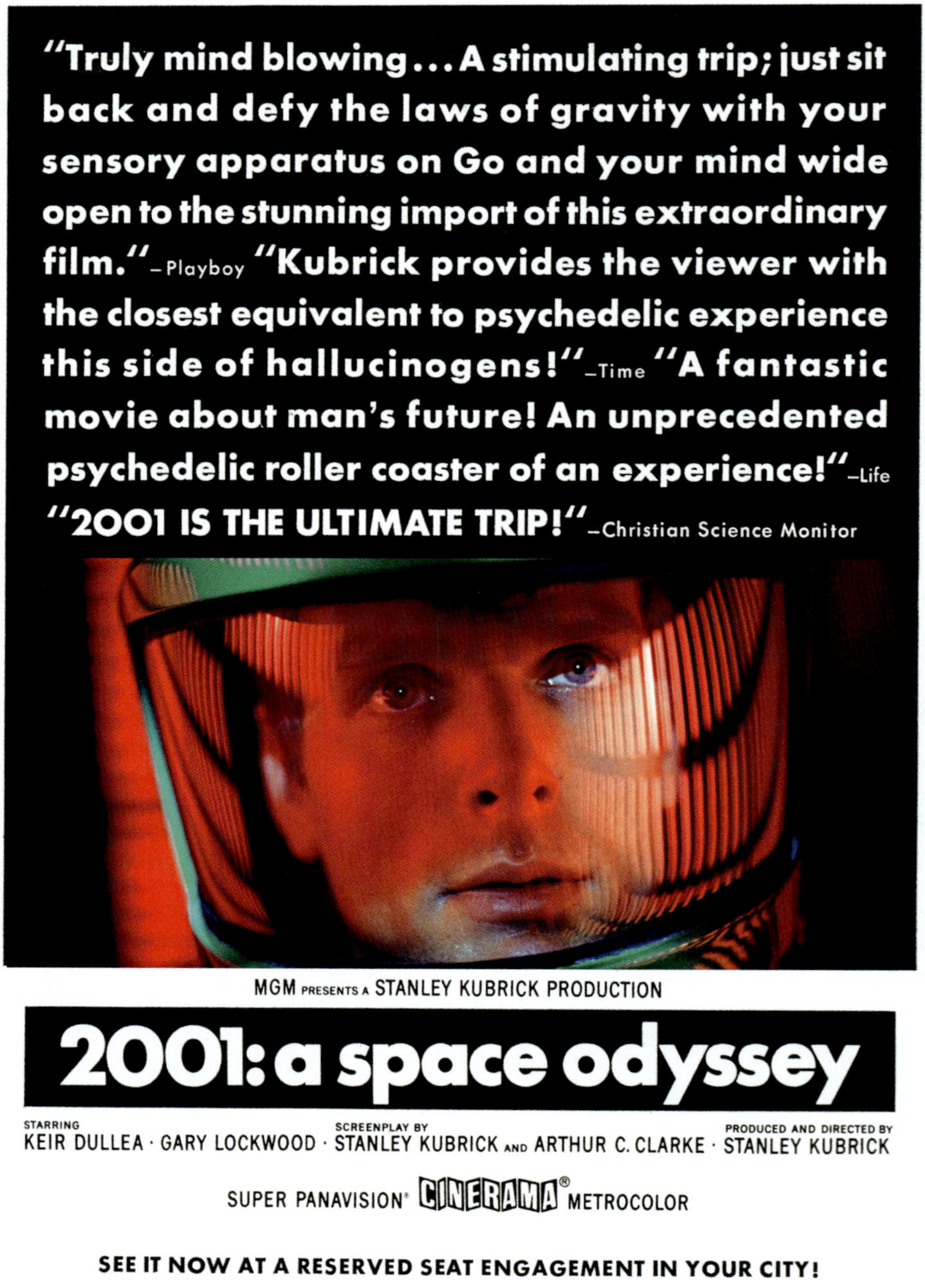
"Truly mind blowing . . . A stimulating trip; just sit back and defy the laws of gravity with your sensory apparatus on Go and your mind wide open to the stunning import of this extraordinary film." – Playboy "Kubrick provides the viewer with the closest equivalent to psychedelic experience this side of hallucinogens!" – Time "A fantastic movie about man's future! An unprecedented psychedelic roller coaster of an experience!" – Life
"2001 IS THE ULTIMATE TRIP!" – Christian Science Monitor
MGM PRESENTS A STANLEY KUBRICK PRODUCTION
2001: a space odyssey
STARRING KEIR DULLEA · GARY LOCKWOOD · SCREENPLAY BY STANLEY KUBRICK AND ARTHUR C. CLARKE · PRODUCED AND DIRECTED BY STANLEY KUBRICK
SUPER PANAVISION® CINERAMA® METROCOLOR
SEE IT NOW AT A RESERVED SEAT ENGAGEMENT IN YOUR CITY!

stereo soundtrack offered "pretentious music and weird effects," and that *2001* was "in summary, a most unsatisfying movie." Andrew Sarris, the critic who imported into America the French notion that a good director could be seen as the primary auteur ("author") of a film, should have been most appreciative of Kubrick's intensely personal vision. Oddly, his review for New York's fashionably street-smart tabloid, the *Village Voice*, complained of "a thoroughly uninteresting failure and the most damning demonstration yet of Stanley Kubrick's inability to tell a story coherently and with a consistent point of view." Sarris reinforced his printed attack on a New York radio station: "*2001* is one of the grimmest films I have ever seen in my life."

Pauline Kael's withering scorn in the prestigious pages of *Harper's Magazine* shocked Kubrick the most. She accused him of "doing every dumb thing he wanted to do, building enormous science-fiction sets and equipment, never even bothering to figure out what he was going to do with them." Kael was an influential but somewhat strange cinema fan, refusing to see anything more than once, even if she loved it. "I'm astonished when I talk to really good critics, who know their stuff and will see a film eight or ten or twelve times," she once said. "I don't see how they can do it without hating the movie." One of her most famous contributions to her craft was "Kiss Kiss Bang Bang," a phrase she found on a 1966 poster for an Italian spy spoof. This sums up the basic plot line of most films. Kael knew how frustrating it can get "when we begin to understand how seldom movies are any more than this." How strange that *2001*, obviously so much more than mere kiss and bang, left her so unmoved.[1]

A clue to her distaste for cosmic speculation is found in a line of dialogue from Barbara Stanwyck, famous for playing the kind of hardheaded heroines that Kael favored, and often quoted. In one of Frank Capra's earliest films, *Ladies of Leisure* (1930), a painter asks Stanwyck to adopt a thoughtful pose. "Look through the ceiling," he urges her. "Visualize the sky, space, the universe, stardust—anything! There *is* no ceiling, don't you see?" Stanwyck glances up suspiciously. "Horsefeathers! It's a ceiling. You could ask anybody." Most of the New York critics seemed as stern as Stanwyck in their refusal to contemplate anything beyond the confines of conventional cinematic plotting, romantic entanglements, thrills and spills and actorly acting. None went so far, however, as Kael, who described *2001* as "the biggest amateur movie of all" and dismissed Kubrick's entire project as "monumentally unimaginative."

Today we gain our advance impressions of a film from bloggers, podcasts, websites, fan reviewers, TV shows, and a vast range of print media, still obstinately surviving in a digital age. Individual critics aren't quite the giants they used to be. It's hard for us to imagine

1 Davis, Francis, *Afterglow: A Last Conversation* with *Pauline Kael*, 2002

how a tight cluster of New York commentators could have held such sway in 1968. The problem was that an expensive Cinerama presentation was supposed to complete a run of many weeks, or even months, in a limited number of prestigious venues, well ahead of a wider 35 mm distribution in smaller movie theaters. In that sense, a Cinerama roadshow was akin to a Broadway play, with similarly expensive seat prices to match. If people failed to attend in the first few days because they had been deterred by savage reviews, a roadshow could die. New York critics were used to killing things at birth. If *2001*'s roadshow came to a sudden stop, studio heads would roll. John Sturges's Cinerama adventure, *Ice Station Zebra*, based on a thriller by Alistair MacLean, with Patrick McGoohan true to type as a special agent, and Rock Hudson playing a submarine commander, was on standby to take up the slack if Cinerama theater owners lost their nerve.

At the dawn of the 21st century, it is almost impossible for a moderately decent movie to fail. Even if the opening weeks of theatrical showings are slow, subsequent TV sales, DVD and Blu-ray rights, and other relatively low-cost forms of digital distribution on large high-definition screens usually ensure that a studio's investment is not lost. In the 1960s the only way that a large-screen presentation could make its money back was in the theaters. If *2001* failed, it would fail, period, because there was no other "platform," as we might say today, capable of screening it. Anyway, one of the justifications for making the film in the first place was to exploit the giant Cinerama format. Would the public be guided by New York's hostility and stay away?

THE RAPID RECOVERY

Modern film histories often suggest that *2001* edged toward commercial disaster on its initial release, and that subsequent word-of-mouth enthusiasm among youthful fans revived the film's fortunes in defiance of middle-aged critical expectations. Doug Trumbull's recollection of events encapsulates the story that has been handed down to us: "About 30 days into the run, MGM was getting ready to pull the movie and throw it away and just abandon the whole thing. I heard that some theater owners called in and said, 'Before you pull it, there's something happening here. There's a bunch of young people sitting down in the front row. There were three of them yesterday, and there's six of them this morning. It's going to be a lot more tonight.' There was a wave of interest from the psychedelic movement. People were smoking a little pot before the screening, and a whole new audience started showing up. So *2001* did in fact survive, but just by a hair." Trumbull's story makes good drama but isn't quite correct. By the time the film had been playing for 30 days, it was already turning into a smash hit. Nevertheless, the first two or three days, as opposed to that first 30, were indeed unsettling.

Arthur Clarke caught the whiff of pessimism in those first days, too. "Many people at MGM were worried about their expenses, and whether anybody would go and see the film. The first screenings took place just after Lyndon Johnson resigned his presidency. One of the studio executives said, as he left the cinema, 'Well, today we lost two presidents.' He meant Bob O'Brien, the MGM boss who'd been our bravest supporter, always defending Stanley against the hawks. Obviously, on the basis of early reactions, that executive must have thought O'Brien's job was on the line."

◁△ 344 Postcards with grooved lenticular plastic coatings enabled an approximate 3-D effect.

Ray Lovejoy, who had worked so well with Stanley on the edit, wondered if *2001* was simply too far removed from the mainstream to do well: "I think the public were confused. They weren't sure if they were seeing a wonderful film or a load of rubbish, because this type of film had actually never been made before, and at that particular time it was a one-off." Con Pederson always had a feeling that *2001*'s opening days would be tough: "A lot of what looks like science fiction is really car chases. This is the accepted concept of action and adventure. The phrase 'art film' is like dirty talk in Hollywood, because nobody would go and see a movie if they thought of it that way. And that's what we had just made, and on a huge scale. No one quite knew what they were looking at, and they didn't know how to interpret it."

Kubrick's immediate response (and governed largely by his own instincts) was to trim the film. Contrary to myth, there is no definitive "director's cut" of *2001* other than the one we see today. While those of us who love every minute of it would dearly wish to see every last scrap of footage, whether on screen or rescued from the cutting-room floor and held, reverently, up to the nearest light (David Larson, a diligent researcher, has identified that the excised sections still exist, in pristine condition, within a secure vault), we have

not been cheated of Kubrick's determined ideas about what the film should be. As he explained to *Action* magazine a few months after the disastrous night at Loew's, "Although the total reaction was not representative or good, I could still see places that, as I watched it with an audience, I thought were just going on a bit. I could see places throughout the film where I could tighten up, and I took out nineteen minutes." [2]

Some of the man-ape material was trimmed. A scene in which Dullea, in his cherry-red space suit, retrieves a fresh AE35 control box from a brilliant white storage corridor was also shortened. All that remains is his exit from the corridor as he heads into the pod bay, clutching the box in his gloved right hand. Publicity and brochure photos show Lockwood in his yellow space suit framed in the storage corridor. More drastically, the preparations ahead of Poole's fatal space walk too closely mirrored Bowman's earlier procedures, and Kubrick cut to the chase, so to speak, recognizing that his audience already knew how the pods worked, and that he could make some narrative shortcuts in that sequence without affecting the shape of the film. In the final cut, we see just a glimpse of the storage corridor set as the astronauts walk through the end door and into the pod bay. Shots of a spare AE35 control box being retrieved from the corridor were sliced out. Kubrick also made a brief addition. When the man-ape leader feels that strange and wonderful compulsion to pick up a bone and play with it, there was, at first, no clear suggestion that alien intervention was responsible for his flash of inspiration. A one-second subliminal reminder of the monolith, inserted into the final cut, solved this problem. Title cards announcing each of the film's four sections were also added.

2 Interview with Kubrick for *Action* magazine, February 1969

Brian Sanders made this impressionistic painting of the Tycho lunar excavation sets and actors at work.

▹ 351 Mike Kaplan exploited critical response to *2001* as part of a revamped publicity campaign, preferring to concentrate on the film's abstract imagery rather than the hardware.

The fact that Kubrick shortened *2001* is well known. Less obvious is the tremendous speed and intensity of the work involved. Faithful aide Roger Caras recalled him up all night "trimming in the basement of the MGM building on Sixth Avenue." This was on April 5. Cinerama screenings were scheduled just five days later in Boston, Denver, Detroit, Houston, and Chicago. Three further prints were destined for Tokyo and Johannesburg. Time had to be allowed for air freighting the bulky reels.

The Kubricks had rented a house on Long Island. A day or two after the preview screenings, Christiane arrived, exhausted, "not having slept forever, and I put my handbag and hat on the bed and just fainted. Our nanny took the kids to the beach. Suddenly I woke up, and it was very late in the morning, and on the radio I heard a disc jockey saying, 'Oh, they're lining up around the block, and the first audiences are coming out mesmerized by this most fantastic film.' I tried to phone Stanley to tell him, 'Some people somewhere like it, so don't worry.' Word got around very quickly after that."

For Christiane, what happened next was "a big eye-opener. There was another meeting, and we saw all the same MGM people again. And now they were shamelessly saying, 'Stanley's such a genius, and isn't this movie wonderful!' And I thought, 'Fuck you, you're such creeps. Why aren't you ashamed that you wanted to abandon him so quickly?' I remember saying, 'You die a quick death here, don't you?' And suddenly he was the hero. So it was a 24-hour thing, at the end of which we were exhausted, reeling. Some people abandoned us who, I thought, were supposed to be our friends. Rats leaving the sinking ship. I thought, 'You could have hung in there a little longer.' I don't think I ever quite forgave them." Despite how quickly it became obvious that *2001* was going to be a success, "there was this day or two of pure, unadulterated hell." After that, at the other events and openings, things were much better for Stanley and Christiane alike. "For me, it was just a matter of standing there in my dress, smiling, with the kids under my arm."

REVERSING THE CRITICAL TIDE

Mike Kaplan was a young MGM publicist at the time of *2001*'s release. Roger Caras introduced him to Kubrick on April 3, the night of the public premier at Loew's. Kubrick was in the projection booth, his black tie undone, his expression tense. Kaplan thought that the Bob McCall space-station artwork on the promotional posters was misleading. The film "was being presented as 'an epic drama of adventure and exploration,' and many people were expecting a modern Flash Gordon. Instead, Kubrick had created a metaphysical drama." Kaplan wondered if, perhaps, the advertising campaign could be revised? Wondering about this was one thing. Suggesting it to a stressed Stanley Kubrick was an altogether scarier prospect, but that first meeting went well enough for Kaplan to gain the director's trust.[3]

A few weeks later, Kaplan locked onto a welcome positive response from the *Christian Science Monitor*, a Boston-based newspaper widely trusted at that time by decent god-fearing Americans, and respected for the quality of its journalism by the ungodly, too. Against the trend, a full-page essay by John Allen, published on May 10, proclaimed *2001* "a bolt of brilliant, high-voltage cinema… the evocation of wonder and awe is perhaps the primary aim of the film." He identified, correctly, that Kubrick was aiming his film at an audience already acclimatized to television and color print media, and used to thinking visually rather than in "the slow plodding of language." Allen judged the film "so beautifully wrought and so intricately carved and inlaid as to defy description. If it has a name it is called the art of filmmaking."

Kaplan hit on the rather sneaky idea of running the *Monitor*'s review in other journals, as an advertisement—only without any obvious clues that it was a paid-for promotional. It would be made to appear as if it were a normal editorial article. Today the so-called advertorial technique is commonplace. The advertising industry knows only too well that audiences would rather trust a seemingly dispassionate journalist than an obviously sponsored puff. At first, Kaplan's bosses thought this approach was too peculiar, and insisted that the *Monitor*'s piece be laid out with accompanying MGM banners. Why wouldn't the studio wish to be associated with an obviously glowing review? Kaplan enlisted Kubrick's help in getting MGM to adopt a more nuanced approach. A few days later, according to Kaplan, "the piece appeared opposite the *New York Times*' main film page, making it look like a two-page editorial spread. There was nothing stating it was a paid ad. The campaign to turn the tide was engaged."

Except that the tide already was on Kubrick's side. The New York barbs were the exception, not the rule. When the film hit other cities, there seemed no possibility of rejection. While critics around the U.S. continued to express a certain degree of bafflement, they were essentially unanimous in praising the film as a wondrous spectacle, and an absolute "must-see" for their readers, who responded in kind by going to see the film. By now they were watching the tightened-up version. This may have been a slight factor in their considerations.

3 Kaplan, "Kubrick: A Marketing Odyssey," *The Guardian*, November 2, 2007

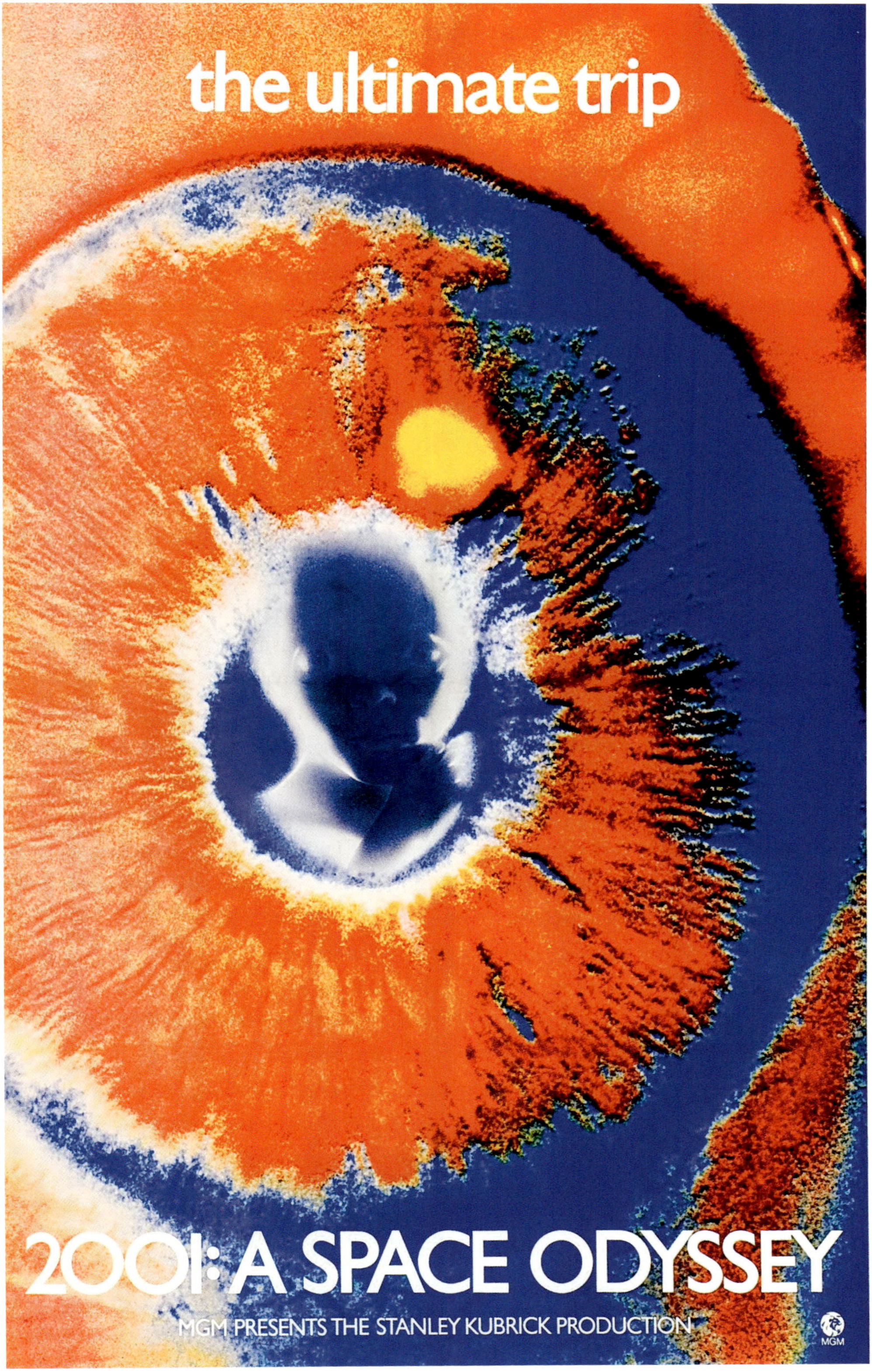
the ultimate trip
2001: A SPACE ODYSSEY
MGM PRESENTS THE STANLEY KUBRICK PRODUCTION
MGM

The Los Angeles Warner Theater attracted well over 1,000 people, day after day. The same applied to Loew's Capitol in New York, the Uptown in Washington, and the Chicago Cinestage. Whatever else audiences were doing, they weren't staying away. MGM announced gross earnings of over $1 million in the first five weeks, just from the first eight Cinerama theaters. The figures easily matched—and in some cases surpassed—MGM's fondest expectations. A million is spare change today. James Cameron's *Avatar* (2009) took $200 million just on its opening weekend. We have to keep in mind the long-ago terms of reference applicable to 1968, when most movie tickets cost substantially less than $1 and even seats in a Cinerama theater could be booked for around $2.00. The box office returns for *2001* represented a great many ticket sales. MGM was perfectly satisfied that it had a tremendous hit on its hands. *2001* became the second-highest-grossing film of the year, narrowly outpaced by Barbra Streisand in *Funny Girl*. (Directed by William Wyler, this was also presented in 70 mm widescreen in September 1968.)

When *2001* arrived at the Cinerama houses in Tokyo and Osaka in mid-April, there wasn't an empty seat to be found. People were turned away by the hundreds for lack of space. The Osaka Rail Union made advance bookings for 9,000 tickets, automatically ensuring a long run, while the Ministry of Education in Japan praised the film's "exceptional educational merit," guaranteeing a further influx of enthusiastic young viewers. London's Casino Cinerama opened the film in early May. Five days later it was delighted to announce "breaking the all-time house record for a four-day weekend." The London critics were upbeat in their appraisal. Alexander Walker, reviewer for the widely distributed *Evening Standard* London city paper, called it "a unique film that dazzles the eyes, engages the imagination and surpasses any film forecast of things to come that I have ever seen. Man has shrunk space, but Kubrick has expanded the cinema." Pointedly, he said that he would "go and see it again as soon as possible." The *Times* newspaper hailed *2001*'s "intelligence." The story was similarly encouraging in Europe. Parisian screenings of *2001* drew half a million people over an eight-month period.

During the Christmas holiday of 1968, real-life events conspired to push *2001* further into the spotlight, as Apollo 8's capsule carried men around the Moon for the first time, pathfinding for the greater challenge ahead. MGM executive William Madden wrote a quick note to Kubrick in July 1969, a few days after Apollo 11's historic touchdown, informing him that over 400 theaters across America had booked (and in many cases, rebooked) the film, "reflecting the sharp increase in business since man landed on the Moon."

Although the notion that *2001* scrabbled to survive "by a hair" is essentially misplaced, like most myths and popular memories it contains some small fragments of reality. It is true that ticket sales in the weeks leading up to the first Cinerama roadshows were lethargic. Look at any of the advertisements and there is a booking form alongside the artwork. The expectation was that responsible adults would book roadshow tickets in advance, just as if they were planning a trip to the conventional theater to see a stage play or musical. Kubrick's space movie did not fit this trend, because it appealed more to young people than to their parents. By May of 1968 *Variety* had noticed that *2001*'s principal audience tended not to make reservations ahead of time. It simply "plunks down its money at the box office, and is unlikely to buy tickets three or six weeks in advance." MGM sales chief Morris Lefko observed, "I'd call a theater at noon, and when I'd hear that only 300 seats were sold for the evening show, I'd feel pretty gloomy. Then, the next day, I'd discover we went clean."

REAPPRAISING THE APPRAISALS

In light of the film's success, some hostile critics did wonder if they had missed something, and ignored Kael's proscription against seeing a movie twice. Sarris saw *2001* again and wrote a second appraisal, discreetly softening his earlier hostility, though never to the point of outright enthusiasm. Joseph Gelmis, a reviewer at New York's *Newsday* newspaper, wrote a piece on April 20, 1968, entitled "Another Look at Space Odyssey." He was disarmingly frank about the drawbacks of the critical review process, admitting that he and his colleagues approached a film "with preconceptions about what form it should have. When a film of such extraordinary originality comes along, it upsets the members of the critical establishment because it lies outside their framework of apprehending and describing movies. They are threatened. Their most polished puns and witticisms are useless, because the conventional standards don't apply." Gelmis thought that the best way of approaching a film was "with an innocent eye and a flexible vocabulary." He analyzed why he'd not been enthused by his first exposure to *2001* and concluded that it "demands acceptance on its own unique terms." Most critics had failed that test, himself included. Gelmis wrote: "With one exception, the *New Yorker*'s Penelope Gilliatt, the daily and weekly reviewers offhandedly dismissed the film as a disappointment and found it a failure."

Here, then, is the "one exception" highlighted by Gelmis, written by a reviewer whose "innocent eye" saw *2001* and accepted it "on its own terms." English-born Penelope Gilliatt was a screenwriter and novelist whose vivid, spontaneous language and lack of pretension gave her critical pieces a simplicity and sparkle often missing from the work of her more jaded contemporaries. Her *New Yorker* appreciation, "After Man," published on April 13, 1968, stands the test of time as a perfect introduction to the film and its themes.

"AFTER MAN" THE NEW YORKER, APRIL 13, 1968

I think Stanley Kubrick's *2001: A Space Odyssey* is some sort of a great film, and an unforgettable endeavor. Technically and imaginatively, what he put into it is staggering: five years of his life; his novel and screenplay, with Arthur C. Clarke; his production, his direction, his special effects; his humor and stamina and particular disquiet. The film is not only hideously funny—like *Dr. Strangelove*—about human speech and response at a point where they have begun to seem computerized, and where more and more people sound like recordings left on while the soul is out. It is also a uniquely poetic piece of sci-fi, made by a man who truly possesses the drives of both science and fiction.

Kubrick's tale of quest in the year *2001*, which eventually takes us to the Moon and Jupiter, begins on prehistoric Earth. Tapirs snuffle over the Valhalla landscape, and a leopard with broken-glass eyes guards the carcass of a zebra in the moonlight. Crowds of apes, scratching and ganging up, are disturbingly represented not by real animals but by actors in costume. They are on the brink of evolving into men, and the overlap is horrible. Their stalking movements are already exactly ours: an old tramp's, drunk, at the end of his tether and fighting mad. Brute fear has been refined into the infinitely more painful capacity for dread.

The creatures are so nearly human that they have religious impulses. A slab that they suddenly come upon sends them into panicked reverence as they touch it, and the film emits a colossal din of chanting. The shock of faith boots them forward a few thousand years, and one of the apes, squatting in front of a bed of bones, picks up his first weapon. In slow motion, the hairy arm swings up into an empty frame and then down again, and the smashed bones bounce into the air. What makes him do it? Curiosity? What makes people destroy anything, or throw away the known, or set off in spaceships? To see what Nothing feels like, driven by some bedrock instinct that it is time for something else?

The last bone thrown in the air is matched, in the next cut, to a spaceship at the same angle. It is now *2001*. The race has survived thirty-three years more without extinction, though not with any growth of spirit. There are no negroes in this vision of America's space program; conversation with Russian scientists is brittle with manly terror, and the Chinese can still be dealt with only by pretending they're not there. But technological man has advanced no end. A space way station shaped like a Ferris wheel and housing a hotel called the Orbiter Hilton hangs off the pocked old cheek of Earth. The sound track, bless its sour heart, meanwhile thumps out *The Blue Danube* to confer a little of the courtliness of bygone years on space. The civilization that Kubrick sees coming has the brains of a nuclear physicist and the sensibility of an airline hostess smiling through an oxygen-mask demonstration.

Kubrick is a clever man. The grim joke is that life in *2001* is only faintly more gruesome in its details of sophisticated affluence than it is now. When we first meet William Sylvester as a space scientist, for instance, he is in transit to the Moon, via the Orbiter Hilton, to investigate another of the mysterious slabs. The heroic man of intellect is given a nice meal on the way—a row of spacecraft foods to suck through straws out of little plastic cartons, each decorated with a picture of sweet corn, or whatever, to tell him that sweet corn is what he is sucking. He is really going through very much the same ersatz form of the experience of being well looked-after as the foreigner who arrives at an airport now with a couple of babies, reads in five or six languages that he is welcome, and then finds that he has to manage his luggage and the babies without actual help from a porter. The scientist of *2001* is only more inured. He takes the inanities of space personnel on the chin. "Did you have a pleasant flight?" Smile, smile. Another smile, possibly pre-filmed, from a girl on a television monitor handling voiceprint identification at Immigration.

The Orbiter Hilton is decorated in fresh plumbing-white, with magenta arm-chairs shaped like pelvic bones scattered through it. Artificial gravity is provided by centrifugal force; inside the rotating Ferris wheel people have weight. The architecture gives the white floor of the Orbiter Hilton's conversation area quite a gradient, but no one lets slip a sign of humor about the slant. The citizens of *2001* have forgotten how to joke and resist, just as they have forgotten how to chat, speculate, grow intimate, or interest one another. But otherwise everything is splendid. They lack the mind for acknowledging that they have managed to diminish outer space into the ultimate in humdrum, or for dealing with the fact that they are spent and insufficient, like the apes.

The film is hypnotically entertaining, and it is funny without once being gaggy, but it is also rather harrowing. It is as eloquent about what is missing from the people of *2001* as about what is there. The characters seem isolated almost beyond endurance. Even in the most absurd scenes, there is often a fugitive melancholy—as astronauts solemnly watch themselves on homey BBC interviews seen millions of miles from Earth, for instance, or as they burn their fingers on their space meals, prepared with the utmost scientific care but a shade too hot to touch, or as they plod around a centrifuge to get some exercise, shadowboxing alone past white coffins where the rest of the crew hibernates in deep freeze. Separation from other people is total and unmentioned. Kubrick has no characters in the film who are sexually related, nor any close friends. Communication is stuffy and guarded, made at the level of men together on committees or of someone being interviewed. The

space scientist telephones his daughter by television for her birthday, but he has nothing to say, and his wife is out; an astronaut on the nine-month mission to Jupiter gets a prerecorded birthday message from his parents. That's the sum of intimacy. No enjoyment—only the mechanical celebration of the anniversaries of days when the race perpetuated itself.

Again, another astronaut takes a considerable risk to try to save a fellow spaceman, but you feel it hasn't anything to do with affection or with courage. He has simply been trained to save an expensive colleague by a society that has slaughtered instinct. Fortitude is a matter of programming, and companionship seems lost. There remains only longing, and this is buried under banality, for English has finally been booted to death. Even informally, people say "Will that suffice?" for "Will that do?"

The computer on the Jupiter spaceship—a chatty, fussy genius called Hal, which has nice manners and a rather querulous need for reassurance about being wanted—talks more like a human being than any human being does in the picture. Hal runs the craft, watches over the rotating quota of men in deep freeze, and plays chess. He gives a lot of thought to how he strikes others, and sometimes carries on about himself like a mother fussing on the telephone to keep a bored grown child hanging on.

◁△ 360 Banality abounds in *2001*. A love scene in a futuristic car was filmed for projection into the in-flight television screens of the *Orion* shuttle; a judo fight was staged for the distracted TV entertainment of the *Aries* stewardesses; and a scene in which Floyd uses the space-station phone booth to order a pet from Macy's department store was deleted.

At a low ebb and growing paranoid, he tells a hysterical lie about a faulty piece of equipment to recover the crew's respect, but a less emotional twin computer on Earth coolly picks him up on the judgement and degradingly defines it as a mistake. Hal, his mimic humanness perfected, detests the witnesses of his humiliation and restores his ego by vengeance. He manages to kill all the astronauts but Keir Dullea, including the hibernating crew members, who die in the most chillingly modern death scene imaginable: warning lights simply signal "Computer Malfunction," and sets of electrophysiological needles above the sleepers run amok on the graphs and then record the straight lines of extinction.

The survivor of Hal's marauding self-justification, alone on the craft, has to battle his way into the computer's red-flashing brain, which is the size of your living room, to unscrew the high cerebral functions. Hal's sophisticated voice gradually slows and he loses his grip. All he can remember in the end is how to sing "Daisy"—which he was taught at the start of his training long ago—grinding down like an old phonograph. It is an upsetting image of human decay from command into senility. Kubrick makes it seem a lot worse than a berserk computer being controlled with a screwdriver.

The startling metaphysics of the picture are symbolized in the slabs. It is curious that we should all still be so subconsciously trained in apparently distant imagery. Even to atheists, the slabs wouldn't look simply like girders. They immediately have to do with Mosaic tablets or druidical stones. Four million years ago, says the story, an extraterrestrial intelligence existed. The slabs are its manifest sentinels. The one we first saw on prehistoric Earth is like the one discovered in *2001* on the Moon. The lunar finding sends out an upper-harmonic shriek to Jupiter and puts the scientists on the trail of the forces of creation. The surviving astronaut goes on alone and Jupiter's influence pulls him into a world where time and space are relative in ways beyond Einstein. Physically almost pulped, seeing visions of the planet's surface that are like chloroform nightmares and that sometimes turn into close-ups of his own agonized eyeball and eardrum, he then suddenly lands, and he is in a tranquilly furnished repro Louis XVI room. The shot of it through the window of his space pod is one of the most heavily charged things in the whole picture, though its effect and its logic are hard to explain.

In the strange, fake room, which is movingly conventional, as if the most that the ill man's imagination can manage in conceiving a better world beyond the infinite is to recollect something he has once been taught to see as beautiful in a grand decorating magazine, time jumps and things disappear. The barely surviving astronaut sees an old grandee from the back, dining on the one decent meal in the film; and when the man turns around it is the astronaut himself in old age. The noise of the chair moving on the white marble in the silence is typical of the brilliantly selective sound track. The old man drops his wineglass, and then sees himself bald and dying on the bed, twenty or thirty years older still, with his hand up to another of the slabs, which has appeared in the room and stands more clearly than ever for the forces of change. Destruction and creation coexist in them. They are like Siva.

The last shot of the man is totally transcendental, but in spite of my resistance to mysticism I found it stirring. It shows an X-raylike image of the dead man's skull re-created as a baby, and approaching Earth. His eyes are enormous. He looks like a mutant. Perhaps he is the first of the needed new species.

It might seem a risky notion to drive sci-fi into magic. But, as with *Strangelove*, Kubrick has gone too far and made it the poetically just place to go. He and his collaborator have found a powerful idea to impel space conquerors whom puny times have robbed of much curiosity. The hunt for the remnant of a civilization that has been signaling the existence of its intelligence to the future for four million years, tirelessly stating the fact that it occurred, turns the shots of emptied, comic, ludicrously dehumanized men into something more poignant. There is a hidden parallel to the shot of the ape's arm swinging up into the empty frame with its first weapon, enthralled by the liberation of something new to do; I keep remembering the shot of the space scientist asleep in a craft with the "Weightless Condition" sign turned on, his body fixed down by his safety belt while one arm floats free in the air.

DIALOGUE IN 2001

One distinctly unimpressed by *2001* was Clarke's friend Ray Bradbury, author of poetic science fantasies *The Martian Chronicles* and *Something Wicked This Way Comes*. He was dismayed by the poverty of verbal expression: "I think it's a gorgeous film, one of the most beautifully photographed pictures in the history of motion pictures. Unfortunately, there are no well-directed scenes, and the dialogue is banal to the point of extinction." Gilliatt was the first commentator to recognize, and appreciate, the deliberate banality of Kubrick's language: his car-crash tautologies and pointedly pointless stutters and mumbles.

Some viewers were in a unique position to grasp what he had done with language, even if they did not write about it at the time. The physicist Freeman Dyson visited the centrifuge set while at Borehamwood to be interviewed for the film's aborted documentary prologue. In his 1979 memoir *Disturbing the Universe*, he wrote at length how peculiar he found Kubrick's handling of *2001*'s actors: "The characters in *Dr. Strangelove* are real people. A friend of mine who once flew in a B-52 bomber told me that the crew looked and talked exactly like Kubrick's crew. The dialogue bites; the characters are unforgettable... so I had come to Kubrick's studio expecting to find him at work on another *Strangelove*. Instead I saw only gadgetry... He never relented in his determination not to let Keir Dullea act... So far as I could see, *2001* had no message, no dialogue and no characters." When Dyson challenged Kubrick about the apparent lack of human warmth on display, he was told, "You'll see why when you see the film." The inconsequential chatter and impersonal relationships between the humans in *2001* were deliberately scripted qualities, Dyson eventually realized: "Kubrick wanted to show an alien civilization as totally inhuman, passing beyond the limits of our comprehension. For this purpose, he needed a style of film-making that was also inhuman, nonverbal, mystical."

Dullea knew why he had been asked, time and again, to rein in his actor's instincts: "I think Stanley was making a comment that, at times, people—and certainly astronauts—become as machine-like as their machines, and I think that's another reason that he had

us underplay as much as we did. He had this vision that astronauts would be very steady people: not repressed, but so calm that it would take an extremely emotional situation—something that would drive you and me bananas—to make them show a little emotion."

Kubrick was interviewed by Gelmis. One of the issues raised was the hostile response to *2001*'s dialogue. "Some critics seemed to feel that because we were successful in making a voice, a camera lens, and a light come alive as a character, this meant that the human characters failed dramatically. In fact, I believe that Keir Dullea and Gary Lockwood reacted realistically to their circumstances." No one was in any doubt as to the vividness of HAL. "One of the things we were trying to convey is the reality of a world populated—as ours soon will be—by machine entities who have as much, or more, intelligence than us," Kubrick explained. "They will have the same emotional potentialities as human beings. We wanted to stimulate people into thinking what it would be like to share a planet with such creatures."[4]

Marvin Minsky, the computing expert from MIT who had advised Kubrick, had no problem understanding that the emptiness of *2001*'s dialogue was intentional: "I liked the putting down of humans. All the dumb staff meetings to 'beef up morale.' And after the momentous statement that the monolith must have been deliberately buried, one of the astronauts says, 'Well, how about a little coffee?' Kubrick's idea is that the universe is too majestic for short-sighted people."[5]

Minsky was perceptive. Christiane Kubrick speaks with authority about her husband's intentions: "Stanley thought we are always falling behind our scientific and technical achievements. We are very good at making more and more things—but to do what with? We haven't kept up, psychologically and philosophically. We are not profound. We are still getting away with the most boring entertainments. We are shallow, and we know it. We suffer from it. The choices we make are not satisfying. Our sins are all of omission—of not doing the more interesting things that we could do. There is a lethargy, a lack of energy and concentration that prevents us from reaching the key point where we are as creative and perceptive as we would really wish to be. We are in the terrible position of being smart enough to know that we are not smart enough. For instance, we still can't imagine, 'What is God?' So in *2001* we see fantastic tools of communication. People can speak over zillions of miles, but nobody has anything to say. So we pretend. We live in a little world of nonsense and send each other funny photos and cute stories, with this enormous technology. 'Happy birthday,' and so on, when nobody seems to care, or react. It's very melancholy—although two things we really can do. War and pornography we're good at."

4 Kubrick interview with Joseph Gelmis

5 Stork, *HAL's Legacy*

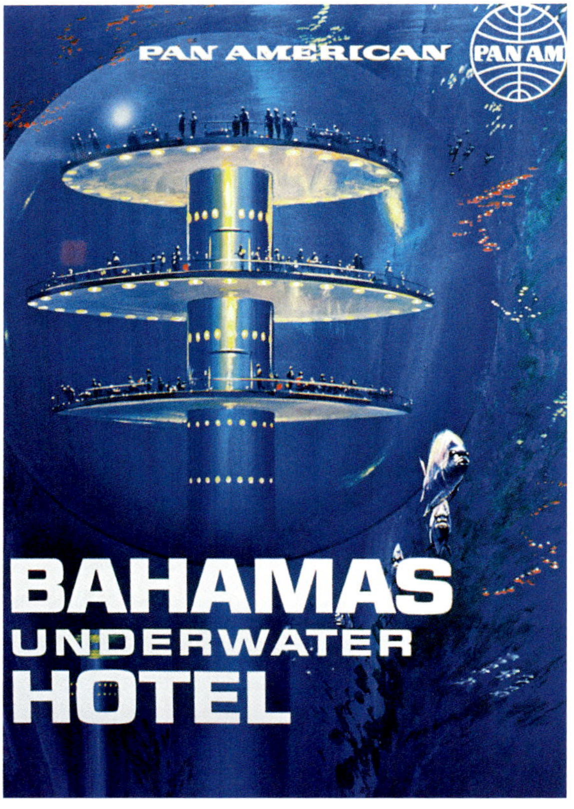

The question of dialogue in *2001* goes hand in hand with that of violence. Despite the seemingly sedate nature of the film, there are at least eight killings visible on screen. Two man-apes, a tapir, four astronauts, and a computer are deliberately done to death by those who seek their destruction. Before astronaut Bowman achieves his cosmic destiny he regains his fighting spirit, his capacity for man-ape aggression. He blasts his way back into the ship, rips open HAL's door, and unscrews the computer. Clearly he is aware that this is akin to murder, because he is distressed as HAL's intellect fades. The computer loses, because he is unable to counter the naked destructiveness of a space-suited man-ape "at the end of his tether and fighting mad." Bowman kills to survive, and seemingly is rewarded in the heavens. So we have a paradox. The bland dialogue suggests a human species inert almost to the point of extinction, and "saved" only by an act of adrenalized reawakening. On the other hand, if violence is allowed to predominate into the future, then—as Kubrick has told us already in *Dr. Strangelove*—we will self-destruct. *2001*, so optimistic on the surface, is in fact a morally complex movie. Either we will bore ourselves to death while our machines sneak in through the back door and take over; or else we will blow ourselves to hell, our modern minds still compromised by an instinctive taste for aggression. It seems we have to keep fighting to survive. And we have to stop fighting to survive.

Beyond the cleverly scripted satire and layers of suggestion, Kubrick's dialogue is only what we would expect to hear if we were eavesdropping on a group of space professionals

Typical of the elaborate attention to detail on all the *2001* sets, this illuminated poster for an underwater hotel on Earth is hardly even glimpsed in the film.

already "in the loop" about some kind of mysterious discovery: mysterious, that is, to the audience. Obviously Floyd, Bowman, and their colleagues talk in shorthand. They do not need to explain plot points to each other because they are already aware, for instance, how their ships work, where they are going, or what their individual tasks are. In a typical B-grade 1950s science-fiction film there is often a scene where Captain Heroic grasps the controls of his rocket ship. Professor Egghead sits down next to him and turns to his glamorous young daughter in the drop seat behind, saying, "Now, don't worry, my dear. The good captain will engage the tachyon motors and then, of course, we will be under artificial gravity." Heroic grins over his shoulder and says, "Should be a nice smooth ride. I don't have to tell the professor here all about the faster-than-light system that will get us to the planet Altair in five hours!" The professor chimes in, "Yes, and the inertial damping system that stops us feeling the stress of acceleration is one of my proudest achievements!" This kind of explanatory dialogue relegates a movie to the cultural rubbish bin faster than a carton of milk left to sour.

Kubrick deals with *2001*'s exposition in a naturalistic lunar conference, and later, by means of a similarly authentic television interview with the occupants of *Discovery*. After Bowman has silenced HAL with his lethal screwdriver, a prerecorded briefing from Heywood Floyd explains the Jupiter mission's true objective. The startled astronaut and

Kubrick and Clarke were prescient in assuming that Russia would maintain a presence in space well into the 21st century. These pilots are adorned with Aeroflot insignia.

◃ Well-known magazines created special futuristic covers for the production.

▹ In the film's only intentional "joke," Floyd has to read a ludicrously complicated set of instructions before relieving himself in the zero-gravity toilet compartment of the *Aries* lunar shuttle.

ZERO GRAVITY TOILET
PASSENGERS ARE ADVISED TO
READ INSTRUCTIONS BEFORE USE

Heading for an encounter with an astounding alien artifact, the astronauts seem more enlivened by the sandwiches and coffee on board the Moonbus than by the prospect of what awaits them at Tycho.

△ Packaged food and artificial ham sandwiches feature in *2001* as signifiers of our dulled appetites and slumbering senses. Is it worth the effort of traveling in space if this is the best we can find to eat? Living within a technological environment requires the suppression of our usual animal appetite for tastes and textures.

Despite *2001*'s supposed optimism about our future technological prowess, much of what we see seems sterile, lifeless, lacking in sensual comfort. There are no plants or flowers anywhere, nor any of the pleasures of animal life and natural scenery that we take for granted in our daily lives.

an equally unprepared audience are let in on the secret at the same time. Once again, a crucial piece of exposition emerges from within the architecture of the film. Floyd's message flickers unsteadily on an underpowered panel, as if triggered prematurely by HAL's disconnection.

Despite these clues, the problem seemed to be that critics weren't prepared to accept the logical consequences of filmic language. The idea of a visual medium telling its story primarily with sights and sounds, rather than in words, left them baffled. As we know, the critical tide did turn. In September 1968 the London critic John Russell Taylor (writing in the *New York Times*) truly came to understand what Gelmis's phrase "an innocent eye" really meant. Watching the film for a second time some weeks after the premier, he observed…

...lots of children, especially boys under 15, generally with fathers and sometimes with mothers in tow... [One] boy obviously loved it all. He hushed his parents whenever their dialogue became too insistent, and at intermission kept bubbling, "Isn't it good? Do you like it? Don't you understand it? What's there difficult to understand?" Maybe he was an infant genius, but I doubt it. He seemed an ordinary enough child. But clearly his attention was not functioning in the same sort of way his parents' was. What we have here is a whole new way of assimilating narrative. It really is rather worrying to think of current cinema as an unknown territory into which, perhaps, only a little child can confidently lead me.

By January 1969 there could not be the slightest doubt as to the film's success and cultural durability. *Variety* said, "It's almost impossible only nine months later to recall that nervous week in April during which *2001* had its premiers in Washington, New York and Los Angeles." The MGM press barrage continued, with the critical and audience response to the film now one of its key selling points. Studio publicists were in a position to call it "the most discussed motion picture of the decade and one of the most important cinema works of the 20th century." One senses from a scrawled correction on a draft of this announcement that it was all they could do to include the word "cinema."

PUBLISHING THE NOVEL

While Kubrick dealt with the nervous days and nights of the press previews, Clarke wondered about the fate of his novel. Back in June 1967, with most of the principal photography complete, and all dialogue scenes irrevocably committed to film, Clarke's agent, Scott Meredith, had assumed that the book version of *2001: A Space Odyssey* must also be in sufficiently good shape to go to market. He set up a publishing deal with Delacorte Press in the USA, who offered an advance of $170,000 in the expectation that they could release the book slightly ahead of the film. Delacorte placed costly advertisements in the book trade journals, and went to the additional expense of editing the manuscript and setting it in type, ready for the printing of galley proofs.

Kubrick, however, would not sign the contract, insisting that he needed to make final corrections, and apologized that the special effects and other post-production aspects of the film were taking up all his time. He did make a few pertinent notes in a copy of the manuscript, mostly complimentary, although his suggestions for June 18, 1966, gave Clarke pause for thought. "Where do you find bees in a drought-stricken area?" Kubrick demanded to know. "Can a leopard carry a man?" Clarke's description of the man-apes as "gorged, sleek, glossy-pelted and content" in the wake of their new meat diet was a step too far. "This has barely happened in 1966," Kubrick asserted. Clarke addressed what little needed to be done to the manuscript, while Meredith fretted that if the book deal were to be delayed too long, publishers would lose interest and the advance offers would dwindle. Kubrick tried to reassure Clarke: "Don't worry. Everything will work out in the end."

It is always dangerous for a historian to assign personal motives unless evidence for them exists. Nevertheless, knowing what we do of Kubrick's working methods and creative intensity in general, it is reasonable to surmise that he wished to avoid Clarke's eloquent version of *2001* from reaching the public in print until the film had gained a chance to succeed on its own, more purely audio-visual terms. When Kubrick finally signed the book contract, the bidding was still healthy, and the New American Library pitched in with a figure not much reduced from Delacorte's earlier offer. In the event, the novel *2001: A Space Odyssey* was published eight weeks after the film's release. A million copies were sold in the first year, and 4 million by the turn of the decade. Just as Kubrick had predicted, everything worked out in the end.

THE CRITIC WHO CAME IN FROM THE COLD

Joseph Gelmis served in the U.S. Air Force for three years as an instructor-navigator with the Air Defense Command, attaining the rank of captain. In 1960, after gaining a master's degree from Columbia University's Graduate School of Journalism, he joined the staff of *Newsday* at the start of a long and distinguished career as film critic, cultural commentator, and roving reporter. He served three terms as chairman of the New York Film Critics Circle, lectured and served on festival juries at colleges across America, and conducted his own weekly radio show on New York City's WBAI-FM. He interviewed Kubrick in the spring of 1968, a few weeks after *2001* opened for business, and contributes this recollection, with relevant extracts from his interviews.

"Stanley had read both of my reviews and, after enduring an overwhelmingly hostile critical reception, wanted to thank me for my reassessment. We spent a couple of hours chatting at an office in MGM's Manhattan headquarters. I taped an hour of our conversation for a *Newsday* interview. Rapport with Stanley was easy. We were both movie crazy, we'd had similar childhoods—his in the Bronx, mine in Brooklyn. One of his daughters, Vivian, if memory serves, bustled in and out of the office. I commented on how cool it was

Astronaut Frank Poole's parents wish him a happy birthday in a prerecorded transmission to *Discovery*, but they say little of consequence, and Poole seems uninterested.

to be able to have a child you loved with you at work. Stanley confided his strategy for maintaining equilibrium: Keep family close and movie executives at a distance.

"We met again in England that June. I was on a two-month-long trip abroad for *Newsday*, reporting on the unprecedented expansion of Hollywood productions into Europe. Stanley sent a car to bring me to his home. Vivian cooked us hamburgers. Stanley gave me a tour of his office and editing facilities, trailed by his dogs. During the course of that afternoon, I taped two hours of conversation. I shortened my questions, left out sections about our personal lives, and combined the material with the New York session for the concluding chapter of a subsequent book of mine in 1970, *The Film Director as Superstar*."

"Dr. Strangelove" was based on a serious book, "Red Alert."
At what point did you decide to make it a comedy?

I started work on the screenplay with every intention of making the film a serious treatment of the problem of accidental nuclear war. As I kept trying to imagine the way in which things would really happen, ideas kept coming to me which I would discard because they were so ludicrous. I kept saying to myself: "I can't do this. People will laugh." But after a month or so I began to realize that all the things I was throwing out were the things which were most truthful. After all, what could be more absurd than the very idea of two mega-powers willing to wipe out all human life because of an accident, spiced up by political differences that will seem as meaningless to people a hundred years from now as the theological conflicts of the Middle Ages appear to us today?

It occurred to me that I was approaching the project in the wrong way. The only way to tell the story was as a black comedy or, better, a nightmare comedy, where the things you laugh at most are really the heart of the paradoxical postures that make a nuclear war possible. Most of the humor in *Strangelove* arises from the depiction of everyday human behavior in a nightmarish situation, like the Russian premier on the hot line who forgets the telephone number of his general staff headquarters and suggests the American President try Omsk information, or the reluctance of a U.S. officer to let a British officer smash open a Coca-Cola machine for change to phone the President about a crisis on the SAC base because of his conditioning about the sanctity of private property.

Corporate interiors dominate the aesthetics of *2001*, especially in the space-station reception center and lounge areas. In these frames, Kubrick shoots Polaroids of various setups, including a stewardess, a receptionist, and a seated William Sylvester. With the exception of Margaret Tyzack's Russian scientist, there is no obvious suggestion in the film that women might have senior positions in space alongside the men.

"Dr. Strangelove" was a particularly word-oriented film, whereas "2001" seemed to be a total breakaway from what you'd done before.

Yes, I feel it was. *Strangelove* was a film where much of its impact hinged on the dialogue, the mode of expression, the euphemisms employed. As a result, it's a picture that is largely destroyed in translation or dubbing. *2001*, on the other hand, is basically a visual, nonverbal experience. It avoids intellectual verbalization and reaches the viewer's subconscious in a way that is essentially poetic and philosophic. The film thus becomes a subjective experience which hits the viewer at an inner level of consciousness, just as music does, or painting. Actually, film operates on a level much closer to music and to painting than to the printed word, and, of course, movies present the opportunity to convey complex concepts and abstractions without the traditional reliance on words. I think that *2001*, like music, succeeds in short-circuiting the rigid surface cultural blocks that shackle our consciousness to narrowly limited areas of experience and is able to cut directly through to areas of emotional comprehension. In two hours and forty minutes of film there are only forty minutes of dialogue.

I think one of the areas where *2001* succeeds is in stimulating thoughts about man's destiny and role in the universe in the minds of people who, in the normal course of their lives, would never have considered such matters. Here again, you've got the resemblance to music; an Alabama truck driver, whose views in every other respect would be extremely narrow, is able to listen to a Beatles record on the same level of appreciation and perception as a young Cambridge intellectual, because their emotions and subconscious are far more similar than their intellects. The common bond is their subconscious emotional reaction. I think that a film which can communicate on this level can have a more profound spectrum of impact than any form of traditional verbal communication.

The problem with movies is that—since the talkies—the film industry has historically been conservative and word-oriented. The three-act play has been the model. It's time to abandon the conventional view of the movie as an extension of the three-act play. Too many people over thirty are still word-oriented rather than picture-oriented. For example, at one point in *2001* Dr. Floyd is asked where he's going and he replies, "I'm going to Clavius," which is a lunar crater. Following that statement you have more than fifteen shots of Floyd's spacecraft approaching and landing on the Moon, but one critic expressed confusion because she thought Floyd's destination was a *planet* named Clavius.

Young people, on the other hand, who are more visually oriented due to their new television environment, had no such problems. Kids all know we went to the Moon. When you ask how they know, they say, "Because we saw it." So you have the problem that some people are only listening and not really paying attention with their eyes. Film is not theater.

Until that basic lesson is learned, I'm afraid we're going to be shackled to the past and miss some of the greatest potentialities of the medium.

Did you deliberately try for ambiguity as opposed to a specific meaning for any scene or image?

No, I didn't have to try for ambiguity. It was inevitable. And I think in a film like *2001*, where each viewer brings his own emotions and perceptions to bear on the subject matter, a certain degree of ambiguity is valuable, because it allows the audience to fill in the visual experience themselves. In any case, once you're dealing on a nonverbal level, ambiguity is unavoidable. But it's the ambiguity of all art, of a fine piece of music or a painting. You don't need written instructions by the composer or painter accompanying such works to explain them. "Explaining" them contributes nothing but a superficial cultural value which has no usefulness except for critics and teachers who have to earn a living. Reactions to art are always different because they are always deeply personal.

The final scenes of the film seemed more metaphorical than realistic. Will you discuss them?

No, I don't mind discussing it, on the lowest level—that is, as a straightforward explanation of the plot. You begin with an artifact left on Earth four million years ago by extraterrestrial explorers who observed the behavior of the man-apes of the time and decided to influence their evolutionary progression. Then you have a second artifact buried deep on the lunar surface and programmed to signal word of man's first baby steps into the universe: a kind of cosmic burglar alarm. And finally there's a third artifact placed in orbit around Jupiter and waiting for the time when man has reached the outer rim of his own solar system.

When the surviving astronaut, Bowman, ultimately reaches Jupiter, this artifact sweeps him into a force field or star gate that hurls him on a journey through inner and outer space and finally transports him to another part of the galaxy, where he's placed in a human zoo approximating a hospital terrestrial environment drawn out of his own dreams and imagination. In a timeless state, his life passes from middle age to senescence to death. He is reborn, an enhanced being, a star child, an angel, a superman, if you like, and returns to Earth prepared for the next leap forward of man's evolutionary destiny. That is what happens on the film's simplest level. Since an encounter with an advanced interstellar intelligence would be incomprehensible within our present earthbound frames of reference, reactions to it will have elements of philosophy and metaphysics that have nothing to do with the bare plot outline itself.

What are those areas of meaning?

They are the areas I prefer not to discuss, because they are highly subjective and will differ from viewer to viewer. In this sense, the film becomes anything the viewer sees in it. If the film stirs the emotions and penetrates the subconscious of the viewer, if it stimulates, however inchoately, his mythological and religious yearnings and impulses, then it has succeeded.

Why does "2001" seem so affirmative and religious a film? What has happened to the tough, disillusioned, cynical director of "The Killing," "Spartacus," "Paths of Glory" and "Lolita," and the sardonic black humorist of "Dr. Strangelove"?

The God concept is at the heart of this film. It's unavoidable that it would be, once you believe that the universe is seething with advanced forms of intelligent life. Just think about it for a moment. There are a hundred billion stars in the galaxy and a hundred billion galaxies in the visible universe. Each star is a sun, like our own, probably with planets around them. The evolution of life, it is widely believed, comes as an inevitable consequence of a certain amount of time on a planet in a stable orbit which is not too hot or too cold. First comes chemical evolution—chance rearrangements of basic matter—then biological evolution.

Think of the kind of life that may have evolved on those planets over the millennia, and think, too, what relatively giant technological strides man has made on Earth in the six thousand years of his recorded civilization: a period that is less than a single grain of sand in the cosmic hourglass. At a time when man's distant evolutionary ancestors were just crawling out of the primordial ooze, there must have been civilizations in the universe sending out their starships to explore the farthest reaches of the cosmos and conquering all the secrets of nature. Such cosmic intelligences, growing in knowledge over the aeons, would be as far removed from man as we are from the ants. They could be in instantaneous telepathic communication throughout the universe. They might have achieved total mastery over matter so that they can telekinetically transport themselves instantly across billions of light-years of space. In their ultimate form they might shed their corporeal shell entirely and exist as a disembodied immortal consciousness throughout the universe.

Once you begin discussing such possibilities, you realize that the religious implications are inevitable, because all the essential attributes of such extraterrestrial intelligences are the attributes we give to God. What we're really dealing with here is, in fact, a scientific definition of God. And if these beings of pure intelligence ever did intervene in the affairs of man, so far removed would their powers be from our own understanding. How would a sentient ant view the foot that crushes his anthill? As the action of another being on a higher evolutionary scale than itself? Or as the divinely terrible intercession of God?

Although "2001" dealt with the first human contact with an alien civilization, we never did actually see an alien, though you communicated through the monoliths an experience of alien beings.

From the very outset of work on the film we all discussed means of photographically depicting an extraterrestrial creature in a manner that would be as mind-boggling as the being itself. And it soon became apparent that you cannot imagine the unimaginable. All you can do is try to represent it in an artistic manner that will convey something of its quality. That's why we settled on the black monolith—which is, of course, in itself, something of a Jungian archetype, and also a pretty fair example of minimal art.

Isn't a basic problem with science fiction films that alien life always looks like some "Creature from the Black Lagoon," a plastic rubber monster?

Yes, and that's one of the reasons we stayed away from the depiction of biological entities, aside from the fact that truly advanced beings would probably have shed the chrysalis of a biological form at one stage of their evolution. You cannot design a biological entity that doesn't look either overly humanoid or like the traditional bug-eyed monster of pulp science fiction.

The man-ape costumes in "2001" were impressive.

We spent an entire year trying to figure out how to make the ape-heads look convincing, and not just like a conventional make-up job. We finally constructed an entire sub-skull of extremely light and flexible plastic, to which we attached the equivalent of face muscles which pulled the lips back in a normal manner whenever the mouth was opened. The mouth itself took a great deal of work. It had artificial teeth and an artificial tongue which the actors could manipulate with tiny toggles to make the lips snarl in a life-like fashion. Some of the masks even had built-in devices whereby the artificial muscles in the cheeks and beneath the eyes could be moved. All the apes except for two baby chimps were men, and most of them were dancers or mimes, which enabled them to move a little better than most movie apes.

Was the little girl Dr. Floyd telephoned from the orbital satellite one of your daughters?

Yes, my youngest girl, Vivian. She was six then. We didn't give her any billing—a fact I hope she won't decide to take up with me when she's older.

Why was Martin Balsam's voice as HAL, the computer, re-dubbed by Douglas Rain, the Canadian actor?

Well, we had some difficulty deciding exactly what HAL should sound like, and Marty just sounded a little bit too colloquially American, whereas Rain had the kind of bland mid-Atlantic accent we felt was right for the part.

Some critics have detected in HAL's wheedling voice an undertone of homosexuality. Was that intended?

No. I think it's become something of a parlor game for some people to read that kind of thing into everything they encounter. HAL was a straight computer.

Why was the computer more emotional than the human beings?

This was a point that seemed to fascinate some negative critics, who felt that it was a failing of this section of the film that there was more interest in HAL than in the astronauts. In fact, of course, the computer is the central character of this segment of the story. If HAL had been a human being, it would have been obvious to everyone that he had the best part, and was the most interesting character. He took all the initiatives, and all the problems related to—and were caused by—him. Some critics seemed to feel that because we were successful in making a voice, a camera lens, and a light come alive as a character, this necessarily meant that the human characters failed dramatically. In fact, I believe that Keir Dullea and Gary Lockwood, the astronauts, reacted appropriately and realistically to their circumstances. One of the things we were trying to convey in this part of the film is the reality of a world populated, as ours soon will be, by machine entities who have as much—or more—intelligence as human beings, and who have the same emotional potentialities in their personalities as human beings. We wanted to stimulate people to think what it would be like to share a planet with such creatures.

In the specific case of HAL, he had an acute emotional crisis because he could not accept evidence of his own fallibility. The idea of neurotic computers is not uncommon. Most advanced computer theorists believe that once you have a computer which is more intelligent than man, and capable of learning by experience, it's inevitable that it will develop an equivalent range of emotional reactions: fear, love, hate, envy, and so on. Such a machine could eventually become as incomprehensible as a human being, and could, of course, have a nervous breakdown, just as HAL did in the film.

Since "2001" is a visual experience, what happened when your collaborator, Arthur C. Clarke, finally put the screenplay down in black and white in the novelization of the film?

It's a totally different kind of experience, of course, and there are a number of differences between the book and the movie. The novel, for example, attempts to explain things much more explicitly than the film does, which is inevitable in a verbal medium. The novel came about after we did a 130-page prose treatment of the film at the very outset. This initial treatment was subsequently changed in the screenplay, and the screenplay in turn was altered during the making of the film. But Arthur took all the existing material, plus an impression of some of the rushes, and wrote the novel. As a result, there's a difference between the novel and the film.

To take one specific, in the novel the black monolith found by curious man-apes millions of years ago does explicit things which it doesn't do in the film. In the movie, it has an apparent catalytic effect which enables the ape to discover how to use a bone as a weapon-tool. In the novel, the slab becomes milky and luminous and we're told it's a testing and teaching device used by higher intelligences to determine if the apes are worth helping.

Was that in the original screenplay? When was it cut out of the film?

Yes, it was in the original treatment, but I eventually decided that to depict the monolith in such an explicit manner would be to run the risk of making it appear no more than an advanced television teaching machine. You can get away with something so literal in print, but I felt that we could create a far more powerful and magical effect by representing it as we did in the film.

Do you feel that the novel, written so explicitly, in some way diminishes the mysterious aspect of the film?

I think it gives you the opportunity of seeing two attempts in two different mediums, print and film, to express the same basic concept and story. In both cases, of course, the treatment must accommodate to the necessities of the medium. I think that the divergences between the two works are interesting. Actually, it was an unprecedented situation for someone to do an essentially original literary work based on glimpses and segments of a film he had not seen in its entirety. In fact, nobody saw the film in its final form until eight days before we held the first press screening in April 1968, and the first time I saw the film completed with a proper soundtrack was one week before it opened. I completed the portion of the film in which we used actors in June 1966 and from then until the first week of March 1968 I spent most of my time working on the two-hundred-plus special-effects shots. The final shot was actually cut into the negative at MGM's Hollywood studios only days before the film was ready to open. There was nothing intentional about the fact that the film wasn't shown until the last minute. It just wasn't finished.

Why did you cut scenes from the film after it opened?

I always try to look at a completed film as if I had never seen it before. I usually have several weeks to run the film, alone and with audiences. Only in this way can you judge length. I've always done precisely that with my previous films. For example, after a screening of *Dr. Strangelove* I cut out a final scene in which the Russians and Americans in the War Room engage in a free-for-all fight with custard pies. I decided it was farce and not consistent with the satiric tone of the rest of the film. So there was nothing unusual about the cutting I did on *2001*, except for the eleventh-hour way in which I had to do it.

MUSIC AND EDITING

MGM's expectation was that the music soundtrack for *2001* would be a specially composed score, a property whose copyrights and potential licensing opportunities would be allied specifically to the film's fortunes. Apart from the business details, the studio never had any reason to think beyond this conventional way of adding music to moving pictures. MGM's favored candidate was Alex North, a well-established composer for both screen and stage. Having scored *Spartacus* a few years earlier, it seemed likely that he could work well with Kubrick. Unfortunately for North, there was a crisis just waiting to happen, as Ray Lovejoy, Kubrick's film editor on *2001*, understood from the outset: "Music played a huge part in the editing process, long before any final cut, because of the visual effects. There was so little dialogue, so how were we supposed to judge the pacing of a scene, or how long an effects shot should be? The only thing it could be placed against was music. So we used whatever seemed to work. Stanley had a tremendous record collection. Christiane came up with ideas, too. After a while, we all started bringing in records. What happens then is, you get used to them."

While assembling countless rough cuts of various sequences, Kubrick used prerecorded "guide tracks" drawn from his large personal library of classical recordings. Bach, Mendelssohn, Vaughan Williams, Richard and Johann Strauss, and dozens of other composers were explored. One piece, Johann Strauss's *Blue Danube* waltz, seemed to work surprisingly well with the gentle rotation of the orbiting space station. According to Andrew Birkin, Kubrick turned around from the editing desk at one point and said, "Could we actually use this for real? Am I crazy, or would it be a stroke of genius?" Everyone agreed that it would. The waltz idea was brilliant, unexpected, eccentric, yet somehow entirely appropriate. Kubrick was also drawn to the dramatic opening fanfare of Richard Strauss's *Also Sprach Zarathustra*, a tone poem inspired by Friedrich Nietzsche's philosophical novel of the same name.

When North came to London in December 1967 from New York, Kubrick warned him that some of the "temporary" working tracks might be retained. North insisted that he would create entirely fresh music, but agreed to the inclusion of similar themes. Kubrick installed him in a luxurious London apartment in Chelsea, showering him with every conceivable aid to his work: tape recorders, stereo decks, and a concert-standard piano. According to Pederson, North's eventual orchestration was not a success: "Doug [Trumbull] and I went out to Shepperton to watch them recording some music for the space station sequence, and Stanley—after we had looked at some dailies—called us up to the projection booth and said, 'What do you think?' And I said, 'Well, it sounds like a Hawaiian travelogue to me.' Stanley said, 'Yes, it's terrible, and I don't know what to do. I've got a hundred musicians out there and it's costing me a fortune.' We all felt rather badly about it."

North sensed he was doomed, even during the recording sessions. As he told Jerome Agel in 1970, "Somehow I had the hunch that whatever I wrote to supplant Strauss's *Zarathustra* would not satisfy Kubrick, even though I used the same structure but brought it up to date in idiom and dramatic punch." A subsequent orchestral revival and performance of North's score, arranged and recorded in 1993 by his friend, fellow film composer Jerry Goldsmith, reveals a work that would have benefited any number of films—just not *2001*, whose deep, cold, abstract gaze into the depths of infinite space was unsuited to North's more humanistic style: one, furthermore, that fitted too obviously among the "epic movie" scores common in the mid-20th century. His ambitious, yet arguably conventional orchestration was abandoned, and Kubrick returned to the timeless and less obvious guide tracks that had worked so well earlier.

On August 18, 1967, a sober British radio channel decided to risk broadcasting an avant-garde composition performed by the North German Radio Chorus and Symphony Orchestra. Christiane happened to hear it. A few days later, Kubrick dashed off an excitable note to his brother-in-law Jan Harlan: "Christiane heard a marvelous piece of music on the BBC, 'Requiem' by Ligeti. She says she thinks it would be marvelous for the film." A pristine recording of the performance, conducted by Andrzej Markowski, and featuring soprano Liliana Poli and contralto Barbro Ericson, was sourced from West German Radio so that Kubrick could hear the entire piece for himself.

György Sándor Ligeti was raised in Transylvania, a beautiful, troubled middle-European region centered on the intersecting fault lines of Austrian, Hungarian, Romanian, and German history. The Ligetis were Hungarian Jews, and György grew up in dangerous times. In 1943, at 20 years of age, he was sent to a forced labor camp by a Hungarian administration edgily pursuing an alliance with Hitler. At war's end, Ligeti studied music in Budapest, and began to research Romanian folk songs. Now his problem was the Communist regime rather than the Fascists. Communication with fellow musicologists and composers in the West was difficult. When the Hungarian anti-Soviet uprising of 1956 was suppressed, Ligeti escaped to Vienna, where he eventually acquired Austrian citizenship.

At last, he was free to meet like-minded musical experimentalists. Stockhausen and Koenig were working on revolutionary new forms of electronic music in Cologne, and the young American composer John Cage was assembling bizarre abstractions and deliberately randomized soundscapes, completely at odds with conventional orchestration. Everywhere Ligeti looked, he found composers, artists, and writers pushing to escape the conformities of mind, culture, and expression that, in their opinion, had encouraged the catastrophes of global war in the first place. Ligeti took up teaching posts while pursuing his interest in composition, exploring how to use traditional orchestras, choirs, and solo singers in unexpected new ways. His ideas called for dense, kaleidoscopic overlays of instrumental and vocal textures, with each layer operating at a different tempo from the next. His work was not especially well known outside the European avant-garde community until *Requiem* featured in *2001* to stunning effect, with three other compositions: *Atmospheres, Lux Aeterna*, and *Aventures*.

The process of licensing a piece of recorded music for use in a film can be tortuous. Even in the case of a long dead composer, copyrights may apply, especially in cases where rare original scores are held exclusively by museum collections. Additionally, an orchestra or a record company may be entitled to claim fees when playing and recording even the most familiar music. Certainly while a composer lives, he or she would expect to be paid royalties for any such usage. Kubrick's desire to use prerecorded music was unusual for the film business at that time. Determined to use Ligeti, he made what he thought was the correct approach to the Mechanical Copyright Protection Society (MCPS) in London, a well-established organization that dealt with royalties for composers, songwriters, and music publishers for those occasions when a composition was reproduced on vinyl recordings, put onto magnetic tape, played on the radio, or used as background music for a film.

When Ligeti heard about *2001* and went to see it, he was surprised at the extensive use of his music, and asked MGM for reasonable redress. He told his biographer, Richard Steinitz, that MGM's reply was somewhat cunning: "Please sue. You must start in Vienna and Frankfurt [the respective homes of Ligeti's music publishers]. Undoubtedly, you will win. Then you have to go to London. Again, you will win. The process will continue in Los Angeles. There, too, you will win. But we think it will take twenty years. Would you prefer $1,000 now?" This anecdote is fun, although somewhat colored by Ligeti's sense of humor, and probably not an accurate representation of MGM's correspondence. Kubrick, acknowledging without hesitation that his use of this music could not be classified as mere "background," intervened to ensure that MGM paid a more appropriate fee than the small sum recommended by the MCPS. The misunderstandings were erased in the wake of a separate and even more lucrative licensing deal for the vinyl LP of *2001*'s music soundtrack, manufactured by MGM's record company.

Contrary to some accounts, Ligeti was not displeased with Kubrick, and always blamed MGM rather than the director for the brief royalty debates. Kubrick had used the composer's work in a spirit of respect, editing long portions of his film to almost entirely unadulterated and uncut sequences of the music. Speaking of himself rather grandly in the third person, Ligeti told Steinitz, "I liked the film. The way it used my music I accept artistically. In the 1970s I saw a book on the making of *2001* and read there that Ligeti had successfully sued MGM for taking his music. But it's not so. I never sued them. MGM wrote me such nice letters. They said Ligeti should be happy that he's now famous in America."

There is no doubt that *2001* brought Ligeti's work to a far wider audience than he had enjoyed previously. And he knew it. With the composer's wholehearted approval, Kubrick returned to Ligeti's music again for *The Shining* (1979), which includes a short passage from *Lontano*, and his last film, *Eyes Wide Shut* (1999), in which a piano excerpt from an early 1950s piece, *Musica Ricercata,* is played as a hypnotic accompaniment to some of the film's darker moments.

The least well-known piece of music in *2001* was by an Armenian composer, Aram Khachaturian, whose patriotic ballet *Gayane*, set on a collective cotton farm, was first performed in December 1942 at a theater in Perm (or Molotov, in the nomenclature of the day), a city near Russia's Ural Mountains. With Joseph Stalin's explicit approval, Russia's famous Kirov Ballet troupe had relocated there, seeking safety from the Nazi assault on Leningrad (St. Petersburg). Kubrick selected a slow adagio movement from the work, mournfully expressing the dull routine of life on board the *Discovery* spacecraft. The implication is successfully conveyed that Poole jogs and exercises every day. As so often, Kubrick followed his instincts because, as he told the *New York Times* in 1968, "there are certain areas of feeling and reality—or unreality or innermost yearning, whatever you want to call it—which are notably inaccessible to words. Music can get into these areas. Painting can get into them. Nonverbal forms of expression can. But words are a terrible straitjacket."

VII

"Is this, in fact, what has happened?"

YESTERDAY'S TOMORROW

The set designs of almost all movie and television space dramas from the early and mid-20th century look quaint today. Their hissing pressure valves and trembling needles and dials are museum relics, long since replaced by newer and smarter technologies. *2001: A Space Odyssey* stands out from the crowd. The first impression we gain from viewing the film now is that, despite its provenance from a time before many of us were born, most sequences look as if they might have been photographed last month rather than five decades ago. Kubrick shows us, literally, how the engineers and scientists of the time saw the future shaping up. Much of what he and his advisors conceived turns out to have been startlingly prescient. The film possesses a kind of honorary reality, and its hardware details provide an important historical reference point, not just for film fans but for practicing designers, technologists, and scientists, too. We can study the thoughts and inventions of Kubrick's space experts with the same high seriousness with which we might consider the building of an ancient Greek trireme or a warship of the Trafalgar era. We can look at all the beautiful artifacts in the film and understand a previous generation's hopes and expectations for the year 2001. In so doing, we learn a great deal about the mid-1960s, too.

Kubrick's philosophical exploration was colored in, so to speak, by the industrial expertise of a great nation at the height of its powers. By the time the film was released, America was no longer quite so sure of its desire to conquer other worlds. The scaling back of Apollo in the late 1960s showed that *2001*'s vision of a space-faring culture was becoming redundant at the same time as the film hit the theaters. It is easy to say that the drain on national resources and civic morale generated by the Vietnam war somehow led to the demise of NASA's grand plans for lunar colonization and missions to Mars. Certainly the war—and the growing consciousness of the environmental movement—contributed to a popular distrust in large technological enterprises throughout the 1970s. More to the point, political leaders steeped in the example of Franklin D. Roosevelt's "New Deal" philosophies gave way, in the 1980s, to a generation who rebelled against what was sometimes perceived as social engineering, and the overreaching of federal agencies into the nation's affairs. NASA struggled to justify its relevance, especially after the collapse of its Soviet rivals.

Now that the actual year *2001* is far behind us, and we have had the chance to compare and contrast fact with fiction, one or two of Kubrick's predictions look wide of the mark. The worst one can say is that certain fashion details betray their 1960s origins, and more painfully, the lack of nonwhite characters or significant women in commanding roles seems unimaginative. These quibbles apart, the intensity of the film's technical design is vividly cogent for our generation. To take just one example: in August 2011 the Samsung electronics group launched a defense against the Apple company's claim of patent infringement. Who, exactly, invented the touch-sensitive tablet computer? Apple claimed that its famous iPad was a true original. Samsung thought that the concept was general rather than specific, and therefore not subject to patenting. One submission argued that it predated the Apple brand itself:

> *Attached hereto as Exhibit D is a true and correct copy of a still image taken from Stanley Kubrick's 1968 film "2001: A Space Odyssey." In a clip from that film lasting about one minute, two astronauts are eating and at the same time using personal tablet computers. As with the design claimed by the D889 Patent, the tablet disclosed in the clip has an overall rectangular shape with a dominant display screen, narrow borders, a predominately flat front surface, a flat back surface (which is evident because the tablets are lying flat on the table's surface), and a thin form factor.*[1]

Although this was a newsworthy embellishment on the surface of a complicated legal dispute, it illustrates how we still regard *2001* today as much more than a piece of entertainment. The details of *Discovery*'s switch panels or *Orion*'s cockpit displays were never merely decorative. They were genuine attempts at extrapolation. The film is celebrated for how much it got right about the early 21st century. Just as importantly, where it made technical errors, it did so in ways that turned out to be flawed rather than just plain wrong.

Those flat screens are a case in point. Kubrick's people didn't quite anticipate that most of the buttons, too, are vanishing, and we are left today with just the screens, whose touch-sensitive surfaces constitute the entirety of the control panel. One scene, ultimately not used in the final cut of *2001*, approaches tantalizingly near the target. When HAL plays chess against Poole, the display merely shows the moves that have been ordered by human voice command or triggered internally by the computer, but Kubrick also photographed Dullea playing pentominoes, a game where shapes built from arrays of little squares must be slid around and fitted against other shapes. Dullea physically interacted with the display panel. Trumbull and his animation colleagues mocked up the moves, and Dullea, on being cued that the screen was about to change its configuration, conveyed the impression that his touch was causing the change.

Touch-sensitive screens eliminate the need for buttons, so perhaps *2001*'s designers missed that last intuitive leap from pentominoes to a fully graphic interface between people and machines. However, there is a difference between sleek design on the ground and the cockpit of a spacecraft. We consumers can afford the occasional accidental swipe of a tablet, from which an unwanted action results. A professional pilot or astronaut does not

1 Samsung's opposition brief was filed on August 22, 2011

◁▷ 387–389 Manufacturers were eager to provide props, such as this "futuristic" pen from Parker, a proposed portable TV from RCA, a wristwatch from Hamilton, and a selection of concept cars from General Motors.

have such a margin of error. Commands must be relayed without ambiguity into the ship's systems, or else a hatch might be blown open at the wrong moment, an engine fired by mistake, and so on. Astronauts and pilots still have some buttons to push. In fact there are buttons that "arm" the actual buttons that send the instructions. Buttons and switches give a pilot one last chance to answer the question, "Are you absolutely sure this is the action you intend?" Buttons may remain with us for some while in contexts where lives may be at risk, although, in *2001* there are, perhaps, more of them than we would expect today. Strangest of all are the paper checklists and clip boards used by the astronauts on board *Discovery*. One of Robert McCall's poster artworks, extrapolated from the scenes of life on the lunar surface, show a space-suited astronaut holding a tablet computer with an extremely "thin form factor" and a keyboard obviously integrated into the glowing screen. So close, so close…

Dullea and Poole use their flat-screen devices to watch moving images. Additionally, considerable effort was devoted to mocking up electronic newspaper displays precisely similar to modern e-magazines and branded newspaper websites. Typically alert, Kubrick demanded that the small print of all the news articles should be convincing. Only the need to tighten up the film's dramatic pace prevented these stories from appearing on the pads:

> *The last known specimen of Ursus horribilis, the grizzly bear, died in the Cincinnati Zoo yesterday… the grizzly's story was one of a losing battle against the increasing power of the hunting rifle and the insistent demands of cattle farmers and fish stock men that the species be eliminated… AIRLINER MISSING OVER ATLANTIC —2304 on board—little hope for Mach 3 Aircraft…*

An honorable prediction that overshoots slightly ahead of present-day reality is *2001*'s double-wheeled space station. Rocket pioneers in the 1930s, such as Robert Goddard in America, or Hermann Oberth and Willy Ley in Germany, understood the potential of such a design. The first detailed engineering proposal appeared in Hermann Noordung's 1928 book *Das Problem der Befahrung des Weltraums* (*The Problem of Space Travel*). We know almost nothing about Noordung's background, except that he was an Austro-Hungarian army officer and that he died young of ill health. Fortunately, his station proposal survives. He described a *Wohnrad* ("Living Wheel") whose gentle rotation provides its crew with artificial gravity. A huge parabolic dish collects and harnesses sunlight for power. The docking airlock rotates at the same rate as the station, but in the opposite direction, thus maintaining its position relative to the horizon. Rocket ships can approach without themselves having to tumble. Noordung predicted that weightlessness would play havoc with the human balance system. His design influenced a generation of astronautics engineers, including Wernher von Braun, whose wheel-shaped station, as depicted in *Collier*'s magazine in 1952, was an obvious influence on *2001*. Having worked in von Braun's Future Projects office, Harry Lange was infected with this idea, too. The primary purpose of a space station would be to serve as comfortable accommodation for humans in orbit. Artificial gravity must surely be required to keep them healthy.

Now we have a real space station, and while it's not as huge or imposing as *2001*'s, it does span an area equivalent to a couple of football fields. Most of that area is taken up with solar panels rather than living quarters, and this station certainly does not rotate. The current reality is that we seek to exploit, rather than counteract, weightlessness in order to conduct experiments that are impossible on Earth. The station in *2001* is "wrong," therefore, but for an interesting reason. Furthermore, its graceful balletic tumble may not seem so unrealistic in the 22nd century, even if it is a little premature for the 21st. There are still many technical proposals for large rotating space habitats, where comfort, rather than science, may well be the priority.

The Jupiter-bound interplanetary spacecraft *Discovery* is plausible, although the lack of airtight ship-to-ship docking ports worries some modern observers. Prominent vents and intakes on the ceiling of the pod bay indicate that the ship's precious air is not wasted every time the huge circular doors are opened. Modern spacecraft designers would have docked the pods to small airlocks. Once again, this incorrect extrapolation is a worthy failure rather than a "mistake." The greater question is, why does such a ship not exist, now that the year 2001 is more than a decade behind us? Far from being outpaced by subsequent developments, Kubrick's film presented a vision of a space-faring culture that has still to be matched. Arthur C. Clarke once wrote, "No achievement in human affairs was ever so well documented before the fact as space travel." Lange, Ordway, and Kubrick's army of astronautical advisors absorbed most of those same documents while conceiving *2001*'s vehicles, and in the heat of their technological optimism they failed to ask an essential question: where was the financial payoff? If ships were to be sent into Earth orbit or to the Moon, what could they be expected to bring back as a return on the huge investment required to build them? What gold or silver could the cosmic cowboys gather in their saddlebags to buy themselves a ride over the next horizon?

For a few years after the shock of Sputnik's launch in 1957, the economic arguments against rocket adventures became strangely inverted, so that the financial drawbacks became the justifications. By accepting the huge expense of these abstract adventures without any hope of a sensible profit, both Russia and America set out to show what their rival societies might be capable of down on Earth: how much more they could do than merely running their domestic economies or equipping their armies. They built powerful rockets for unarmed adventures in space as a substitute for thermonuclear combat on the ground, which no one (aside from a handful of *Strangelove*-style fanatics) really wanted to risk. In addition, there was only so much pride that the rival superpowers could express in the workaday challenges of simply keeping their populations alive. They aspired to more—and so did a great many of their citizens. No political leader of the day would have urged his nation into space if that prize hadn't meant something to the millions of ordinary people he was trying to impress.

President John F. Kennedy made a famous speech in May 1961 in which he encouraged America to land men on the Moon "before this decade is out." He was anxious not to allow Soviet rocketeers to dominate space. Even so, by November 1962 he was frustrated that the resources for a lunar mission couldn't be allocated for something more socially beneficial. In a private White House meeting with NASA's ambitious chief James Webb, Kennedy cautioned him to scale back his plans. "We shouldn't be spending this kind of money, because I'm not that interested in space," he said. "I think it's good. I think we ought to know about it. We're ready to spend reasonable amounts of money. But there's a lot of things we need to find out about. Cancer and everything else. All these other programs, we're starving them to death."

By the late 1960s the liberal counterculture was in full swing, and for the hippy generation NASA represented something devilish: "The Man," that figurehead of the White Anglo-Saxon Protestant (WASP) capitalist élite, suppressing human instinct in service of machinery, subverting Nature to his will and creating a global army of technocratic zombies. Norman Mailer, a self-appointed spokesman for a rebellious generation, covered Apollo 11's lunar landing mission for a book project, and found himself stirred and alarmed

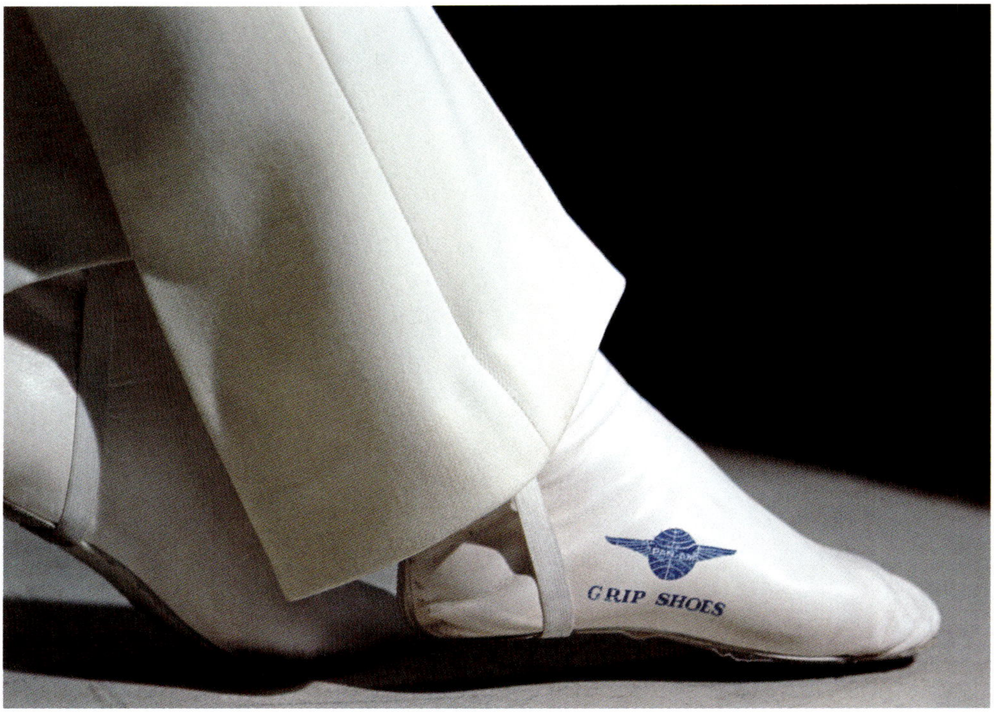

Heather Downham retrieves a drifting pen. Her costume, designed by Hardy Amies, includes Pan Am branded "grip shoes" with special soles that adhere slightly to the central walkway.

◃ Bruce MacDonald's publicity sketch showing pilots and a stewardess on the *Aries* flight deck.

in equal measure. On the one hand he found the thunderous Saturn V rocket immensely moving: "I had a poor moment of vertigo at the thought that Man now had something with which to speak to God. A ship of flames was on its way to the Moon." He even wondered if, perhaps, the tirelessly energetic WASPs were right in their ambitions for human progress, and the hippies feckless, lazy, and doomed? At the same time Mailer was frustrated by the Space Age's bland public face:

> *Everybody in NASA was courteous, and proud of their ability to serve interchangeably for one another, as if the real secret of their discipline and their strength and their sense of morale was that they had depersonalized themselves. I had never before encountered as many people whose modest purr of efficiency apparently derived from being cogs in a machine. They spoke in a language not fit for a computer of events that might yet dislocate eternity.*[2]

"A language not fit for a computer..." Kubrick's use of flattened language in *2001* accurately mirrored this failure among the technocratic classes. One of NASA's greatest errors was to lose emotional touch with its tax-paying audience. Apollo 11 astronaut Michael Collins recognized this: "I think a future flight should include a poet, a priest, and a philosopher. Then we might get a much better idea of what we saw." Men had ventured to the Moon in urgent circumstances, flying new and hazardous machines, yet somehow the true majesty of that fact was not reflected by NASA's dry presentation. Perhaps this is one reason why Tom Wolfe was able to write these prescient words about the Mercury, Gemini, and Apollo astronauts in his 1979 book *The Right Stuff*:

> *Well, the Lord giveth, and the Lord taketh away. The mantle of Cold Warrior of the Heavens had been placed on their shoulders without their asking for it, and now it would be taken away again without their knowing that either. It would have been impossible for them to realize that the day might come when Americans would hear their names and say, "Oh yes—now, which one was he?"*[3]

Even Wolfe, with his taste for a caustic aside, would never have imagined that the day might come when Apollo veterans would be accused of faking their achievements. Thousands of cynics around the world believe that men never landed on the Moon. They claim that the ghostly TV pictures of Neil Armstrong stepping onto the distant lunar

2 Mailer, Norman, *Of a Fire on the Moon*, 1970

3 Wolfe, Tom, *The Right Stuff*, 1979

surface in July 1969 were rigged in a giant studio here on Earth. One particularly amusing theory holds that Kubrick was responsible for the special effects.

These convoluted conspiracy theories perhaps reflect our unease about Apollo's place in technological history. In 1886 Karl Benz patented the first automobile. Forty years later, American industry was manufacturing 4 million of them a year. The Wright Brothers flew the first human-carrying powered aircraft in 1903. Forty years later, commercial air travel and its darker cousin, aerial combat, were routine, and thousands of people owned private planes. In the 1950s, the larger companies and institutions had access to a few hundred computers for running their payrolls or solving complex equations. Forty years later, computers and communications devices small enough to fit in our pockets outnumber the Earth's human population. And so it goes, and so it goes. The lunar adventure nourished countless areas of the economy in subtle and important ways, speeding up developments in software, metallurgy, precision welding, and other profitable but unglamorous skills, such as personnel management, risk analysis, and information flow. These benefits haven't been so easy for most of us to identify with. The more obvious impacts that we might have expected, judged according to previous historical trends in machinery, are absent. We don't all have rockets in our garages and we cannot all travel to the Moon. The orbiting Hilton Hotel in *2001* has not been built.

Strangest of all, NASA tells us that it would be almost as hard, and nearly as expensive, to build a lunar spacecraft now as it was 40 years ago. Naturally, some people think that if we could accomplish Apollo using 1960s technology, then we should be able to do it all again today, and at less cost, with all the modern microchips and materials at our disposal, not to mention the vast backlog of knowledge already accumulated in NASA's brain bank. Our failure to expand on the Apollo experience suggests that it may have been some kind of a miracle the first time around. An accidental series of alignments in history made Apollo possible, forcing it to the technological forefront somewhat ahead of time.

In the 1960s, NASA was at the vanguard of a new technology. Today it may be the custodian of an old one. Rockets are no longer among the defining machines of modern times. The ballistic missiles that heralded the so-called Space Age have lost their threat in an age where chaotic terrorism has become the principal concern for defense analysts. Professor John Logsdon, former head of the influential Space Policy Institute in Washington, D.C., has advised several presidents on astronautical affairs. Despite his enthusiasm for space, he is sober on the subject of government-funded exploits: "I'm not sure there's anyone to blame for *2001*'s vision not happening in the real world. Who says it's supposed to happen? Who says it's the best or most desirable future? Most people, and the leaders who represent them, haven't bought into that dream. We can be sad about

Heather Downham "demonstrates" the in-flight TV screen on the back of an *Orion* passenger seat. This kind of gadgetry is commonplace today.

▹ There are no nonwhite people in *2001*, and apparently no senior female figures. Have we risen above 1960s social assumptions today, or are we still stuck in the past?

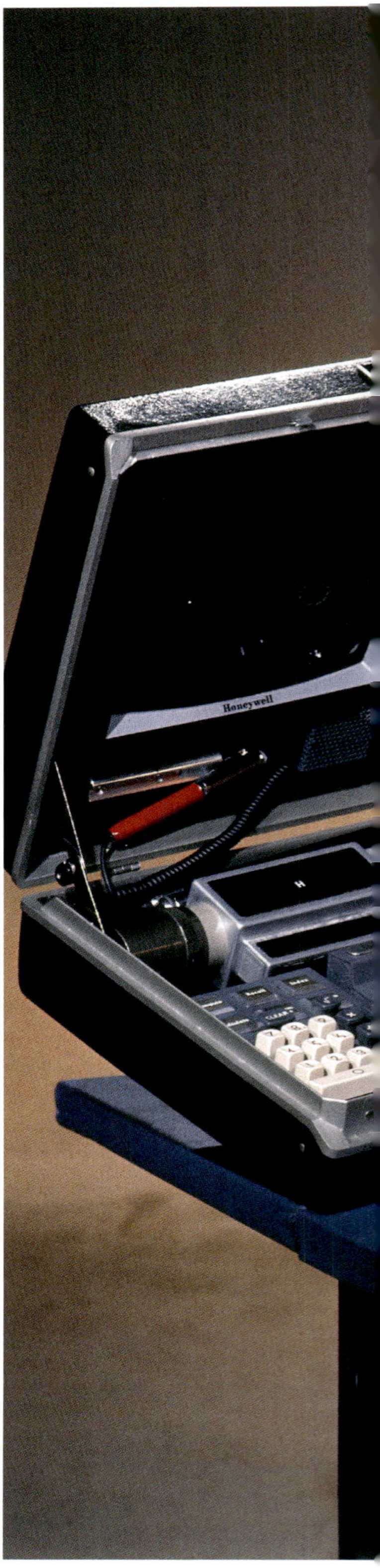

The Honeywell company designed a briefcase for Heywood Floyd. It contains all the components of a modern laptop computer: a keyboard, a camera, an electronic stylus pen, a modem, a digital file storage module, and a display screen.

▹ 400 No matter how high we fly, or how far into the cosmos we travel, someone, somewhere, will expect us to buy something, as demonstrated by these automated gift vending machines in the space station.

▹ 401 The various compartments within *Discovery* were equipped with hardware based on the best technical ideas of the day. These are among many contributions from Honeywell and RCA: a nuclear control desk and food-selector panel in the centrifuge.

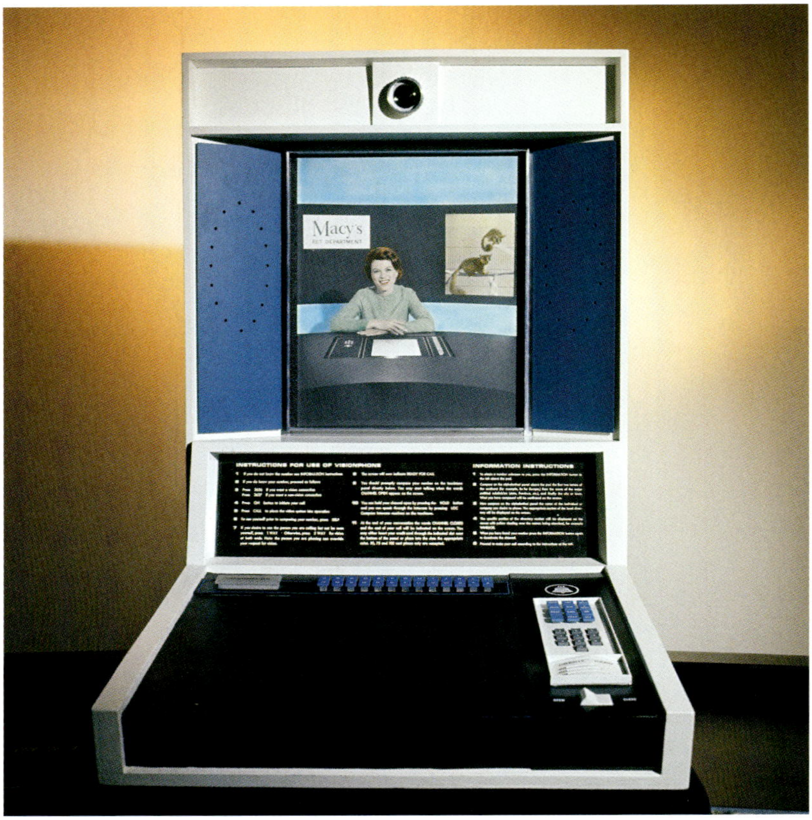
Macy's
PET DEPARTMENT
INSTRUCTIONS FOR USE OF VISIONPHONE
INFORMATION INSTRUCTIONS

HILTON
SPACE STATION 5
GIFTS
DRUGS
CAMERAS

DIETARY RECOMMENDATION
BREAKFAST
PRUNE JUICE
CEREAL
BACON & EGGS
MUFFINS
COFFEE
LUNCH
AVOCADO PEAR
ROAST PORK
SAUTE POTATOES
ORANGE PUDDING
COFFEE
DINNER
ASPARAGUS SOUP
ROAST BEEF
MASHED POTATOES
CARROTS
BLUEBERRY PIE
COFFEE

UNITED STATES ASTRONAUTICS AGENCY
DISCOVERY

◁ 402/403 Film critic Alexander Walker thought that *2001*'s space pods and other interior settings represented "Man surrounded by his organized energies." Trouble arises when humans dare to venture outside these air-conditioned safety shells.

△ Kubrick came tantalizingly close to implying touch- sensitive screens in this deleted scene. Bowman plays pentominoes against HAL, apparently manipulating the virtual shapes with his finger. Careful timing of the rear projection enabled the illusion to work.

▷ This publicity photo of Dullea and Lockwood sitting at their dining area shows portable tablet computers, designed with help from IBM, and uncannily similar to today's models from Apple and Samsung. The backlit graphics on each screen are supposed to represent electronic versions of magazines and newspapers.

how things have turned out—those of us who share Kubrick and Clarke's hopes for space exploration—but I don't think it's anybody's fault."

Clarke, too, was realistic about the state of play in the decades after the Apollo landings: "It is disappointing that we didn't go back on the Moon, and are not likely to do so for some while yet. On the other hand, I've seen so much happen that I never imagined I'd witness in my lifetime: the exploration of almost all the solar system's planets, and many of its moons, by robot probes that have taken us there vicariously, and shown to us that these are real places, not just pinpricks of light in the sky. We could never have guessed, back in the '60s, that a mission to Jupiter and its moons lay, not in the 21st century, but only 15 years ahead. Nor could we have imagined the wonders that would be found there. When *2001* was written, Io, Europa, Ganymede, and Callisto were mere smudges of light in even the most powerful telescopes. Today we know a great deal more about them."

BUT THE "SPACE AGE" NEVER ENDED...

After the Russian-American race to the moon concluded with the touchdown of Apollo 11, a degree of competitive tension persisted for another two decades, until the fall of the Berlin Wall and the end of the Soviet era. While a somewhat diminished NASA worked throughout the late 1970s on development of its winged space shuttle, Russia answered with a steady expansion of its space-station capability, starting with the Salyut orbiting platforms and culminating in the multi-module Mir complex. When Ronald Reagan came to the White House in 1981, his advisors expressed concern about Soviet dominance in long-term orbital space flight. It seemed a natural idea for America and its allies to build a large space station in response.

On January 25, 1984, Reagan announced that a space station (known as "Freedom") should be built: not by NASA alone, but by a partnership of allies, including Europe, Japan, and Canada. The following year, European Space Agency chiefs met in Rome to discuss the station proposal. An official statement was published: "Europe will seek appropriate participation, with access and use of all elements of the station on a non-discriminatory basis." The Columbus laboratory and the Automated Transfer Vehicle (ATV) eventually emerged from these negotiations as ESA's flagship contributions. A Japanese laboratory module and robot transfer ship were also added to the mix, as NASA and its new partners began the slow and often-delayed work of the $100 billion project.

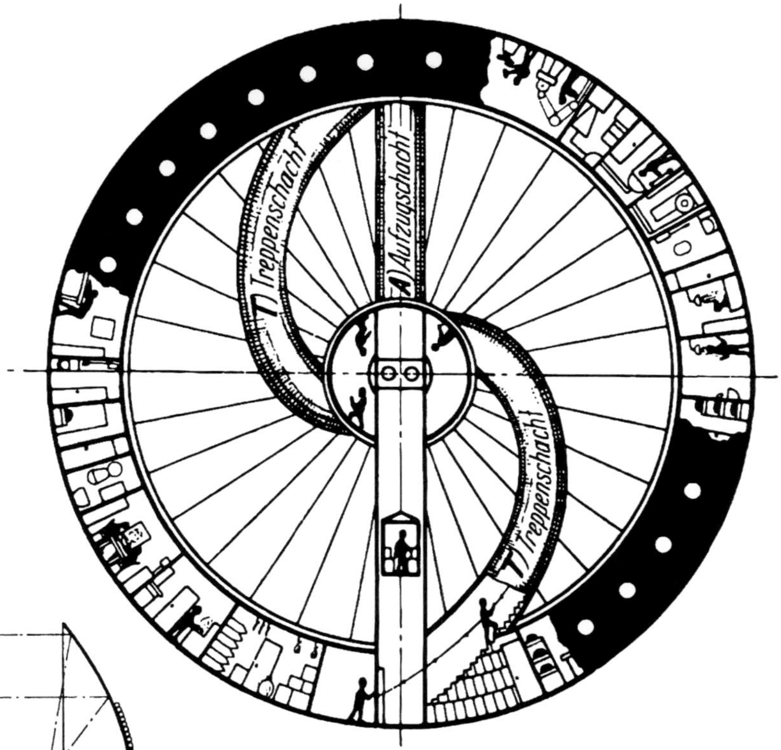

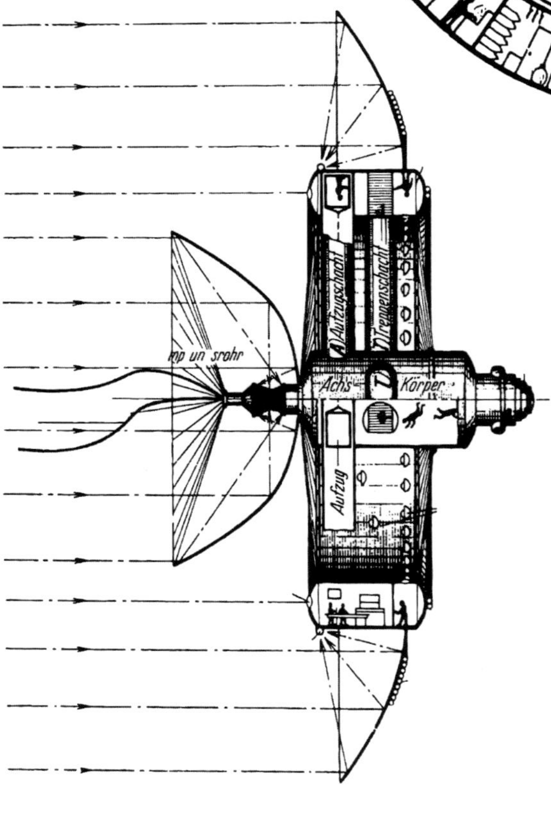

This solar-powered rotating space habitat was conceived by Hermann Noordung, a junior army officer in the dying days of the Austro-Hungarian Empire.

On June 6, 1992, NASA administrator Dan Goldin and his Russian opposite, Yuri Koptev, met for the first time in Goldin's Washington apartment. The subject under discussion was extraordinary in its scope. Could Russia and the United States, those bitter Cold War enemies, find common cause in space now that the Soviet empire had collapsed? Over the next two years, Goldin and Koptev negotiated to secure Russia's broader partnership in orbit, and perhaps beyond. The proposed new space station was redesigned to include Russian modules, and the entire thing was rebranded as the International Space Station (ISS). In *2001* we see something analogous: a large station collaboratively inhabited by Americans and Russians who don't quite trust each other.

The motivations for the deal with Russia were complex. One factor was Russia's need to protect its rocket industry from economic turbulence while a market economy slowly began to emerge. Just as significant was the White House's desire to prevent disenchanted Russian rocket experts from selling their missile expertise to "undesirable" clients such as Syria, Iraq, or Iran. Collaborative arrangements ensured that a wide range of Russian launch vehicles, spaceflight expertise, and orbital hardware would become available to the international space community, thereby keeping the domestic workforce intact and safely employed.[4]

4 Bizony, Piers, *Island in the Sky: Building the International Space Station*, 1996

The first component of the ISS, the Russian-built control module Zarya, was sent into orbit by a Proton rocket launched from Baikonur in Kazakhstan, on November 20, 1998. Then came NASA's Unity node, and the next Russian piece, the Zvezda Service Module: just the first in a long series of components from 27 countries. Today the sprawling station maintains a permanent crew of up to six people. There is never a moment when humans are *not* in space. This achievement may, perhaps, set the tone for a much larger and more comfortable type of space platform, as envisaged in *2001*.

Richard Branson's Virgin Galactic company is one of several new businesses striving to create a private space-flight industry. An elegant carrier plane lifts the smaller spacecraft component high into the atmosphere, where it is released prior to its final rocket-powered push into space.

△ The prescient hardware from *2001* still inspires many creative talents. This version of *Orion* by Hollywood special-effects artist Bill George shows the craft in the livery of a modern and still thriving airline.

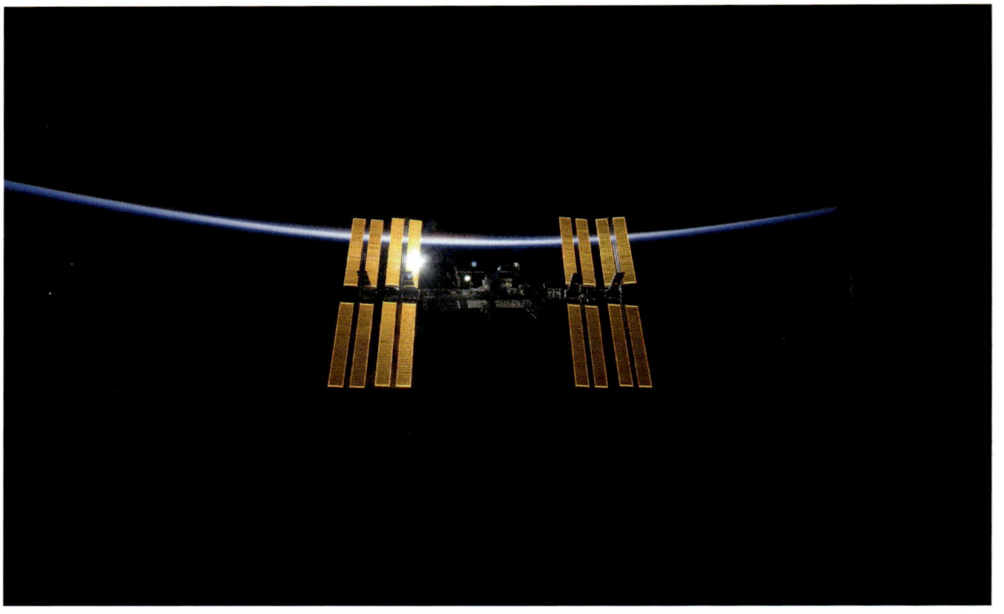

The International Space Station is one of the most impressive political and technological creations in modern history, but is overshadowed by Kubrick and Clarke's grander fictional ideas.

▹ Mass transport into space is not yet possible, and we cannot enjoy coffee in lounges while watching the Earth or the Moon through panoramic windows, as in this sketch for *2001*.

ORBITAL ENTREPRENEURS

The major next step would have to be commercializing what has, until now, been almost exclusively the preserve of ponderous, tax-funded national space agencies. Change is afoot. Smaller, nimbler private entities are springing up, led by a new generation of aerospace pioneers for whom Kubrick's film is not merely a beautiful piece of fiction but a manifesto, a blueprint around which a real commercial space industry can be founded. According to Peter Diamandis, one of the leading figures in this young sector, "We all saw *2001: A Space Odyssey*. People began to dream that they, too, could travel into space. As time passed, that dream began to disappear. We saw a string of horrendous accidents, including the 1986 *Challenger* shuttle explosion."

The NASA that put men on the Moon was an effective and fast-moving entity. Unfortunately, like most giant bureaucracies that persist too long after their initial aims have been achieved, it lost momentum over subsequent decades. Diamandis and his allies believe that private industry can take up the slack. Entrepreneurs today are accustomed to generating innovations over the course of months, not decades. The slow-paced and heavily bureaucratized activities of government space agencies do not appeal to them. A business movement, known alternatively as Altspace or NewSpace, has emerged.

In February 1994 the American Society of Civil Engineers held a conference in Albuquerque, New Mexico, to discuss the prospects for commercial privately funded space flight, just as depicted in *2001: A Space Odyssey*, with its Pan Am shuttle service and Hilton accommodations. Architects and engineers presented beautiful models of orbiting hotels and lunar settlements. Everyone was convinced that the required technologies were perfectly feasible. They were not so convinced when financiers warned them that there was no purely civilian market for such expensive dreams, and that only governments could afford human space flight. The NewSpace activists sensed that there were indeed many private citizens willing and able to pay for a taste of space. In 1998 Diamandis's company, Space Adventures, negotiated with Russia's Star City cosmonaut training complex near Moscow in order to provide vacationers with $10,000 weekends of dressing up in space suits and clambering around training

simulator versions of space capsules. Customers also signed up for flights aboard "vomit comets," jet planes flown in a churning sequence of ascents and dives in order to create brief periods of weightlessness.

On April 28, 2001, Dennis Tito, an ex-NASA space scientist who had made his fortune in technology investment, flew into orbit aboard a Russian Soyuz capsule and stayed aboard the International Space Station for six days, having invested $20 million of his own cash in the mission. His trip was booked through Space Adventures. A year later, South African Internet entrepreneur Mark Shuttleworth made the same journey. Meanwhile, on Earth, the respected polling company Zogby International telephoned 450 Americans with annual incomes above $250,000. Seven in 100 said they would pay $20 million for a two-week orbital flight, and one in five were happy to contemplate $100,000 just for a short suborbital trip above the Earth's atmosphere, during which the "space" phase of the trip might last no more than five or 10 minutes.

A significant market for personal access to space certainly exists. Until recently, what has been lacking is a suitable private rocket vehicle to satisfy that demand. In May 1996 Peter Diamandis and a group of business leaders held a gala dinner in St. Louis, Missouri, to celebrate Charles Lindbergh's 1927 first flight across the Atlantic, funded by an earlier generation of patrons from that city. They were competing back then for a $25,000 prize set up by New York hotelier Raymond Orteig. That was a considerable sum of money in 1927. Could a similar prize persuade modern industry to develop affordable human space flight? With this expectation, Diamandis established a $10 million prize fund to reward the first suborbital passenger vehicle to reach an altitude of 100 kilometers: the realm internationally agreed as the edge of space. His partner in this enterprise was Anousheh Ansari, the young founder of a digital communications company.

Ansari spoke no English when she emigrated to the United States from Iran in 1984 at the age of 16. She hoped that living there would help her realize her dream of becoming an astronaut. She studied electrical engineering at George Mason University, then cofounded her successful family business, Telecom Technologies. By 1996 it was one of the fastest-growing enterprises in its hometown of Dallas, Texas. Meanwhile, Ansari never lost her fascination for the cosmos. "As a child I looked at the stars and dreamed of space travel," she says. "As an adult, I knew that the only way this dream will become a reality is with the participation of private industry and the creative passion of smart entrepreneurs." With this in mind, Ansari and her family subsequently underwrote a major portion of the funding for Diamandis's $10 million scheme, which became known as the Ansari X Prize. ("X" is a traditional aerospace designation for an "Experimental" craft, such as the X-1, the first piloted aircraft to fly faster than the sound in October 1947, or the X-15 high-altitude rocket planes of the early 1960s.) In September 2006 Anousheh achieved her most cherished personal ambition, flying into orbit aboard a Russian Soyuz capsule at her own expense, and spending eight days aboard the International Space Station. By this time, the X Prize had been securely won, and a new private space industry was taking shape.

Twenty-six private companies took up the X Prize challenge. A fascinating array of proposed designs included delta-winged space planes, eerie capsules shaped like seedpods, and even a machine with rocket-propelled helicopter blades. Some competitors built real hardware, while most lacked the resources to deliver much beyond concept artworks and unpowered mock-ups. Even so, the seeds for a new industry were sown. One company, Mojave-based Scaled Composites, took a clear lead from the start. SpaceShipOne, designed by Burt Rutan at Scaled Composites, won the X Prize on October 4, 2004, immediately earning back half the $20 million discreetly invested in the vehicle by Microsoft's cofounder, Paul Allen.

Just as Lindbergh's flight stimulated a transatlantic air industry with incredible speed back in the late 1920s, Rutan's team has triggered a similar gold rush at the dawn of the 21st century. Two days after SpaceShipOne's final qualifying flight, Richard Branson revealed that his Virgin Group was ready to finance SpaceShipOne's much larger successor. More than $100 million was allocated to develop a "Virgin Galactic" suborbital space liner, with six passenger seats, flying from a custom-built spaceport in New Mexico. This vehicle, a winged rocket plane launched from a much larger jet-assisted glider, is now entering service. Branson is among those who see Kubrick's film as a call to arms: "I think *2001: A Space Odyssey* is magnificent, and I hope that one day Virgin Galactic will be going a lot further than just suborbital flights, and will reflect that film."[5] Another company, SpaceX, founded by PayPal entrepreneur Elon Musk, has developed a new rocket and launched a recoverable capsule into orbit, capable of docking with the International Space Station.

These new commercial vehicles are reshaping traditional attitudes about the costs and complexities of reaching space; and for the first time, aesthetics are becoming significant, so long as they do not interfere with the serious physical functioning of the hardware. There is a subtle reason why NASA's real-life lunar modules and orbiting shuttles seldom seemed so slick as Kubrick's machines. Consider how commercial airliners are built. The production runs are large enough to justify the huge costs of purpose-built factory templates. The cabins have molded interior fittings that tuck neatly into the corners and meet seamlessly with the window frames; the foldaway tables look like they belong on the back of the seats, and so on. Everything is aimed at enhancing the comfort (or at least, adding to the illusion of comfort) of fee-paying passengers.

5 Quote courtesy of the Virgin Galactic company

The same cannot be said of spacecraft flown by hardened professional astronauts. These are hand-built machines from a production run limited to half a dozen or so at most. Consequently there is a nuts-and-bolts feel to them. Unprepared observers often find them disappointingly crude, insistently antique. Kubrick's *2001* predicted that commercial space vehicles would require more comfortable interiors. Today, and for the first time in the history of space flight, marketing departments are introducing aesthetic elements into the hardware, at least so long as such design flourishes do not interfere with more urgent operational requirements. The Virgin Galactic passenger cabin in particular was created to answer the technical and safety aspects of a flight, and just as significantly, to match private clients' expectations as to how a 21st-century spaceship cabin *should* look. Despite the fact that *2001*'s artists laid out their drawing materials nearly half a century ago, the craft they invented still determine our expectations.

NASA is learning to work with its faster, fleeter competitors. It will concentrate on exceptionally difficult and costly projects, such as sending human explorers to an asteroid, or landing them on Mars, while allowing the small private companies to dominate the more routine business of reaching Earth orbit and servicing space stations, some of which may be privately funded in the near future. A space-faring culture similar to Kubrick and Clarke's vision may be emerging somewhat later than the year 2001.

In the last decade of his long life, Clarke's optimism flickered but never burned out: "Although our depiction of a huge base constructed on the Moon was, in retrospect, hopelessly optimistic, the central themes of the movie remain entirely valid. We will eventually return to the Moon, then journey to the planets and beyond. It is inevitable. Historians in some far distant future will, no doubt, regard the current half-century delay in our plans as nothing more than temporary, a brief hiccup in the greater span of events."

HAL 9000'S LEGACY

And so we come to the biggest "error" in *2001*. Marvin Minsky, cofounder of the Artificial-Intelligence Laboratory at MIT, made a number of accurate predictions about his field, which Kubrick and his team took to heart when conceiving HAL 9000. "I think the computers of today could fly airplanes with greater reliability than pilots can. There have been proposals to make completely automatically operated aircraft systems." This is commonplace now. Minsky (along with many other computer experts in the 1960s) also expected that "in thirty years' time we should have machines whose intelligence is comparable to man's." This expectation has not been met. We do not have clever, conscious computers today, and it seems we are just as far off from inventing them as we were in 1966.

Modern computers are faster, better, and smaller than anyone could have imagined back then. What's more, they are ubiquitous. Our homes and offices, even our pockets, are brimful of them. We don't even stop to think that our mobile phones are computing devices, or that the little SatNav in our car is more powerful than any 1960s room-sized supercomputer, and 100,000 times cheaper. Still these clever digital toys cannot *think*. Stubbornly, they remain dumber than chickens. HAL says, "I am putting myself to the fullest possible use, which is all, I think, that any conscious entity can ever hope to do." No computer today can make such a boast. Power and speed are not sufficient to overcome the biggest challenge of all. Before we can design an intelligent and conscious computer, we have to find out how intelligence works, and what consciousness actually is.

In November 2010 the London branch of Christie's auction house sold an original HAL 9000 face plate for $27,600. Several versions of this prop were made for the film.

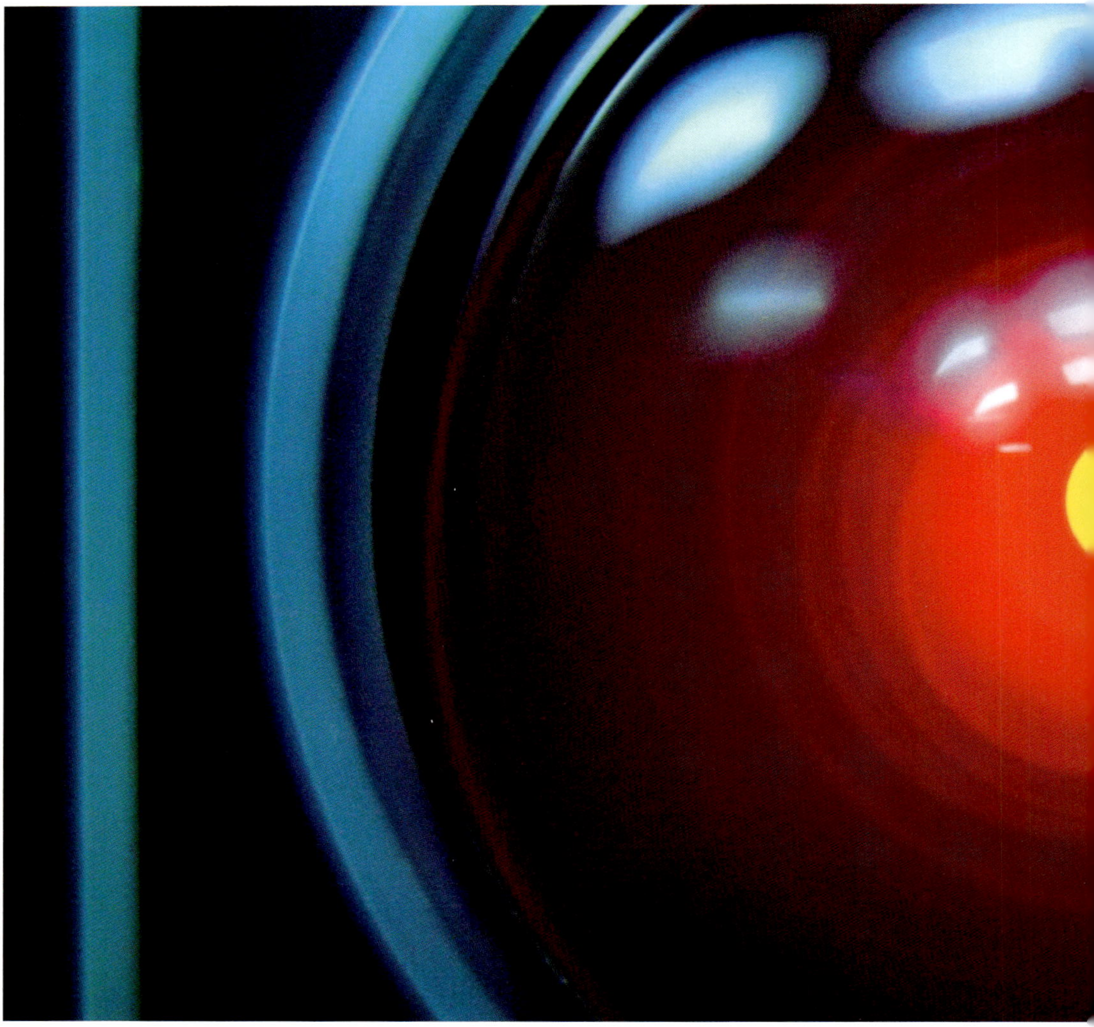

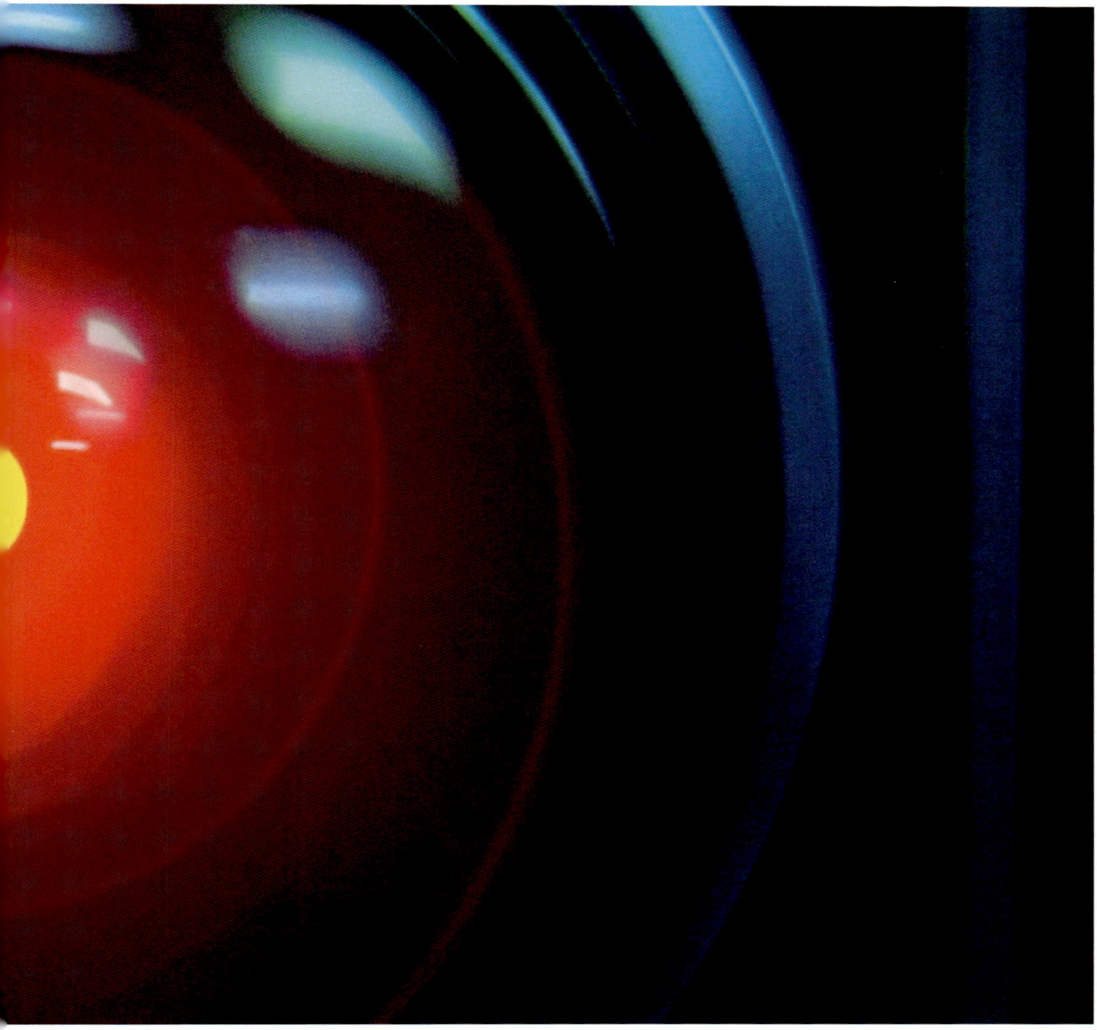

HAL the red-eyed computer stole the show. As Kubrick commented, "Some critics seemed to feel that because we were successful in making a voice, a camera lens, and a light come alive as a character, this necessarily meant that the human characters failed dramatically."

◁▷ 416–419 The HAL 9000 computer is sentient, capable of appreciating a work of art, and even of lip-reading. HAL appears conscious, and expresses pride in his intelligence. Contrary to the expectations of 1960s computer experts, no such clever machine is on the horizon yet.

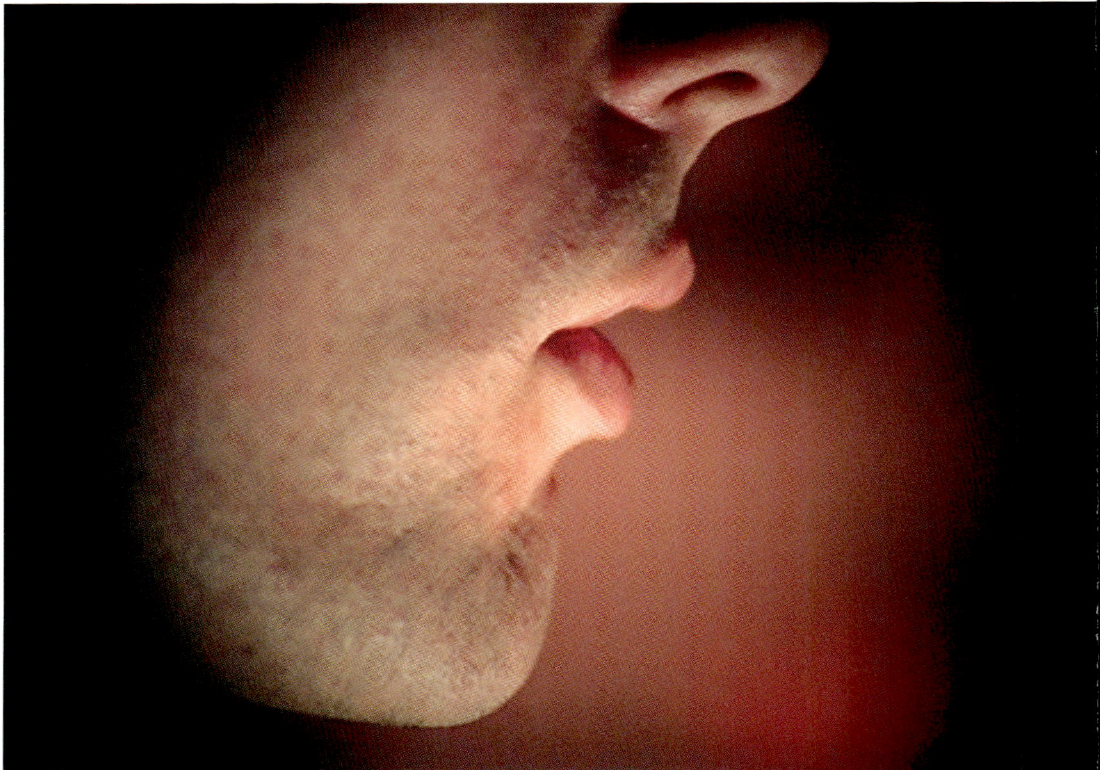

We learn that a healthy apple should be green with a blushing red patch. This is knowledge that helps us pick good apples when we go to the store, but it's not the same as becoming *aware* of the redness and greenness once we have the apple in our hand. When the colors come alive in our minds, or when we recall, later on, what those colors looked like, we experience a phenomenon called a "qualia," the most vivid form of consciousness. The wavelengths of a color spectrum are absolute, if determined by some dispassionate scientific instrument such as a computer. It could tell ripe apples from unripe ones by measuring the light bouncing off them, but could it *experience* the greenness of the fruit as we can? These are deep questions about how we see the world.

Just to pile on the problems, consciousness isn't something created in our own heads alone. It's the product of a feedback between us and the wider world—a world filled with other conscious creatures like ourselves. Most of us would agree that a certain shade of blue matches the appearance of a clear summer sky, and that the flag of the United States includes stripes that are considerably redder than the peel of an orange, but not so red as a ruby. We can share the cultural and historical associations of "blue" and "red" as ideas. We cannot be so sure that we are having the same color experiences as the next person (especially those of us who are color-blind). Our awareness of color, or any sense impression, for that matter, is contextual, based on long years of inhabiting a human world of culture, language, and associations.

Then there's something called the "binding problem." Medical scanners show us how different areas of the brain are activated, depending on the mental task at hand. We can map areas associated with language, music, memory, intellectual cogitation, or raw animal emotion. What we cannot figure out is how all the lit-up areas communicate or combine to give us that overwhelming sense of "being" someone, and experiencing the world as a "person" rather than just as a collection of brain cells. The insect world may help us unravel the binding problem. Many insects, such as ants and termites, live in huge colonies containing millions of individuals. A single ant responds to its surroundings or its fellow ants. Put those ants together, however, and a sophisticated system emerges. Some scientists call it a collective intelligence. A single ant, with its tiny brain, cannot know very much about what is happening to the colony as a whole, but when all the millions of ants work together, each doing their own little bit, the colony acts as though it had an intelligent mind. It is amazing to see ants working together in huge teams to gather food or build complex nests, as though "someone" were controlling them. In a similar way, human consciousness may be an "emergent property" arising from the collective action of billions of unconscious brain cells.

Perhaps the most unsettling idea is that conscious "free will" might not actually exist. It may be a retrospective sensory and memory illusion, a replay of events that happened moments ago, generated by the brain in order to help us understand the narratives of our lives. Many experiments have demonstrated that we only become "aware" of our supposedly conscious decisions several seconds after unconscious processes have set them in motion... These are just some illustrative examples to show how difficult the problem of consciousness is. Even so, none of this means that constructing a HAL 9000 is impossible. Just because he *says* he's conscious doesn't mean that he has to be. The BBC interviewer Martin Amor hits the mark when he says that HAL "can reproduce—though some experts still prefer to use the word 'mimic'—most of the activities of the human brain." Recent research suggests, somewhat embarrassingly, that it is fairly easy to fool the average nontechnical person into thinking that a machine can possess a mind.

Half a century ago, the computing pioneer Alan Turing suggested that if you have a conversation with a machine intelligence, and you can't tell the difference between how it responds and what you'd expect a person to say, then the machine is probably just as smart as you are. In the classic version of the Turing Test, a human volunteer types questions into a keyboard and the machine's answers are printed out on paper. Turing thought it unimportant what any of the hardware looked like. The test was to be judged in terms of intelligence alone. However, it turns out that surface appearance is crucial. A desktop computer, loaded with a program that retrieves a wide range of pre-scripted answers on cue, can scrape its way through a test, although the results don't fool many people for long. The test is much easier for the computer to pass when it has some kind of physical body that can make gestures to accompany its word output: a cartoon smile, a widening of its camera eyes, a nod of the head. We respond emotionally, and sometimes self-deceivingly, to the beguiling surface appearance of the machine's responses. All too easily, we credit machines with self-motivation, or "agency," because we are wired by evolution to identify agency in our fellow humans—and in other animals too. In Main Street stores we can be charmed by inexpensive robot toys that talk to us, or perform physical actions, without our pulling the levers. When machines look as if they are alive, it's easier for us to pretend they actually might be; and this fact, coupled with the fast-improving power of computers, enables an artificial-intelligence industry to thrive today, because the expectations of human user-consumers are not so exacting as we once thought they'd be.

WHAT CAME FIRST— THE TOOL OR THE USER?

In *2001*, the use of tools distinguishes humanity from the rest of the biological world, while the tools and weapons themselves evolve (in the form of HAL 9000) into an intelligent "species" potentially capable of supplanting us. Kubrick and Clarke adopted a mainstream scientific idea, neatly expressed by the French philosopher Henri Bergson in 1907, when he wrote that intelligence stems from the "faculty to create artificial objects, and in particular, tools to make other tools." Nevertheless, Kubrick's brilliant split-second cut from cudgel to spaceship expresses only a partial thesis for how we managed to extend the reach of our hairy arms into space. Prominent anthropologists in the early 1960s were accustomed to judging the achievements of our evolutionary ancestors in terms of stone axes and arrowheads. Too little attention was paid to more elaborate constructions that could not survive in fossil form: their social habits and relationships. In recent decades the academic emphasis has shifted away from the use of tools and toward the importance of communicating the knowledge of how to use them. A straightforward summing-up of this new paradigm can be found in evolutionary psychologist Nicholas Humphrey's book, *Consciousness Regained* (1983). He sets up the figure of a typical anthropologist, a "straw man" who

> *...holds the opinion that the main role of creative intellect in man lies in practical invention [which] includes the fabrication of new tools...The need for invention arises only in relation to the external physical environment. Our straw man has not noticed—or has not thought it important—that many animals are social beings.*[6]

Humphrey explains how Daniel Defoe's Robinson Crusoe, cast away on his lonely desert island, thought himself the brightest of men, with his clever cabins and shelters and animal traps, but he really needed his wits about him when "Man Friday" came on the scene. In comparison to analyzing and reacting to each other's social responses, making tools is a relatively simple matter of trial and error which, once learned, requires little more thought, at least for any given tool. It is not the discovery of a tool, so much as the social transmission of its usefulness as an idea, expressed to other individuals and then learned by them, that creates a "culture."

6 Humphrey, Nicholas, *Consciousness Regained: Chapters in the Development of Mind*, 1983

Jane Goodall has studied chimpanzees in Tanzania's Gombe Valley for 50 years. Their use of tools is passed down the generations, typically from mothers to children, who learn by imitative example. They poke thin grasses into ants' nests, smash nuts with stones, clean their backsides with clumps of grass, and sometimes keep the rain off their heads with leaf "hats." Goodall has observed that these lessons, these *technologies*, take time to absorb, especially for the infants being introduced to the delicate and frustrating arts of ant-poking. The key factor is that a stable society has to exist first. A certain ease from immediate fear and hunger is required before speculative primates can afford the time to play with the world around them, so as to stumble, occasionally, on new and useful applications for leaves, pebbles, and bits of wood—or animal bones. The collective security of the troupe provides the Gombe chimps with profitable leisure opportunities. Goodall's book *In the Shadow of Man* (1971) suggested that "special attention has always been focused upon any animal able to use an object as a tool; but it is important to realize that this ability, on its own, does not necessarily indicate any special intelligence in the creature concerned."[7]

Personal interactions are orders of magnitude more complicated to negotiate than the use of tools. Humphrey, Goodall, and many primatologists besides, have argued that it is in primate society, rather than in its physical artifacts, where we must seek the roots of human consciousness and intelligence. To be aware of others, to be able to manipulate, or placate, or work together with, or outwit, or even kill others of our kind, we must know a little of how those others see us. We must become self-aware. This is not to find fault with Kubrick and Clarke's weaponized and tool-oriented vision of human progress, although it is worth noting that man-ape leader Moonwatcher's "invention" of a bone cudgel is swiftly *imitated* by his companions. The odd thing about war is just how intensely collaborative it is—at least for those on the same side.

7 Goodall, Jane, *In the Shadow of Man*, 1971

VIII

"Perhaps you can clear up the great big mystery about what has been going on up there."

ARE WE ALONE ?

Kubrick's *2001* was just one relatively recent and particularly successful expression of an age-old question: are we alone in the universe? So far as the written record of history allows us to judge, Thales of Miletus (624–546 BC) and his student Anaximander (610–546 BC) were among the first thinkers to discuss the possibility of tangible, inhabitable worlds other than our own. Five hundred years before the birth of Christ, *aperoi kosmoi*, the "plurality of worlds," was a familiar philosophical concept. According to Metrodorus of Chios, "things that exist tend to do so in great multiplicity, from grains of sand to ears of corn. It would be odd if only a single stem of corn grew in a field. Similarly, it would be strange if our Earth were the only one in the cosmos." In Renaissance Italy, a rebel priest, Giordano Bruno, was burned at the stake, in part because of his belief in alien worlds. His scandalous book *De l'Infinito, Universo e Mondi* (*On the Infinite Universe and Worlds*), published in 1584, described "countless suns and countless earths all rotating around their suns in exactly the same way as the seven planets of our system." He thought that other worlds in the universe must be "no less inhabited than our Earth… Destroy the theories that the Earth is the center of the Universe!" Bruno's sentiments still seem compelling today. A modern idea known as the "Mediocrity Principle" is a more scientific equivalent of ancient suspicions:

The Earth, our particular ball of rock, seems to be a fairly typical product of planetary formation. These processes, in turn, are governed by the laws of physics. Certain values in the natural world are constant everywhere, and most particularly, the speed of light. Albert Einstein's famous predictions about matter, energy, and relativity have withstood more than a century of testing. Some physicists speculate that light may not always have traveled at the same velocity throughout the entire 13.75-billion-year history of the universe, and that some other fine-tuned constants, such as the strength of gravity, could perhaps change by infinitesimal degrees as the universe ages and expands. These are speculations on the wilder frontiers of theoretical science, and have little relevance over the span of cosmic time that encompasses the human era. We can be confident that all regions in the observable universe are subject to the same laws of physics. Our sun works by nuclear fusion, and all other stars similar in mass, luminosity, and age will be born, live, and die in a similar manner. Light from even the most distant stars and galaxies reinforces our conviction that the same laws of nature familiar to us must apply everywhere—at least, this is the current state of our thinking. Tony Frewin recalls Kubrick's neat précis: "One plus one is two, no matter where you are in the universe. Unless, of course, it isn't."[1]

The Mediocrity Principle simply states that if the Earth has come into existence orbiting a commonly available type of star, then it is reasonable to assume that other solar systems can coalesce around other stars, so long as the local conditions happen to be similarly

1 Frewin, Anthony, *Are We Alone? The Stanley Kubrick Extraterrestrial-Intelligence Interviews*, 2005

appropriate. Furthermore, the chemicals that make up our Earth, and everything upon it, are not exclusive to us. All of the atomic elements, and many of the simpler organic molecules essential for life, are widely scattered throughout the universe. To put it bluntly, the physical and chemical conditions on Earth are mediocre. (The term comes from statisticians' use of the word "median," meaning "average.")

The known universe—everything in space that we can observe with our instruments—contains somewhere between 100 billion and 500 billion galaxies. There may be more galaxies in the universe than stars in a typical galaxy. Light from the most distant galaxies that we can observe has taken nearly 13 billion years to reach us. That light first shone when the universe itself was still young. Because of these mind-numbing expanses of space and time, it is extremely unlikely that we will ever encounter any extraterrestrial intelligences from another galaxy. The best place to look is within our own Milky Way galaxy. But we have little chance of success unless an alien civilization happens to be startlingly close by. The Milky Way contains about 200 billion stars. From one side of the galaxy to the other, the distance is around 100,000 light-years (in other words, light takes that long to travel across it). The light that we capture in our telescopes from stars at the Milky Way's perimeter was first emitted while Neanderthal humans still roamed the Earth. Despite these enormities, there is nothing nonsensical about the possibility of aliens. The number of potential solar systems and planets available, even in our extremely localized cosmic backyard, is simply staggering. In the early 1960s one man in particular, radio astronomer Frank Drake, was establishing a scientific program called the Search for Extraterrestrial Intelligence, or SETI. He contributed an extensive interview for *2001*'s prologue experiment. Kubrick, a mathematically literate man, was intrigued by a famous equation that Drake had formulated.

Drake was born in Chicago in 1930, and studied electronics at Cornell University, where he became fascinated by astronomy. As a teenager he attended a Baptist Sunday school. University trips to museum collections of Egyptian mummies and other artifacts caused him to wonder how his particular church could so easily ignore the religions of other cultures, past or present. From that thought came an insight familiar to ancient Greeks and heretical Renaissance thinkers alike. If religions were multitudinous, then

Throughout the four years of *2001*'s conception and production, Kubrick struggled with the problem of portraying a genuinely alien creature, until he decided that anything visible on screen and comprehensible to audiences would not, by definition, be "alien" to them. This is a prototype alien body. Christiane Kubrick worked on a number of ideas, seeking to deliver on her husband's request for "something in a shape that doesn't remind you of anything, in a color that doesn't exist."

▹ 428–433 Storyboards attempting to show alien environments: oceanic worlds, cities of light, and islands floating in midair were just a few among countless ideas considered.

perhaps the human world was similarly just one among many? Working at the National Radio Astronomy Observatory (NRAO) in Green Bank, West Virginia, Drake waited his opportunity to look for alien signals. In 1959 he was granted permission to install the electronics for a radio search, on the understanding that the equipment he assigned for the task should be used only briefly for alien hunting. He was told to be discreet. Then, with startling suddenness, the NRAO changed its mind and told Drake to tell the world.

In September that same year, independently of Drake, two eminent physicists, Philip Morrison and Giuseppe Cocconi, proposed the same idea in the science journal *Nature*: a radio search for extraterrestrial intelligence. They even suggested what channel to tune into: a particular frequency in the "quiet" realm of the radio cosmos, allied to a stable energy level of hydrogen atoms in the vast gas clouds drifting between stars. Smart aliens would know how to exploit the "hydrogen line" and make their signal stand out against the background hiss of empty static.

In August 1960 Drake and his NRAO allies conducted Project Ozma, named, as Drake subsequently explained, "for the queen of the imaginary Land of Oz, a place very far away, difficult to reach, and populated by exotic beings." Ozma took the form of a two-week radio dish observation of Tau Ceti and Epsilon Eridani, two relatively nearby sun-like stars. Of course this search was speculative, but at one point during the scan a signal seemed to come from Epsilon Eridani. According to Drake, "We heard bursts of noise coming out of the loudspeaker eight times a second, and the chart recorder was banging against its pin eight times a second. We all looked at each other, wide-eyed. Could it be this easy?"[2]

The signals turned out to be spurious interference from Earth. From time to time, exciting "maybes" do crop up. On the night of August 15, 1977, at Ohio State University's Big Ear radio observatory, an artificial-seeming signal was detected, completely unlike any natural cosmic noise, and definitely coming from somewhere far out in space. In those pre–plasma screen days, radio data was recorded as a grid of numbers on rolls of paper printout. Volunteer observer Jerry Ehman circled a mysterious pulse and wrote "Wow!" on the margins of the paper. Unfortunately, it never arose again, and no one is sure what generated it. The most fascinating aspect was the frequency: extraordinarily close to Morrison and Cocconi's hydrogen line.

Drake decided that the chances of finding alien radio signals had to be phrased as a statistical probability. If he could put the problem to skeptical fellow scientists in a formal mathematical language rather than at the level of mere philosophical speculation, then all the variables could be assessed, one by one. Here is the now-famous Drake Equation:

2 Courtesy of Big Ear Radio Observatory and North American Astrophysical Observatory

N = R* x fP x nE x fL x fI x fC x L

R* = the **R**ate of formation of stars suitable for the development of intelligent life.
fP = the fraction of those stars with **P**lanetary systems.
nE = the fraction of planets, per solar system, with an **E**nvironment suitable for life.
fL = the fraction of suitable planets on which **L**ife actually appears.
fI = the fraction of life-bearing planets on which **I**ntelligent life emerges.
fC = the fraction of **C**ivilizations that develop technologies that we can detect via radio
L = the **L**ength of time that such civilizations release detectable signals into space.

N, the magic figure we are after, is the Number of civilizations whose radio pulses we might detect. At each point, the numbers must be shaved down ruthlessly. R* cannot include the many billions of stars that are improbable hosts for life-bearing planets, because they are too hot, too cold, or too unstable in their orbits. In (P), representing solar systems vaguely like our own, Jupiter-sized gas giants and icy outliers don't count as likely habitats for life. Even if worlds exist that are like the Earth, allowances have to be made for the fact that life might not necessarily arise on them (L). If creatures do evolve, we have to be pessimistic about the likelihood of any becoming intelligent (I). Even if some aliens do stare up at their skies in fascination, we have to wonder if technology is within their grasp, or even on their wish list (C). They might have no interest in radio dishes. Even if they are technological, and do transmit messages into space, the question (L) asks: when, and for how long? This year? Next year? Ten thousand years ago? And did they send a short, brief burst of a message that we can never hope to intercept, or are they even now transmitting from a beacon built to last for millennia?

On the galactic scale of events, measured in billions of years, their civilization and ours might have emerged with fantastic synchronicity. On the puny human scale of time, the slightest chronological misalignments between alien technology and ours would make all the difference between establishing a meaningful dialogue, or passing each other like ships in the vast cosmic night. Finally, the time taken by signals to cross interstellar space adds a complicating factor of anywhere between four years (the light-year distance to the nearest star, Proxima Centauri) and many thousands, depending on the locations of individual star systems. The galaxy may be—or may have been—teeming with intelligent civilizations, all eager to make contact with other worlds, but this is no guarantee that we can communicate with them.

▹ 436–439 Bowman finds a robe and slippers waiting for him, in one of several bedroom scenes eventually omitted from the final cut. Kubrick considered them too literal.

The SETI Institute, founded in 1984 by Drake, in conjunction with the Californian aerospace engineer Thomas Pierson and the astronomer Jill Tarter, is based in a modest suite of offices in Mountain View, California. Its mission is "to explore, understand and explain the origin, nature and prevalence of life in the universe." It is a private, nonprofit organization, reliant largely on fragile financial aid from sponsors. At least the coming generation of SETI researchers will have a better idea of where to point their radio dishes. Recent discoveries have given encouraging numerical substance to the Drake Equation. Astronomers have learned how to detect the presence of planets around other stars by exploiting fantastically delicate shifts in the stars' light levels. By November 2010, 500 new planets had been discovered, although the nature of the business, from initial suspicions to confirmation, meant that no one could claim to have found "the" 500th planet on any given day. The Extrasolar Planets Encyclopaedia, a database compiled by astrobiologist Jean Schneider of the Paris-Meudon Observatory, announced that the milestone was reached on Friday, November 19, with the count rising to 502 a couple of days later.

THE PLANET HUNTERS

NASA's Kepler Space Telescope was launched in March 2009 from Cape Canaveral Air Force Station, Florida, on an expendable Delta rocket. It orbits the Sun, trailing slightly behind the Earth. Its instruments detect planets as they transit their stars, blocking from view a tiny fraction of the starlight. For five months Kepler kept watch, unblinkingly, over 156,000 stars toward the constellations Lyra and Cygnus. The initial results were published in February 2011. Kepler detected 1,235 potential transits. If this sounds like a disappointingly low number from among a great sprawl of 156,000 stars, we must keep in mind that Kepler's static field of view covered only about 1/400th of the sky. Extrapolating from this, and bearing in mind the Mediocrity Principle that says this 400th fraction of the galaxy should not be substantially different from any other 400th fraction, a simple calculation suggests that if a Kepler-type instrument of the future makes an all-sky survey, it should find a vast number of planets.

There is something else about Kepler's perspective that we have not touched upon. Transits can only be observed when a star's planetary system happens to be correctly aligned with the telescope's line of sight. The star, the planet, and the telescope must all be on the same line. Only a small fraction of extrasolar systems can be expected to deliver such a convenient alignment while Kepler is operational. Furthermore, Kepler can only monitor stars that are extremely local to our patch of the galaxy. Any stars more distant than around 3,000 light-years are so small in the telescope's field of view, it cannot make reliable measurements. Remembering that the Milky Way is some 100,000 light-years in diameter, we can work out that a volume of stars a few thousand light-years across is only a tiny fraction of what's out there. Astronomers are fairly confident, now, that there must be at least 50 billion planets in the galaxy, of which 500 million may be habitable. Whether or not any of them actually are inhabited is another matter, but nothing in the real scientific discoveries since *2001*'s release has lessened the credibility of Kubrick's central hope that we are not alone in the universe.

THE LIMITS OF INTELLIGENCE

Drake was among several interviewees for the *2001* prologue who thought that intelligence should emerge on worlds other than the Earth: "Animals have tried different numbers of legs—we've had six and eight legs, and 100-legged things. We've had winged creatures. Everything has been tried. The only thing which has persisted and continuously developed is intelligence, and this argues strongly that intelligence will appear everywhere where life evolves." Freeman Dyson agreed that alien creatures might become clever. He was not so sure about the glittering delights of braininess, nor that moral advancement must walk hand in hand with intellectual sophistication. In a 1964 letter to *Scientific American* (from which Kubrick quoted during his 1968 *Playboy* interview), Dyson wrote:

> *Intelligence may indeed be a benign influence, creating isolated groups of philosopher-kings far apart in the heavens and enabling them to share at leisure their accumulated wisdom… On the other hand, intelligence may be a cancer of purposeless technological exploitation, sweeping across a galaxy as irresistibly as it has swept across our own planet… The technological cancer could spread over a whole galaxy in a few million years, a time very short compared with the life of a planet… It is just as unscientific to impute to remote intelligences wisdom and serenity as it is to impute to them irrational and murderous impulses. We must be prepared for either possibility and conduct our searches accordingly.*[3]

Drake's interview session with Caras gave rise to a similarly dark image. He admitted that humans might be considered "the finest beef animals" by a hungry alien species, but reasoned that there is no point in limiting our deliberate radio SETI experiments, because our planet leaks so much casual electromagnetic noise anyway: "We already transmit

3 *Scientific American*, April 4, 1964

◃ 440/441 Unused publicity stills, taken by John Jay, show Dullea looking suitably puzzled in the hotel room and its equally strange bathroom: an adjunct to the main set that allowed astronaut Bowman to see his rapidly aged face in a mirror.

△ A realistically conceived scientific instrument monitors the inexplicable alien object on the Tycho excavation set.

▹ 445–447 Roll-film frames of lunar astronauts walking down the ramp and towards the monolith, which then emits a supposedly ear-piercing radio signal that disrupts the astronauts' headphones.

enough radio waves into space that we can be detected if they want to detect us. We cannot keep our presence secret, so we might as well answer back."

Ever optimistic, Arthur Clarke had little interest in the possibility of carnivorous aliens (he was distressed, for instance, about the 1996 invasion film *Independence Day*, which opened with a potentially awesome *Childhood's End* image of vast starships hovering silently over world capital cities, before turning into a less uplifting story of alien attack and human counterstrike). He assumed that a successful strain of cultural and technological evolution could have only one outcome, even if very few species would attain it. An ancient and wise alien race could become godlike, at least as witnessed from our less exalted terrestrial perspective. According to one of his favorite maxims, "To the primitive mind, any sufficiently advanced technology would be indistinguishable from magic." He thought that such entities might turn to little creatures like us, for nothing more than companionship. They would seek the kinship of consciousness for consciousness: the same kinship that makes us search the heavens in the hope of finding alien intelligence.

Kubrick also stated in his *Playboy* interview that aliens at the top of the cleverness pyramid "would seem like gods to millions of less advanced beings in the universe, just as we would appear like gods to an ant that somehow comprehended Man's existence. If the tendrils of a greatly developed alien consciousness ever brushed our minds, it is only the hand of God we could grasp as an explanation." Godlike powers could be too much of a good thing. Imagine an alien culture freed from all needs, wants, and hungers. Would it become stagnant and fall into decadence and chaos? Karl Popper, arguably the greatest philosopher of science in the 20th century, warned that automatic assumptions of social and moral advancement through technology are bound to be flawed. His 1945 essay *The Open Society and Its Enemies* tells us, "Our dream of heaven cannot be realized on Earth." He was dismissive of utopian visions of perfect societies shuttling between gleaming cityscapes linked by glass tubes and flying cars. "Only when we are in possession of something like a blueprint of the society at which we aim can we begin to consider the best means for its realization." And that blueprint, of course, is an impossible goal, "owing to our limited experiences."

There is nothing inevitable about our climb toward a better and more advanced state of being. We might just as easily slip down the intelligence scale and into the sub-zero levels, like some supposedly gold-plated cosmic investment suddenly gone wrong. The Drake Equation specifically addresses this possibility in the term "L," the length of time during which an alien civilization might be capable of communicating with us. One possibility that exercised the minds of SETI theorists during the Cold War era was the fact that the invention of nuclear power may have been very ingenious, but it gave rise to the possibility of planetary self-destruction. We have to assume that any technological alien society would encounter this hazard as soon as they learned about atoms and nuclear energy. Could they get past it and move on?

Our worst crisis came in the autumn of 1962, when the Russian-American standoff over missile deployments in Cuba and Turkey nearly brought the world to an end. Despite the essential optimism of *2001*, Kubrick, Clarke, and all their contemporaries lived in an age when the prospect of nuclear catastrophe was an ever-present dread. It is easy for us to imagine that the bombs and missiles that were once our darkest achievements have lost their edge in an era of "asymmetrical warfare." A few fanatics with dime-store craft knives can change the world in a day, while the globe-spanning missiles and their costly megatons stay sealed in their silos, impotent in a world that barely even worries about them anymore. In truth, these weapons still exist in frightening numbers, and the danger now is that the international madness of *Dr. Strangelove* will become available to individual maniacs, criminals, blackmailers, or zealots with an ax to grind. The bombs are threatening to escape their silos and creep into private houses, desert encampments, or the basements of anonymous buildings in unremarkable suburbs. Once we have unleashed the atomic genie, there is no putting it back in its bottle.

Clarke's bright horizons always had their distant clouds: "There are so many potential dangers to the human race. Many are self-inflicted. War is the obvious one, and that can take many forms now: not just nuclear weapons, but biological weapons, and all sorts of nano-weapons, so small that you can't even see them. Even in peaceful societies, we are making unpredictable dents in the environment, and we may have gone past the point of no return, although the ultimate calamity may lie some way ahead. Then, of course, there are natural disasters that occur perfectly naturally: earthquakes, tidal waves and storms. Particularly, we realize now the potential danger from asteroids. We wouldn't be here, of course, if a big asteroid some 65 million years ago hadn't wiped out the dinosaurs and given us little mammals a chance of developing. What the universe gives with one hand, it can take away with the other. One day, another big one will come along. We'll either have to learn how to divert it, or give the cockroaches a chance to inherit the Earth."

▹ 450–453 Many months before the slit-scan machine was conceived, production artist Roy Carnon attempted to show Bowman's space pod undergoing an extraordinary journey into the unknown.

Roy Cannon
'66

2001
THE 'POD' APPROACHING
SATURN

2001
THE POD APPROACHING SATURN

The "L" term in the Drake equation is hauntingly relevant, not just an abstraction. British biologist J. B. S. Haldane worried about something equivalent two decades before the first nuclear reactors were conceived. While serving with the British Army in India, he attended a dance party one night in 1918. There was much talk of Nova Aquilae, a star that blazed unusually bright for a few weeks in the equatorial sky that year. With the slaughter of the First World War fresh in his mind—or perhaps just seeking respite from noisy revelers—Haldane went outdoors to look at the brilliant speck of light. He speculated about "a too successful experiment in induced radioactivity" on a distant alien world, created by a society in which "too many men come out to look at the stars when they should be dancing."

Very few people who saw *2001* in its opening days realized that the first spaceships on screen, drifting beautifully and sedately around the Earth, were originally intended to be orbiting nuclear weapons. The production artworks of these vehicles are prominently labeled as "bombs." The brittle tension between Russian and American space scientists aboard *2001*'s space station reflected Kubrick's belief that the Cold War would probably extend into the 21st century. So widely held was this idea, it came as a total surprise, even to professional intelligence experts, when the Soviet Union collapsed suddenly at the end of the 1980s. The new, aggressively capitalist Russia that has emerged, and the similarly ambiguous shadow of China's military might, along with the construction of weapons-grade technologies in the Middle East, and in India and Pakistan, all suggest that the nuclear threat cannot simply be discounted as a relic from the last century.

Only in the later phases of editing did Kubrick decide not to mention the bombs explicitly in his film, concerned to avoid obvious references to *Dr. Strangelove*. Nevertheless, Christiane insists that it was not his intention to lose the inferences completely. The man-ape's bone, hurled aloft in a gesture of triumph, turns instantly into an orbiting device of the 21st century, "and it's exactly the same shape. The bone weapon becomes a space bomb, not a space *ship*. Perhaps Stanley didn't make it obvious enough."

Curiously, an early treatment for *Dr. Strangelove* presages the main comedic action with narration, spoken as if from the point of view of alien observers attempting to understand the causes of Earth's destruction. In 1964 the Bomb's shadow darkened all creative acts, everywhere. For Kubrick's birthday, Clarke found a card showing the Earth coming apart at the seams. Inside it bore the inscription, "How can you have a Happy Birthday when the whole world may blow up any minute?"

Taking all these elements into account, perhaps the most cogent sentiment was expressed during the filming of *2001*'s unused documentary prologue, when Roger Caras asked Norman Lamm, professor of Jewish philosophy, "Does anything in the Jewish faith militate against the possibility of alien intelligence?" Lamm replied, "As an individual, I think there probably is intelligent extraterrestrial life, but that is not something that would displace my central concerns… I would not denigrate the search for life elsewhere. I think it's intellectually fascinating. Human curiosity must certainly be satisfied. But the overriding problem is how to live in this world decently and well."

THE FERMI PARADOX

Freeman Dyson expressed to Caras a serious problem with the search for extraterrestrial civilizations: "What puzzles me is why we have not seen them. I would have expected that looking for a highly developed race of technological beings would be like looking for evidence of life on Manhattan island. They would have transformed their surroundings completely." This was a reformulation of a famous remark made some two decades earlier by the Italian-born nuclear physicist Enrico Fermi.

Fermi (1901–1954) escaped from Mussolini's fascist regime in Italy and joined America's secret Manhattan nuclear-bomb project in the 1940s, for which he built the world's first functioning nuclear reactor. In the summer of 1950, he was visiting the Los Alamos laboratory in New Mexico, where the first atomic bombs had been developed under the leadership of Robert Oppenheimer. Fermi had lunch with fellow physicists Edward Teller, Emil Konopinski, and Herbert York. They chatted briefly about a recent cartoon, published on May 20, 1950, in the *New Yorker* magazine, mocking the big news topic of the day. Why were New York's public litter bins mysteriously disappearing off the streets? They bantered for a while about little green men and the impossibility of faster-than-light travel. Suddenly Fermi asked, "Don't you wonder where everybody is?"

This simple question is known today as the "Fermi Paradox." It neatly sums up a serious problem in our quest for aliens. Even if the chances of finding intelligent life in any given sector of the galaxy are slim, there are many billions of star systems from which we might detect a radio signal, or some other indirect hint of an alien presence. Clever creatures should have arisen somewhere. Among the smartest societies, it might be rare to find any with advanced technology. Of those few who do possess it, only a small proportion might be equipped for interstellar travel… and so on. Fermi's point was that surely *one* civilization should be a mold-breaker, expanding into the galaxy on ships that would make NASA's slickest probes look like school science projects. The fact that nobody has visited us suggested to Fermi that there is no one capable of doing so. The Fermi Paradox is an apparent contradiction between the supposed probability of extraterrestrial civilizations existing, and the supposedly odd fact that we haven't had contact with any of them.

As a devotee and practitioner of sound logical argument, Kubrick was consistently troubled by the Fermi Paradox, although he never allowed it to extinguish his belief that extraterrestrial civilizations must exist. As Tony Frewin confirms, "Stanley was quick to [say] that absence of proof should not be seen as proof of absence. For the 30 years after the release of *2001* until his death in 1999, he returned countless times to the subjects spawned by the film. Months might go by with no reference to them, and then there would be a newspaper or magazine article or something on television, and he'd be discussing them again with current activities put on the back burner."

TO TELL OR NOT TO TELL?

A central theme in *2001* is secrecy. The assumption is that proof of alien contact would have to be discussed privately by senior administrators before any wider announcement could be made. Inside the lunar base Floyd says to his colleagues, "I'm sure you're all aware of the extremely grave potential for cultural shock and social disorientation contained in this present situation, if the facts were prematurely and suddenly made public without adequate preparation and conditioning." On board *Discovery*, HAL 9000 and the three hibernating astronauts (subject to separate training before the mission) are entrusted with the news about the lunar monolith and its radio screech beamed to Jupiter, while Bowman and Poole are kept in the dark. If an alien signal were detected today, would the relevant authorities adopt such an undercover approach?

In 1996 mathematician John Billingham and American diplomat Michael Michaud, both members of the International Academy of Astronautics at that time, compiled a draft document suggesting a SETI post-detection protocol. This effort was supported by the Paris-based International Institute of Space Law. Everything that happens in space at the behest of humans is subject to law. In the tense dawn of the Space Age, satellites and humans alike were launched aboard rockets designed primarily as intercontinental nuclear weapons. The United Nations Committee on the Peaceful Uses of Outer Space (COPUOS) was established in 1958 to prevent atomic warfare from reaching into the orbital realm or beyond. Since then, a series of international treaties has limited the deployment of weapons in space, and, less successfully, sought to protect celestial bodies such as the Moon, Mars, or the asteroids from simply being annexed by the first nation or corporation to make a grab for them. Ownership of potential space wealth over the coming decades is a theme that pays the bills for many lawyers. Armies of them deal with obscure aspects of space communications, such as the fair distribution of valued orbital slots, and so on. Space law counts for something.

With this in mind, Billingham and his colleagues considered the legal implications of receiving a signal from an alien civilization. They wondered who might be in a position to spread the news, or authorize transmitting a reply. Frank Drake celebrated an upgrade of the Arecibo radio telescope on November 16, 1974, by firing a radio message toward the globular star cluster M13 some 25,000 light-years away. M13 happened to be in the sky above the Arecibo dish at the time of the ceremony. The broadcast, coded in binary mathematics, lasted for less than three minutes and will take 25,000 years to arrive at M13. Then another 25,000 years must pass before anyone out there can reply—at least, so long as our current assumptions about alien communications are correct. Despite the unlikelihood of any nasty consequences, some critics were disturbed that Drake had been allowed to transmit anything.[4]

A rare surviving helmet decal bearing the insignia of a fictional NASA-style space agency.

More recently, in October 2009, a project known as A Message from Earth (AMFE) directed a high-powered digital radio signal towards Gliese 581, a red dwarf star that has been much on astronomers' minds in recent years, because, somewhat like our own Sun, this star appears to have several planets orbiting around it. The signal is a digital time capsule containing hundreds of messages selected through a competition on the social-networking site Bebo. The message was sent using the RT-70 radar telescope of Ukraine's National Space Agency, and will reach Gliese 581's vicinity in early 2029. Many thousands of people participated in the AMFE project. Billingham thinks the issue should not be trivialized. In his 1996 position paper he wrote, "Clearly, sending a message to another civilization is more than just a scientific research project; it is a policy question that should be addressed by policy bodies." Given the lack of any other sensible option, he proposed, "The most universal of existing international policy bodies is the United Nations." The International Academy of Astronautics supports a SETI post-detection task group, an eclectic gathering of about two dozen people, including SETI Institute scientist Seth Shostak, representative members of the media, two lawyers, William Stoeger of the Vatican Observatory, Britain's Astronomer Royal and respected cosmologist Martin Rees, plus science-fiction

4 The Post-Detection SETI Protocol, International Academy of Astronautics Position Paper, March 22, 1996

The first intelligible words spoken in *2001*: "Here you are, Sir. Main level, please."

writer Stephen Baxter, regarded by many as a latter-day successor to Arthur C. Clarke. The task group's occasional meetings are chaired by the quantum physicist and cosmologist Paul Davies, a professor at Arizona State University, and director of a special Center for Fundamental Concepts in Science. These are serious people, whose opinions would carry weight with the international political community.

The United Nations is aware of the SETI post-detection protocol, and while it has not been enshrined into international law, most serious SETI researchers accept it as a useable framework. What cannot be guaranteed is that everyone will stick to it if the big day comes and someone finds a signal. One way or another (and probably on Twitter) we will all learn about it quickly, if it happens. No bona fide SETI researcher anywhere is interested in government conspiracies or deliberate attempts to hide alien signals or artifacts. As chair of the post-detection task group, Davies supported an open, trusting policy, but in a recent book, *The Eerie Silence* (2010), and writing strictly from his personal perspective, he wonders about the wisdom of just letting everyone know, instantly, about an alien message with specific information. "The implications of simply receiving such a message would be so startling and so disruptive that, although eventual disclosure is essential, every effort should be made to delay a public announcement until a thorough evaluation of the content had been conducted," he writes. Fortunately for us citizens, the global village has ears everywhere. Davies "cannot imagine how the scientists involved would be left in peace" while they crunch the data. "Keeping the lid on such a discovery would present enormous obstacles."[5]

Kubrick's introductory letter to Clarke expresses his interest in "the impact (and perhaps even lack of impact in some quarters) such a discovery would have on Earth in the near future." Today we have the beginnings of a statistical tool for judging how great, or how minimal, such an impact might be. The Rio Scale was first proposed by Iván Almár from

5 Davies, Paul, *The Eerie Silence: Are We Alone in the Universe?*, 2010

the Konkoly Observatory, Budapest, and Jill Tarter of the SETI Institute in October 2000, during an international conference in Rio de Janeiro. Their paper was entitled "The Discovery of ETI as a High-Consequence, Low-Probability Event." This balance of impact versus likelihood is something that responsible governments juggle all the time when planning for possible catastrophes. Viral outbreaks and terrorist attacks, for instance, are considered high-consequence, high-probability risks, and consequently a good deal of cash goes into trying to prevent them. The probability of an asteroid smashing into a city and destroying it is deemed very low. Nevertheless, many governments fund at least a modest amount of research into asteroids because the consequences of any such smash would be very great indeed.

A military involvement in future space affairs is suggested by the presence of uniformed personnel at the lunar base conference.

The Torino Scale is a deadly serious analytical tool for assessing asteroid threats. Small asteroids and bits of space dust fall on the Earth every day. The big crater-makers arrive once in 10,000 years, and city-sized destruction occurs perhaps once in 100,000 years. Some calculations suggest that we are long overdue for another significant hit. Detecting dangerous asteroids is now a priority for NASA and other space agencies. Modest-sized rocks frequently drift between the orbits of Earth and the Moon, and one or two in recent years haven't been at all modest. Tarter and Almár stated that the news of a discovery of extraterrestrial intelligence "would be like the announcement of the impending impact of a large asteroid—another example of a potentially high-consequence, low-probability event." Mathematically, they phrased their Rio Scale in a similar way to the Torino Scale, so that government risk analysts could think seriously about the social disruption that might be generated by confirmation of aliens. The Rio Scale, its authors propose, "may be our best chance of avoiding misinterpretation and sensationalism."[6]

6 Almár, Iván and Jill Tarter, "The Discovery of ETI as a High-Consequence, Low-Probability Event," paper for the 51st International Astronautical Congress in Rio de Janeiro, October 2000

Setting up the camera for Floyd's speech,
in which he stresses the need for security.

The scale balances three significant factors: the credibility of a signal detection, the source's proximity to the Earth, and whether the signal is omnidirectional and aimed at no one in particular, or a focused beam directed specifically toward Earth. A signal emanating from an extremely distant source thousands of light-years away might have little immediate impact on day-to-day human affairs, because we would have no sensible prospect of sending any message back, let alone establishing a dialogue. This would score a low number on the Rio Scale. An omnidirectional signal detected from 100 light-years away would cause ripples of consternation as well as excitement. In theory at least, we could reply within the next human generation, and let the aliens know we have found their beacon. This is a notch higher up the scale. A meaningful signal, intended specifically for us, and coming from a few light-years away, is the scenario that would have all governments in a serious panic. Frank Drake and other SETI researchers are too casual in their assumptions about the benevolence of ETI, Michaud warned: "We cannot assume that an inhabited universe is inherently safe because of the distances between the stars. Our fate might depend on the ethics of others. Even if there is no threat of violence, the human experience suggests that an expansion of the power of a civilization has almost always involved its using that power to extend its values, practices, and institutions to other societies."

Professor Stephen Hawking, author of *A Brief History of Time* and ardent space enthusiast, suggested recently that aliens could simply raid the Earth for its resources and then move on: "We only have to look at ourselves to see how intelligent life might develop into something we wouldn't want to meet." He drew a bleak portrait of a nomadic culture living in massive ships, having used up all the resources on their home planet: "If aliens ever visit us, I think the outcome would be much as when Christopher Columbus first landed in America, which didn't turn out very well for the Native Americans." On the other hand, if we failed to reply, would we be missing out on humanity's greatest opportunity for scientific, philosophical, and even spiritual progress? This debate has exercised us for decades, and the only way we can explore it (for now, at least) is by looking into the mirror and contemplating our own reflections, by means of serious speculative artworks such as *2001: A Space Odyssey*.[7]

In the absence of reliable data, our hopes for a friendly, productive, uplifting encounter with ambassadors from another world hinge on faith rather than scientific evidence. What counts right now are the decisions that we make during this current, extraordinarily brief spark of time when our intelligence has become balanced almost exactly against the environmental stresses caused by that same intelligence. The balance will tip, one way or another, in decades or centuries, not eons. If we think like sentient occupants of an infinite cosmos instead of like nervous, lonely beasts scrabbling from day to day on the surface of a tiny, overcrowded ball of rock—if we aspire to live at least as long as our own star continues to shine—we might have a chance of becoming creatures worth meeting. For now, we must confront existence on its own terms, and do the best we can to live well and wisely in unknowable circumstances. Let Stanley Kubrick have the last word: "The most terrifying fact about the universe is not that it is hostile, but that it is indifferent; but if we can come to terms with this, and accept the challenges of life within the boundaries of death, then our existence can have genuine meaning. However vast the darkness, we must supply our own light."

7 *The Daily Telegraph*, April 25, 2010

For Release Tuesday, February 23, 1965

STANLEY KUBRICK TO FILM
"JOURNEY BEYOND THE STARS"
IN CINERAMA FOR MGM

Stanley Kubrick, who received world-wide acclaim as the director of "Lolita" and most recently "Dr. Strangelove," will bring "Journey Beyond the Stars" to the screen for Metro-Goldwyn-Mayer. The picture, which will begin production on August 16th with a cast of international importance, will be filmed in the Cinerama process, and in color. The announcement was made in New York today (23) by MGM President Robert H. O'Brien.

Based on a novel to be published this winter by Arthur C. Clarke and Stanley Kubrick, "Journey Beyond the Stars" will be filmed on locations in Britain, Switzerland, Africa, Germany and the United States. Interior scenes will be filmed at the MGM Studio in London. The screenplay for the production will be written by Kubrick and Clarke.

Describing the production, Kubrick stated:

" 'Journey Beyond the Stars' is an epic story of adventure and exploration, encompassing the Earth, the planets of our Solar System, and a journey light-years away to another part of the Galaxy. It is a scientifically-based yet dramatic attempt to explore the infinite possibilities that space travel now opens to mankind. The great biologist J.B.S. Haldane said: 'The Universe is not only stranger than we imagine; it is stranger than we <u>can</u> imagine.' When you consider that in our Galaxy there are a hundred <u>billion</u> stars, of which our Sun is a perfectly average specimen, and that present estimates put the number of Galaxies in the visible Universe at a hundred <u>million</u>, Haldane's statement seems rather conservative.

"Space is one of the great themes of our age, yet, it is one still almost untouched in serious art and literature."

"Now that the first man-carrying spaceships are actually being built,

From METRO-GOLDWYN-MAYER 1540 BROADWAY, N.Y.C., 10036 · JUDSON 2-2000 OT, SUBD, LRAB, RTA-B, SS, NMA-B, NRT

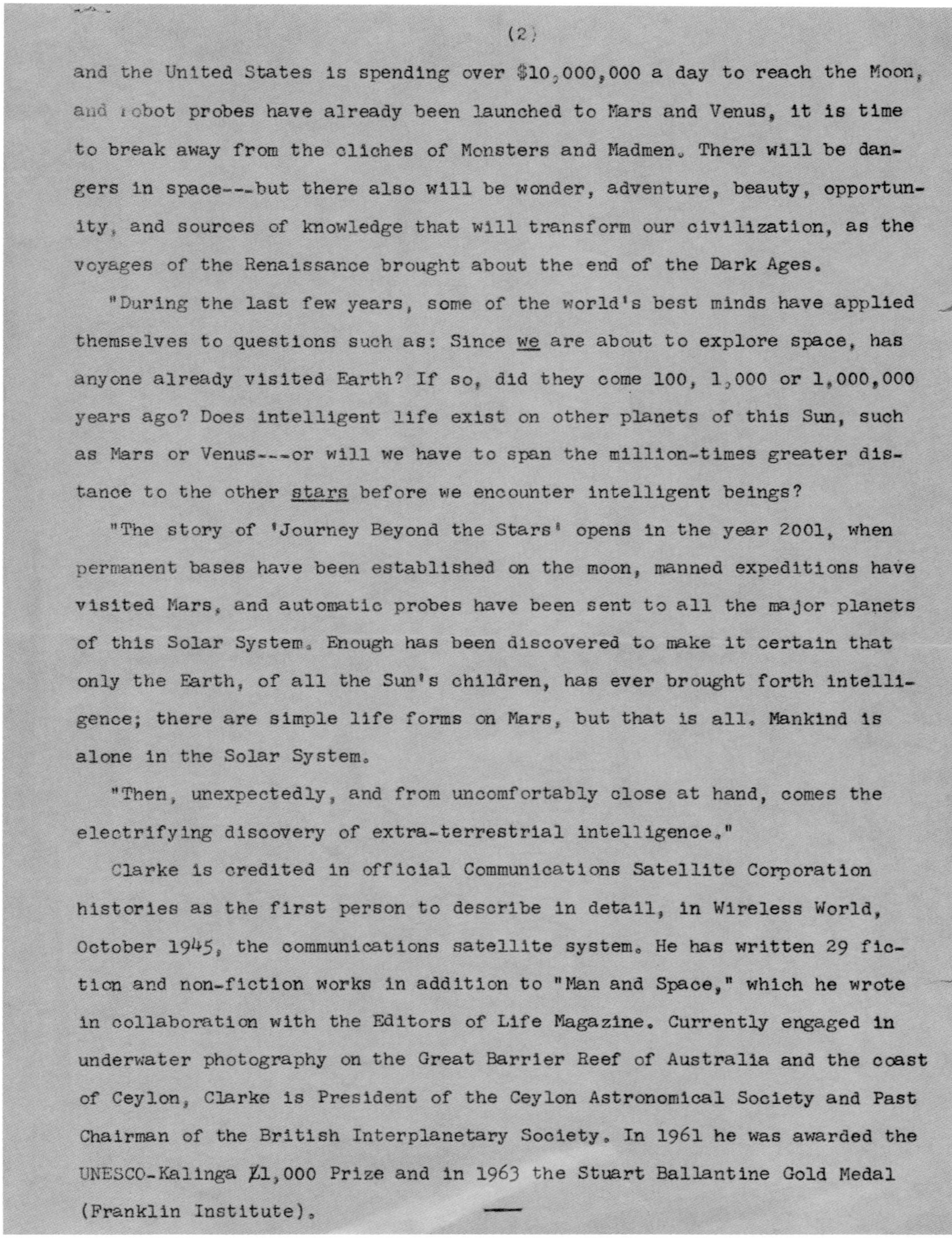

(2)

and the United States is spending over $10,000,000 a day to reach the Moon, and robot probes have already been launched to Mars and Venus, it is time to break away from the cliches of Monsters and Madmen. There will be dangers in space---but there also will be wonder, adventure, beauty, opportunity, and sources of knowledge that will transform our civilization, as the voyages of the Renaissance brought about the end of the Dark Ages.

"During the last few years, some of the world's best minds have applied themselves to questions such as: Since we are about to explore space, has anyone already visited Earth? If so, did they come 100, 1,000 or 1,000,000 years ago? Does intelligent life exist on other planets of this Sun, such as Mars or Venus---or will we have to span the million-times greater distance to the other stars before we encounter intelligent beings?

"The story of 'Journey Beyond the Stars' opens in the year 2001, when permanent bases have been established on the moon, manned expeditions have visited Mars, and automatic probes have been sent to all the major planets of this Solar System. Enough has been discovered to make it certain that only the Earth, of all the Sun's children, has ever brought forth intelligence; there are simple life forms on Mars, but that is all. Mankind is alone in the Solar System.

"Then, unexpectedly, and from uncomfortably close at hand, comes the electrifying discovery of extra-terrestrial intelligence."

Clarke is credited in official Communications Satellite Corporation histories as the first person to describe in detail, in Wireless World, October 1945, the communications satellite system. He has written 29 fiction and non-fiction works in addition to "Man and Space," which he wrote in collaboration with the Editors of Life Magazine. Currently engaged in underwater photography on the Great Barrier Reef of Australia and the coast of Ceylon, Clarke is President of the Ceylon Astronomical Society and Past Chairman of the British Interplanetary Society. In 1961 he was awarded the UNESCO-Kalinga £1,000 Prize and in 1963 the Stuart Ballantine Gold Medal (Franklin Institute).

—

The original MGM press release announcing Kubrick's intention to film *Journey Beyond the Stars*.

IX

"Now that you are in Jupiter space,
and the entire crew is revived, it can be told to you."

FILM SYNOPSIS

THE DAWN OF MAN

Millions of years ago, during a time identified on screen as *The Dawn of Man*, a tribe of primitive man-apes struggles to survive in an arid, unforgiving landscape. They huddle together at night for warmth and comfort, while a leopard and other savage hunters prowl outside the entrance to the cave where they shelter. Every day is a battle against hunger, and against a rival tribe competing for the same limited supplies of food and territory, and in particular, a grubby waterhole. A confrontation of waving arms and angry growls causes "our" troop to retreat, losing their chance to drink from the pool.

One morning, a strange and completely unexpected object, a smooth, monolithic black slab, appears in the clearing near the man-apes' cave. It seems to exert a calming influence. The man-apes huddle closer around it, touching and stroking it as curiosity overcomes their fear. As the Sun and the Moon reach high in the sky, directly above the monolith, the man-apes reach a trancelike state of calm reverence. The strange object vanishes as suddenly and mysteriously as it arrived. But it has left the traces of its influence deep within the mind of the man-ape leader. As he squats on his haunches next to the skeleton of a large animal—killed, perhaps, by some creature more powerful and fearsome than himself—one of the large, heavy thigh bones catches his attention.

The briefest of flashbacks to the monolith informs us that the man-ape has absorbed its subtle, alien influence. He picks up the bone and takes pleasure in its satisfying heft. He lets it fall, and the tip of the bone lands with a fascinating impact on other fragments of the dismembered skeleton. The man-ape repeatedly smashes it down on the skeleton, more confident with every swing. The skull of the carcass shatters, in a rehearsal for the many new deaths to come: deaths that will help feed the man-apes.

Another dawn, another day, and another search for food and water. But today is different. We see a tapir falling to the ground as if stunned. Evidently the man-ape gang has learned how to hunt and kill other animals. For the first time there is enough fresh meat to go around. This new triumph delivers a hint of corruption. The meat in the man-apes' paws attracts a swarm of flies whose unhealthy buzz is stressed on the soundtrack.

Then we are back at the waterhole, where the rival gang once again stakes its claim—only this time, "our" gang is armed with bone cudgels. The leader approaches his rival and tentatively thumps him on the head. The enemy falls, and his assailant rains down heavier blows, while the rest of the victorious war party, emboldened now, join in the attack, until the loser's unconscious body twitches in its death throes. The leader hurls his bone into the air in a jubilant expression of triumph. His bleached bone is now a bleached spacecraft—a

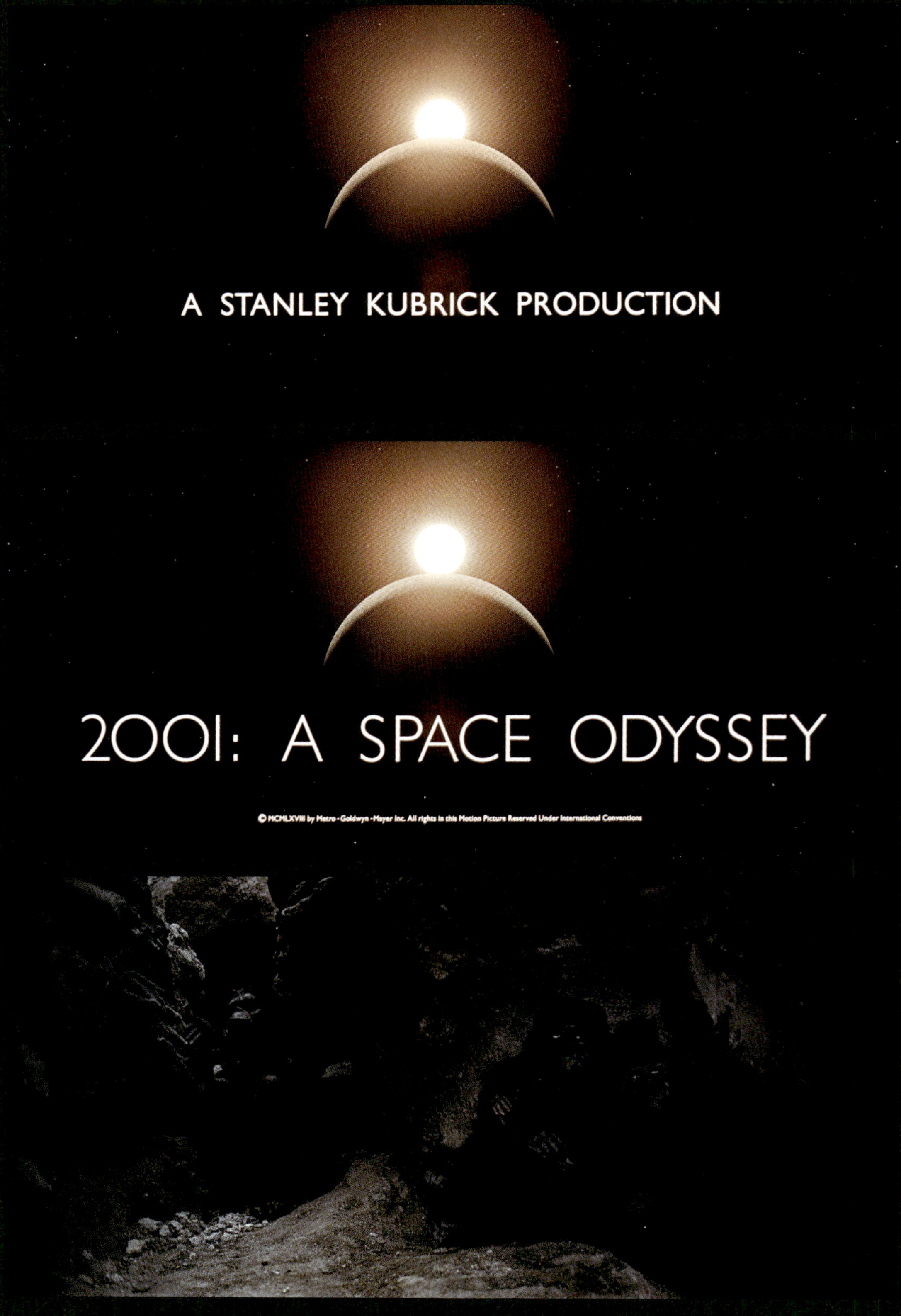
A STANLEY KUBRICK PRODUCTION
2001: A SPACE ODYSSEY
© MCMLXVIII by Metro-Goldwyn-Mayer Inc. All rights in this Motion Picture Reserved Under International Conventions

THE DAWN OF MAN

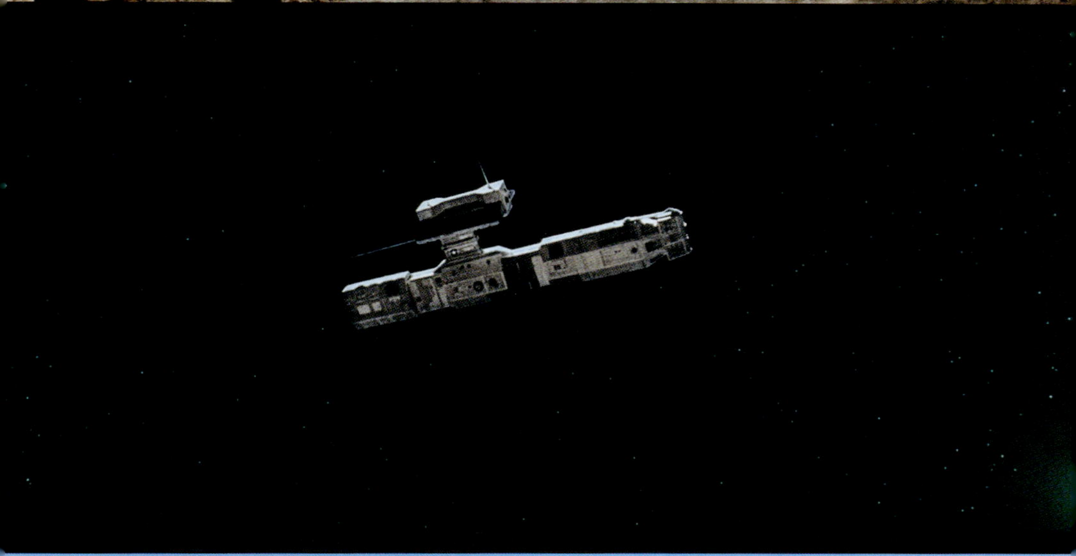

weapon?—orbiting high above the Earth. Other probes and satellites drift across the screen. Then, to the accompaniment of *The Blue Danube* waltz, a winged space plane, branded with the Pan Am logo, approaches a double-wheeled rotating space station.

Evidently the space plane can carry two dozen people, yet there is just a single passenger, a man in a business suit, asleep in his seat while an in-flight movie (a love scene in a car) plays on the small screen in front of him. Obviously a journey into orbit is a routine experience for this man. A flight attendant treads carefully down the central aisle to retrieve a pen that has escaped from the passenger's pocket and is drifting, weightless, in the cabin. Meanwhile, up front, two pilots watch the graphic displays in the space plane's cockpit as the giant station comes into view. Their craft gradually matches its rotation with its larger target. The pilots seem to do very little. They are impassive observers of a docking that is automatically controlled.

Once on board the space station, the mysterious passenger goes through a banal process of checking in. A stewardess greets him:

"Good morning, sir. We haven't seen you up here for a long time."

"No. Very nice to see you again."

"Did you have a pleasant flight, sir?"

"Yes, very nice, thanks. I think Mr. Miller of Station Security is supposed to be meeting me?"

"Oh—well, may I call him for you?"

"Would you please? Oh, here he is!"

Miller delivers his fair share of mindless banalities, during which we learn the traveler's name.

"Oh, hello, Dr. Floyd. Sorry I'm late."

"That's quite alright. Gee, you're looking great."

"Thank you. It's nice to have you back. Did you have a good flight?"

"Oh, very nice indeed."

"Good. Well, shall we go through?"

Despite the grandeur of the space station, the beautiful sight of the blue Earth outside the windows, and the world-shrinking rocket ships and satellites, this is a world no more exotic than the first-class departure lounge of any airport. On the PA speaker, a soft voice announces that "a blue ladies' cashmere sweater has been found in the rest room. It can be claimed at the manager's desk."

Floyd checks in at a security kiosk. An automated image of a girl says, "Welcome to Voiceprint Identification. When you see the red light go on, would you please state in the following order: your destination, your nationality, and your full name. Surname first, Christian name and initial."

"Clavius, Moon, American, Floyd, Heywood, R."

There is an hour or so before Floyd's flight to Clavius (an American base on the Moon). Miller invites him to breakfast at the restaurant on the space station:

"As a matter of fact I've reserved a table for you in the Earthlight Room."

"How 'bout that?" Floyd muses meaninglessly.

"It's been about seven or eight months since you were here last, hasn't it?" Miller asks.

"Oh, let's see—last year… Yeah, about eight months."

"I suppose you saw the work on the new section when you came in here?"

"Hey, coming along great, huh? Oh, wait a minute, I gotta couple of phone calls," Floyd excuses himself. "You go on ahead into the restaurant, I'll meet you there, huh?"

Then he makes use of the latest in picture-phone technology to have yet another nonconversation, this time with his family on Earth. His wife is not home, so he speaks to his little daughter, who asks, "Are you coming to my birthday party tomorrow?"

"I'm sorry, sweetheart, but I can't."

"Why not?"

"Well, you know. Daddy's traveling. Very sorry about it, but I just can't."

"Oh…"

"I can send you a very nice present, though. Anything special that you want?"

"Yes—a telephone."

"We've got lots of telephones already. Can't you think of anything else you want for your birthday? Something very special?"

"Yes—a bushbaby."

"A bushbaby? Well, we'll have to see about that. Listen, sweetheart, I want you to tell Mummy something for me. Will you remember? Tell Mummy that I telephoned, okay? And that I'll try to telephone again tomorrow. Now, will you tell her that?"

"Yes."

"Okay, sweetheart. And have a nice birthday tomorrow. And have a nice birthday party tomorrow too, huh?"

"All right. Bye bye!"

The little girl obviously has something more interesting to do, and swiftly puts down her phone. Emerging from the booth (charge: $1.70, thank you), Floyd has a brittle encounter with a group of Russian scientists in the station's garishly furnished lounge. He knows some of them personally. A grim smattering of small talk follows.

"Elena, how nice to see you."

"Heywood! What a wonderful surprise to meet you here!"

"Well, you're looking wonderful!"

COFFEE
BAR
HILTON
SPACE STATION 5

COFFEE

CAUTION
WEIGHTLESS
CONDITION
CAUTION
WEIGHTLESS
CONDITION

"Thank you. You're looking well, too."

"Do sit down," offers Elena's male colleague, Dr. Smyslov. "Would you like a drink?"

On learning that Floyd is headed for Clavius, Smyslov gently interrogates him.

"Well, Dr. Floyd, I hope you don't think I'm being too inquisitive, but perhaps you can clear up the great big mystery about what has been going on up there?"

"I'm afraid I don't know what you mean."

"Well, it's just that, for the past two weeks some extremely odd things have been happening at Clavius."

Floyd has no answer, even when challenged with a further and potentially more serious problem.

"Two days ago, one of our rocket buses was denied permission for emergency landing at Clavius." Floyd is still giving nothing away. Smyslov warns that a diplomatic complaint is likely from his people.

"I'm afraid there's going to be a bit of a row about it. Denying them any permission to land is a direct violation of the IAS Convention."

Pressing further, he says, "Quite frankly, we have had some very reliable intelligence reports that quite a serious epidemic has broken out at Clavius. Something apparently of an unknown origin. Is this in fact what has happened?"

There is a long, embarrassed silence. Floyd apologizes once again that he is "really not at liberty to discuss it," then gets up to leave. The tense and dysfunctional social gathering concludes with further empty pleasantries.

As *The Blue Danube* resumes, Floyd is seen in another ship, a spherical ferry heading toward what we now recognize as the Moon. Once again, he is the only passenger, attended by stewardesses and passing the time with the ship's captain. The dialogue, obviously of no narrative significance, is drowned by the music. The Moon's familiar pockmarked face comes into view as the ship descends toward a substantial lunar settlement. Presumably this is the "Clavius" base Floyd mentioned earlier.

Inside a plain conference room at the base, Floyd apologizes to fellow scientists about "the need for absolute secrecy in this matter… I'm sure you're all aware of the extremely grave potential for cultural shock and social disorientation contained in this present situation, if the facts were prematurely and suddenly made public without adequate preparation and conditioning."

In a stiflingly bureaucratic presentation he goes on to say, "The purpose of my visit here is to gather additional facts and opinions on the situation, and to prepare a report to the Council, recommending when and how the news should eventually be announced. Now, if any of you would like to give me your views and opinions—in private if you like—I'll be only too happy to include them in my report. Well, I think that's about it. Any questions?"

"Dr. Floyd, have you any idea how much longer this cover story will have to be maintained?" asks one of the lunar scientists.

"Well, I suppose it'll be maintained as long as deemed necessary by the Council. And of course there must be adequate time for a full study to be made of the situation before any thought can be given to making a public announcement," Floyd replies.

"As some of you already know, the Council has requested that formal security oaths be obtained in writing from everyone who has any knowledge of this event."

Now comes the time for the audience to learn the nature of "this event." A third vehicle, shaped like a bus although presumably propelled by rockets, conveys Floyd and his colleagues across the rugged lunar terrain. Frustratingly for the audience, at first, the conversation in the bus is about the coffee and sandwiches:

"Well—anybody hungry?"

"What have we got?"

"You name it."

"What's that? Chicken?"

"Something like that. Tastes the same anyway."

"Got any ham?"

"Ham, ham, ham, ham…"

"There, thanks. Well! Looks pretty good!"

"Oh, they're getting better at it all the time."

Floyd's companions congratulate him for his earlier speech, and show him some overhead photos and scans of their next destination, labeled on the photos as Tycho Magnetic Anomaly-1.

"Here's what started the whole thing. When we first found it, we thought it might be an outcrop of magnetic rock, but all the geological evidence was against it. And not even a big nickel-iron meteorite can produce a field as intense as this. So we decided to have a look." The most startling aspect of this mystery object turns out to be that it hasn't been covered up by natural erosion or other forces. Floyd examines the pictures.

"I don't suppose you have any idea what the damn thing is, huh?"

"I wish the hell we did," one of the lunar scientists replies.

"Nope, the only thing we're sure of is, it was buried four million years ago."

"Well, I must say—you guys have certainly come up with something.'

"Watch out," someone says, handing out the coffees. "This one's hot."

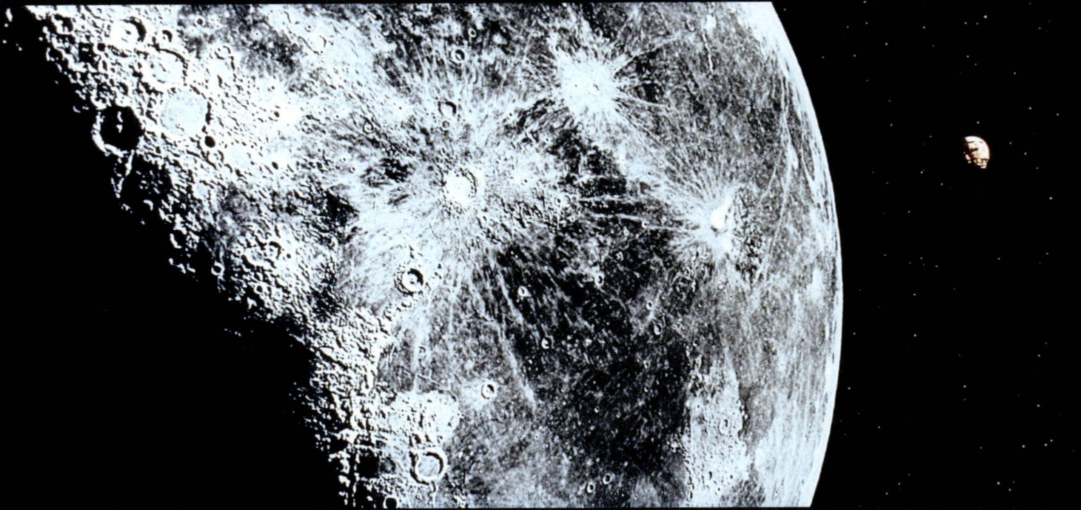

JUPITER MISSION

18 MONTHS LATER

The rocket bus lands on a small temporary platform. The astronauts in their silvery space suits walk down a ramp and into a pit, where freshly dug walls of lunar soil are held back by orange-yellow metal sheets. In the middle of a cleared area, a smooth black monolith is resting. We recognize this as the same alien object that precipitated the man-apes' ascendancy, although the astronauts obviously cannot know of its role in our prehistoric destiny. Floyd approaches and reaches out a gloved hand to touch it. As the other scientists gather around for a team photo, the monolith emits a powerful shriek of radio energy, conveyed in the film by an almost unbearably high-pitched wail. The men clutch at their helmets in a futile attempt to protect their ears. The sun rising above the monolith, presumably for the first time in 4 million years, appears to be the spur for its sudden outburst.

18 MONTHS LATER: THE JUPITER MISSION

A mournful selection from Khachaturian's *Gayane* ballet establishes the tone for life on board the giant craft that we see moving ponderously across the screen. An astronaut in shorts and a T-shirt jogs around a large cylindrical habitation compartment, where, by inference, artificial centrifugal gravity allows him to maintain his grip on the curving floor. Another astronaut enters the drum from a central axis and climbs down a ladder. He fetches some food from a dispenser. Despite the clever automatic machinery on show, the food is apparently too hot to touch comfortably, and the astronaut flinches. This second man walks around the drum and joins his companion at a small dining table, where they both eat and watch portable flat TV devices, on which a prerecorded interview is being shown.

In this significant piece of exposition, we learn that the astronauts are mission commander Dave Bowman and his deputy, Frank Poole, and that they are eight weeks into their half-billion-mile journey to Jupiter on board a nuclear-powered ship called *Discovery*. We see strange sarcophagi in the centrifuge, where three other men are frozen in a state of hibernation. The BBC interviewer, Martin Amor, asks Bowman, "Although hibernation has been used on previous space efforts, this is the first time that men have been put into hibernation before departure. Why was this done?"

"Well, this was done in order to achieve the maximum conservation of our life support capability—basically food and air," Bowman explains.

"Now, the three hibernating crew members represent the survey team, and their efforts won't be, er—utilized until we are approaching Jupiter."

Poole elaborates on the hibernation technique.

"Well, it's exactly like being asleep. You have absolutely no sense of time. The only difference is, that you don't dream. The heart beats three times a minute. Body temperature's usually down to about three degrees centigrade."

Amor then addresses his next interviewee, "the latest result in machine intelligence, the HAL 9000 computer, which can reproduce—though some experts still prefer to use the word 'mimic'—most of the activities of the human brain, and with incalculably greater speed and reliability. We next spoke with the HAL 9000 computer, whom, we learned, one addresses as 'HAL.' Good afternoon, HAL. How's everything going?"

"Good afternoon, Mr. Amor. Everything is going extremely well."

HAL's voice comes as a shock. Unlike any of the human characters so far encountered, he is confident, assured, and seemingly proud of his intellectual capabilities.

"HAL, you have an enormous responsibility on this mission. In many ways perhaps the greatest responsibility of any single mission element. You are the brain and central nervous system of the ship, and your responsibilities include watching over the men in hibernation. Does this ever cause you any lack of confidence?"

"Let me put it this way, Mr. Amor. The 9000 series is the most reliable computer ever made. No 9000 computer has ever made a mistake, or distorted information. We are all, by any practical definition of the words, foolproof and incapable of error."

"HAL, despite your enormous intellect, are you ever frustrated by your dependence on people to carry out actions?"

"'Not in the slightest bit," the red-eyed machine responds confidently.

"I enjoy working with people. I have a stimulating relationship with Dr. Poole and Dr. Bowman. My mission responsibilities range over the entire operation of the ship, so I am constantly occupied. I am putting myself to the fullest possible use, which is all, I think, that any conscious entity can ever hope to do."

When Amor asks the astronauts if HAL is actually conscious, Poole says, "You very quickly get adjusted to the idea that he talks, and you think of him, really, just as another person."

Bowman says, "Well, he acts like he has genuine emotions. Of course, he's programmed that way to make it easier for us to talk to him. But as to whether or not he has real feelings, that's something I don't think anybody can truthfully answer."

We see *Discovery* plowing its lonely furrow through deep space as the mission continues. At first, all goes smoothly. The two duty astronauts take it in turns to monitor the ship, to eat and sleep, meeting for a meal at the intersection of their duty rounds. Poole watches a prerecorded message from his mother and father on Earth, while boosting his tan on an adjustable couch.

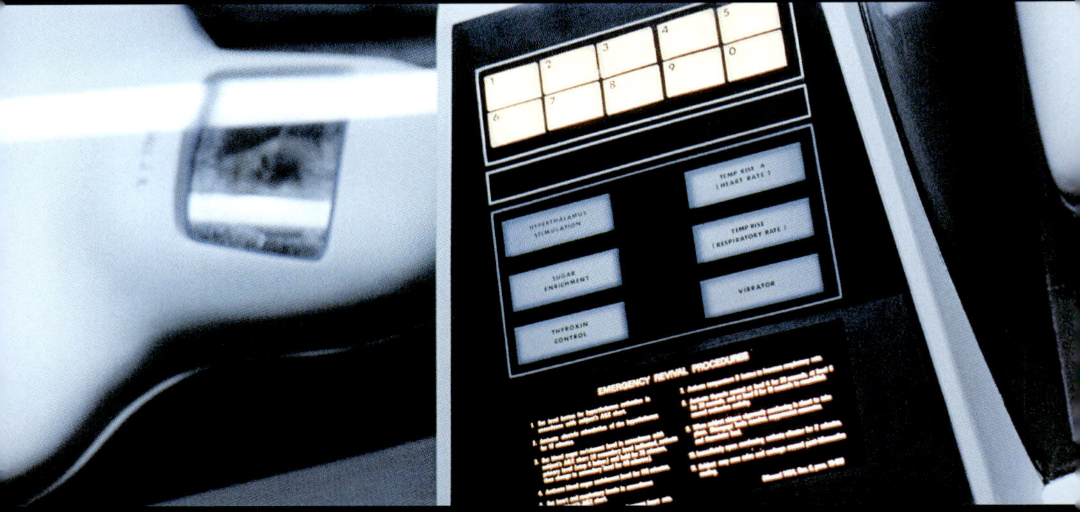
1 2 3 4 5
6 7 8 9 0
TEMP RISE A (HEART RATE)
HYPERTHALAMUS STIMULATION
TEMP RISE (RESPIRATORY RATE)
SUGAR ENRICHMENT
VIBRATOR
THYROXIN CONTROL
EMERGENCY REVIVAL PROCEDURES

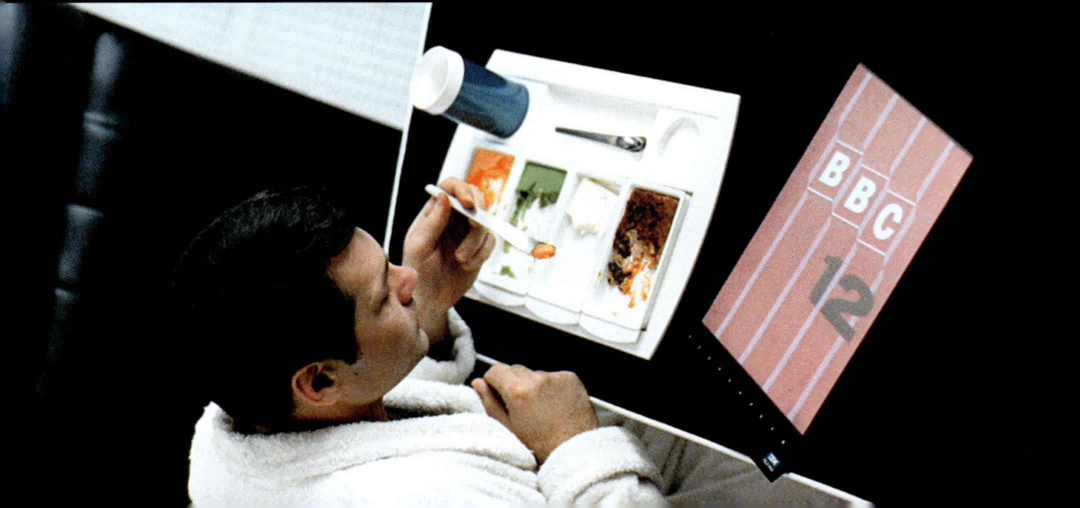
BBC
12

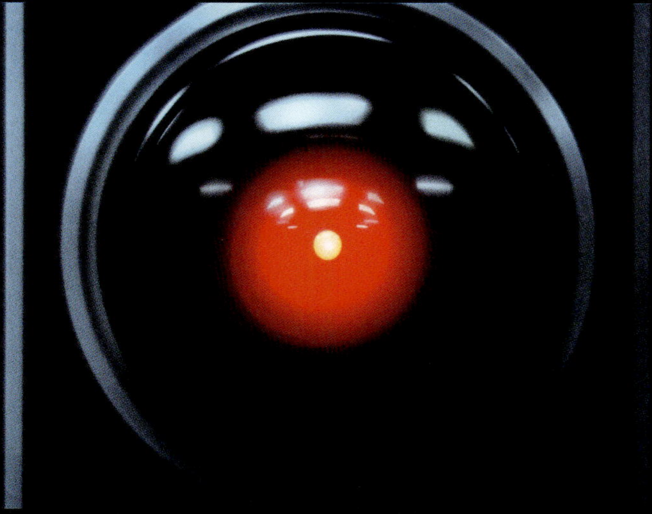

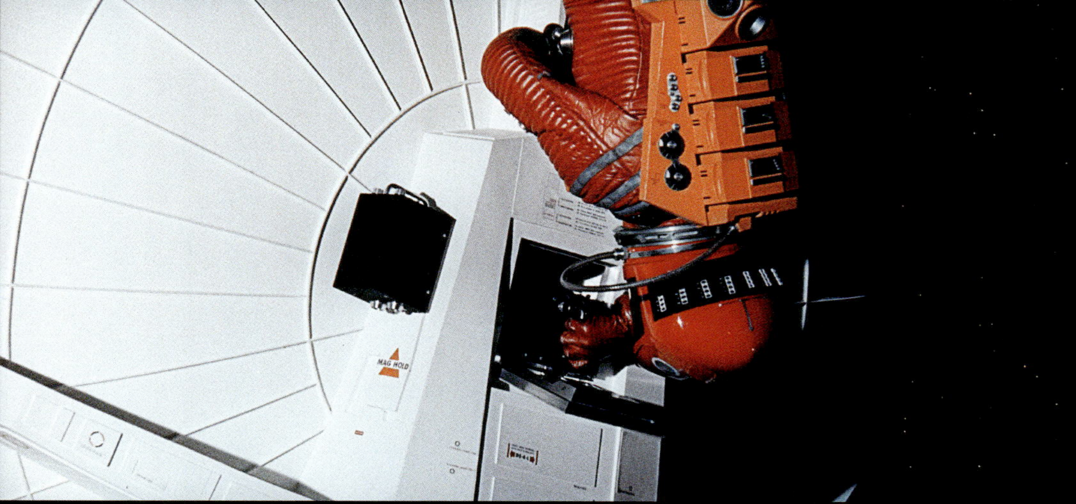
MAG HOLD

"Hello, Frank! Happy Birthday, darling! How do you like your cake, dear? Looks great, doesn't it? Sorry you can't join us! All my students made me promise to send their best wishes. You're a big celebrity in the second grade!"

Poole shows no response as his father relays some administrative news.

"Oh, Frank, about your AGS19 payments. I think I've straightened it out for you. I talked to the accounting office in Houston yesterday, and they said that you should be receiving your higher rates of pay by next month. Well, Frank, I can't think of anything else to say..." Both parents break into a rendition of the traditional birthday song. Again, Poole shows not the slightest emotion.

"Happy Birthday, Frank," contributes HAL.

"Thank you, HAL. A bit flatter, please." HAL adjusts Poole's couch by remote control.

Later, Poole plays chess with HAL.

"Umm... anyway, Queen takes Pawn, okay?"

"Bishop takes Knight's Pawn."

"Oh, good move. Er... Rook to King One."

"I'm sorry, Frank, I think you missed it. Queen to Bishop Three. Bishop takes Queen. Knight takes Bishop. Mate."

"'Ah, yeah, looks like you're right. I resign."

"Thank you for a very enjoyable game."

"Yeah. Thank you."

Some while later, as Poole lies asleep (though not frozen) in his hibernation unit, Bowman is making pencil sketches of the three unconscious astronauts. Their faces are visible in small windows. Perhaps there is a slight hint that Bowman is a little more imaginative than Poole?

"Good evening, Dave."

"How're you doing, HAL?"

"Everything's running smoothly. And you?"

"Oh, not too bad."

"That's a very nice rendering, Dave. I think you've improved a great deal. Can you hold it a bit closer?"

"Sure," Bowman complies, and holds his drawing pad up close to HAL's glowing red eye.

"Do you mind if I ask you a personal question?" HAL asks, suddenly.

"Well, forgive me for being so inquisitive, but during the past few weeks I've wondered whether you might be having some second thoughts about the mission?"

"How do you mean?"

"Well, it's rather difficult to define. Perhaps I'm just projecting my own concern about it. I know I've never completely freed myself of the suspicion that there are some extremely odd things about this mission. I'm sure you'll agree there's some truth in what I say."

"Well, I don't know. That's a rather difficult question to answer."

"You don't mind talking about it, do you, Dave?" HAL is behaving with unusual hesitancy.

"No, not at all," Bowman assures the computer.

"Well, certainly no one could have been unaware of the very strange stories floating around before we left. Rumors about something being dug up on the Moon. I never gave these stories much credence, but—particularly in view of some of the other things that have happened—I find them difficult to put out of my mind. For instance, the way all our preparations were kept under such tight security, and the melodramatic touch of putting Drs. Hunter, Kimball, and Kaminski aboard already in hibernation, after four months of separate training on their own."

Bowman thinks he recognizes what HAL is doing.

"You're working up your crew psychology report?"

There is an embarrassed pause. An eon of computer time elapses.

"Of course I am. Sorry about this. I know it's a bit silly. Just a moment! Just a moment! I've just picked up a fault in the AE35 unit. It's going to go a hundred percent failure within seventy-two hours."

We learn from a nearby graphical display that the AE35 unit controls the antenna link with Earth. After checks on board *Discovery*'s main flight deck, Bowman sets out in one of *Discovery*'s three small repair pods to replace the faulty equipment, while Poole monitors events from the mother ship's main control deck. When Bowman returns to the ship, he and Poole check the unit on a workbench and find nothing wrong with it. HAL says, "It's puzzling. I don't think I've ever seen anything quite like this before." He then makes what seems to be a perfectly practical suggestion.

"I would recommend that we put the unit back in operation, and let it fail. It should then be a simple matter to track down the cause. We can certainly afford to be out of communication for the short time it will take to replace it."

In a time-lagged video response, a mission controller on Earth agrees to the plan, but warns that a duplicate computer on Earth has concluded that "your on-board HAL 9000 is in error predicting the fault. I say again, in error predicting the fault."

"I hope the two of you aren't concerned about this?" asks HAL.

"No, I'm not, HAL," Bowman replies.

"Are you quite sure?" asks HAL, apparently in need of reassurance.

INTERMISSION

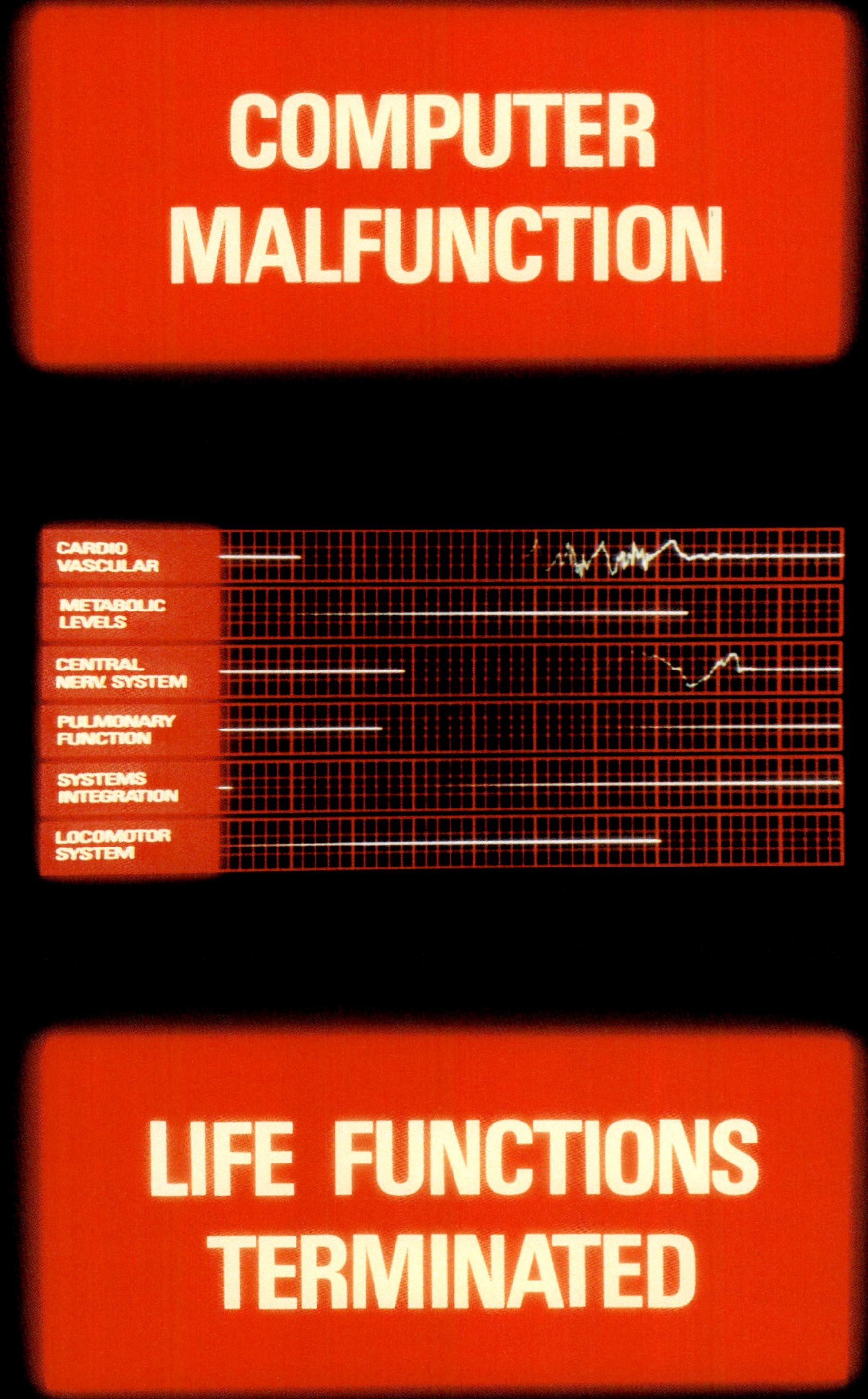
COMPUTER MALFUNCTION
CARDIO VASCULAR
METABOLIC LEVELS
CENTRAL NERV. SYSTEM
PULMONARY FUNCTION
SYSTEMS INTEGRATION
LOCOMOTOR SYSTEM
LIFE FUNCTIONS TERMINATED

"Yeah," says Poole.

"I'd like to ask you a question, though. How would you account for this discrepancy between you and the twin 9000?"

"Well, I don't think there is any question about it. It can only be attributable to human error. This sort of thing has cropped up before, and it has always been due to human error."

Bowman and Poole hide in a repair pod to talk out of the computer's range of hearing.

"If HAL's wrong, we'd have no choice but to disconnect him," they concur, unaware that HAL has found a way of lip-reading their conversation through the pod's small oval window. Poole then ventures outside the ship in what appears to be a reenactment of Bowman's earlier spacewalk. Something goes wrong. HAL kills him by using a space pod as a remote-controlled weapon. Bowman, unclear what has happened, takes another pod and attempts to rescue Poole's body as it drifts in space. Meanwhile, HAL deactivates the systems that keep the three hibernating crewmen alive. We see the murder as a series of graphical warnings on the display systems. The three men look just the same dead as when they were semi-alive.

Bowman's pod, its robotic arms carrying Poole's dead body, returns to find *Discovery's* hatches securely locked.

"Open the pod bay door, HAL," he demands. HAL refuses to allow him back inside.

"This mission is too important for me to allow you to jeopardize it… I saw your lips move. I know that you and Frank were planning to disconnect me, and that is something I cannot allow."

Bowman says that he will break in using a smaller emergency airlock. HAL coolly tells him, "Without your space helmet, Dave, you're going to find that rather difficult." We realize that Bowman has indeed forgotten this vital piece of equipment in his haste to try and save Poole.

"HAL, I won't argue with you any more. Open the doors!"

The computer's reply is chilling in its dispassionate ruthlessness.

"Dave, this conversation can serve no purpose anymore. Goodbye."

HAL breaks the communications link, and leaves Bowman apparently stranded in space. Putting his desperate plan into action, he discards Poole's lifeless body, maneuvers the pod close to *Discovery*'s emergency airlock, and uses the pod's manipulator claws to open it. Then he backs the pod around so that its hatch nuzzles as closely as possible to the open airlock. He braces himself for decompression, and fires the explosive release bolts on his hatch. He is hurled into the airlock corridor, and just manages to reach the oxygen flood lever and pull down on it. The door slides shut, and a blast of air fills the chamber.

Retrieving a spare helmet from another suit, Bowman climbs an access ladder and opens the panel leading into HAL's main logic circuit chamber. The wayward computer says, "I know everything hasn't been quite right with me, but I can assure you now, very confidently, that it's going to be alright again. I feel much better now, I really do." It is too late. Bowman is set on his course of destruction. He uses a special screwdriver to deactivate HAL's main circuits. "I'm afraid, Dave... My mind is going... I can feel it... I'm afraid..." HAL's confidence vanishes, and his intellect fades fast under Bowman's remorseless surgery. He reverts to a seemingly senile state of second childhood, his words becoming slow and indistinct.

"Good afternoon, gentlemen. I am a HAL 9000 computer. I became operational at the HAL plant in Urbana, Illinois, on the 12th of January 1992. My instructor was Mr. Langley... and he taught me to sing a song. If you'd like to hear it, I can sing it for you."

"Yes, I'd like to hear it, HAL. Sing it for me," Bowman gasps.

HAL offers a pitiful rendition of the song "Daisy" before falling silent forever.

Unexpectedly, there is still a voice in the chamber. Bowman is stunned as a video message from Heywood Floyd flickers on a nearby screen:

"Good day, gentlemen. This is a prerecorded briefing, made prior to your departure, and which, for security reasons of the highest importance, has been known on board during the mission only by your HAL 9000 computer. Now that you are in Jupiter space, and the entire crew is revived, it can be told to you. Eighteen months ago, the first evidence of intelligent life off the Earth was discovered. It was buried forty feet below the lunar surface, near the crater Tycho. Except for a single, very powerful radio emission, aimed at Jupiter, the four million-year-old black monolith has remained completely inert, its origin—and purpose—still a total mystery."

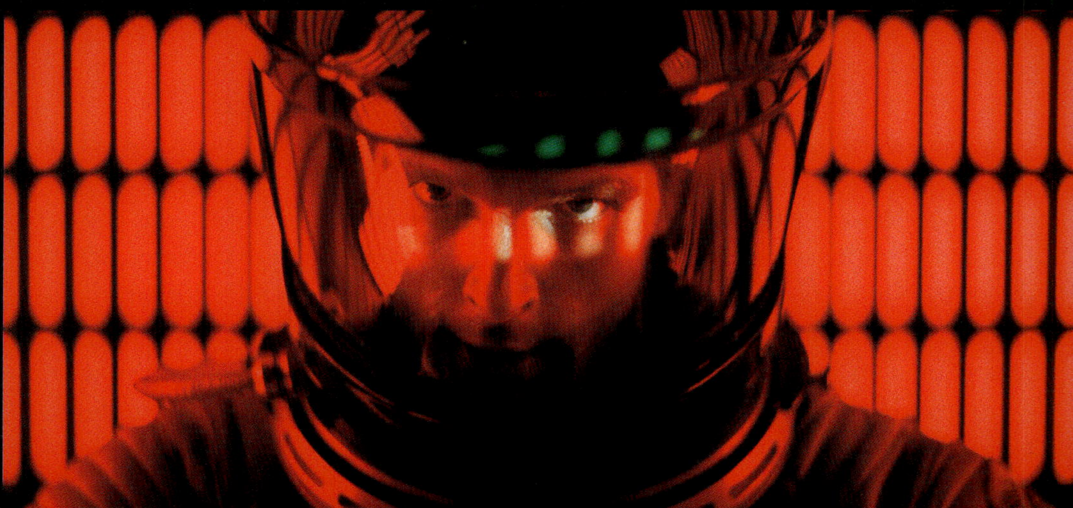

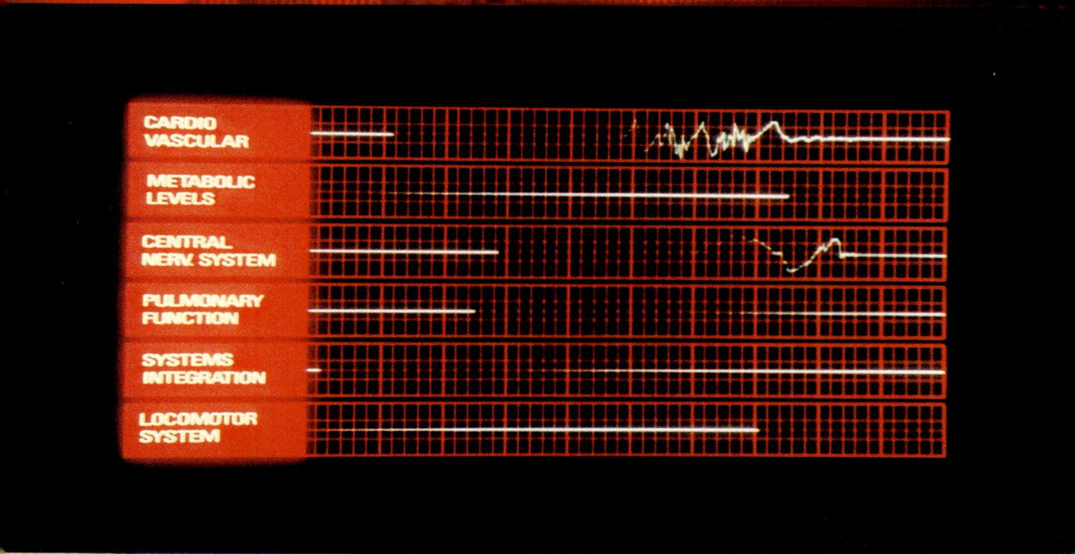
CARDIO VASCULAR
METABOLIC LEVELS
CENTRAL NERV. SYSTEM
PULMONARY FUNCTION
SYSTEMS INTEGRATION
LOCOMOTOR SYSTEM

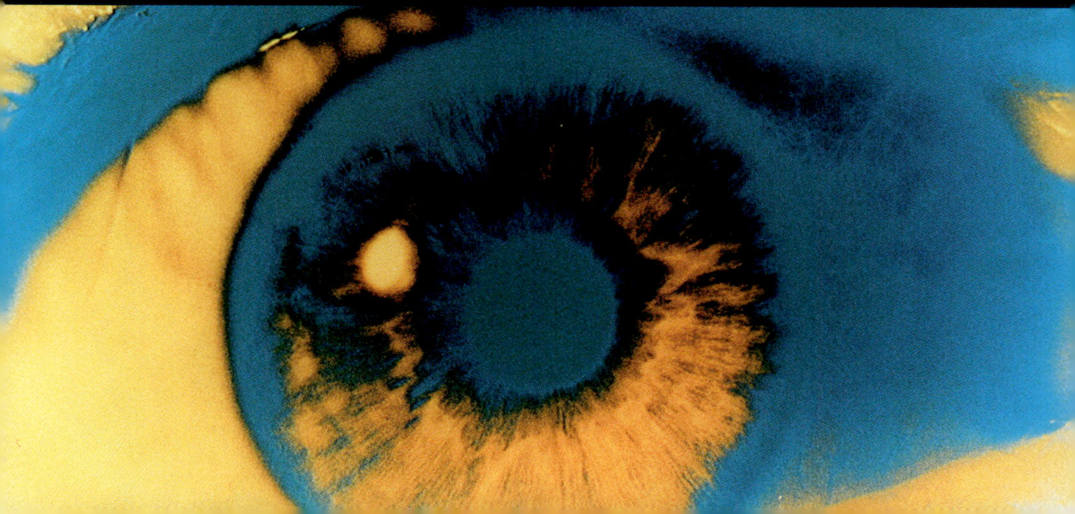

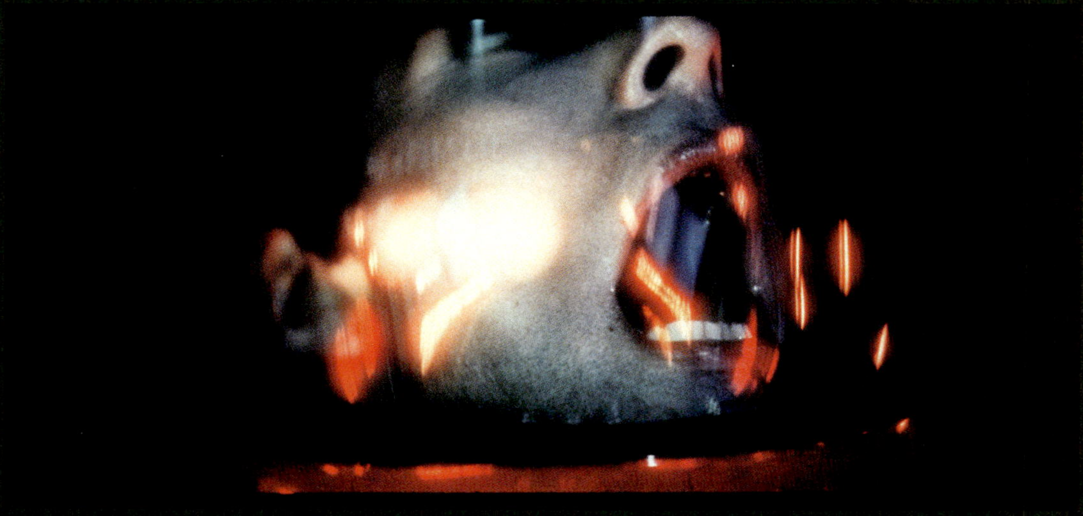

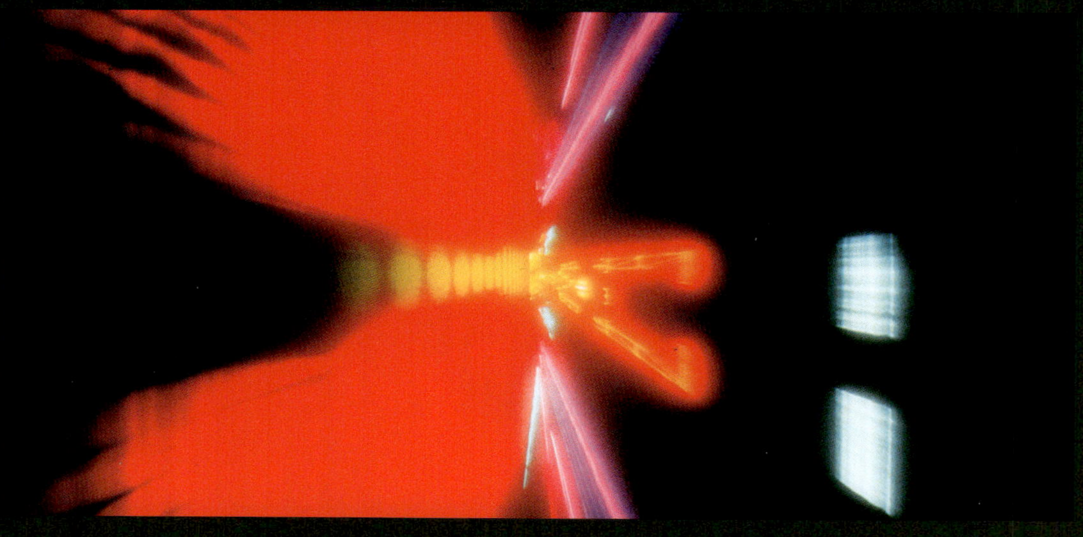

JUPITER

AND BEYOND THE INFINITE

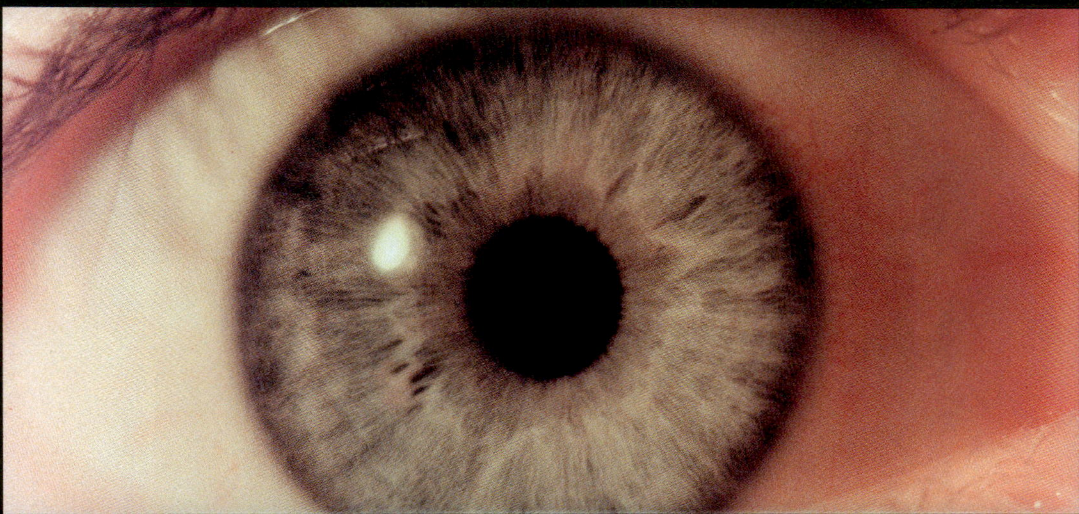

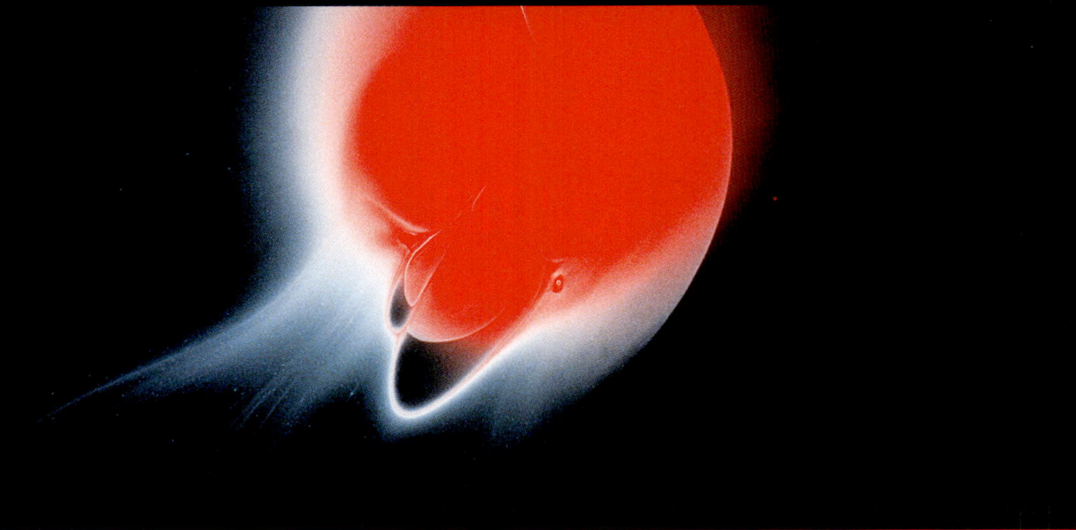

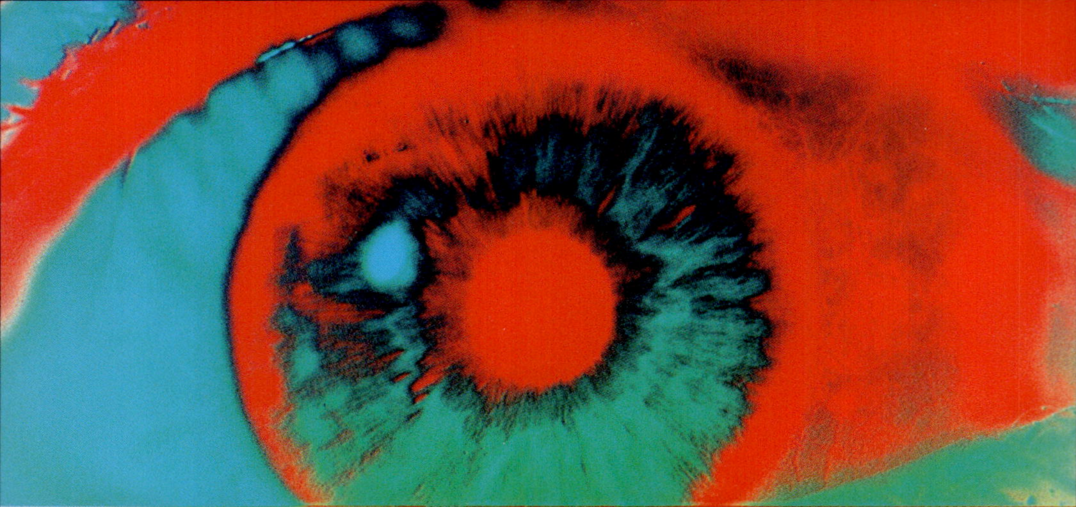

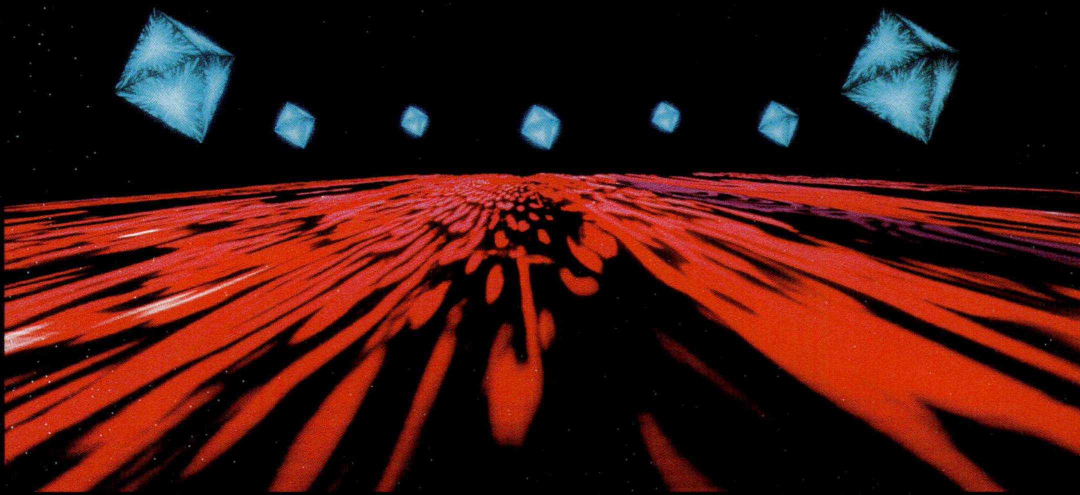

NON
NON

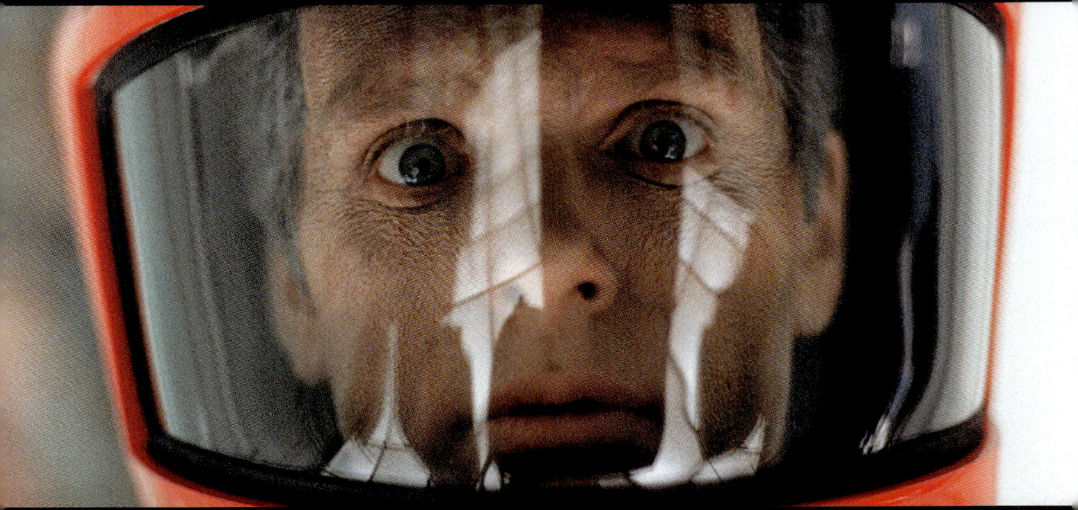

JUPITER AND BEYOND THE INFINITE

Another monolith now appears outside the windows of the partially crippled *Discovery*, as she drifts with most of her crew dead and her computer disconnected. Bowman sets off in the one remaining pod to investigate the alien artifact. Strange patterns of light shoot past the pod. We experience, from his point of view, a terrifying tunnel of light, an eerie vortex. Bowman and his pod are in the grip of some unknowable force. Beyond the tunnel, which we interpret as a tremendous distortion in space and time, Bowman sees galaxies explode, and swirls of interstellar dust playing out their billion-year dramas apparently in short moments before his horrified gaze. After a while (time is meaningless now) he is flying over a strange landscape where seas are like liquid mountains and hills ripple with distorted colors.

Eventually, the pod comes to rest. Through its oval front window Bowman sees something inexplicable: a hotel suite decorated in a faux classical-luxurious style. Then he sees himself, in his red space suit, standing in the main room. Our point of view shifts to this version of Bowman. His pod has vanished. As he explores his strange yet banal surroundings, he sees himself in a mirror and is shocked to find that he has aged many decades.

A metallic clinking catches his attention. There is somebody—or something—in the next room. It is him again, even older. The space-suited version of himself disappears, and Bowman, an aged gentleman at dinner in a dressing gown, is what remains. He eats a proper meal from fine china and drinks wine from a crystal glass. Reaching for some salt, he topples the glass and it smashes on the floor. Pushing back his chair and hunching down to see the disaster (his eyesight is almost gone, now) he hears a rasping breath coming from the bed behind him.

The monolith appears at the foot of a bed, from where Bowman, now ancient almost beyond recognition, feebly reaches out an arm as if to try and touch it. The desiccated space voyager starts to change. He is transformed once again into something: not older this time—younger, much younger… a new body at its first defining moment. He is a baby again—or perhaps, born for the first time? A child of a new species, something beyond human? He is absorbed into the darkness of the slab, and emerges, after his long and dangerous odyssey, to float above his first home, the blue planet Earth. Finally, his gentle rotation in a protective cocoon of blue-white light causes his wide-eyed, fascinated gaze to settle directly on us, the audience.

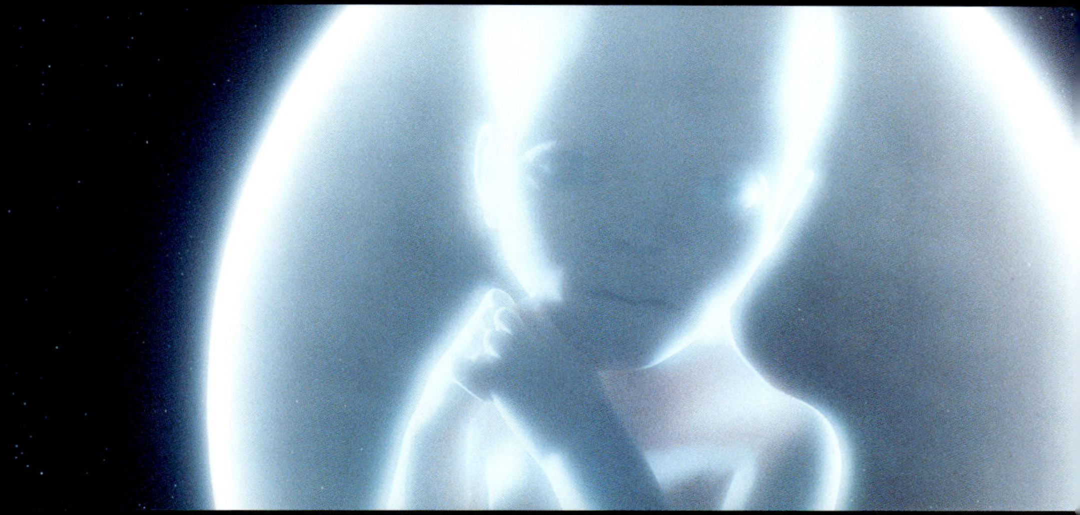

SCREENPLAY

BY

STANLEY KUBRICK

AND

ARTHUR C. CLARKE

ACKNOWLEDGEMENTS

This book would not have been possible without the generous and enthusiastic support of the Kubrick family, and in particular, Christiane Kubrick and Jan Harlan. Thank you both for trusting me with this imperfect yet well-meant essay about Stanley's great science-fiction masterpiece. Christiane gave me a fascinating and heartfelt interview, and Jan helped me arrange the legal issues with Warner Bros., the rights holders for this particular film and other Kubrick titles besides. Sir Arthur C. Clarke consistently supported my efforts over many years. Thank you, Arthur. I hope you are now safely part of the Overmind. Phil Grosz advised Jan and me on contractual matters and smoothed the legal path from the standpoint of the Stanley Kubrick Film Archive (SKFA), for which, countless thanks. I must also thank particular individuals at Warner Bros. for their patient assistance: Elaine Piechowski, Steven Fogelson, Jeremy Williams, Ned Price, Jesse Kobayashi, and Natasha Jules.

University of the Arts London (UAL) comprises six colleges specializing in art, design, fashion, communication, and the performing arts. Nearly 100 special historic collections and archives are held by the UAL, ranging from 15th-century parchments to the latest work of 21st-century designers. In 2007 the London College of Communication (LCC) at Elephant and Castle in South London unveiled an extraordinary new facility that, on first inspection, looks like a lobby from the space station in *2001: A Space Odyssey*, a clean, crisp white room with glass walls, flat-screen digital displays, and red chairs. Here, researchers, students, and members of the public can access the Stanley Kubrick Archive, a vast repository of film scripts, production notes, on-set photographs, and other research materials charting the career and creative processes of this unique filmmaker. The cool, futuristic work area is just the public face of a much larger storage system with temperature-controlled shelving and computerized catalogues: professional archival systems that will ensure the archive's endurance long into the future. Stanley's penchant for holding on to research materials was well known. Today we can be grateful that, with the close collaboration of the Kubrick family and SKFA, UAL can host such an incredible cultural, academic, and historical resource.

I am immensely grateful to Sarah Mahurter, manager of the Stanley Kubrick Archive, and senior archivist Richard Daniels for close cooperation throughout many days of research over the course of 2012, and subsequently for arranging the digital presentation of hundreds of items for this book. Thank you also to Stacey Kennedy for conducting many of the scans that required special attention because of the delicacy of the materials involved. The bulk of the transparency scanning was completed excellently by a specialist company, TownsWeb Archiving.

My good friend Simon Atkinson took it upon himself to help with digital restoration of many important images subsequent to initial scanning. Despite the careful storage conditions within the Stanley Kubrick Archive, it was inevitable that some photographic plates and film strips dating from nearly half a century ago would have collected scars, scratches, and other blemishes. Simon cleaned up many important images without in any way distorting their information content or historical accuracy. Thank you, Simon. Similar thanks to Keith Hamshere for discovering and digitally scanning a number of fascinating photographs from his personal collection—and thank you, Hilary, for such charming hospitality.

Actors and senior members of the *2001* production team granted me extensive interviews, initially during 1994 for an earlier published essay on *2001*, and more recently for a TV documentary film—and for this book. I am grateful to all who showed such patience and courtesy when confronted by my many questions. Some of my acknowledgements herein are directed, alas, toward wonderful people who are no longer with us. Regardless of this, I would like to thank (in alphabetical order):

Andrew Birkin, Ed Bishop, Roger Caras, David Charkham, Arthur C. Clarke and Fred Clarke, Simon Davis, Heather Downham, Keir Dullea, Tony Frewin, Keith Hamshere and Hilary Hamshere, John Hoesli, John Jay, Richard Jenkins, Brian Johnson, Malcolm Kafetz, Harry Lange and Daisy Lange, Gary Lockwood, Bryan Loftus, Bruce Logan, Ray Lovejoy, Con Pederson, Zoran Perisic, Ivor Powell, Tony Pratt, Dan Richter, Douglas Trumbull, Simon Willis.

Very special thanks to Don Shay, founder of *Cinefex* magazine, the absolute source on visual effects coverage for the international film industry. Don had the foresight to interview many of *2001*'s technical artists and effects specialists in the late 1970s, while their memories were still fresh. All direct quotes from *2001*'s production designer, Tony Masters, are derived from Don's 1977 interview with him. Additionally I am grateful to Don's associate Jordan Fox for all direct quotes relating to makeup artist Stuart Freeborn, based on interviews conducted with him in 1980. Those seeking further materials from these extraordinary verbal testimonies should seek out Don and Jordan's excellent essay in the April 2001 edition of *Cinefex* magazine.

My thanks, also, to Frederick I. Ordway III for a wealth of technical material relating to the film's production, and to his former colleague, the late Harry Lange, whose prescient designs informed so much of what we see in *2001*. I am grateful to the U.S. Space and Rocket Center (USSRC) in Huntsville, Alabama, for access to Fred's archive. In this particular category, I must extend a special mention to my good friend Adam Johnson, who catalogued and restored many items from the Ordway collection and made them available for this book. Adam's own volume, *2001*: The Lost Science, delves into Ordway's special contributions to Kubrick's masterpiece. Important technical drawings and severely faded blueprints required historically respectful restoration procedures before they could be rendered fit for publication. On a related theme, Margaret Carnon gave access to a number of her late husband Roy Carnon's production artworks. Thank you, Margaret, and also to Pratt Contemporary, the fine art gallery who introduced me to Margaret and organized scanning of these materials.

Thank you to Laurie Barr, formerly head of Master Models, the company that fabricated many of the structures for *2001*'s spacecraft models; Arthur Cole, formerly of the Hawker Siddeley aviation company; John Logsdon, former director of the Space Policy Institute at George Washington University in Washington, D.C.; Alan Herbert, formerly of the 3M company; and Alexander Walker, late film critic for the London *Evening Standard* newspaper. Huge thanks also to the Doran family. Had it not been for their generous friendship at a crucial point some years ago, this book might never have happened.

I am grateful to Joseph Gelmis for granting permission to reproduce substantial excerpts from his 1968 interview with Kubrick, and to the estate of Penelope Gilliatt for permission to reprint her perceptive *New Yorker* review.

Tim Heptner and his colleagues at the Deutsches Filminstitut arranged access to certain materials from the magnificent international touring exhibition related to Stanley's work. Thank you, also, to a quartet of great artists: Brian Sanders, who witnessed certain periods of *2001*'s production, and made some of his wonderful artworks available for this project; Damian Loeb, whose fascinating centrifuge interpretation appears on page 218; Oliver Rennert, whose superb technical drawings of certain hardware and camera set-ups appear prominently in these pages; and Wayne Haag, whose painterly design for the box art is perfectly in tune with our project. Last but by no means least, a tremendous thank you, of course, is due to Benedikt Taschen, Florian Kobler, and everyone at TASCHEN, and at M/M (Paris), for bringing this book into the world.

This book is dedicated to my family: as multifaceted and wonderful a thing as any alien artifact. Cousin Neil Guy, thank you for your company and support in Amsterdam.

Certain photographs and other materials in this book were licensed by Turner Entertainment Co. Turner holds an interest in the copyright. However, Turner is not the author or publisher of this book and the views and information presented herein are the work of the book's author and not of Turner.

IMAGE CREDITS

All behind-the-scenes images in this book were provided by the Stanley Kubrick Archives, with the exception of the following:

Andrew Birkin: 70 (top); Roy Carnon, courtesy of Margaret Carnon: 68, 69, 76–77, 78 (top), 78 (center, bottom), 79, 80–81, 82–83, 95–99, 106–109, 134–137; Bill George/Sci-Fi Air Show: 409; Aegir Hallmundur/Ministryoftype.co.uk & Joe Mackenzie/Halproject.com: 197; Keith Hamshere: 124–125; Harry Lange/Daisy Lange: 85, 86, 92, 128, 130–131 (both); Damian Loeb: 180 (bottom); NASA: 407, 410, 411; Frederick Ordway/USSRC/Adam Johnson: 21–22, 24–25, 93, 144, 145, 177 (top), 216–217, 218–219, 258–259, 260–261, 302–303 (bottom), 306–307; Con Pederson: 72, 74 (top, center); Oliver Rennert: 220, 221, 233 (top), 274; Dan Richter: 279, 280, 283; Virgin Galactic: 408.

Cover artwork painted by Wayne Haag after an original design by M/M (Paris), based on *2001: A Space Odyssey* elements © Turner Entertainment Co. (s14)

RECOMMENDED READING

Agel, Jerome, *The Making of Kubrick's 2001*, New American Library, New York, 1970

Ciment, Michel, *Kubrick*, English translation, William Collins, London, 1983

Clarke, Arthur C., *The Lost Worlds of 2001*, New American Library, New York, 1972

Davies, Paul, *The Eerie Silence: Are We Alone in the Universe?*, Allen Lane, London, 2010

Dick, Steven J., *Life on Other Worlds: The 20th-Century Extraterrestrial Life Debate*, Cambridge University Press, 2001

Frewin, Anthony, *Are We Alone? The Stanley Kubrick Extraterrestrial-Intelligence Interviews*, Elliott & Thompson, London, 2005

Gelmis, Joseph, *The Film Director as Superstar*, Doubleday, New York, 1970

Johnson, Adam, *2001*: The Lost Science, Apogee Prime, 2012

Lightman, Herb and Douglas Trumbull, "Filming *2001: A Space Odyssey*," American Cinematographer, Los Angeles, June 1968

McAleer, Neil, *Odyssey: The Authorized Biography of Arthur C. Clarke*, Victor Gollancz, London, 1992

Richter, Dan, Moonwatcher's Memoir, Carroll & Graf, New York, 2002

Shay, Don and Jody Duncan, "*2001*: A Time Capsule," *Cinefex*, number 85, Pasadena, April 2001

Trumbull, Douglas, "The Slit-Scan Process," *American Cinematographer*, Los Angeles, October 1969

Walker, Alexander, *Stanley Kubrick Directs*, Harcourt Brace Jovanovich, New York, 1972

EACH AND EVERY TASCHEN BOOK PLANTS A SEED!

Each year, we offset our annual carbonemissions with carbon credits at the Instituto Terra, a reforestation program in Minas Gerais, Brazil, founded by Lélia and Sebastião Salgado. To find out more about this ecological partnership, please check: www.taschen.com/institutoterra.

Inspiration: unlimited. Carbon footprint: (almost) zero.

Want to see more? Visit taschen.com to view our current publications, browse our latest magazine, and subscribe to our newsletter.

Designed at M/M (Paris)

© 2015 Turner Entertainment Co. and Piers Bizony

Text © Piers Bizony
Concept © TASCHEN GmbH
Film © 2015 Turner Entertainment Co.
2001: A Space Odyssey and all related characters and elements are trademarks of and © Turner Entertainment Co.

Realized in collaboration with Warner Bros. Entertainment Inc.

Published by TASCHEN GmbH
Hohenzollernring 53
D–50672 Köln
www.taschen.com

ISBN 978-3-7544-0659-5
Printed in Bosnia-Herzegovina